Advanced Lectures in
Quantitative Economics II

Advanced Lectures in Quantitative Economics II

Edited by

Aart J. de Zeeuw

CentER for Economic Research,
Faculty of Economics,
Tilburg University,
The Netherlands

ACADEMIC PRESS
Harcourt Brace & Company, Publishers
London   San Diego   New York   Boston
Sydney   Tokyo   Toronto

ACADEMIC PRESS LIMITED
24/28 Oval Road
LONDON NWI 7DX

United States Edition published by
ACADEMIC PRESS INC.
San Diego, CA 92101

A catalogue record for this book is available from the British Library

ISBN 0-12-214685-9

Typeset by Mathematical Composition Setters Ltd, Salisbury, Wiltshire
Printed in Great Britain by Hartnolls Limited, Bodmin, Cornwall

Contents

Preface

In the spring of 1986 a group of academics from each of the economics faculties in the Netherlands took the initiative of founding the 'Network Quantitative Economics', in order to provide a nationwide doctoral programme in economics and econometrics. The Network was given a start-up grant by the Ministry of Education and Sciences, which made it possible to attract a director and to develop a teaching programme with the best teachers from inside and outside the Netherlands.

This volume contains a selection of lecture notes of courses given for the doctoral students of the Network Quantitative Economics in the period 1989–91. The topics are at the forefront of recent developments in research in economics and econometrics, and will be of interest not only to doctoral students but also to others who want to keep abreast of recent research. This is the second such volume; the first was edited by Rick van der Ploeg, who was the first director of the Network, from September 1986 until January 1989.

I had the privilege of being the second director of the Network Quantitative Economics. In September 1991 the Network merged with another network, to become the Netherlands Graduate School of Economics. Since I will be relinquishing my position on 1 August 1992, I would like to take the opportunity of expressing my gratitude to everyone who has eased my task as director. I would like especially to thank Gerard van der Laan, chairman of the board of the Network, and my secretary, Jeanine Leijtens. I wish my successor, Casper van Ewijk, all the best.

I am very grateful to the authors of the chapters in this volume, who were willing to write down parts of their lectures in a comprehensible form. Finally, I want to thank Josette Janssen, Robert de Jong, Theo van de Klundert, Gerard van der Laan, Rick van der Ploeg and Peter Schotman for their help and advice in the editorial process.

Aart de Zeeuw
27 July 1992

List of Contributors

Microeconomics:

Partha S. Dasgupta, Faculty of Economics, University of Cambridge, Sidgwick Avenue, Cambridge CB3 9DD, UK.

Frank H. Hahn, Faculty of Economics, University of Cambridge, Sidgwick Avenue, Cambridge CB3 9DD, UK.

Macroeconomics:

Charles R. Bean, Faculty of Economics, London School of Economics, Houghton Street, London WC2A 2AE, UK.

Stephen J. Turnovsky, Department of Economics, University of Washington, 301 Savery Hall, Seattle, Washington 98195, USA.

Econometrics:

Alberto Holly, DEEP, Université de Lausanne, École des HEC, 1015 Lausanne, Switzerland.

Grayham E. Mizon, Department of Economics, European University Institute, Badia Fiesolana, 50016 San Domenico di Fiesole, Italy.

Theo E. Nijman, Faculty of Economics, Tilburg University, Postbox 90153, 5000 LE Tilburg, The Netherlands.

Franz C. Palm, Faculty of Economics, Limburg University, Postbox 616, 6200 MD Maastricht, The Netherlands.

Introduction

At the beginning of the 1980s there was a significant change in the system of university education in The Netherlands. Prior to 1982, each student entering university had studied for an 'old-style doctorandus' degree in the subject of their choice. Formally, for most studies this could be accomplished in five years, although in practice it took longer because students were encouraged to also develop other skills. To a large extent the curriculum was intended for those few students who would go on to write a doctoral thesis, rather than for the vast majority of students who would go on to work in the private sector or for government. In The Netherlands the only requirement for a doctorate degree is to write and argue a doctoral thesis. In the old system this was mainly done by people who were either employed as assistant professors by one of the universities or who had a temporary contract with the Dutch Organization for Scientific Research. The doctorate degree was not a requirement to get a permanent position as assistant professor or even professor, which has led to the situation in which quite a few faculty members at Dutch universities do not have a doctorate degree. Another problem was that under the old system, only during the public defence of the doctoral thesis was there any significant critical feedback, by a committee of several people. The research was mainly carried out in a one-to-one relationship with the supervisor, so that the researcher got very little feedback from others.

In September 1982, university education in The Netherlands was reorganized in a two-phase system. The first phase of the system leads to a 'new-style doctorandus' degree, and should take four years. This is the final degree for the vast majority of students. The second phase of the system is a four-year doctoral programme, for only a minority of students. These doctoral students are university employees who are expected to complete the doctoral programme and to provide some teaching or research assistance in return for a salary, which is low in the beginning but which increases by annual increments to the starting salary of an assistant professor in the final year.

Since the new system of university education started in September 1982, the second phase of the system had to be implemented for the first time in 1986. In order to stimulate the development of doctoral programmes the Ministry of Education and Sciences gave start-up grants to promising initiatives. How to set up the doctoral programmes was left to the profession. One of the few initiatives that received a start-up grant for five years was the 'Network Quantitative Economics'. The Network is in fact a group of academics from each of the Dutch universities, who are active in research and who are willing to teach and supervise in a national doctoral programme. Because econometrics has a strong tradition in The Netherlands, a large part of the group

Table 1: Workshops organized by NQE, 1986–92

University of Groningen, 15–19 December, 1986
Professor Willem H. Buiter (Yale University):
'Dynamic rational expectations models and macroeconomic theory'
Professor John Sutton (London School of Economics):
'Analysis of price behaviour in oligopolies: some recent approaches'
Professor M. Hashem Pesaran (University of Cambridge):
'Econometric analysis of linear rational expectations models'

Limburg University, Maastricht, 6–11 April, 1987
Professor Sweder van Wijnbergen (World Bank):
'Structural adjustment and disequilibrium in open economies'
Professor Christopher A. Pissarides (London School of Economics):
'Equilibrium unemployment theory'
Professor Robert F. Engle (University of California at San Diego):
'Co-integration and related issues'

University of Amsterdam, 14–18 December, 1987
Professor Jeffrey D. Sachs (Harvard University):
'Macroeconomic policy issues in open economies'
Professor Roger Guesnerie (CEQC, Paris):
'Rational expectations, learning and sun-spot equilibria in OLG and
other models'
Professor Thomas J. Rothenberg (University of California at Berkeley):
'Structural econometric models'

Tilburg University, 21–25 March, 1988
Professor Rudiger Dornbusch (Massachusetts Institute of Technology):
'The dollar, debt and deficits & LDC debt problems'
Professor Peter J. Hammond (Stanford University):
'Incentives and allocation mechanisms'
Professor Stephen J. Nickell (University of Oxford):
'Topics in applied microeconometrics'

Free University, Amsterdam, 12–16 December, 1988
Professor Peter Neary (Trinity College, Dublin):
'International trade and resource allocation'
Professor Joseph E. Stiglitz (Stanford University):
'The economics of imperfect information'
Professor Whitney Newey (Princeton University):
'Semi-parametric efficiency bounds'

Leiden University, 10–14 April, 1989
Professor Stephen J. Turnovsky (University of Washington):
'Recent developments in international macrodynamics'
Professor Partha S. Dasgupta (University of Cambridge):
'The economics of deprivation'
Professor Grayham E. Mizon (University of Southampton):
'Practical econometric modelling'

University of Nijmegen, 11–15 December, 1989
Professor Torsten Persson (University of Stockholm):
'Macroeconomic policy, credibility and politics'
Professor Frank H. Hahn (University of Cambridge):
'Recent general equilibrium theory'
Professor Alberto Holly (University of Lausanne):

'Asymptotic theory for nonlinear econometric models: estimation, asymptotic distribution and hypothesis testing'

Erasmus University, Rotterdam, 28 May–1 June, 1990
Professor Angus S. Deaton (Princeton University):
'Consumption, saving and income'
Professor Martin Hellwig (University of Basel):
'Financial markets and financial institutions under incomplete information'
Professor Edward E. Leamer (University of California at Los Angeles):
'Bayesian analysis of economic data'

Wageningen Agricultural University, 10–14 December, 1990
Professor N. Gregory Mankiw (Harvard University):
'Topics in macroeconomics'
Professor Alvin E. Roth (University of Pittsburgh):
'Two-sided matching'
Professor John Geweke (University of Minnesota):
'Bayesian inference and dynamic econometric models'

University of Utrecht, 27–31 May, 1991
Professor Charles R. Bean (London School of Economics):
'Government policy and economic growth'
Professor Eric S. Maskin (Harvard University):
'Lectures on repeated games'
Professor Andrew D. Chesher (University of Bristol):
'The effect, detection and correction of specification error in microeconometric modelling'

Institute of Social Studies, den Haag, 9–13 December, 1991
Professor Richard A. Jackman (London School of Economics):
'The macroeconomic effects of unions'
Professor Jacques H. Drèze (CORE, Louvain-la-Neuve):
'Supply and demand influences on output and employment'
Professor Orley C. Ashenfelter (Princeton University):
'Labour supply, schooling, training and earnings'

University of Groningen, 1–5 June, 1992
Professor Kenneth F. Wallis (University of Warwick):
'Macroeconometric modelling'
Professor Oliver D. Hart (Massachusetts Institute of Technology):
'Theory of the firm and firms' financial structure'
Professor Daniel L. McFadden (University of California at Berkeley):
'Econometric analysis of qualitative choice'

consists of econometricians. The main other group in the Network is working in economic theory.

The teaching of the doctoral programme of the Network Quantitative Economics can be split into three parts. Firstly, at each of the six economics faculties in the Netherlands, basic semester courses are organized in micro-economics, macroeconomics and econometrics. Secondly, each year a programme of twelve specialized modules is run in the town of Utrecht, which is situated in the centre of the country. Each module consists of four two-hour lectures, and each doctoral student has to pass at least eight modules. Thirdly,

twice a year a workshop is organized at one of the Dutch universities where
three well-known professors from abroad each teach a mini-course. Such
a workshop lasts one week and each mini-course consists of five two-hour
lectures. Each doctoral student has to participate in at least four workshops.
The teaching programme is intended to lead to both a broad and a deep understanding of economics and econometrics.

During the first two years of the four-year programme the doctoral students
follow their courses and start their research under the guidance of one of the
fellows of the Network Quantitative Economics. At the end of this period the
doctoral students submit a thesis proposal which is evaluated by two other
fellows of the Network. They also present their first results at one of the twice-
yearly research seminars in Utrecht, with a fellow of the Network as discus-
sant. In this way the doctoral students get more feedback in an earlier stage
of their research than in the old system. The last two years of the programme
are used to complete the research and to write the thesis. The doctoral students
are of course encouraged to try to present their work at international
conferences.

The Netherlands is a small country, which makes it possible to organize such
a national doctoral programme. Clearly, the advantage is that the programme
can draw upon the expertise of the best people in all Dutch universities for
teaching and supervision, and that a wide variety of doctoral courses can be
offered in an efficient manner. Moreover, the biannual workshops ensure that
the doctoral students are brought into contact with leading researchers in
economics from all over the world, and that their education matches the best
education that can be found elsewhere. Table 1 lists the workshops which the
Network Quantitative Economics organized in the first six years of its
existence.

This book contains the lecture notes of some of the courses that were given
at the workshops in the period 1989–91. One chapter is based on the material
that was presented in that period as one of the specialized modules in the
teaching programme at Utrecht.

Of the book's seven chapters, four can be classified as economics and three
as econometrics. Two of the economics chapters concern microeconomic
topics, and the other two macroeconomic, although this distinction is ques-
tionable. The chapters describe in a comprehensive way recent developments
which received considerable attention in the literature and at conferences.

In chapter 1 Partha Dasgupta develops the economics of destitution by
means of a resource allocation theory which accommodates the possibility that
a sizeable fraction of a population may be bereft of endowments. By distinguishing potential and actual labour power, an analytical construct is provided
which makes essential use of the phenomenon of undernourishment. In this
way a language is constructed in which policies for alleviating extreme poverty
can be discussed.

In chapter 2 Frank Hahn gives an overview of general equilibrium theory
with incomplete markets, in which agents are unable to carry out all the trades

they will ever wish to make at the initial date. He defines a sequence economy as one in which there is trading at every date. In such an economy, agents need to form price expectations, which they do not need to do when every good has all the required contingent future markets. Incomplete markets throw doubt on the robustness of the co-ordinating power of market economies.

In chapter 3 Charles Bean presents a survey of classical growth theory and the new endogenous growth theory, which seeks to generate unbounded growth in output per head without relying on exogenous labour-augmenting technical progress. Endogenous growth models all have the feature of endogenizing the process by which the efficiency of labour is enhanced over time, either through the expansion of knowledge, or else through investment in human, rather than purely physical, capital. He describes several endogenous growth models and discusses the impact of government policy on the equilibrium growth rate.

In chapter 4 Stephen Turnovsky deals with the microeconomic underpinning of dynamic international macroeconomic models. Essentially, this has come to mean that the underlying behavioural relationships are derived from some form of intertemporal optimization by representative agents. In this way much of the arbitrariness of macroeconomic modelling is eliminated, and by explicitly introducing some intertemporal measure of welfare, a framework is provided for performing macroeconomic welfare analysis and for discussing optimal macroeconomic policy-making.

In chapter 5 Theo Nijman and Franz Palm present the state of the art in the rapidly expanding literature on GARCH models for time-varying volatility measures. In a way, GARCH models are natural extensions of ARMA schemes to describe the time dependencies in second moments of many economic series. These non-linear models are fairly easily implemented, estimated and tested. They discuss the properties of these models and they show the relevance for the analysis of financial series by treating a number of applications from the finance literature in detail.

In chapter 6 Grayham Mizon shows how simulated data are used to illustrate the properties of the major types of time series process. This knowledge helps in the choice of data-admissible model classes when modelling time series variables. Knowledge of the data-generating process for simulated data enables the calculation of the properties of statistics of interest. The analogous role of the congruent general model in a modelling strategy which seeks to develop simple, economically interpretable models, which parsimoniously encompass the general model, is also illustrated.

In chapter 7 Alberto Holly develops asymptotic estimation theory for non-linear econometric models. The purpose is to describe general conditions for the strong consistency of extremum estimators, that is estimators obtained by either maximizing or minimizing a stochastic criterion function defined over the parameter space. The special cases of both the maximum likelihood estimator and the method of moments estimator are treated as illustrations of some of the general results.

The book covers a wide variety of topics. It is intended for doctoral students and other researchers who wish to be acquainted with some important recent developments in economics and econometrics. The doctoral students of the Network Quantitative Economics have already benefited from the efforts of these leading researchers sharing their knowledge.

PART I:
Microeconomics

PART 1
Microeconomics

1

The Economics of Destitution[*]

Partha S. Dasgupta

University of Cambridge

1. Introduction

In this chapter I shall develop the economics of destitution. By this term I refer to a resource allocation theory which accommodates the possibility that a sizeable fraction of a population may be bereft of resource endowments. This needs doing, because in its general form modern resource allocation theory (e.g. Koopmans, 1957; Debreu, 1959; Arrow and Hahn, 1971) assumes that people have sufficient resources at their command as initial endowments. Indeed, even in its specialized garbs, the theory assumes that even when a person owns no physical assets he still has one inalienable asset, namely labour power. But the science of nutrition has revealed the important truth that this presumption is false (see Dasgupta, 1992a, chapters 14–15). What an assetless person owns is *potential* labour power, nothing more. Conversion of potential into actual labour power can be realized if the person finds the means of making the conversion, not otherwise. Nutrition and health-care are a necessary means to this. The economics of destitution enquires into the circumstances in which this conversion is realizable, and those when it is not.

The inability of modern resource allocation theory to address the phenomenon of destitution goes deeper: it is oblivious of even minimal physiological truths. It takes no account of the fact that there are fixed energy costs,

---

[*] An early version of this lecture was prepared in 1986 as part of the E.S. Woodward Memorial Lectures at the University of British Columbia. Portions of what appears here were also delivered as the Walras–Bowley Lecture to the Econometric Society at its Ann Arbor Meeting in June 1989. The material was subsequently collated in chapters 16–16[*] of my book, *An Inquiry into Well-Being and Destitution*, Clarendon Press, Oxford, forthcoming, 1993. In preparing this chapter I have taken the physiological basis of the economics of destitution as given; I have not substantiated it. The nutrition literature is the appropriate source of information for this, and I have provided the material in my book in a form which is, I hope, suitable for social scientists. In particular, chapters 14–15 of my book have an account of food needs and work capacity, and of the various adaptive mechanisms human beings resort to for coping with food deficiency.

measured by what is referred to as 'maintenance requirements' in the nutrition literature (see below), which individuals must cover before they can do anything else over the medium and long run. Maintenance requirements consist of: (i) the basal metabolic rate (sometimes also called the resting metabolic rate), (ii) the energy expended in the process of assimilating food (often called dietary thermogenesis), and (iii) the energy spent in those minimal activities necessary for personal hygiene.[1] Maintenance requirements comprise something like 60–75 per cent of an individual's daily energy expenditure. To be sure, it has been noted before that resource allocation theory is vulnerable to the charge that it ignores maintenance energy requirements (Bliss and Stern, 1978a,b) but little has been done to rectify this shortcoming. Admittedly, it is also possible that in many circumstances, for example where the economy under review is rich in assets, the theory is not at risk from this fixed cost (Dasgupta and Ray, 1986, 1987). But the matter needs to be proved; it can't be taken for granted.

The matter is more awkward for the economics of poor countries, or what is otherwise known as development economics, since this has serious ramifications for development policy. It is to me curious that a large literature should have been erected on the concept of absolute poverty, have it then related to the phenomenon of undernourishment, and yet the literature has not gone on to provide an analytical construct which makes essential use of the physiological phenomenon of undernourishment. Thus, the concept of malnutrition has made repeated appearances in recent works on development economics (e.g. Underwood, 1983; Biswas and Pinstrup-Andersen, 1985; Reutlinger and Pellekaan, 1986; Berg, 1987; Bell and Reich, 1988; George, 1988; Dreze and Sen, 1990; UNDP, 1990; World Bank, 1990), but it has found little to no operational room in it. By this I mean that the underlying models on the basis of which these authors derive policies to alleviate undernourishment do not have undernourishment as a phenomenon in them. If you were to replace the term 'undernourishment' by 'low income', or 'hunger', or 'low utility', you would notice no difference. Among other things, this has prevented policy-makers and academic economists from asking in clear contexts whether there is a necessary trade-off between growth in the standard of living, as caught, say, in estimates of national income per head, and reductions in poverty among contemporaries. To put it in different words, it has prevented them from asking the related question whether 'trickle down' is the most appropriate route to take for the elimination of poverty. That there need not be a trade-off between growth and redistribution if redistributive policies are judiciously chosen is a point which has, of course, on occasion been made, most notably by Amiya Dasgupta (1975, 1976), Adelman (1979) and Streeten *et al.* (1981). (See also Chenery *et al.*, 1974; Hicks, 1979). But they were not

---

[1] The basal metabolic rate (BMR) is the energy expenditure of an individual who is at complete rest in a thermo-neutral environment, and who has fasted for a period of at least 13 hours. For practical purposes WHO (1985) takes maintenance requirements to be approximately $1.4 \times$ BMR.

provided with formal constructions built on adequate physiological foundations in which to undertake such inquiries, so they were unable to discuss the
issue in any quantitative manner through the use of such a construct. For this
reason their claims are ultimately not convincing. If quantitative models glide
over the phenomenon of undernourishment, as for example do current com-
putable general equilibrium models, they are by implication incapable of
asking if growth in productivity is possible through redistributive measures.
The claim that it is remains an act of faith, backed only by unquantified
intuition.

The economics of destitution redresses these lacunae. My aim in this chapter
will be to use basic physiological notions for extending modern resource allocation theory for the purpose of constructing a language in which policies for
alleviating extreme poverty can be discussed. Along the way I shall also be
interested in demonstrating that the resulting theory is capable of explaining
a number of phenomena uncovered by recent empirical studies of the rural
labour market in poor countries. In doing this I shall proceed in steps. The
following section will provide a heuristic account of the theory. Subsequent
sections will develop the theory in increasing generality. All along, I shall
simultaneously keep an eye on description, explanation, prediction, and
prescription.

2. Asset Ownership, Maintenance Costs, and Labour Power

Consumption possibility sets are non-convex. Maintenance requirements make
them so. Even although these costs are person-specific, the non-convexity
appears in the same region in everyone's consumption possibility set. In this
crucial sense people are similar, not different. It means that large numbers of
people taken together can't iron out the non-convexity, in a sense that will be
made precise below.[2]

The standard theory of resource allocation assumes each person's consumption possibility set to be convex. The theory therefore needs to be
reconstructed, with physiology taken into account. To do so in any generality
requires formidable mathematical machinery (for confirmation of which, see
Hammond, 1992). I want to avoid this here. So with one hand tied behind our
backs we will proceed initially by considering a timeless model; that is, we will
restrict ourselves to stationary nutritional states. By this I will mean that
people's body weight and composition will be taken to be given and fixed. The
model will be capable of linking a person's physical productivity to nutrition
intakes when the latter are considered only as a *flow* (e.g. daily calorie intake).

---

[2] Contrast Farrell (1959), Aumann (1964, 1966), Starr (1969), and Arrow and Hahn (1971), who
showed that non-convexities in utility orderings disappear in the aggregate when there are large
numbers of diverse people. The non-convexity we are dealing with is different.

However, a person can be in long-term energy balance (i.e. maintain constant body weight) and yet be undernourished. This means we won't lose much by our restriction, but we should bear in mind that it *is* a restriction. It doesn't leave room for an analysis of changes in a person's nutritional status over time. In sections 9 and 10 we will extend the model to incorporate non-stationary nutritional states. This way we will be able to regard nutritional status (e.g. the 'body mass index', see Dasgupta 1992a, chapter 14) as a *stock*, and study variations in nutritional status in response to experience in the economic world which people inhabit.[3] We will discover that this extended theory is immune to a number of criticisms levelled recently against nutrition-based accounts of the conditions of living among the rural poor. These criticisms (e.g. Bliss and Stern, 1982; Rosenzweig, 1988; Dreze and Mukherjee, 1989) have been prompted by too literal a reading of the simple, atemporal model. It will be confirmed that the substance of the intertemporal model is embedded in the one which is atemporal. Restriction to stationary nutritional states and a timeless framework may be draconian, but it isn't misleading. That is why we will study it in detail.

Earlier we noted that the only thing assetless people own is *potential* labour power. Conversion of potential into actual labour power can be realized if the person finds the means of making the conversion, not otherwise. Now, someone with an income that does not depend upon their doing work ('unearned income') is capable of bringing about at least a part of the conversion without having to work. In a poor economy they enjoy an advantage over their assetless counterparts, in that they can undercut the assetless in the labour market.[4] A theory of economic disenfranchisement and undernourishment, which links their incidence and extent to the distribution of assets can be fashioned out of these ingredients. The theory makes precise the intuitive idea we carry with us when we use the term 'economic disenfranchisement'; it also identifies the assetless as those who are particularly vulnerable. The economic outcasts are for the most part from this segment of the population.

A simple, stylized example may help. Suppose everyone needs 2,000 kcal of energy per day to be able to function: anything less and their productivity is nil, anything more and their productivity is unaffected. (The nutrition–productivity curve is a step-function in this case. See the Appendix, section A2.) Consider two people, one of whom has no non-wage income, while the other enjoys 1,500 kcal per day of non-wage income. The first person needs

---

[3] The body mass index is a person's weight divided by the square of their height. It is the most reliable index of nutritional status. Units in which weight and height are customarily measured are kilograms and metres respectively. A wide battery of empirical evidence (see Waterlow, 1986; James, Ferro-Luzzi and Waterlow, 1988; James, *et al.*, 1992) suggests that the body mass index of healthy people lies in the range 18.5–25. A person would be regarded as overweight above the range, and would be subject to the risks associated with undernourishment below the range.

[4] Whether they do undercut, or whether social norms prevent them from doing so, is a different matter and will not affect the thrust of what follows. One of my goals here is to demonstrate the existence of involuntary unemployment. Were undercutting socially not permitted, the volume of unemployment would be that much higher.

a full 2,000 kcal of wages per day to be employable, while the latter requires only 500 kcal per day. The former is *prima facie* disadvantaged.

We will initially be studying a decentralized market economy. As we should be mainly interested in agrarian societies, it will be as well to aggregate and think only of markets for land, labour and final output (e.g. food crops). Our aim is to explore the limits people face in their ability to convert potential labour power into actual labour power, so the market for labour will come up for scrutiny. Economic disenfranchisement will be interpreted here as the inability to participate in the labour market. We will think of the outcasts as living on common property resources (or alternatively, as beggars). They get wasted gradually, their life expectancy is low even by the standards prevailing in poor countries. Such people exist in large numbers, they are the outsiders. Our analysis will provide an explanation of how this can come about.

The nutrition-based models we will develop here have very special structures; but they possess a number of general features. I shall be especially interested in those conclusions that are robust. This is a point of importance. The institutional arrangements underlying agricultural work in poor countries are immeasurably complex and so specific to regions that no single model can entirely do. One thing is certain though: models which are dissonant with physiological truths are hopelessly incomplete.

For tractibility we will postulate frictionless markets for land (more generally, all capital assets) and crops. A large body of empirical work has shown that within villages in a number of poor countries (e.g. the Indian subcontinent) the casual labour market is competitive, that if the market for land is dormant it is in great part because land offers a vital form of insurance to its owner, and not because the land market is absent. So we will postulate a flawless competitive spirit among employers and workers.

Even as a research strategy this makes sense, because at the level of theoretical discourse it doesn't do to explain malnutrition and disenfranchisement by an appeal to monopsonistic landlords, or predatory capitalists, or a tradition-bound labouring class and to leave it at that. For one thing, this is far too easy a route. For another, to do so would leave us exposed to the argument that this merely proves that governments should concentrate their attention on freeing markets from restrictive practices. It does not provide an immediate instrumental reason as to why governments, if they are able to, should also intervene to ensure that people are not undernourished.

If an economy is vastly poor in assets, it is technologically not feasible for all citizens to enjoy adequate diet and health-care. There has to be a sufficient accumulation of productive capability before this is possible. Thus, to say that an economy is 'vastly poor' is to say that population size exceeds the land's carrying capacity. Consider then an economy which is neither rich in assets nor vastly poor. The theory to be developed will show that were such an economy to rely on the market mechanism, the initial distribution of assets would play a crucial role in determining if all citizens have their basic needs met. For example, we will confirm that if a large fraction of the population were to be assetless, markets on their own would be incapable of enabling all to obtain an adequate diet (result (v) below). On the other hand, were the distribution of assets sufficiently equal, the labour market would be capable of absorbing all, and no one would suffer from malnutrition (result (ix)).

The formal constructions in this lecture will be classical ones. In particular, the involuntary unemployment to be shown to be a feature of our model economy will not be due to demand deficiency. To seal this point we will note that all the equilibria in the timeless economy are Pareto efficient (result (vi) below). This means, among other things, that there are no policies open to the government for alleviating the extent of undernourishment other than those which amount to consumption or asset transfers. A common wisdom is that such policies impede the growth of an economy's productive capacity because of their detrimental effect on saving and investment, incentives, and so forth. But this is only one side of the picture. The other is what our model will stress, which is that a transfer from the well-off to the undernourished can enhance output via the increased productivity of the impoverished (results (vii) and (viii)). We don't know in advance which is the greater effect, but to ignore the latter yields biased estimates of the effects of redistributive policies. One of my aims (see the Appendix, section A3) is to provide sample calculations which tell on the matter.

Asset transfers in a rural context suggest agrarian reform. This is what we will study here. But as always, it is as well to rise beyond the immediate confines of a theoretical construct and to seek the general message. Agrarian reform should be taken to be a metaphor here. In the world as we know it this is only one route open to governments. There are other ways of redistributing benefits and burdens, and they include the provision of consumption transfers, public health-care, education, and rural infrastructure, which are typically financed by taxes imposed on the relatively wealthy. Each of these types of redistribution should ideally be established in parallel. A number of basic needs are collective goods, and modern resource allocation theory has for long found a role for governments in the supply of collective goods. Here we are concentrating on nutrition, which is a private good *par excellence*. By developing the economics of destitution we will offer a justification for the thesis that it is the singular responsibility of government to be an active participant in the allocation mechanism guiding the production and distribution of food and primary health-care. This justification is built on the idea that in a poor economy, markets on their own are incapable of empowering all people with the opportunity to convert their potential labour power into actual labour power. As a resource allocation mechanism, markets on their own simply won't do. The theory we will develop below also shows how a group of similar, poor people can become fragmented over time into distinct classes, facing widely different opportunities. Risk and uncertainty will play no role in this. It is a pristine theory of class formation.

3. The Labour Market and Involuntary Unemployment[5]

We will be studying an economy capable of producing a single (composite) commodity called 'food crop'. (We could think of this commodity as a set of cash crops which are traded internationally at fixed prices.) For simplicity of exposition, we assume that only two inputs, land and labour power, are involved in the production of food crop (generalization to more inputs is a trivial matter). Labour power is required to accomplish agricultural tasks. Again, for ease of exposition, we will assume that agricultural work involves a single, composite task (but see section 8). This means that we can identify the amount of labour power a worker exerts with the amount of agricultural work he/she performs; or, in other words, we may identify the labour power a worker exerts in agriculture with the number of units of the composite task the person accomplishes. Let E denote the aggregate amount of agricultural work performed. It is the sum of the amounts of work performed by all who are employed in agricultural production; or, in other words, it is the aggregate amount of labour power deployed. Let T denote the total quantity of land, and let $F(E, T)$ be the output of food crop, where $F(E, T)$ is assumed to be a concave function, displaying diminishing marginal products, and is both constant-returns-to-scale and increasing in each of E and T. The total quantity of land is assumed to be fixed, and is $\hat{T}$. Aggregate labour power deployed in agriculture is not given. It is endogenous to the construction.

The model is timeless. Total population, assumed without loss of generality to be equal to the potential work force, is M, which is taken to be large. We can therefore approximate and consider a continuum of people. So we number people along the unit interval $[0, 1]$. Each person has a label, n, where n is a real number between 0 and 1. In this interval population density is constant, and is equal to M. We may then normalize and set $M = 1$, so as not to have to refer to the population size. A person with label n will often be called an n-person.

We are studying a private ownership economy. The proportion of land person n owns is $t(n)$, so that $\hat{T}t(n)$ is the total amount of land that person possesses (i.e. $t(n)$ is a density function). Without loss of generality, we label people in such a way that $t(n)$ is non-decreasing in n. So $t(n)$ is the distribution of land, and we take it to be a continuous function. In Fig. 1 a typical distribution is drawn. Persons labelled 0 to $\bar{n}$ are landless, and $t(n)$ is an increasing function beyond $\bar{n}$. Thus, all persons numbered in excess of $\bar{n}$ own land, and the higher the n-value of a person, the greater is the amount of land they own. $\bar{n}$ can be substantial. In the early 1970s the proportion of the rural populations of Brazil and Bangladesh that was landless or nearly landless was in the range 70–75 per cent. In Bolivia and Guatemala the proportion is about 85 per cent,

---

[5] The analysis in sections 3–7 is taken from Dasgupta and Ray (1986, 1987).

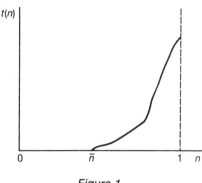

Figure 1.

and in India it is something like 50 per cent (Sinha, 1984). A value of $\bar{n}$ in the region 0.5–0.7 does not appear to be uncommon.[6]

I now turn to the crucial nutrition–productivity relationship. We will be studying a timeless framework until Section 8. Figure 2 presents the link between a person's energy intake x (which I will identify with that person's income) and the maximum amount of agricultural work they are capable of accomplishing, $\Phi(x)$, in an atemporal world (see sections 8–10 for extensions). As a matter of convention I have set $\Phi(x) = 0$ for $x < r$, where r is the person's maintenance requirement. It bears emphasis that it *is* a mere convention I am following here, nothing more, and there will be nothing amiss in my doing so. The reason is that we are assuming here that the person is in energy balance (i.e. they maintain their body weight). So we are not entitled to study the region $x < r$ in Fig. 2. Were $x < r$, the individual would not be in energy balance, and something would have to give: they would either lose weight, or would have to cut down on some other activity, and I am supposing that they do not experience either sort of loss.

Figure 2 is a particular idealization, in that I have assumed $\Phi(x)$ to be strictly concave for $x > r$. Nothing will hang on this, so long as $\Phi''(x) < 0$ for large enough x, which is patently the correct assumption to make, since there is a limit to the pace at which a person can work at a task, no matter what their energy intake. Of course, we are entitled to consider only a limited range of values of x here; between maintenance requirement, r, and some upper limit. At large levels of daily intake the person's health suffers. As they over-eat, they are unable to maintain energy balance. Subject to the

---

[6] This specification asserts that the frequency distribution of owners over landholdings of different sizes, *excluding zero*, is flat. This is unrealistic. For example, Rudra and Chakraborty (1991) have found that for landholdings of size 2 hectares or more in India the Pareto curve fits nicely. It is a trivial matter to incorporate general distributions in the model being developed in the text. For instance, were there to be a ceiling on landholdings, $t(n)$ would be flat for large n. And so on. But our chosen specification has the virtue that the resulting notation is uncomplicated. Since nothing would be gained were we to generalize the specification, we won't.

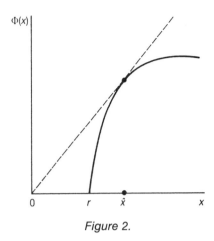

Figure 2.

restriction that x lies in a limited interval (say, in the region 2,000–3,500 kcal per day for an adult male), $\Phi(x)$ can be regarded as the nutrition–productivity curve.

It cannot be emphasized strongly enough that the nutrition–productivity curve drawn in Fig. 2 is an idealization. The functional relationship is certainly not deterministic, and in all probability not of uniform curvature either. Bliss and Stern (1978b) explored the then existing literature to see what one could say about the slope of $\Phi(x)$ slightly to the right of $x = r$. They collated some limited evidence to suggest that the curve is a straight line in this region. 'Increasing returns' to energy intake immediately to the right of $x = r$, is yet another possibility, and we could easily work with this in what follows, even at the expense of some expositional ease. But none of these finer details is a matter of any significance to the theory we will develop.

It is important to distinguish critical from inessential assumptions. The theory does not rest on the special properties of Fig. 2, and we should bear this in mind when we come to develop it. What is critical for the theory are two assumptions: (i) maintenance requirement is a significant fraction of total energy expenditure, and (ii) at levels of intake somewhat in excess of maintenance requirement there are diminishing gains in productivity from further increases in consumption (i.e. $\Phi''(x) < 0$). As both are incontrovertible, we are on firm ground.

We will assume for simplicity that a person either does not work in the agricultural sector or works there for one unit of 'time'. Each person has a reservation wage which must as a minimum be offered if he is to accept a job in the labour market. For high n-persons this reservation wage will be high because their rental incomes are large. For low n-persons, most especially the landless, this reservation wage is low, but it isn't nil. The thought here is that if they find no employment they live on the fruits of local common property resources (gathering, hunting, tapping, and so forth; see Falconer and Arnold,

1991; Dasgupta, 1992a, chapter 10), or survive by begging. This involves work, but it doesn't require as much endurance as agricultural work. The landless don't starve when they fail to obtain jobs in agriculture: they are destitutes and become undernourished. We aren't modelling famines here, we are thinking of normal times.

Since we wish to study the agricultural sector, it will help enormously to treat it in isolation. So I shall assume that the goods and services obtainable from common property resources are not exchangeable with food crops in the market. The cleanest way of formalizing this is to say that food crops are purchased by each person with only that part of his income which is derived from agriculture. The way to think about this is that both wages and land rents are paid in terms of food crops.

Let us assume that there are competitive markets for both land and labour power (but see section 8). Now let ρ denote the rent on land. (As this is a timeless economy, ρ can also be thought of as the price of land.) Person n's rental income is therefore $\rho \hat{T} t(n)$.

The reservation wage is written as $\bar{w}(R)$, where R is non-wage income, including the value of leisure. $\bar{w}(R)$, although not R, is exogenously given in our timeless model. (But see sections 9–10.) We take it that $\bar{w}(R)$ is continuous and increasing in R. For a landless person, R is income from common property resources. Should such persons find and accept employment in agriculture, they have to forgo R (there is no time left for scavenging). For those owning a tiny piece of land, R is the sum of their rental income and income from common property resources. If they find and accept employment in agriculture, they have to forgo income from common property resources, but not rental income. Finally, someone owning a large piece of property can afford leisure. Their non-wage income consists simply of rental income. They will not be involved in scavenging. It would be pedantic to model all this formally. So we construct a 'reduced form' of $\bar{w}(R)$, and write it as $\bar{w}(n, \rho)$. We assume it is non-decreasing as a function of n, non-decreasing as a function of ρ, and a positive constant in the interval $[0, \bar{n}]$. This means that the landless are identical. It also means that the commons provide a fixed quantity of sustenance per person, no matter how many live on them. While it is hallowed by intellectual tradition (an exception is Guha, 1989), the assumption has little to commend it. For the moment, however, we make it. A typical form of $\bar{w}(n, \rho)$ is drawn in Fig. 3. In sections 9–10 we will dispense with it to fruitful effect.

Our first aim is to study the link between the distribution of physical assets and the incidence and extent of undernourishment and economic disenfranchisement. The analysis would be contaminated were we to suppose that people differ physiologically. Therefore, we take it that they differ only in terms of the quantity of land they own. The nutrition–productivity curve of the representative person is drawn in Fig. 2. We are to think of the ordinate of the curve as measuring the maximum labour power, Φ, a person is capable of offering in agricultural production. In keeping with our interpretation, we

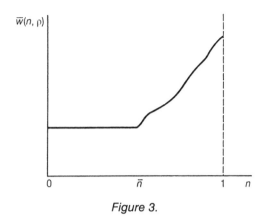

Figure 3.

can also think of it as the maximum amount of agricultural work the person is able to accomplish; or, in other words, the maximum number of units of the composite agricultural task the individual is capable of performing. We now make the crucial assumption that an employer can observe the amount of work done by a labourer. With our interpretation, this means that wages can be paid on a *piece-rate* basis. Now, labour time is not a factor of production, but agricultural work is. It follows that labour will be remunerated on a piece-rate basis. To be sure, we can compute a worker's take-home pay (which we will denote by w). This we are able to do by multiplying the piece-rate by the amount of work the person accomplishes (equation (5.4) below). But the worker is not paid a time wage; rather, payment is made on the basis of the amount of work done.

As noted earlier, the horizontal axis in Fig. 2 measures nutrition intake (or consumption), x, which we identify with income. $\hat{x}$ denotes the level of nutrition intake at which marginal labour power equals average labour power. A person will be said to attain their efficient-productivity at $\hat{x}$. I have deliberately chosen the nutrition–productivity curve to display a large curvature at $\hat{x}$. This is consonant with the findings in Viterie (1974), Immink and Viterie (1981a, b) and Immink *et al.* (1984a, b). Our analysis is not dependent upon this specification, but it helps to interpret things in a sharp manner. For example, it allows us to regard $\hat{x}$ as someone's nutrition requirement (the level of energy intake from food that will balance energy expenditure when the individual has a body size and composition, and level of physical activity consistent with long-term good health; and that will allow for the maintenance of economically necessary and socially desirable physical activity; WHO, 1985, p. 12). By the same token, it enables us to say that someone consuming less than $\hat{x}$ in this timeless economy is undernourished. The key assumption I now make is that the reservation wage of a landless person is less than $\hat{x}$. The thought here is that income from common property resources is less than $\hat{x}$, and that it is quite inadequate even when allowance is made of the fact that gathering and tapping involve less work than agriculture.

We are now left with the concept of involuntary unemployment, which has yet to be defined. It is a sharper notion than surplus labour, much discussed in the development literature.[7] We have assumed the existence of a continuum of people for good reason. Involuntary unemployment has to do with differential treatment meted out to similar people. Formally, we will say that a person is involuntarily unemployed who cannot find employment in a market that employs someone else very similar, and if the latter person, by virtue of their employment in this market, is distinctly better off. Notice that this subsumes the situation where individuals are identical, in which case dissimilar treatment may arise due to rationing in the labour market (see section 6). It is, however, frequently noted by thinkers that no two people are ever identical. Our definition accommodates this thought.

There is overwhelming evidence from village studies of involuntary unemployment in the Indian sub-continent. One way of measuring this is to ask for information on the number of days spent by a respondent in seeking employment at the prevailing wage and the number of days the respondent was successful. The ratio of the latter to the former would give the probability of employment in the casual labour market. One minus this ratio, when averaged over respondents, would then be a measure of involuntary unemployment.[8] Data from the famous ICRISAT study revealed, for example, that in the mid-1970s average involuntary unemployment rates for males were about 12 per cent and 39 per cent during the busy and slack seasons respectively. The corresponding estimates for females were 11 per cent and 50 per cent.[9] The seasonal nature of agricultural employment bears re-stressing, as does the extent of gender differences in the figures for the slack season. We will deploy these observations later in this chapter.

The definition of involuntary unemployment has been cast within the context of markets only because we are studying the competitive market mechanism here. Moreover, it has been focused on unemployment only because we are studying labour allocation. But the underlying idea is of general significance. A weak ethical principle, much discussed in public economics, is that resource allocation mechanisms should be horizontally equitable, by which is meant that individuals who are the same in all relevant

---

[7] On surplus labour, see Leibenstein (1957a,b), Mazumdar (1959), Georgescu-Roegen (1960), Schultz (1964), Sen (1966), and Guha (1989). We will define the notion in section 9 and develop a model economy in which involuntary unemployment and surplus labour are simultaneously present.

[8] Mazumdar (1989) has a good discussion of this. See also Rudra (1982) and Bardhan (1984).

[9] ICRISAT is the acronym for the International Crops Research Institute for the Semi-Arid Tropics, in Hydrabad, India. Its panel data initially covered 240 households in six villages in the semi-arid regions of two states (Andhra Pradesh and Maharashtra), over an extended period starting in the mid-1970s. It is a pioneering investigation. Accounts of its findings on credit, tenancy and labour relations in this data-set are in Binswanger et al. (1984), Jodha (1984), Ryan and Ghodake (1984), and in an excellent synthesis by Walker and Ryan (1990).

The most extensive accounts of land and labour relations in the broader context of South Asia with which I am familiar are Singh (1988a,b,c, 1990; Mazumdar, 1989), which include analyses of the ICRISAT data.

respects should be treated equally. (Musgrave, 1959; Stiglitz, 1988.) Involuntary unemployment is an instance of horizontal *in*equity. We will discover that the involuntarily unemployed in our model economy are for the most part undernourished as well. The phenomenon is repugnant.

4. Efficiency Wages and Piece-Rates

Leibenstein (1957a, b), Mazumdar (1959), Prasad (1970), Mirrlees (1975), Rodgers (1975), Stiglitz (1976), and Bliss and Stern (1978a, b) have studied special cases of the construction we are developing here. Their analyses suggest that in our model economy the labour market does not necessarily clear. So I shall assume that there is a mechanism built into the market system which *rations* labour power if supply exceeds demand and if flexibility in the piece-rate is incapable of clearing the market. We don't need to be explicit about the mechanism, but some form of 'queuing' can be taken to be the process by which the rationing is realized. Queuing can vary in its mode of operation. Rudra (1982), for example, reports in his study of a large number of villages in West Bengal, India, that search on the casual labour market is undertaken by employers (and *not* by the workers), who typically visit labourers in their homes the evening before the day when work is to be undertaken. In the busy agricultural season employers aren't overly selective about the quality of workers they hire. In the slack season they are. There is overwhelming evidence there of labour rationing excepting for those few days of the year when agricultural activity is particularly intense.[10]

We begin with some technical preliminaries, involving no economics. They will prove essential when we come to the economics. Define $w^*(n, \rho)$ as:

$$w^*(n, \rho) \equiv \arg \min [w/\Phi(w + \rho \hat{T} t(n)), \text{ subject to } w \geq \bar{w}(n, \rho)] \quad (4.1)$$

In words, $w^*(n, \rho)$ is that wage rate (i.e. wage paid to a labourer) which, at the land-rental rate ρ, minimizes the wage per unit of agricultural work person n can accomplish, conditional on their being willing to work at this wage rate.[11] $w^*(n, \rho)$ is called the 'efficiency-wage' of person n. It is a function of n, not because people differ physiologically (in our model they don't), but because different people possess different landholdings. This explains why a person's efficiency wage depends in general on the rental rate on land, i.e. on 'unearned' income. By hypothesis $\hat{x}$ exceeds the reservation wage of the landless. So $w^*(n, \rho) = \hat{x}$ for landless people. In words, the efficiency wage of a landless worker is that person's nutritional requirement. By continuity,

---

[10] See Bardhan and Rudra (1981, 1986) and Dreze and Mukherjee (1989) for additional village studies.

[11] If Φ is of the form depicted in Fig. 2, the right-hand side of equation (4.1) has a unique value. If it is not, then the right-hand side of the equation is not necessarily unique. When not, we should choose the largest solution and define $w^*(n, \rho)$ as the largest solution.

we may conclude that for someone who owns only a tiny piece of land, $\bar{w}(n, \rho) < w^*(n, \rho) < \hat{x}$.[12]

To fix ideas, let us suppose that the reservation-wage schedule, $\bar{w}(n, \rho)$, is such that for an individual who owns somewhat more than just a tiny plot of land, $\bar{w}(n, \rho) = w^*(n, \rho) < \hat{x}$. (The efficiency wage equals the reservation wage, which in turn is less than the nutritional requirement.) Let us also assume that the reservation-wage schedule is such that for someone who owns a vast amount of land, $\bar{w}(n, \rho) = w^*(n, \rho) > \hat{x}$. These latter two features aren't necessary for the analysis (see the example analysed in sections A2 and A3), but they help motivate it by bringing the model economy closer to the world as we know it. They stress that the efficiency wage of an individual can be high for one of two reasons: (i) that person enjoys no unearned income, so that their entire labour power in agriculture has to be fuelled by wages; and (ii) their reservation wage is high. In an intertemporal economy (i) would encompass the case where the person's nutritional status is low. We will demonstrate that the economically disenfranchised are in this state not because they don't wish to work, but because they are unable to offer the labour power the market demands. The rich are also too costly to hire as agricultural workers, but for reason (ii): they prefer to do other things.

In my exposition here I shall take it that labour is paid on a piece-rate basis. This means that an employer can observe the amount of work any given employee of his accomplishes. So the way the contract is agreed upon is a matter of no substance. For example, we could alternatively assume that payment is on a wage basis, but that there is agreement on what the job entails; that is, how much work the worker is expected to accomplish. The key assumption is that contracts are honoured.

We may now define $\mu^*(n, \rho)$ as:

$$\mu^*(n, \rho) \equiv w^*(n, \rho)/\Phi(w^*(n, \rho) + \rho \hat{T} t(n)) \qquad (4.2)$$

For any given ρ, $\mu^*(n, \rho)$ is the minimum value of wage per unit of agricultural work to which person n can be forced. Now $\Phi(x)$ is the maximum amount of work a labourer can accomplish when their nutrition intake is x. Recall also that we are identifying a person's intake with their income. Therefore, $\mu^*(n, \rho)$ in equation (4.2) may be thought of as the efficiency piece-rate for person n. Since it is a function of n's non-wage income, it depends on ρ for those owning land. In Fig. 4 a typical shape of $\mu^*(n, \rho)$ has been drawn. It is relatively 'high' for the landless because they enjoy no rental income. For them, $\mu^*(n, \rho) = \hat{x}/\Phi(\hat{x})$. This is the nutrition intake per unit of agricultural work an individual is capable of performing when their intake equals their requirement. It is also the inverse of a person's efficient-productivity. Thus, other things being the same, the efficiency piece-rate of a person with a good nutritional

---

[12] To confirm this, translate $\Phi(.)$ in Fig. 2 to the left by the tiny amount $\rho \hat{T} t(n)$, and then use equation (4.1).

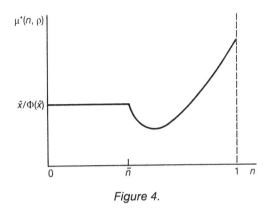

Figure 4.

status would be expected to be less than that of an individual with a bad nutritional status. In section 2 we provided an intuitive explanation for the fact that the landless are costly workers; they can be undercut by people having access to rental income. We will confirm this below.

Using the reservation-wage function in Fig. 3, it is an easy matter to check from equation (4.2) that $\mu^*(n, \rho)$ is a shade lower than $\hat{x}/\Phi(\hat{x})$ for 'small' landholders. To see why, recall that $\bar{w}(n, \rho)$ has been assumed to be a continuous function of n. This means that the reservation wage of a small landholder is lower than $\hat{x}$. As with landless people, the constraint in equation (4.1) is not binding for small landowners. Moreover, small landowners enjoy rental income. Taken together, these two facts imply that the efficiency piece-rate of a small landowner is lower than that of a landless individual.

I suggested earlier that we should think of the reservation wage schedule as rising steeply with n. It lends empirical credence to the model. It means that for large n the constraint in equation (1) binds when we compute n's efficiency wage. In short, n's efficiency wage equals the reservation wage. It also means that $\mu^*(n, \rho)$ is large for large n. In Fig. 4, $\mu^*(n, \rho)$ has been drawn as something like a U-shaped curve. We will use this depiction to illustrate the outcome of the competitive market mechanism in our model economy. The figure is consonant with the assumptions we have so far made. But they don't guarantee this shape. In sections 9 and A1 we will see that this shape isn't necessary for the analysis.

5. Competitive Market Allocations

As there are two factors of production (land and labour power), two factor markets have to be reckoned with. The market for food crops and the factor markets are all assumed to be competitive. By this we will mean that all decision units take prices as given. Our aim in this chapter is to extend the standard theory of resource allocation by acknowledging physiology. So it makes sense to stay close to the most pristine version of the theory (the Arrow–Debreu construct) in all other respects.

We will assume that market prices are public knowledge. Each 'agricultural enterprise' (we will often use the term 'employer') knows its own technology of production ($F(.)$ is the aggregate technology), knows how much land it is operating, and can observe the amount of work accomplished by each worker employed by it. It does *not* need to know anything about the nutrition–productivity curves of workers.[13] Each individual knows how much land they own (if any), and their own capabilities, which in the context of our model means their nutrition–productivity curve (but see section 8). They need know nothing about other people's capabilities, nor about technological possibilities. As in the Arrow–Debreu theory, we assume that all contracts are honoured. In an intertemporal setting the corresponding assumption would be that there is a complete set of forward markets. We will drop this assumption in sections 9–10.

The price of food crops can be set equal to unity by normalization. ρ is the rental rate on land. Let μ denote the price of a unit of labour power. We have been identifying a unit of labour power with a unit of agricultural work. Therefore, μ is the piece-rate. Employers (which may be households) are profit-maximizing and each individual aims to maximize their total income given the opportunities faced.[14] In the Appendix (section A1) we will provide a formal definition of competitive equilibrium allocations in our model economy. Here we will take the informal route when defining an equilibrium. Having done that, I shall characterize equilibrium allocations.[15]

We will use a 'tilde' over economic variables to denote their values in equilibrium. Thus $\tilde{\rho}$ and $\tilde{\mu}$ denote the rental rate on land and the piece-rate, respectively. Since prices are taken as given by all agents, $\tilde{\mu}$ must equal the marginal product of aggregate labour power ($\tilde{E}$), and $\tilde{\rho}$ the marginal product of land. In short,

$$\tilde{\mu} = \partial F(\tilde{E}, \hat{T})/\partial E \tag{5.1}$$

---

[13] This is often misunderstood. In commenting on models making use of the links between nutrition and productivity, Rosenzweig (1988, p. 723) says: 'If the … model is modified to include alternative sources of consumption other than wage income for some workers, the model predicts diversity in time wages among workers, as long as employers have information about individual workers' circumstances (a likely scenario in the village economy).' Basu (1992, p. 109) makes the same mistake, but to worse effect, in that he builds an alternative construction so as to avoid this non-existent weakness of the theory.

[14] More precisely, individuals compare their maximal income if they work in agriculture to the sum of their reservation wage and maximal rental income if they are not working in agriculture.

[15] Rodgers (1975) and Stiglitz (1976) analysed an economy where landowners' reservation wage is in effect infinity. Thus, the only possible labourers are the landless. In this case it makes no difference whether there is a single employer (i.e. labour monopoly) or many: the outcome is the same. Because of this happy analytical coincidence Rodgers and Stiglitz did not need to develop the apparatus required to discuss non-monopsonistic markets, a need which cannot be avoided if we wish to explore the implications of agrarian reform (section 7); for after such a reform, the labour market cannot be monopsonistic.

and

$$\tilde{\rho} = \partial F(\tilde{E}, \hat{T})/\partial T \qquad (5.2)$$

As $F(.)$ is constant-returns-to-scale, employers earn no profits after factor payments have been made or imputed. Formally,

$$F(\tilde{E}, \hat{T}) = \tilde{\mu}\tilde{E} + \tilde{\rho}\hat{T} \qquad (5.3)$$

Equation (5.1) allows us to compute aggregate demand for labour power.[16] (We will come to the question of labour supply presently.) Land is supplied inelastically. The value of $\tilde{\rho}$ is such that at $\tilde{E}$ equation (5.2) holds. The land market clears. So does the market for food crops. By assumption, demand for agricultural produce is made by people with only that part of their income which comes from the agricultural sector. Aggregate demand equals aggregate supply. This is given by equation (5.3).

So far the description of an equilibrium has been conventional. The novel bit concerns the labour market. Labour is a differentiated commodity here: people differ in their efficiency wages. Let $D(n)$ be the market demand for the labour time of person n, and let that person's supply of labour-time be $S(n)$. By assumption $S(n)$ is either zero or unity. Let $\tilde{G}$ denote the set of persons who are employed in agriculture, and let $\tilde{w}(n)$ be the wage rate for every n-person in $\tilde{G}$. Who belongs to $\tilde{G}$?

To answer this, notice that the market demand must be nil for someone whose efficiency piece-rate exceeds $\tilde{\mu}$. Equally, this person cannot (or given his reservation wage, will not) supply the labour quality the market can bear at the going rate $\tilde{\mu}$.[17] Therefore, this person supplies no labour time. For this n-person $S(n) = D(n)$. The labour market clears for all such people.

What of someone whose efficiency piece-rate is less than $\tilde{\mu}$? Plainly, every employer desires this person's service. There is demand for his/her time. Speaking metaphorically, this person's wage ($w(n)$) is bid up to the point where the piece-rate received equals $\tilde{\mu}$. Since for this n-person $\tilde{\mu} > \mu^*(n, \tilde{\rho})$, we may conclude that $\tilde{w}(n) > w^*(n, \tilde{\rho}) \geqslant \bar{w}(n, \tilde{\rho})$. This means in turn that the person supplies their unit of labour time (i.e. $S(n) = 1$) most willingly. Employers may as well demand this amount (they make no profit from hiring the person, so they are indifferent between hiring them and not hiring them). Demand equals supply for any such individual's service. The labour market clears for this category of people as well.

We come finally to someone whose efficiency piece-rate equals $\tilde{\mu}$. This category is of especial interest. Employers are indifferent between hiring

---

[16] The right-hand side of the equation is a declining function of E. Its intersection with $\tilde{\mu}$ yields $\tilde{E}$. See Fig. 8.

[17] To confirm this, suppose the person were to be employed at a wage rate $w \geqslant \bar{w}(n, \tilde{\rho})$. For this to be feasible, it must be that $w + \tilde{\rho}\hat{T}t(n) \leqslant \tilde{\mu}\Phi(w + \tilde{\rho}\hat{T}t(n)) + \tilde{\rho}\hat{T}t(n)$; and so $w \leqslant \tilde{\mu}\Phi(w + \tilde{\rho}\hat{T}t(n))$. This contradicts the fact that for this person $\mu^*(n, \tilde{\rho}) > \tilde{\mu}$.

someone in this category and not hiring them. Moreover, such a person is willing to supply their labour time: with eagerness if the wage to be received exceeds their reservation wage, and as a matter of indifference if it equals it.

How large is this class of people? The answer is: very large if $\tilde{\mu} = \hat{x}/\Phi(\hat{x})$, and infinitesimally small if $\tilde{\mu} \neq \hat{x}/\Phi(\hat{x})$; (see section 6). If $\tilde{\mu} = \hat{x}/\Phi(\hat{x})$, all the landless fall into this category. Agricultural enterprises are indifferent between employing and not employing a landless person, whereas every landless person is most eager to be hired.[18] The problem is that there are an awful lot of land-less people (all n-persons in the range $[0, \bar{n}]$, to be precise), and if all were to be employed condition (5.1) would almost surely be violated. To confirm this, notice that when $\tilde{\mu} = \hat{x}/\Phi(\hat{x})$ the left-hand side of equation (5.1) is fixed by physiology. Once we know what $\tilde{\mu}$ is, we can determine $\tilde{E}$ from the equation. Now recall that in equilibrium all n-persons whose efficiency piece-rates are less than $\tilde{\mu}$ are employed. It is an easy matter to compute their supply of aggregate labour power in terms of $\tilde{\mu}$. (see the Appendix.) Call this $\tilde{E}_1$ and define $\tilde{E}_2 = \tilde{E} - \tilde{E}_1$. In equilibrium just that mass of landless persons finds employment as is needed to supply $\tilde{E}_2$.[19] The remaining mass of the landless is rationed out of the labour market. It is forced to live on common property resources. These people are involuntarily unemployed. The economy equilibrates by rationing the labour market.[20]

We have defined equilibrium allocations. But do they exist? Our first result affirms this:

Result (i): In the economy under review a competitive equilibrium exists.[21]

Agricultural workers may as well be paid at a piece-rate. A person's wage equals the product of the piece-rate and the amount of work they perform. The problem is that this equality doesn't necessarily specify the wage: there

---

[18] The latter follows from the fact that a landless person would earn $\tilde{\mu}\Phi(\hat{x}) = \hat{x}$ in wages, and by assumption, $\hat{x} > \bar{w}(n, \tilde{\rho})$ for $n \in [0, \bar{n}]$.

[19] Without loss of generality, suppose those who find employment in agriculture are in the interval $[0, \tilde{n}]$, with $\tilde{n} < \bar{n}$. Then $\tilde{E}_2 = \tilde{n}\Phi(\hat{x})$. $\tilde{n}$ gets determined from this equality.

[20] What we are calling a competitive equilibrium here is called a 'quasi-equilibrium' in general equilibrium theory (Debreu, 1962) or alternatively, a 'compensated equilibrium' (Arrow and Hahn, 1971). The difference between an Arrow–Debreu equilibrium and a quasi-equilibrium lies in the way household demand is defined. (We will for simplicity think of demand as being uniquely given at each price vector.) Let p be the price vector and e the vector of initial endowments of a household whose utility function of consumption is $u(x)$, where x is a consumption bundle. The demand vector, $x^*(p, e)$, in the Arrow–Debreu theory is defined as: $u(x^*(p, e)) \geqslant u(x)$ for all consumption bundles x such that $px \leqslant px^*(p, e) = pe$. In contrast, a commodity bundle $\tilde{x}(p, e)$ is the household's quasi-demand if $px \geqslant p\tilde{x}(p, e)$ for all consumption bundles x such that $u(x) > u(\tilde{x}(p, e))$. Notice that there may be a consumption bundle costing the same as the one which is quasi-demanded and is strictly preferred. So at given prices a household may have a number of quasi-demands even when its demand is unique. Labour rationing is a way of splitting identical households into distinct groups, each group consuming different quasi-demand vectors. Rationing accomplishes this by getting identical people to face different budget constraints.

[21] We will not provide a formal proof of this (for which see Dasgupta and Ray, 1986). It will be simpler to study the matter diagrammatically.

may be more than one wage at which the equality holds.[22] Competition among employers drives the wage up to the largest solution. Formally, this is stated as:

Result (ii): For all $n \in \tilde{G}$, $\tilde{w}(n)$ is the larger of the (possibly) two
solutions of the equation: $w/\Phi(w + \tilde{\rho}\hat{T}t(n)) = \tilde{\mu}$ (5.4)

Thus far a definition of equilibrium allocations; we have yet to characterize them. Before doing this it will prove useful to note that among those who are employed in agriculture, larger landholders earn higher wages. Formally, this is stated as:

Result (iii): For all n_1, $n_2 \in \tilde{G}$, $t(n_1) < t(n_2)$ implies $\tilde{w}(n_1) < \tilde{w}(n_2)$ (5.5)

This has proved to be a contested result (see Rosenzweig, 1988). In a sample of rural households in India, Rosenzweig (1980) found no link between an agricultural worker's wage and the amount of land owned. Notice that the finding would be consistent with Result (iii) were household size an increasing function of the size of landholding. Unfortunately, the study did not investigate this question. In any event, since the model is timeless, land ownership should be thought of as a surrogate for ownership of productive assets, in particular nutritional status. When this switch is made the matter is not so controversial. Deolalikar (1988) has found in his study of ICRISAT data that nutritional status is positively associated with wage.

If they are employed, an n-person's income (i.e. nutrition intake) is $x(n) = \tilde{w}(n) + \tilde{\rho}\hat{T}t(n)$. The income of an n-person who doesn't work as an agricultural labourer is $x(n) = \bar{w}(n, \tilde{\rho}) + \tilde{\rho}\hat{T}t(n)$.[23] Now $\bar{w}(n, \tilde{\rho})$ is an increasing function of n for $n \geqslant \bar{n}$. Moreover, Result (ii) reflects the fact that competition bids up the wages of those with more land. Their rental incomes are, of course, greater. They are doubly fortunate. This is stated as:

Result (iv): For all n_1, $n_2 \in [0, 1]$, $t(n_1) < t(n_2)$ implies $x(n_1) < x(n_2)$ (5.6)

6. Development Regimes

Superimpose the horizontal curve $\mu = \tilde{\mu}$ on to Fig. 4. There are three equilibrium regimes (Figs 5–7). Population density and the distribution of landholdings together determine to which of the three the economy belongs. In this section we will hold fixed the distribution of land ($t(n)$). We will increase $\hat{T}$ and study its effect on equilibrium allocation. In the following

---

[22] The reader can confirm that there can be at most two wages at which the equality holds.
[23] $\bar{w}(n, \tilde{\rho})$ represents income from common property resources for the rural poor. For the rich it reflects the income-equivalent of leisure.

section we shall vary the distribution of land and then discuss the efficacy of economic growth with redistribution. The central result concerning growth is:

Result (v): For any given distribution of land, $t(n)$, a competitive equilibrium allocation exists, and is in one of three possible regimes:

(1)   If $\hat{T}$ is sufficiently small, $\tilde{\mu} < \hat{x}/\Phi(\hat{x})$, and the economy is characterized by malnutrition among all the landless and some of the near-landless (Fig. 5).
(2)   There are ranges of moderate values of $\hat{T}$ within which $\tilde{\mu} = \hat{x}/\Phi(\hat{x})$, and the economy is characterized by malnutrition and involuntary unemployment among a fraction of the landless (Fig. 6).
(3)   If $\hat{T}$ is sufficiently large, $\tilde{\mu} > \hat{x}/\Phi(\hat{x})$, and the economy is characterized by full employment and an absence of malnutrition (Fig. 7).

Let us study each regime in turn.
Regime 1: $\tilde{\mu} < \hat{x}/\Phi(\hat{x})$. The regime is described in Fig. 5. All n-persons

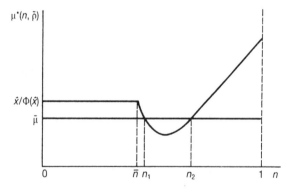

Figure 5.

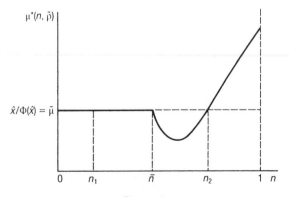

Figure 6.

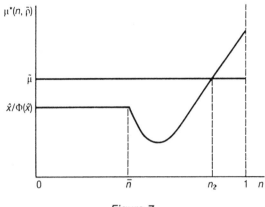

Figure 7.

between n_1 and n_2 are employed in agriculture.[24] Unless $\hat{T}$ is exceptionally low, the borderline n_1-person is one for whom the market wage $\tilde{w}(n_1)$ exceeds that person's reservation wage $\bar{w}(n_1, \tilde{\rho})$. I shall assume this in the exposition. All n-persons below n_1 and above n_2 are out of the labour market: the former because their labour power is too expensive, the latter because their reservation wages are too high (they are rich).

All the landless are undernourished ($\tilde{x}(n) < \hat{x}$). It can be verified that people between $\bar{n}$ and n_1 are also undernourished: their rental incomes are too meagre. Persons slightly to the right of n_1 consume less than $\hat{x}$. So some of the employed are undernourished as well.

Admittedly, there are no job queues in the labour market; nevertheless, the economy suffers from involuntary unemployment. To confirm this, note $\tilde{w}(n_1) > \bar{w}(n_1, \tilde{\rho})$. By continuity, we may infer that $\tilde{w}(n) > \bar{w}(n, \tilde{\rho})$ for all n in a neighbourhood to the right of n_1. These people are employed. They are distinctly better off than n-persons in a neighbourhood to the left of n_1, who suffer their reservation wages. The income schedule, $\tilde{x}(n)$, is discontinuous at n_1. Persons with labels just to the left of n_1 are involuntarily unemployed.

Note finally that persons to the right of n_2 are voluntarily unemployed. Call them pure *rentiers* (or the gentry). They are capable of supplying productive labour power at the going piece-rate $\tilde{\mu}$, but choose not to: their reservation wages are too high. They are to be contrasted with unemployed people to the left of n_1, who are incapable of supplying labour at $\tilde{\mu}$. Despite the discontinuity of $\tilde{x}(n)$, the economy in Regime 1 is at an Arrow–Debreu equilibrium: all markets clear.

Regime 2: $\tilde{\mu} = \hat{x}/\Phi(\hat{x})$. The regime is described in Fig. 6. It was argued earlier that this is not a fluke case: the economy is in this regime for certain

---

[24] I am assuming implicitly that the marginal product of labour power in agriculture is large when aggregate labour power employed in it is small. This means agriculture is viable, and equilibrium $\tilde{\mu}$ does not lie entirely below the curve $\mu^*(n, \tilde{\rho})$.

intermediate ranges of $\hat{T}$. All persons between n_1 and n_2 are employed. Those to the right of n_2 remain out of agricultural work because their reservation wages are too high. The economy equilibrates by rationing landless people in the labour market. A fraction of the landless, $n_1/\bar{n}$, is involuntarily unemployed, and they live on common property resources. They are the destitutes here, and they are undernourished. The remaining fraction, $1 - n_1/\bar{n}$, finds employment at the wage rate $\hat{x}$, which meets their nutritional requirements. It is also their efficiency wage. The unemployed and the malnourished are the same set of people. The proportion of the undernourished is a function of $\hat{T}$. The economy in Regime 2 is not in an Arrow–Debreu equilibrium, it is in quasi-equilibrium. Out of an originally homogeneous group of landless people two classes are created in the regime: one consists of the employed, the other the outcasts. Since those among the landless who are employed are paid their efficiency wage, this theory is often called an 'efficiency-wage theory'.

Regime 3: $\bar{\mu} > \hat{x}/\Phi(\hat{x})$. Figure 7 depicts this regime. Persons from 0 to n_2 are employed, and those to the right of n_2 price themselves out of the labour market; their reservation wages are too high. $\tilde{x}(n)$ is a continuous function. There is full employment. When in Regime 3, the economy is in an Arrow–Debreu equilibrium.

A simple way of illustrating the regimes is to resort to a 'partial equilibrium' diagram, hold constant the rental on land, and study the aggregate supply and demand functions of labour power. In Fig. 8 aggregate labour power, E, has been plotted along the horizontal axis and the piece-rate on the vertical axis. Aggregate demand is $\partial F(E, \hat{T})/\partial E$ and is downward-sloping. Aggregate supply is upward sloping, but has a discontinuity at $\mu = \hat{x}/\Phi(\hat{x})$, displaying a horizontal jump amounting to $\bar{n}\Phi(\hat{x})$. (This is where having a mass of identical landless people plays its role.) If the aggregate demand curve goes through the the gap (as does CD), the economy is in Regime 2. If it cuts the supply curve

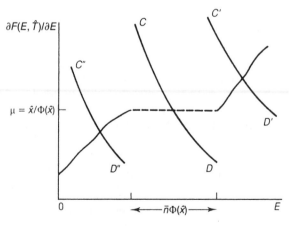

Figure 8.

beyond the gap on the right (as does $C'D'$), the economy is in Regime 3; and if before the gap on the left (as does $C''D''$), it is in Regime 1.

Before discussing the menu of feasible public policies in this economy, it is important to note:

> Result (vi): No matter which regime the economy is in, equilibrium allocations are Pareto-efficient. (For a proof, see Dasgupta and Ray, 1987.)

This sets limits on the public agenda. Policies aiming at alleviating malnutrition in the short run simply have to involve a redistribution of benefits and burdens, in which some parties emerge worse off. Over the long run, matters are different of course, because there is the prospect that growth in net national product will trickle down to the poorest of the poor. So public policy needs to be founded on some combination of asset (or consumption) redistribution and income growth. We will study the two polar routes separately in the next section. In section A3 I shall present a sample calculation so as to illustrate how we may test their relative efficacy.

7. Growth with Redistribution

So as to provide a streamlined account let us assume that for every possible $\hat{T}$ and $t(n)$, competitive equilibrium is uniquely given. This way we avoid having to select among equilibrium allocations.

We imagine a very poor economy ($\hat{T}$ is very small) and a given distribution of land, $t(n)$. Equilibrium allocation is in Regime 1 (Fig. 5). If the gentry accumulates in land improvement, $\hat{T}$ increases. For ease of exposition let us suppose that the distribution of land remains approximately the same. With $\hat{T}$ increasing, after some time the economy enters Regime 2 (Fig. 6), and eventually Regime 3 (Fig. 7).[25] It is only in Regime 3 that no one is malnourished. In the long run, growth in net national product trickles down even to the poorest of the poor, but it may be a slow process. In section A3 I shall estimate its speed with the help of a simple example.

As we have introduced time, we should think also of a credit market, and allow people to borrow. That the ability of peasants to do so is severely restricted in poor countries only means that our account of the growth process passing through successive regimes is more than a metaphor. Nevertheless, assume now that there is a credit market where peasants can obtain consumption loans. As accumulation occurs in Regime 1 the piece-rate increases. Thus, borrowing *cet. par.* accelerates the transition from Regime 1 to Regime 2, because the peasant who obtains a consumption loan in effect has a non-wage income for that period. (He consumes in excess of his current income so as to

---

[25] I do not have a proof that under general conditions the economy moves monotonically from Regime 1 to 2 and then to 3 with increasing $\hat{T}$. The example we will study in section A2 displays this feature.

raise his productivity.) On the other hand, if the economy is closed, this borrowing must be from the gentry, and making loans are an alternative to land improvement. This will retard the growth in $\hat{T}$. In Regime 2 accumulation raises the volume of employment rather than the piece-rate. As the end of Regime 2 approaches, all landless people will wish to borrow. I conclude that a credit market will modify the 'trickle', but it will not eliminate any of the regimes.

Amiya Dasgupta (1975, 1976), Adelman (1979), Hicks (1979), Sen (1981), and Streeten *et al.* (1981) have made a plea for policies which seek redistribution with growth. They have suggested that certain patterns of egalitarian redistribution of benefits and burdens (e.g. agrarian reform, ensuring an economy-wide distribution of health-care, education, and so forth) enhance growth in net national product. At an extreme is the thought that some minimal redistributive measure is necessary even to generate growth. It is possible to test these ideas in our laboratory.

Begin with marginal agrarian reforms. Consider a transfer of a bit of land from the gentry to a group of involuntarily unemployed people and to a group of those who are 'on the margin' of being unemployed. This is shown in Fig. 9. The reform is so fashioned that the new distribution of land is more egalitarian than the old, in the sense that the Lorenz curve of land distribution after the reform lies above that of the old one. The pre-reform equilibrium is in Regime 1. Since the reform is marginal, equilibrium is in Regime 1 even after the transfer. The figure displays changes evaluated at the original equilibrium pair of prices $(\tilde{\mu}, \tilde{\rho})$. People between n_a and n_b gain land. Their efficiency piece-rates decline, because their rental income increases even while their efficiency wages remain higher than their reservation wages. Efficiency piece-rates of those from whom land is taken (people between n_c and n_d) also decline, but for a different reason: their reservation wages are now slightly lower.

This pattern of redistribution has three effects. First, because their rental income increases, the unemployed become more attractive to employers. Second, those among the poor who are employed become more productive to the extent that they too receive land. And third, by taking land away from the gentry, their reservation wages are lowered, and when this effect is strong enough it induces them to forsake leisure and enter the agricultural labour market, however, this is not so in Fig. 9. These three effects in combination ensure that aggregate output after the reform is higher. (For a proof, see Dasgupta and Ray, 1987.) This gives us:

Result (vii): If the distribution of assets in a poor economy is very unequal, there are marginal agrarian reforms which are not only egalitarian but which result in an increase in the rate of growth of net national product.

Partial agrarian reforms of the kind just studied have a possible displacement effect, whereby 'newly' productive workers displace previously employed, less

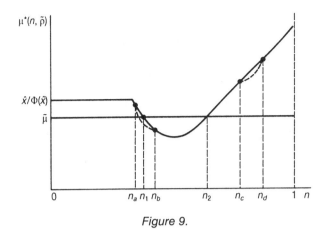

Figure 9.

productive workers.[26] Even when aggregate agricultural output increases following a Lorenz-improving land redistribution, the mass of involuntarily unemployed people may increase. This is a shortcoming. Fortunately, there is no such effect in the case of full agrarian reforms, which we will now discuss.

In order to highlight the detrimental effects of unequal asset distribution on productivity and output, we will assume that there is enough land to feed everyone adequately. To make this notion precise, imagine that everyone consumes the same amount. If x is each person's nutrition intake, aggregate output is $F(\Phi(x), \hat{T})$.[27] For the allocation to be viable, x must be a solution of

$$x = F(\Phi(x), \hat{T}) \tag{7.1}$$

If equation (7.1) has a solution, it typically has two solutions. We will concentrate on the larger of the two values and call it $x(\hat{T})$. Let $\hat{T}_1$ be the value of $\hat{T}$ for which $x(\hat{T}) = \hat{x}$, where $\hat{x}$, as before, is nutritional requirement. Equation (7.1) has a unique solution only in a fluke case. One can show that the smallest value of $\hat{T}$ for which a solution to equation (7.1) exists involves an $x(\hat{T}) < \hat{x}$. So $\hat{T}_1$ is uniquely defined.

At $\hat{T}_1$ the existing population size can be thought of as the land's carrying capacity. If $\hat{T} < \hat{T}_1$, population size exceeds the carrying capacity. If $\hat{T} > \hat{T}_1$, the economy can in principle support more people. We may now state (see Dasgupta and Ray, 1987):

Result (viii): Consider an economy where $\hat{T} \geqslant \hat{T}_1$. Provided reservation wages are low enough, an equal division of consumption ($x(\hat{T}) \geqslant \hat{x}$) is

---

[26] In being 'less productive' I mean being associated with a higher efficiency piece-rate.
[27] Recall that by normalization, we have set the population size at unity.

achievable as a competitive equilibrium allocation if there is equality in landholdings.

This result, in alliance with the characteristics of Regime 3, comes close to establishing that if an economy is neither rich nor very poor in the aggregate, large inequalities in the distribution of assets are the cause of malnutrition and involuntary unemployment. Even so, they just miss the target. Fortunately, the next two results in conjunction with result (viii) nail the intuitive idea completely.[28]

Result (ix): There exists an interval $[\hat{T}_1, \hat{T}_2]$ such that if $\hat{T} \in [\hat{T}_1, \hat{T}_2]$, there are unequal distributions of land for which competitive equilibrium allocation is in Regime 2.

Result (x): If $\hat{T} \geqslant \hat{T}_2$, no matter how unequal the distribution of land, competitive equilibrium is in Regime 3.

When discussing marginal agrarian reforms we noted that they can have perverse effects on employment. Result (viii) says that if population is below the carrying capacity of land, a full agrarian reform eliminates unemployment and malnutrition. This and Result (ix) imply that unless an economy is well endowed (i.e. $\hat{T}$ is just short of $\hat{T}_2$) marginal reforms cannot accomplish what an aggressive reform can. Result (x) provides the link between our nutrition-based resource allocation theory and the now-standard Arrow–Debreu theory, by implying that the chain connecting asset distribution and aggregate employment is snapped if the economy is richly endowed with assets.

Now some of the most influential doctrines today concerning material prospects for poor countries are based on the efficacy of the market mechanism. (See e.g. World Bank, 1986.) It should not be doubted that 'getting prices right' is a desirable objective, but it is the singular responsibility of governments to ensure that basic needs, such as health-care and primary and secondary education, are within the reach of all. The market mechanism on its own is far from capable of ensuring this. Moreover, it is a finding of modern resource allocation theory that natural monopolies, such as infrastructure, ought not to be left to the market mechanism. We are now going beyond this. Even if prices were to be got right in a poor economy, the market mechanism, unless acting upon a reasonable distribution of productive assets, can be relied upon to be an unmitigated disaster. The development of smoothly-functioning anonymous markets is necessary, but by no means sufficient, for general well-being in poor economies.

---

[28] For proofs see Dasgupta and Ray (1987). As an exercise the reader may wish to confirm these results in the context of the example in section A2 of the Appendix.

8. Robustness and Extensions

How robust are our general conclusions against relaxation of the underlying assumptions to meet observations from the world as we know it? Ten extensions suggest themselves; eight can be discussed in a non-technical manner without loss, and we do so here. The remaining two are a shade more complex: they introduce new issues. We will discuss them in the next two sections.

8.1. Heterogeneity of Agricultural Tasks

Contrary to our assumption, there are many tasks involved in agricultural production. Let us take it that there are N tasks. They can be so measured that a unit task of each type involves a unit of labour power. The production function will now be of the form $F(E_1, ..., E_N, \hat{T})$, where E_1 is aggregate labour power employed in the first task, and so forth. In competitive equilibrium the marginal product of labour power in each task equals its piece-rate. The analysis otherwise remains the same.

There are strong empirical correlates of this. In his surveys in West Bengal villages, Rudra (1982) found wage rates to depend upon the nature of agricultural tasks. There are specific rates for male ploughmen in the busy season, female weeders in the slack season, and so forth. Significantly, wages attached to female tasks are lower. (See also Bardhan, 1984.)

8.2. Heterogeneity of People

People differ physiologically. So the nutrition–productivity curve should differ from person to person. Let H (for simplicity, a real number) denote a person's nutritional status. An individual is now defined by a pair of numbers (H, n), and using the earlier notation, we have $\Phi(.) = \Phi(x_n, H)$. If no two people are physiologically the same, we can define the population spread as a uniform bivariate distribution on (H, n) pairs and reconstruct our analysis. This means there is no mass of people at any point on the space of (H, n) pairs. It also means that there is no regime corresponding to Regime 2. Aside from this, nothing in the analysis changes. (See section 9.)

If innate skills for different tasks differ (some are more adept at weeding, some at threshing, and so forth), the same technique of labelling may be used. Once again, nothing in the analysis changes.

8.3. Household Decisions

Notice that this device can also be used to distinguish people by their family size and thus their household commitments. A person with a family doesn't consume their entire income. They share with their family. *Ceteris paribus* the larger is their family, the less they themselves consume of their income. If it is a reasonable approximation to simplify and assume that members in a household share total income in some fixed manner, introducing an additional index to reflect family size suffices. If not, we need also to specify how the allocation of food is reached within a household (via household-welfare maximization, or bargaining, or whatever; see Dasgupta, 1992a, chapters 11–12). The number of dependants (and this will be endogenous to the model, because the person in question may have a spouse or sibling who also is in search of a job outside) and the sharing rule will tell us how much of a person's income that person will themselves consume. The rest of the argument is monumentally tedious, but routine.

It is often thought that the concept of involuntary unemployment is necessarily restricted to a wage economy. Recognition that people do household chores and cultivate family plots will spell ruin for the concept, or so it is argued; and I have heard it suggested that in extending it we will need to rethink the entire issue. This is not so. The term 'involuntary unemployment' has to do with work options open to a person and to those who are similar. It is a special case of a concern with a person's activity options and of the options facing those who are similar to them. The concept has to do with horizontal inequity. The notion of involuntary unemployment can be extended in such a way as to be relevant for any resource allocation mechanism.

A family in abject poverty not only has to make do with little, it cannot even afford to share its poverty equally. In his highly original analytical work, Mirrlees (1975) pointed out that when a welfare-maximizing family is very poor, it is forced to divide its consumption unequally among its members. The reason is the non-convexity of nutrition–productivity sets, the most well-known and extreme version of which is reflected by the problem of food allocation between two on a lifeboat with food enough for only one. Rich households don't face this dilemma, they can afford to provide all members with their nutritional requirements. (See Mirrlees, 1975; Stiglitz, 1976; Martorell *et al.*, 1979; Payne, 1985; Dasgupta, 1988; Haddad and Kanbur, 1989.)

Admittedly, non-convexity may not be the sole reason for unequal shares within poor, welfare-maximizing households. Pitt, Rosenzweig and Hassan (1990) have found evidence in Bangladesh that despite considerable intra-household disparity in calorie intake, households are averse to inequality. They have argued that both the higher level and greater variance in the calorie intake of men relative to women reflect in part the fact that men are engaged in activities where productivity is sensitive to a person's state of health.

There is, finally, the possibility that unequal shares are also an outcome of uneven bargaining powers among members of a household. (See Dasgupta, 1992a, chapter 11.) It seems plausible that all these causes of inequality are active in poor households. But no matter what is the process by which intra-household allocations are reached, including it in our present analysis will not affect the general findings here, which have to do with inter-household transactions.

8.4. Monopsony

The agricultural labour market in many poor regions is competitive. This was one of the most significant findings of the village studies reported earlier. (See Dasgupta, 1992a, chapter 9, for details.) It should nevertheless be asked how the theory we have developed here would change were the number of employers to be small; in the extreme were employers to collude and form a cartel.

Bliss and Stern (1978a) have analysed a labour market not dissimilar to ours, excepting that there is a single employer; or in other words, a monopsonist. They assumed that the employer knows the nutrition–productivity curve of all potential workers, and so is able to compute a person's efficiency wage, which is then offered to the person. This is an unacceptably strong assumption, and it is necessary that we do away with it. In fact if people are identical, the Bliss–Stern analysis does not require the monopsonist to know the common nutrition–productivity curve: competition between workers could be expected to bid down the wage to its efficiency level.

But suppose workers are not identical. We need then to ask what the employer may be presumed to know. If he knows the distribution of workers according to different productivity 'types' (where a 'type' is defined, say, by a worker's nutritional status, which is unobservable to the employer) we are in an analytical terrain similar to the one made familiar in the literature on screening (Maskin and Riley, 1984a,b). It would be in the interest of the employer to offer an entire wage schedule, where wage is a non-decreasing function of the amount of work that is accomplished. Each worker would be permitted to select their most-prefered point on the schedule. (I am assuming workers know their own capabilities; but see 8.6 below.) Depending upon the details of the model, equilibrium either has all employed workers 'pooling' (everyone but those remaining out chooses the same point), or it 'separates' (no two types choose the same point), or it is a mixture of the two (e.g. a mass of the employed choose the same point while others separate; and so forth). Non-convexity of the nutrition–productivity curve makes for complications; otherwise the analysis follows a path which is now routine.

8.5. Moral Hazard

How can an employer tell how much of their income workers will themselves consume? Should the employer not expect leakage? What guarantee is there that workers will not waste calories by spending more time on leisure activities? Neither matters for the theory if, as we have assumed so far, contracts are always honoured. An employer need not care what workers do with their calories so long as the piece-rate paid does not exceed the market rate. (Of course, the employer must be able to observe the amount of work actually completed; otherwise piece-rates cannot be implemented.) We have been developing a theory of competitive markets. A monopsonistic employer cares, and will take steps to see that wages are not thrown away in frivolous activities.[29] But that is a different matter.

8.6. Noisy Φ

People cannot possibly know their own $\Phi(.)$ function. So then how can people commit themselves to performing the amounts of work they have undertaken to accomplish? They cannot, of course. Like the employer for whom they work, they take risks whenever agreeing on a contract. Attitudes towards risk, the availability of insurance, family support, and so forth, will influence the final outcome. These are familiar terrains, similar to the uncertainty one faces in production theory. They introduce additional complexities to the analysis here. They don't annul its central conclusions.

8.7. Time and History

Nutritional status is a capital asset. If we don't allow for the possibility of accumulation in other forms of capital, and if we allow for long-term contracts, competitive equilibrium in our timeless model can be viewed as a stationary equilibrium in an economy comprising dynasties (Ray and Streufert, 1992). However, if someone's nutritional status alters through time, intertemporal externalities rear their heads. Unless long-term contracts can be signed, employers will not be able to appropriate all the future benefits from employing a person now. (You hesitate to fatten a calf if you can't ensure it will not run away in the next period.) The problem has been avoided by our assuming in effect that all contracts are long-term. In the remaining two sections we will develop an analysis of economies functioning through time, where nutritional status matters. It will be confirmed that the theory can easily account for the existence of the casual labour market. It can also account for the coexistence of casual and long-term employment contracts.

An individual worker's history can be telling and very pernicious. It has been suggested to me by a number of colleagues that if our model economy were to languish in a stationary state (no accumulation) in Regime 2, the concept of involuntary unemployment would cease to have bite, because on average all the landless could be employed the same number of periods. (This would be so if in each period a lottery were to be in use for rationing the labour market.) Over the long run then, horizontal equity would be preserved.

This may well have some validity. Rudra (1982), Bardhan (1984) and Ryan and Ghodake (1984), for example, have observed from village studies that the probability of being unemployed in a given season is not the same for all people. However, they have collected no longitudinal data to check if people get shuffled around over time in such a way as to face the same probability of

---

[29] An extreme case is slavery. On the constraints imposed on the activities of slaves, see Genovese (1974).

being employed over the long haul. One may doubt if they do so shuffle, since relatively unproductive agricultural workers in the Indian sub-continent would appear to be gradually weeded out of the casual labour market. (See Mazumdar, 1989.) Here is how this will work in the efficiency-wage theory.

When we introduce time into a model, we should introduce history as well. So now introduce a tiny bit of history. Suppose the landless are all identical to begin with. Assume too that living on common property resources involves an ever-so-slight deterioration in nutritional status, and therefore in their efficient-productivity. In the first period a fraction of the landless are employed (Regime 2). We can't tell in advance which particular fraction, because a lottery is in use. But in the next period the previously-employed enjoy an ever-so-slight advantage because of their better nutritional history. Subsequently most of these same people will find employment, and all who languished in the first period through bad luck will continue to languish; no longer through bad luck, but through cumulative causation.

Long-term contracts in our model here have served the purpose of ensuring that in the future employers will be able to obtain the services of workers with better nutritional histories.[30] The phenomenon of cumulative causation (due to positive feedback) can occur in economies with 'network externalities' (Farrell and Saloner, 1986). The source of cumulative causation here is different. It has appeared here because of the maintenance costs of living, and not because of externalities. Thus, there are forces at work which pull poor people away from one another in the space which matters most: the space of well-being. Some propel themselves into higher income groups, while others remain in the mire. A similar phenomenon has been noted in models of learning. The growing divergence can be between initially similar firms producing the same commodity (Dasgupta and Stiglitz, 1988), or between the market shares enjoyed by rival products which were to begin with equally placed (Arthur, 1989; David, 1991). Here we are providing an account of the growing divergence in people's well-being. It is consistent with the positive association that has been observed between nutritional status and the owner-ship of land. (See, e.g. Valverde *et al.*, 1977; Bairagi, 1983.) Admittedly, unless the size of the population gallops alongside, accumulation (e.g. improvement in land) should ensure that unemployment and malnutrition will disappear in time. The non-convexity of the nutrition–productivity set should cease to have a stranglehold over people's lives. We confirmed this in our basic model (results (v) and (x)), but it can be a long while before this happens. In the interim the government must be urged to consider redistributive policies. If they are judiciously chosen, they may even enhance economic growth.

8.8. Food and Feed

Food has been aggregated here into a single commodity. But there is no single

---

[30] Such contracts serve other purposes as well. See Dasgupta (1992a), chapter 9.

thing called food; there are various kinds of food, each possessing a different mix of characteristics. Cereals (wheat, rice, maize, barley) are a source of protein and energy, both directly (as food) and indirectly (e.g. corn as animal feed). Among the world's poor, cereals as food are the main source of nutrition, accounting for about 50 per cent of their total calorie intake (Valdes and Konandreas, 1981). As people grow richer their food basket (among non-vegetarians, that is) changes from plant to animal protein. Income growth alters the composition of demand, from necessities to luxuries.[31] As Table 1 shows, in 1980 consumption of cereals in forty of the poorest countries was 208 million metric tonnes, whereas cereals as feed amounted to only 5 million tonnes. In contrast, the corresponding figures in twenty-six industrial market economies were 104 and 288 million metric tonnes. As the table also shows, income elasticities of demand for cereals as food and feed in the poorest countries are 0.23 and 0.75, respectively, and in industrial market economies they are 0.03 and 0.14. All this is in accordance with what one would expect.

The problem is that animal metabolism is not very efficient in the conversion of plant food. It requires 7 kcal of energy in grains in order to obtain 1 kcal of energy from grain-fed beef. (The corresponding ratio for poultry is 2:1.) Thus, growth in average income generates an incentive for farmers to shift land away from the production of food-grain towards that of cereals as feed-grain and as grazing grounds. On the basis of calories, the shift is

Table 1: Consumption of cereals.

	Poor countries	Industrial market economies
(1) Aggregate cereal demand (million metric tonnes)		
food	208	104
feed	5	288
(2) Rate of growth of demand for cereals (1966–80)		
food	2.9	1.0
feed	3.8	1.3
(3) Rate of growth of *per capita* demand for cereals (1966–80)		
food	0.4	0.1
feed	1.3	0.4
(4) Income elasticity of demand for cereals		
food	0.23	0.03
feed	0.75	0.14

Source: Yotopoulos (1985), Tables 1–2.

---

[31] For an account of the effect of growing world income on the composition of demand for resources, see Keyfitz (1976).

disproportionate because of the inefficient conversion process.[32]. This goes to impoverish the poor further, either because grain prices rise to equilibrate the market (Yotopoulos, 1985), or because involuntary unemployment increase (as it would in the natural extension of our basic model here; see Baland and Ray, 1991), thereby reducing the demand for food grain.

In his work on Latin American poverty, Feder (1977, 1979) saw the process of rural impoverishment as being generated in great part by the rising international demand for meat products. (See also Barraclough, 1977.) In a notable article, Yotopoulos (1985) has argued that when growth in national income in a poor country is unevenly shared, an additional source of the problem lies within the domestic economy itself: increases in the number of middle-income people exacerbate the incidence of malnutrition among those without assets, because the composition of demand shifts in an adverse way. There are indications that this is a potent force. For example, the annual rate of growth of cereal consumption in the poorest countries during 1966–80 was 2.9 per cent, whereas that of feed was 3.8 per cent. The introduction of necessities and luxuries into our basic model affects its detailed operations (e.g. it tends to retard the 'trickle-down' effect); it does't alter its wider implications.

9. Involuntary Unemployment and Surplus Labour[33]

The model economy studied formally so far in this chapter has been timeless. However, a person's physical productivity is a function of their nutritional status (e.g. body mass index; maximal oxygen uptake, or VO_2 max; see Dasgupta, 1992a, chapter 14), and alterations in this take time to be realized. Nutritional status is a stock, not a flow. If employers are at all able to reap the benefits of paying high wages, they can do so in the future, but not today. This means that they would have an incentive to pay efficiency-wages were the labour contract to cover a long period (say the agricultural cycle), but not otherwise. Taken at face value the theory we have developed does not appear to speak to the operations of the casual labour market, which in many parts of the agrarian world is a daily happening, contributing as it does the bulk of the hired labour force. For this reason the focus on permanent contracts has been seen to be a chief shortcoming of the efficiency-wage theory:

> ... the theory must be considered more plausible in the longer term than in the short run. The effects on strength and energy would be expected to show after weeks and months rather than a day or two. Thus one would, under the theory, expect permanent labour contracts to be rather common.
>
> (Bliss and Stern, 1982: p. 67)

What then of our construct?

---

[32] The world food crisis of 1972–4 involved a 3 per cent shortfall in grain production, accompanied by a 250 per cent price increase.

[33] This and the following section are based on Dasgupta (1992b).

In an innovative recent work Guha (1989) has used the fact of seasonality in labour requirements in agriculture to show how casual and permanent labour can coexist in a world where the nutrition–productivity link makes itself felt. In hiring a permanent worker, an employer can internalize the gains from paying high wages. But the employee has to be paid even during the slack season, when there is little work to be done. In contrast, casual workers are paid only when they are hired, which is typically during the busy season. This suggests that they are cheaper. However, they may well be less productive because of the deprivation from which they suffer during the slack season. If their nutritional status were just that much worse, employers would be indifferent between hiring workers on a long-term basis and waiting to hire less productive casual labourers when the busy season arrives. This would mean also that in certain situations only short-term employment would prevail, while in others only permanent contracts would be found profitable.

In Dasgupta (1992a, chapter 16*) I have extended Guha's analysis in such a way as to absorb nutritional models which capture something of the world as we now know it, and show that the central messages of our timeless construct carry over even when the model economy sustains both casual and permanent workers. Here I want to go a slightly different route to meet two other criticisms, which together would appear to deliver a fatal blow to the efficiency-wage theory. The first is that there are seasonal variations in the daily wage of casual workers; and the second is that the daily wage varies across regions (indeed, across villages short distances apart; see Rudra, 1982, 1984; Bardhan and Rudra, 1986). If the nutrition–productivity relationship is stable, based as it is on physiological grounds, one would expect the minimum of real wages across the year to be similar across regions. This is the criticism (Rosenzweig, 1988: p.726).

This is not quite the case. Consider a two-period world where nutrition intake in the first period (the slack season), x, affects a person's nutritional status in the second period (the busy season). I assume for simplicity that agricultural work is required only in the busy season, and that only casual labourers are hired. Formally, if y is consumption in the second period, let the person's second-period agricultural productivity be a continuous function $\Phi(x, y)$ with the properties (Fig. 10):

$$\Phi(x, y) > 0 \qquad \text{if } y \geqslant r(x)$$

$$= 0 \qquad \text{if } y < r(x),$$

$$\text{with } r(x), \ r'(x) > 0; \ \partial\Phi/\partial y > 0; \ \partial^2\Phi/\partial^2 y < 0. \qquad (9.1)$$

Notice that the maintenance requirement, $r(.)$, of a person in the second period is an increasing function of first-period consumption, x.[34]

---

[34] As always, the functional form makes sense only within the relevant range of intakes (e.g. the range which does not sustain obesity). The parameters of the model economy to be studied are so chosen that intakes will lie inside the range.

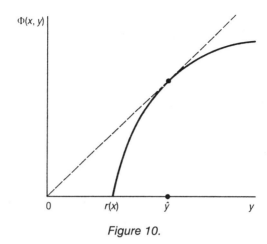

Figure 10.

For simplicity of exposition we will concentrate on the landless. We may as well then assume that the reservation wages of those who own land are so high that they don't work as labourers. This way we can ignore them. Let $\overline{M}$ be the population size of the landless. As before, we take $\overline{M}$ to be large, and regard it a continuous variable.

If the population living on the commons in any season is M, their average consumption is given by the function $\gamma f(M)$, where γ is a scale factor, and f is a positive-valued, declining function of M. During the slack season all the landless live on the commons. So $x = \gamma f(\overline{M})$. Imagine that M_e people are employed as casual workers during the busy season. Their reservation wage is then $\gamma f(\overline{M} - M_e)$. As before, let us denote by $\hat{y}$ the efficiency wage of a worker; that is:

$$\hat{y} \equiv \arg \min [y/\Phi(\gamma f(\overline{M}), y), \text{ subject to } y \geqslant \gamma f(\overline{M} - M_e)] \qquad (9.2)$$

Assume that the reservation-wage constraint in (9.2) does not bind. Then $\hat{y} > \gamma f(\overline{M} - M_e)$. (We will justify this presently.) Clearly $\hat{y}$ is a function of x. When we need to, we will write this as $\hat{y}(x)$; or alternatively, as $\hat{y}(\gamma, \overline{M})$. Now use equation (9.2) to define the efficiency piece-rate:

$$\mu^*(x) = \mu^*(\gamma f(\overline{M})) \equiv \hat{y}/\Phi(\gamma f(\overline{M}), \hat{y}) \qquad (9.3)$$

The efficiency piece-rate of a person is the inverse of their efficient productivity. Earlier, we observed that people enjoying superior nutritional status appear to be more productive. The way to formalize this here is to say that their efficient productivity is higher. In short, $\partial \mu^*(x)/\partial x < 0$. This means:

$$\partial \mu^*(\gamma f(\overline{M}))/\partial \gamma < 0, \quad \text{and} \quad \partial \mu^*(\gamma f(\overline{M}))/\partial \overline{M} > 0 \qquad (9.4)$$

Inequalities (9.4) tell us nothing about the sign of $\hat{y}'(x)$. But one can show that if $\Phi(x, y)$ has a steep curvature in the neighbourhood of $\hat{y}$, then $\hat{y}'(x) > 0$. (See section A3.) We will assume this is so.

We seek equilibrium allocations in what corresponds to Regime 2 in the timeless model (section 6). This implies we should study the class of situations where the equilibrium piece-rate, $\tilde{\mu}$, equals the efficiency piece-rate of the landless. From our earlier discussion in this chapter we know that they are equal when the total quantity of agricultural land, $\hat{T}$, is not too large. Let us assume this. As before, let agricultural output equal $F(E, \hat{T})$, where E is aggregate labour power deployed. Then $\tilde{\mu}$ is given by the condition:

$$\tilde{\mu} = \mu^*(\gamma f(\overline{M})) = \partial F(\tilde{E}, \hat{T})/\partial E \qquad (9.5)$$

Denote by $\tilde{M}_e$ the number of employed people in equilibrium. Unless $f(\overline{M})$ is a steeply declining function, equation (9.5) holds with $\overline{M} > \tilde{M}_e > 0$ and $\hat{y} > \gamma f(\overline{M} - \tilde{M}_e)$. When this is so, the volume of involuntary unemployment amounts to $\overline{M} - \tilde{M}_e$. The prevailing casual wage is $\hat{y} = \mu^*(\gamma f(\overline{M}))\Phi(\gamma f(\overline{M}), \hat{y}(\gamma, \overline{M}))$. It is a function of γ and $\overline{M}$. But $\hat{y}'(x) > 0$, so a marginal increase in the productivity of the commons, or a decline in the size of the population, leads to a rise in wages. In poor countries mobility costs are high, to such an extent that even villages are often production enclaves (Rudra, 1984; Bardhan and Rudra, 1986). This being so, we should not expect population density $(\overline{M}/\hat{T})$ to be geographically uniform. Nor should we expect the local commons to provide a uniform source of sustenance across regions. Thus Bardhan's observation in West Bengal, that the casual wage rate is positively associated with normal rainfall (Bardhan, 1984: p. 53), is consistent with our model.

The model has generated testable propositions. Perhaps the most interesting is the one we have just deduced, that in any cross-section of villages, those possessing a richer stock of common property resources per person during the slack season are the ones that would be expected to sustain higher casual wages during the busy season. I do not know of any empirical study on this.

This is not to suggest that the generalized efficiency-wage model we have developed here can provide an adequate explanation for all that has been observed in agricultural labour markets in the Indian sub-continent or Latin America. No single model can do that. For example, the persistent finding in Indian villages, that seasonal wages are remarkably uniform across labourers of a given sex, working at a given task, even when their productivities are known to differ, is belied by our model (or for that matter any simple model) and may have something to do with the difficulty of enforcing wage differentials on a fine-tuned basis. In any event, the link between nutrition and productivity should only be seen as providing an underlying structure of the conditions of living among the poorest of the poor. Superimposed on the theory lies a whole host of considerations shaping the detailed workings of the market for raw labour. (See Dasgupta, 1992a, chapter 9.) We should not expect any basic theory to do more.

The efficiency-wage theory, even in its general form, requires wages to depend on physiological considerations; but only in part. Current nutritional status is a function of past consumption, and among rural folk in poor countries nutrition intakes to a great extent are influenced by what the local commons have to offer. The hybrid model we have developed here is thus shaped by both physiology and ecological possibilities. To me, this is one of its attractions.

We have now at hand a theoretical explanation for involuntary unemployment even in the casual labour market. This is a central feature of our model. It also harbours an account of surplus labour, which is a different notion altogether. The agricultural sector is said to have surplus labour if a reduction in population leads to no decline in crop production. (See Leibenstein, 1957a, b; Mazumdar, 1959; Sen, 1966; Guha, 1989.) Suppose then that a few of the landless migrate out of the region under study. This amounts to a marginal decline in $\overline{M}$. From equation (9.4) we conclude that μ^* too declines marginally, and from equation (9.5) that $\tilde{E}$ increases slightly. But this means F increases marginally; thus, agricultural output would be expected to increase were population to decline in size. This is surplus labour with a vengeance.

10. Who Resists Wage Cuts?

Village surveys can be an intellectual minefield. The theory we have developed here sees competitive employers refusing to hire workers at a piece-rate in excess of the rate prevailing in the market. The theory also has it that workers would be *unable* to work at a lower wage rate, were they required to provide comparable labour power.[35] This latter feature has often gone unnoticed by people writing on the subject. For example, in their survey of village studies of the labour market in India, Dreze and Mukherjee (1989) think *all* efficiency-wage theories are doomed to failure. They do so because they attribute the resistance to wage cuts in these theories to employers rather than to workers. The authors cite their own observations in a North Indian village, which were consonant with the earlier findings of Bardhan and Rudra (1981,1986) and Rudra (1982) in a sample of over 100 villages in West Bengal. When asked, employers said they did not pay less than the prevailing wage because of resistance from labourers. Workers in turn, when asked, responded by saying that they would indeed so resist, because earnings from lower wages would be insufficient.

But resistance to what? To a wage cut accompanied by a reduction in the labour effort characterizing a day's work, or to a cut *un*accompanied by any such decline? Field studies with which I am familiar do not distinguish between the two, but the distinction is vital. In the model we have developed, a cut in wages *per se* would be attractive to employers, but workers would be unable

---

[35] I am supposing that the worker's efficiency wage exceeds his reservation wage.

to provide the labour power expected of them in the market, so they would
be forced to resist the cut. On the other hand, employers would find unattrac-
tive a wage cut which is accompanied by a reduction in the supply of labour
power commensurate with workers' physiological capabilities. (It would
increase the piece-rate to a level in excess of the market-equilibrium value.)
The question that field-workers asked of employers and workers did not
pertain to this latter option, but rather, to a wage cut *per se*. Their answers
support the efficiency-wage theory.

To make the point more sharply than our timeless framework was capable
of, we extend the model of the previous section.[36] Let s be a worker's body
mass index at the beginning of the busy season, and s' the index at the end
of it. Let y denote the calorie-equivalent of the casual wage; $r(x)$ the maintenance requirement (where x is slack-season consumption); and $q(\Phi)$ the
energy expended in completing Φ units of the composite agricultural task.
Then the energy conservation equation for a person (that over any time period
energy intake must equal energy expended) reads:

$$y = r + q(\Phi) - \sigma(s - s') \tag{10.1}$$

where σ is the coefficient of transformation of body mass into work. As before,
let M_e be the number who are employed during the busy season. Now denote
by m the representative person's body-mass index at the end of the busy season
were that person to continue to live on the commons. As this is a function of
$(\overline{M} - M_e)$, we write it as $m(\overline{M} - M_e)$. I take it this is a decreasing function
of its argument. Given the person's circumstances, nutritional status is of
primary importance; he cannot afford to accept employment if his body-mass
index is to fall below $m(\overline{M} - M_e)$. This we capture by the postulate that he will
not accept a condition of employment involving $s' < m(\overline{M} - M_e)$. Assume,
however, that subject to the condition $s' \geq m(\overline{M} - M_e)$, the individual prefers
higher income to a lower one. Such 'preferences' are lexicographic.

We are now home. The analysis of the previous section can be repeated to
show that if $\hat{T}$ is not large and if average consumption from the commons,
$f(M)$, doesn't decline too rapidly with M, competitive equilibrium in the casual
labour market during the busy season sustains involuntary unemployment:
people prefer to be employed in agriculture than to remain on the commons.
In particular, the number employed, $\widetilde{M}_e$, is such that $s' = m(\overline{M} - \widetilde{M}_e)$, and the
casual wage $\hat{y} > f(\overline{M} - \widetilde{M}_e)$. Finally, equation (10.1) reads:

$$\hat{y} = r(x) + q(\Phi) - \sigma(s - m(\overline{M} - \widetilde{M}_e))$$

where Φ is given by (9.1) and $x = f(\overline{M})$. The casual wage is rigid. Were any
of the employed to be asked if they would be willing to work for less while

---

[36] The analysis which follows is an extension of the one in section 7.4b in Dasgupta and Ray
(1990).

performing the same tasks, they would say 'no'. Were any of the unemployed to be asked if they would be willing to work for something less than the prevailing wage while performing the same number of tasks as the employed, they would say 'no'. Dreze and Mukherjee (1989) have simply misinterpreted the nutrition-based efficiency-wage theory. There is no contradiction here with the answers to their questionnaires.

11.   The Appeal of Nutrition-Based Theories of the Labour Market

Why have we found it necessary to dig so deeply into the structure of those resource allocation mechanisms where the nutrition–productivity link plays a crucial role? Recall the answer: the science of nutrition says it must play a role among the poorest of the poor. Moreover, we have found that resource allocation theory built on the link makes contact with a number of observed features of the labour market in the Indian sub-continent. It accounts for differences in wage rates in neighbouring villages; and it does so in a satisfying way, in that it provides an intimate connection between the availability of local common property environmental resources and the seasonality of agriculture. The theory provides one explanation (there are others; see Eswaran and Kotwal, 1985; Dasgupta, 1992a, chapter 9) for the coexistence of casual and permanent labour contracts; and it explains the empirical finding that it is the workers who resist cuts in wages, even in the midst of involuntary unemployment. The theory furthermore provides a coherent explanation of the presence of surplus labour; and most important of all, it offers a rigorous account of involuntary unemployment, a pervasive phenomenon not only in the Indian sub-continent, but in Latin America as well.

These are empirical observations of the broad brush. The agricultural labour market is so bewilderingly complex that it has revealed any number of detailed features which no model should be required to explain. It is therefore as well to conclude by noting an attitude which is essential to any enquiry into well-being and destitution. The institutional arrangements underlying agricultural work in poor countries are so complex and so specific to regions that no single model can entirely get off the ground. We can but nibble at an understanding, and that too only from various ends. To do this it is best to suspend disbelief and capture a few compelling features of the conditions of living among the rural poor in poor countries and see what they together tell us. We should not, of course, take any of the constructions literally, but we should take them seriously.

Appendix

A1.   Technicalities and Definitions

In sections 2–6 a resource allocation mechanism in which nutrition intake affects the capacity for work was analysed. The model developed was timeless. We began with the notion of efficiency wage ($w^*(n, \rho)$) and efficiency piece-rate ($\mu^*(n, \rho)$) for each person (equations (4.1) and (4.2)), and in our exposition we assumed for simplicity that $\mu^*(n, \rho)$ has the shape depicted in Fig. 4. However, the underlying assumptions of the model do not guarantee this shape. What they do imply more generally, is:

For any given ρ:

(i) $\mu^*(n, \rho)$ is constant in the interval $n \in [0, \bar{n}]$, and is a decreasing function of n in the region immediately to the right of $\bar{n}$.

(ii) $\mu^*(n, \rho)$ is a decreasing function of n to the right of $\bar{n}$ so long as the reservation-wage constraint in equation (4.1) does not bind. (From this it follows that the reservation-wage constraint in equation (4.1) binds in any region of n where $\mu^*(n, \rho)$ is an increasing function of n.)

(iii) If the reservation-wage constraint in equation (4.1) binds for some n-person, it binds for all persons who own more land.

(iv) For large values of n, $\mu^*(n, \rho)$ is an increasing function of n, because the effect of a higher reservation wage ultimately outweighs the diminishing increments to labour power associated with larger income.

Recall that $S(n)$ is the supply of labour-time by n (it can be either 0 or 1), and that $D(n)$ denotes market demand for n's labour time. Competitive equilibrium allocations were defined informally in the body of this chapter. We now provide a formal definition:

A rental rate $\tilde{\rho}$, a piece rate $\tilde{\mu}$, a subset $\tilde{G}$ of the interval $[0, 1]$, and a real-valued function $\tilde{w}(n)$ on $\tilde{G}$ sustain a competitive equilibrium allocation if (and only if):

(1) for all n-persons for whom $\tilde{\mu} > \mu^*(n, \tilde{\rho})$, $S(n) = D(n) = 1$;

(2) for all n-persons for whom $\tilde{\mu} < \mu^*(n, \tilde{\rho})$, $S(n) = D(n) = 0$;

(3) for all n-persons for whom $\tilde{\mu} = \mu^*(n, \tilde{\rho})$, $S(n) \geqslant D(n)$, where $D(n)$ is either 0 or 1, and where $S(n) = 1$ if $\tilde{w}(n) > \bar{w}(n, \tilde{\rho})$;

(4) $\tilde{G} = [n \mid D(n) = 1]$, and $\tilde{w}(n)$ is the larger of the (possibly) two solutions of $w/\Phi(w + \tilde{\rho}\hat{T}t(n)) = \tilde{\mu}$ for all n with $D(n) = 1$;[37]

(5) $\tilde{\mu} = \partial F(\tilde{E}, \hat{T})/\partial E$, where $\tilde{E}$ is aggregate labour power supplied by all who are employed in agriculture; that is,

$$\tilde{E} = \int \Phi(\tilde{w}(n) + \tilde{\rho}\hat{T}t(n)) \, d\nu(n);$$

and

(6) $\tilde{\rho} = \partial F(\tilde{E}, \hat{T})/\partial T$.

---

[37] I should add that all relevant functions, such as $D(n)$, are taken to be measurable. Lebesgue measure is denoted by $\nu(.)$. Observe that the two stated conditions regarding $\tilde{w}(n)$ define it uniquely for each person in agriculture.

Proofs of all results quoted in the body of the chapter are in Dasgupta and Ray (1986,1987).

A2.   A Two-Class Example

It will be illuminating to study an example in which equilibrium allocations can be solved for explicitly. I consider what is initially a two-class economy in which the aggregate production function is of the Cobb–Douglas form. The nutrition–productivity curve is taken to be a step function, and the reservation wage is assumed to be nil for all. Thus, assume:

$$\Phi(x) = \bar{\Phi} > 0 \qquad \text{if } x \geqslant \hat{x} > 0,$$
$$= 0 \qquad \text{if } x < \hat{x}, \qquad \text{(A2.1)}$$

$$t(n) = 1/(1 - \bar{n}) \qquad \text{for } 1 \geqslant n \geqslant \bar{n} \geqslant 0,$$
$$= 0 \qquad \text{for } 0 \leqslant n < \bar{n}, \qquad \text{(A2.2)}$$

$$\bar{w}(R) = 0 \qquad \text{for all } R \geqslant 0, \qquad \text{(A2.3)}$$

$$F(E, T) = E^{\alpha} T^{(1-\alpha)} \qquad \text{where } 0 < \alpha < 1. \qquad \text{(A2.4)}$$

Using equation (4.1) we may confirm that the efficiency wage of n-person is:

$$w^*(n, \rho) = \hat{x} \text{ for } 0 \leqslant n < \bar{n}$$
$$= \max\{0, \hat{x} - \rho \hat{T}/(1 - \bar{n})\} \text{ for } \bar{n} \leqslant n \leqslant 1. \qquad \text{(A2.5)}$$

Similarly, on using equations (4.2) and (A2.5) it is immediate that the efficiency piece-rate assumes the form:

$$\mu^*(n, \rho) = \hat{x}/\bar{\Phi} \text{ for } 0 \leqslant n < \bar{n}$$
$$= \max\{0, \hat{x} - \rho \hat{T}/(1 - \bar{n})\}/\bar{\Phi} \text{ for } \bar{n} \leqslant n \leqslant 1. \qquad \text{(A2.6)}$$

We will keep fixed the distribution of land and vary $\hat{T}$ so as to illustrate Result (v). We will then illustrate Results (vii)–(x). We will finally do a sample calculation to see the speed of the 'trickle-down' phenomenon.

Because $\tilde{\mu}$ is anchored at $\hat{x}/\bar{\Phi}$ in Regime 2, we begin with it. The equilibrium conditions in this regime are:

$$\tilde{E} = \bar{\Phi}(1 - n_1) \qquad \text{where } 0 < n_1 < \bar{n} < 1 \quad \text{(A2.7)}$$

$$\tilde{\rho} = \bar{\Phi}^{\alpha}(1 - n_1)^{\alpha}(1 - \alpha)\hat{T}^{-\alpha} \qquad \text{(A2.8)}$$

$$\tilde{\mu} = \alpha \bar{\Phi}^{(\alpha-1)}(1-n_1)^{(\alpha-1)}\hat{T}^{(1-\alpha)} \tag{A2.9}$$

$$\tilde{\mu} = \hat{x}/\bar{\Phi}.^{[38]} \tag{A2.10}$$

Equations (A2.7)–(A2.10) are four in number, and there are four unknowns, $\tilde{E}$, $\tilde{\rho}$, $\tilde{\mu}$ and n_1, to solve for. Using equations (A2.9)–(A2.10), we find

$$n_1 = 1 - [\alpha\bar{\Phi}^\alpha\hat{T}^{(1-\alpha)}/\hat{x}]^{1/(1-\alpha)}. \tag{A2.11}$$

Now $0 < n_1 < \bar{n} < 1$ in Regime 2. Using this fact in equation (A2.11) we may conclude that given $\bar{n}$, if the economy is to be in Regime 2, $\hat{T}$ must satisfy the inequalities:

$$(1-\bar{n})[\hat{x}/\alpha\bar{\Phi}^\alpha]^{1/(1-\alpha)} < \hat{T} < (\hat{x}/\alpha\bar{\Phi}^\alpha)^{1/(1-\alpha)} \tag{A2.12}$$

that is, $\hat{T}$ must be neither too small nor too large.

From (A2.12) I conclude that the economy is in Regime 3 if $\hat{T} \geqslant (\hat{x}/\alpha\bar{\Phi}^\alpha)^{1/(1-\alpha)}$, irrespective of the distribution of landholdings. In the language of Result (x),

$$\hat{T}_2 = (\hat{x}/\alpha\bar{\Phi}^\alpha)^{1/(1-\alpha)} \tag{A2.13}$$

Since $n_1 = 0$ in Regime 3 (Fig. 7), equilibrium allocation can be computed explicitly as:

$$\tilde{E} = \bar{\Phi}; \quad \tilde{\rho} = (1-\alpha)\bar{\Phi}^\alpha\hat{T}^{-\alpha};$$

$$\text{and } \tilde{\mu} = \alpha\bar{\Phi}^{(\alpha-1)}\hat{T}^{(1-\alpha)} > \hat{x}/\bar{\Phi} \tag{A2.14}$$

From (A2.12) we may conclude as well that the economy is in Regime 1 (Fig. 5) if $\hat{T} \leqslant (1-\bar{n})[\hat{x}/\alpha\bar{\Phi}^\alpha]^{1/(1-\alpha)}$.

Equilibrium in Regime 1 is a bit more complicated to solve for. It exhibits employment for all $n \in [\bar{n}, 1]$ so long as $\hat{T}$ is not too small. To calculate this bound, assume first that $\tilde{G} = [\bar{n}, 1]$. Then

$$\tilde{E} = \bar{\Phi}(1-\bar{n}); \quad \tilde{\rho} = (1-\alpha)\bar{\Phi}^\alpha(1-\bar{n})^\alpha\hat{T}^{-\alpha}$$

$$\text{and } \tilde{\mu} = \alpha[\bar{\Phi}(1-\bar{n})]^{\alpha-1}\hat{T}^{-\alpha} < \hat{x}/\bar{\Phi} \tag{A2.15}$$

This is an equilibrium as long as $\tilde{\mu} \geqslant \mu^*(n, \tilde{\rho})$ for all $n \in [\bar{n}, 1]$; or in other words, if

$$\alpha[\bar{\Phi}(1-\bar{n})]^{\alpha-1}\hat{T}^{1-\alpha} \geqslant [\hat{x} - \tilde{\rho}\hat{T}/(1-\bar{n})]/\bar{\Phi} \tag{A2.16}$$

---

[38] Notice that $\tilde{G} = [n \mid D(n) = 1] = [n_1, 1]$.

Since $\alpha < 1$, the right-hand side of (A2.16) is smaller than the left-hand side of (A2.12) which is the borderline for Regime 1.

If $\hat{T}$ does not satisfy (A2.16), we are in Regime 1 with only a subset of $[\bar{n}, 1]$ in employment. Without loss of generality, choose the subset to be $[n_1, 1]$, where $n_1 > \bar{n}$. For such an equilibrium, $\tilde{\mu} = \mu^*(n, \tilde{\rho})$ for $n \geqslant n_1$. So we define

$$\tilde{E} = \bar{\Phi}(1 - n_1); \quad \tilde{\rho} = (1 - \alpha)\bar{\Phi}^\alpha(1 - n_1)^\alpha \hat{T}^{-\alpha};$$

$$\text{and } \tilde{\mu} = \alpha[\bar{\Phi}(1 - n_1)]^{\alpha - 1}\hat{T}^{1-\alpha} < \hat{x}/\bar{\Phi} \quad (A2.17)$$

as the equilibrium values. Now solve for n_1 by using (A2.16) and (A2.17) to obtain:

$$\alpha[\bar{\Phi}(1 - n_1)]^{\alpha - 1}\hat{T}^{1-\alpha} = [\hat{x} - \tilde{\rho}\hat{T}/(1 - \bar{n})]/\bar{\Phi}$$

Rearranging, we conclude that n_1 is the solution of

$$\alpha\bar{\Phi}^\alpha(1 - n_1)^{\alpha - 1}\hat{T}^{1-\alpha} + [(1 - \alpha)\bar{\Phi}^\alpha(1 - n_1)^\alpha\hat{T}^{1-\alpha}]/(1 - \bar{n}) = \hat{x}$$

This describes the regimes.

A3 The Speed of 'Trickle-Down'

In section 6 we observed that asset or consumption redistribution is one route towards the alleviation of malnutrition and involuntary unemployment. Growth is another. The model we have developed here is a good laboratory in which to ask how long it takes for increases in aggregate wealth to trickle down to the poorest of the poor. To draw out the answer in a sharp form I shall consider extreme circumstances. For example, when studying the efficacy of redistributive measures I shall suppose that they can be implemented instantaneously and without cost. When discussing the speed of the 'trickle-down' phenomenon I shall take it that the distribution of land remains unchanged during the process of growth. So consider the economy modelled in equations (A2.1)–(A2.4). Given that population by normalization is of size unity, the quantity of land capable in principle of meeting everyone's nutritional requirement can be calculated to be (see equation (7.1)):

$$\hat{T}_1 = (\hat{x}/\bar{\Phi}^\alpha)^{1/(1-\alpha)}.$$

Let $\hat{T} = \hat{T}_1$. Were land to be distributed equally, no one would be undernourished. Imagine instead that land is distributed according to equation (A2.2). Now use equation (A2.11) to show that $n_1 = 1 - \alpha^{1/(1-\alpha)}$. A plausible figure for α (the share of wages in agriculture in a poor country) is 0.8. This means $n_1 \approx 0.67$. Let us assume $\bar{n} > n_1 \approx 0.67$, so that the economy is in

Regime 2 to begin with. We have seen that the regime ends (and the economy enters Regime 3) at the point when $\hat{T} = \hat{T}_2 = (\hat{x}/\alpha\bar{\Phi}^\alpha)^{1/(1-\alpha)}$.
Therefore,

$$\hat{T}_2/\hat{T}_1 = \alpha^{-1/(1-\alpha)} \approx 3 \tag{A2.18}$$

Thus, if unassisted 'trickle-down' is to be relied upon, assets have to grow by a factor of 300 per cent in order that malnutrition is eliminated. This means that were capital to grow at, say, 3 per cent per year, it would take about 37 years before destitution was a thing of the past. Now 3 per cent per year is a generous figure to assume for a typical poor country. I conclude that the fruits of economic growth trickle down slowly under the market mechanism.

Admittedly, the example is special. It has a number of unusual features, for example, that $\hat{T}_2/\hat{T}_1$ in equation (A2.18) is independent of $\bar{n}$ as long as $\bar{n} > 0.67$. But the moral, though banal, is important: there are redistributive measures on offer which enhance growth in output even while they alleviate the extent of undernourishment in the immediate future.

References

Adelman, I. (1979): *Redistribution before Growth*, University of Leiden, Leiden.

Arrow, K.J. and Hahn, F.H. (1971): *General Competitive Analysis*, Holden Day, San Francisco.

Arthur, W.B. (1989): 'Competing Technologies, Increasing Returns, and Lock-In by Historical Events', *Economic Journal*, 99.

Aumann, R. (1964): 'Markets with a Continuum of Traders', *Econometrica*, 32.

Aumann, R. (1966): 'Existence of Competitive Equilibria with Markets with a Continuum of Traders', *Econometrica*, 34.

Bairagi, R. (1983): 'Dynamics of Child Nutrition in Rural Bangladesh', *Ecology of Food and Nutrition*, 13.

Baland, J.-M. and Ray, D. (1991): 'Why Does Asset Inequality Affect Unemployment?: A Study of the Demand Composition Problem', *Journal of Development Economics*, 35.

Bardhan, P.K. (1984): *Land, Labour and Rural Poverty*, Columbia University Press, New York.

Bardhan, P.K. and Rudra, A. (1981): 'Terms and Conditions of Labour Contracts in Agriculture, 1979', *Oxford Bulletin of Economics and Statistics*, 43.

Bardhan, P.K. and Rudra, A. (1986): 'Labour Mobility and the Boundaries of the Village Economy', *Journal of Peasant Studies*, 13.

Barraclough, S. (1977): *Agrarian Structure in Latin America*, Lexington Books, Lexington, MA.

Basu, K. (1992): 'The Broth and the Cooks: A Theory of Surplus Labour', *World Development*, 20.

Bell, D.E. and Reich, M.R. (eds) (1988): *Health, Nutrition and Economic Crises*, Auburn House, Dover, MA.

Berg, A. (1987): *Malnutrition: What Can be Done?* Johns Hopkins University Press, Baltimore.

Binswanger, H. *et al.* (1984): 'Common Features and Contrasts in Labour Relations in the Semiarid Tropics of India', in H. Binswanger, and M.R. Rosenzweig (eds), 1984.

Binswanger, H. and Rosenzweig, M.R. (eds) (1984): *Contractual Arrangements, Employment and Wages in Rural Labour Markets in Asia*, Yale University Press, New Haven.

Biswas, M. and Pinstrup-Andersen, P. (eds) (1985): *Nutrition and Development*, Oxford University Press, Oxford.

Bliss, C.J. and Stern, N.H. (1978a): 'Productivity, Wages and Nutrition, 1: The Theory', *Journal of Development Economics*, 5.

Bliss, C.J. and Stern, N.H. (1978b): 'Productivity, Wages and Nutrition, 2: Some Observations', *Journal of Development Economics*, 5.

Bliss, C.J. and Stern, N.H. (1982): *Palanpur: The Economy of an Indian Village*, Clarendon Press, Oxford.

Chenery, H. *et al.* (1974): *Redistribution with Growth*, Oxford University Press, New York.

Dasgupta, Amiya (1975): *The Economics of Austerity*, Oxford University Press, Delhi.

Dasgupta, Amiya (1976): *A Theory of Wage Policy*, Oxford University Press, Delhi.

Dasgupta, P. (1988): 'Poverty as a Determinant of Inequality', in W.M. Keynes, D.A. Coleman and N.H. Dinsdale (eds), *The Political Economy of Health and Welfare*, Macmillan, London.

Dasgupta, P. (1992a): *An Inquiry into Well-Being and Destitution*, Clarendon Press, Oxford, (forthcoming, 1993).

Dasgupta, P. (1992b): 'The Allocation of Hunger', Walras–Bowley Lecture, Econometric Society, mimeo., University of Cambridge.

Dasgupta, P. and Ray, D. (1986): 'Inequality as a Determinant of Malnutrition and Unemployment: Theory', *Economic Journal*, 96.

Dasgupta, P. and Ray, D.(1987): 'Inequality as a Determinant of Malnutrition and Unemployment: Policy', *Economic Journal*, 97.

Dasgupta, P. and Ray, D. (1990): 'Adapting to Undernourishment: The Biological Evidence and its Implications', in J. Dreze and A. Sen (eds), *The Political Economy of Hunger: Entitlement and Well-Being*, Clarendon Press, Oxford.

Dasgupta, P. and Stiglitz, J. E. (1988): 'Learning-by-Doing, Market Structure, and Industrial and Trade Policies', *Oxford Economic Papers*, 40.

David, P. (1991): 'So, How Would it Matter if "History Mattered"?: Path Dependence in Economics and its Long-run Implications', mimeo., Department of Economics, Stanford University.

Debreu, G. (1959): *Theory of Value*, John Wiley, New York.

Debreu, G. (1962): 'New Concepts and Techniques for Equilibrium Analysis', *International Economic Review*, 3.

Deolalikar, A.B. (1988): 'Nutrition and Labour Productivity in Agriculture: Estimates for Rural South India', *Review of Economics and Statistics*, 70.

Dreze, J. and Mukherjee, A. (1989): 'Labour Contracts in Rural India: Theories and Evidence', in S. Chakravarty (ed), *The Balance between Industry and Agriculture in Economic Development, 3: Manpower and Transfers*, Macmillan, London.

Dreze, J. and Sen, A. (1990): *Hunger and Public Action*, Clarendon Press, Oxford.

Eswaran, M. and Kotwal, A. (1985): 'A Theory of Two-Tier Labour Markets in Agrarian Economies', *American Economic Review*, 75.

Farrell, J. and Saloner, G. (1986): 'Installed Base and Compatibility: Innovation, Product Preannouncements and Predation', *American Economic Review*, 76.

Farrell, M. (1959): 'The Convexity Assumption in the Theory of Competitive Markets', *Journal of Political Economy*, 67.

Feder, E. (1977): 'Agribusiness and the Elimination of Latin America's Rural Proletariat', *World Development*, 5.

Feder, E. (1979): 'Agricultural Resources in Underdeveloped Countries: Competition between Man and Animal', *Economic and Political Weekly*, 14.

Genovese, E.D. (1974): *Plantation, Inequality and Development: Essays on the Local History of American Slave Society*, in E. Miller and E.D. Genovese (eds), University of Illinois Press, Urbana, Illinois.

George, V. (1988): *Wealth, Poverty and Starvation: An International Perspective*, Wheatsheaf, Hemel Hempstead, Herts.

Georgescu-Roegen, N. (1960): 'Economic Theory and Agrarian Reforms', *Oxford Economic Papers*, 12.

Guha, A. (1989): 'Consumption, Efficiency and Surplus Labour', *Journal of Development Economics*, 31.

Haddad, L. and Kanbur, R. (1989): 'Are Better Off Households More Unequal or Less Unequal? A Bargaining Theoretic Approach to "Kuznets Effects" at the Micro Level', mimeo., World Bank, Washington, DC.

Hammond, P.J. (1992): 'Compensated Equilibria in Continuum Economies with Individual Non-Convexities', mimeo., Department of Economics, Stanford University.

Hicks, N. (1979): 'Growth vs. Basic Needs: Is there a Trade-off?', *World Development*, 7.

Immink, M.D.C. and Viterie, F.E. (1981a,b): 'Energy Intake and Productivity of Guatemalan Sugarcane Cutters: An Empirical Test of the Efficiency Wage Hypothesis, Parts I and II', *Journal of Development Economics*, 9.

Immink, M.D.C. *et al.* (1984a): 'Microeconomic Consequences of Energy Deficiency in Rural Populations in Developing Countries', in E. Pollitt and P. Amante (eds), *Energy Intake and Activity*, Alan R. Liss, New York.

Immink, M.D.C. *et al.* (1984b): 'Functional Consequences of Marginal Malnutrition Among Agricultural Workers in Guatemala, II: Economics and Human Capital Formation', *Food and Nutrition Bulletin*, 6.

James, W.P.T. *et al.* (1992): *Body Mass Index: An Objective Measure of Chronic Energy Deficiency in Adults*, FAO, Rome.

James, W.P.T., Ferro-Luzzi, A. and Waterlow, J.C. (1988): 'Definition of Chronic Energy Deficiency in Adults', *European Journal of Clinical Nutrition*, 42.

Jodha, N.S. (1984): 'Agricultural Tenancy in Semiarid Tropical India', in H. Binswanger and M.R. Rosenzweig (eds), 1984.

Jodha, N.S. (1986): 'Common Property Resources and the Rural Poor', *Economic and Political Weekly*, 21.

Keyfitz, N. (1976): 'World Resources and the World Middle Class', *Scientific American*, 235.

Koopmans, T.C. (1957): 'The Price System and the Allocation of Resources', in *Three Essays on the State of Economic Science*, McGraw Hill, New York.

Leibenstein, H. (1957a): 'The Theory of Underemployment in Backward Economies', *Journal of Political Economy*, 65.

Leibenstein, H. (1957b): *Economic Backwardness and Economic Growth*, John Wiley, New York.

Martorell, R. *et al.* (1979): 'Protein Energy Intakes in a Malnourished Population after Increasing the Supply of Dietary Staples', *Ecology of Food and Nutrition*, 8.

Maskin, E. and Riley, J. (1984a): 'Monopoly with Incomplete Information', *Rand Journal of Economics*, 15.

Maskin, E. and Riley, J. (1984b): 'Optimal Auctions with Risk Averse Buyers', *Econometrica*, 52.

Mazumdar, D. (1959): 'The Marginal Productivity Theory of Wages and Disguised Unemployment', *Review of Economic Studies*, 26.

Mazumdar, D. (1989): 'Microeconomic Issues of Labour Markets in Developing

Countries: Analysis and Policy Implications', EDI Seminar Paper #40, World Bank, Washington, DC.

Mirrlees, J.A. (1975): 'A Pure Theory of Underdeveloped Economies', in L. Reynolds (ed), *Agriculture in Development Theory*, Yale University Press, New Haven.

Musgrave, R. (1959): *Theory of Public Finance*, McGraw Hill, New York.

Payne, P.R. (1985): 'Nutritional Adaptation in Man: Social Adjustments and their Nutritional Implications', in K. Blaxter and J.C. Waterlow (eds), *Nutritional Adaptation in Man*, John Libbey, London.

Pitt, M.M., Rosenzweig, M.R. and Hassan, M.N. (1990): 'Productivity, Health and Inequality in the Intrahousehold Distribution of Food in Low-Income Countries', *American Economic Review*, 80.

Prasad, P.H. (1970): *Growth with Full Employment*, Allied Publishers, Bombay.

Ray, D. and Streufert, P. (1992): 'Dynamic Equilibria with Unemployment due to Undernourishment', *Economic Theory*, 2.

Reutlinger, S. and Pellekaan, H. (1986): *Poverty and Hunger: Issues and Options for Food Security in Developing Countries*, World Bank Publication, Washington, DC.

Rodgers, G. (1975): 'Nutritionally Based Wage Determination in the Low-Income Labour Markets', *Oxford Economic Papers*, 27.

Rosenzweig, M.R. (1980): 'Neoclassical Theory and the Optimizing Peasant: An Econometric Analysis of Market Family Labour Supply in a Developing Country', *Quarterly Journal of Economics*, 94.

Rosenzweig, M.R. (1988): 'Labour Markets in Low Income Countries', in H. Chenery and T.N. Srinivasan (eds), *Handbook of Development Economics*, North Holland, Amsterdam.

Rudra, A. (1982): *Indian Agricultural Economics: Myths and Realities*, Allied Publishers, New Delhi.

Rudra, A. (1984): 'Local Power and Farm-Level Decision-Making', in M. Desai, S.H. Rudolph and A. Rudra (eds), *Agrarian Power and Agricultural Productivity in South Asia*, University of California Press, Berkeley, CA.

Rudra, A. and Chakraborty, U. (1991): 'Distribution of Landholdings in India: 1961–62 to 1982', *Journal of Indian School of Political Economy*, 3.

Ryan, G. and Ghodake, R. D. (1984): 'Labour Market Behaviour in Rural Villages in South India: Effects of Season, Sex and Socioeconomic Status', in H. Binswanger and M.R. Rosenzweig (eds), 1984.

Schultz, T.W. (1964): *Transforming Traditional Agriculture*, Yale University Press, New Haven.

Sen, A. (1966): 'Peasants and Dualism: With or Without Surplus Labour', *Journal of Political Economy*, 74.

Sen, A. (1981): 'Public Action and the Quality of Life in Developing Countries', *Oxford Bulletin of Economics and Statistics*, 43.

Singh, I. (1988a): 'Small Farmers in South Asia: Their Characteristics, Productivity and Efficiency', World Bank Discussion Paper 31, Washington, DC.

Singh, I. (1988b): 'Tenancy in South Asia', World Bank Discussion Paper 32, Washington, DC.

Singh, I. (1988c): 'Land and Labour in South Asia', World Bank Discussion Paper 33, Washington, DC.

Singh, I. (1990): *The Great Ascent: The Rural Poor in South Asia*, Johns Hopkins University Press, Baltimore.

Sinha, R. (1984): *Landlessness: A Growing Problem*, FAO, Rome.

Starr, R. (1969): 'Quasi-Equilibria in Markets with Non-Convex Preferences', *Econometrica*, 37.

Stiglitz, J.E. (1976): 'The Efficiency Wage Hypothesis, Surplus Labour and the Distribution of Income in LDCs', *Oxford Economic Papers*, 28

Stiglitz, J.E. (1988): *Economics of the Public Sector*, 2nd Edn, W.W. Norton, New York.

Streeten, P. *et al.* (1981): *First Things First: Meeting Basic Needs in Developing Countries*, Oxford University Press, Oxford.

Underwood, B.A. (ed.) (1983): *Nutrition Intervention Strategies in National Development*, Academic Press, New York.

UNDP (1990): *Human Development Report*, United Nations Development Programme, New York.

Valdes, A. and Konandreas, P. (1981): 'Assessing Food Insecurity Based on National Aggregates in Developing Countries', in A. Valdes (ed.), *Food Security in Developing Countries*, Westview Press, Boulder, CO.

Valverde, V. *et al.* (1977): 'Relationship between Family Land Availability and Nutritional Status', *Ecology of Food and Nutrition*, 6.

Viterie, F.E. (1974): 'Definition of the Nutrition Problem in the Labour Force', in N.S. Scrimshaw and M. Behar (eds), *Nutrition and Agricultural Development*, Plenum Press, New York.

Walker, T.S. and Ryan, J.G. (1990): *Village and Household Economies in India's Semi-Arid Tropics*, Johns Hopkins University Press, Baltimore.

Waterlow, J.C. (1986): 'Metabolic Adaptation to Low Intakes of Energy and Protein', *Annual Reviews of Nutrition*, 6.

WHO (1985): *Energy and Protein Requirements*, World Health Organization, Technical Report Series 724, Geneva.

World Bank (1986, 1990): *World Development Report*, Oxford University Press, New York.

Yotopoulos, P. (1985): 'Middle-Income Classes and Food Crises: The "New" Food-Feed Competition', *Economic Development and Cultural Change*, 33.

2

Sequence Economies and Incomplete Markets

Frank H. Hahn

University of Cambridge

1. Introduction

What follows is an account of some lectures given in Nijmegen in 1989 under the sponsorship of the NQE. At that time no good survey of the subject had been published. Now, however, that is no longer the case: we now have the outstanding survey by Geanakoplos (1990), a whole issue of the *Journal of Mathematical Economics* (1990) is devoted to this topic, and numerous other articles are either published or in pre-print. In writing these notes I have been very conscious of this rich literature (and, of course, have used it), so that what is now offered is not just a precise account of the lectures I gave. I have judged it unnecessary to repeat some of the less intuitive or esoteric proofs: readers who want these are asked to consult the references. In particular I have neglected proofs of genericity, on the grounds that they are so easily available to readers who want them. For the others it seemed unnecessarily technical. This is also true of some existence proofs. My aim has been to give as much of the economic intuition as possible which is sometimes lacking in the technical literature.

We have been accustomed, ever since Adam Smith, to think of markets as co-ordinating the self-interested actions of agents. Markets turn what might otherwise be chaos into order. In our theories on these matters we think of a market for a particular good and mean by that that there are trading opportunities in that good at a known price. This, of course, is an abstraction, but many believe that it does not lead to serious errors in understanding. But ever since Arrow–Debreu provided us with the proper way of distinguishing goods by physical characteristics, location, date of delivery and state of nature, economists who understand the need for these distinctions have also been aware that many goods may not have markets at all. This has had two effects:

in the first instance it is no longer possible to suppose that the economy could be described as if it only had one transaction date: there would have to be transactions at every date. An economy of this kind is a 'sequence economy'. In such an economy agents need to form price expectations, which they do not need to do when every good has at the given date all the required contingent futures markets (see section 4 below). The second effect has been that 'co-ordination failure' now looks a possibility. Incomplete markets throw doubt on the robustness of the co-ordinating power of market economies.

Some of this, of course, has been known for a long time. There is an extensive literature on incomplete markets resulting from incomplete property rights when there are externalities. Incompleteness of this sort is of great practical importance, but I do not discuss it because it is so well known. But there is an important literature which relates incompleteness in markets for goods to policies required to deal with incompleteness arising from externalities (Newbery and Stiglitz, 1982). The reader is advised to consult it. In these notes I have chosen to concentrate on the 'pure case', which is not only free from externalities but is also characterized by perfect competition and equilibrium.

There are several reasons for this. Almost all of the recent literature proceeds in this way and these notes are designed as an introduction to that literature. Secondly, there are good grounds for the strategy of starting with what is well known to explore the new. The Arrow–Debreu theory is both well known and understood. If the exploration leads to important modifications of what were much-used propositions based on that theory, then that will have consequential effects—say in policy discussions. Lastly there is clarity. If one were to abandon perfect competition, equilibrium and complete markets at the same time, not only would that be an enormously difficult project but, even if accomplished, it would be hard to disentangle which of the abandoned postulates was responsible for which of the new conclusions.

But my procedure has a danger, to which the literature testifies—its provisional nature may be forgotten. In the theory we are exploring logical entailments and not describing the world. It may be a starting point for organizing our knowledge about the world. For instance, as Robert Solow has pointed out to me, we gain a better understanding of Keynes' assertion that savings do not constitute a demand for goods when we relate this to the incompleteness of markets. Similar remarks apply to the relation between incomplete (forward) labour markets and labour contracts. It is the sign of a fastidious and mature economist that he can move from the abstract and descriptively false to 'real' problems without confusing his starting point with where he wants to get to. Much of recent macroeconomic theory, for instance, has failed this test.

It is for these reasons that I have thought it useful to start with a summary of the complete market case. Anyone who understands the proof of the two welfare theorems for this situation will also quickly understand why the theorems do not apply to 'essential sequence economies', even in modified form. By an essential sequence economy I mean one which cannot be brought into one-to-one correspondence with another which has trading only at one date. I have not repeated existence proofs, but have noted what they require. I have also not attempted a proof of Debreu's theorem that, generically, equilibria are locally isolated. I have stated it so as to allow a comparison with some indeterminacy results (see section 7). Particular importance is given to the fact that this economy can be described by endowments, preferences and technology—that is, it can be described without specifying agents' beliefs. We shall see that this is not possible for sequence economies.

I then (section 3) discuss some of the reasons which have been put forward for markets to be incomplete. These are suggestive, but still await adequate formalization and integration into the theoretical model. As will be seen in everything that follows, the markets which are available are taken as exogenous. This is unsatisfactory, and leaves some fascinating questions open for research. For instance, it might be possible to show that when the welfare loss from the lack of some market is sufficiently 'large', there will be a strong inducement to create one.

I then go on to describe a simple sequence economy in which only goods are traded but contingent markets are incomplete. This is close to Radner (1972), which is of the nature of a foundation paper for this whole topic. It is shown how incompleteness leads to a failure to equalize the marginal rates of substitution of wealth over states amongst agents. We shall also show how completeness would make the sequence structure inessential. Two important assumptions are made. Firstly it is supposed that agents have perfect foresight of prices for each state. Secondly, no restriction is placed on short sales. Both of these assumptions are, of course, highly debatable, and the reader is urged not to forget that they have been made.

Next (in section 5) we make a beginning with the recent literature by considering Arrow's suggestion of 'economizing' on markets by means of securities which span the states of nature. We show (as he did) that this leads to an inessential sequence economy—we can describe the economy 'as if' all transactions were at a single date. The crucial step here is the 'no-arbitrage theorem' which is stated and proved. However, it should be noted that the economy with Arrow securities is not the same economy as that described by Arrow–Debreu. This is so for two reasons. In the description of the former it is necessary to specify price beliefs of agents; this is not required in the latter. Secondly, although the complete Arrow securities economy can be studied 'as if' all transactions took place at a single date, they in fact occur sequentially. So there will be spot markets in one which are not available in the other and, of course, transactions in securities. If one took account of transaction costs this would matter.

If Arrow securities do not span the states of nature, then the no-arbitrage theorem still allows us to consider agents as maximizing subject to only one budget constraint. That is because one can implicitly buy today a good for delivery tomorrow in state s by buying the appropriate securities. However, in addition to the budget there will be a constraint due to incompleteness. That constraint restricts the agents' wealth profiles over states. We discuss how this inhibits equalization of marginal rates of substitution.

In discussing Arrow securities we distinguished three pure cases: securities pay in a good which enters the utility functions (numeraire) or in a bundle of goods (real) or in unit of account (nominal). It turns out that these distinctions matter for a proof of existence, and that is discussed next (section 6). It transpires that with numeraire and nominal securities the proof is pretty straightforward, except that one needs a special 'trick' (Cass, 1984) to demonstrate that a boundary condition is satisfied. Real securities give more serious difficulties. This was first noted by Hart (1975) and arose from a possible span change in the return matrix (as prices change in a fixed point map). Rather highbrow work has now shown that these difficulties are not generic. That is, for 'almost all economies', there exists an equilibrium with real securities. I have not reproduced the proofs, which are difficult unless one knows the relevant (and almost surely unfamiliar) mathematics. But I offer some intuitive remarks.

Section 7 discusses welfare economics. The most important result here, which is due to Geanakoplos and Polemarchakis (1986), is that generically the equilibria are not 'constrained Pareto-efficient'. That is, they can be Pareto-improved upon when policy is restricted to operating through the securities which exist. I provide all that is required for an understanding, except for genericity.

Section 8 is largely taken up with the result of Geanakoplos and Mas-Colell (1989) that for incomplete nominal securities the set of equilibria can be parametrized by $(S - 1)$ parameters in $\mathbb{R}^{S-1}$. (Here S is the cardinality of S the set of states of nature.)[1] That is, there is a continuum of equilibria, which is indeterminacy with a vengeance. The remarkable feature of this result is that this degree of indeterminacy does not depend on the number of securities there are, as long as they do not span. In the literature, nominal securities are referred to as financial securities, and one says that their pay-off is in 'money'. This nomenclature has the potential for generating much confusion. I discuss this matter with reference to Patinkin's (1965) well-known work on the 'Classical Dichotomy'.

Before leaving this introduction, two remarks are in order. First it should not be assumed that those who have provided the new insights are unaware of the distance which remains between the theory and the world. The reader should bear this in mind, and not content him or herself with dismissing the whole enterprise as irrelevant. What is needed is to identify carefully where the next move to greater realism is likely to be possible and fruitfully researched. The second remark may be otiose. These notes provide an 'overview'. Anyone seriously interested, and particularly anyone interested in research in the area, must read and understand some of the more important references which I have given.

---

[1] It will be clear from the context whether S refers to the set or to its cardinality.

2. The Canonical Model

Arrow and Debreu answered an intellectual question: is it possible for a decentralized economy of entirely self-interested agents to be 'orderly'? By 'orderly' I shall mean both 'be in equilibrium' and 'be Pareto-efficient'. The first of these characteristics requires that all agents can carry out their market and production plans, with no wish to deviate from these. The second means that there is no other feasible state of the economy preferred by some and not dispreferred by anyone. It is important to understand at the outset that the Arrow–Debreu question is not: 'are decentralized economies orderly?', nor even 'do decentralized economies tend to orderliness?' Accomplished economists have been known to muddle these questions, with occasionally costly consequences.

In this section I intend to give a very brief account of the main features of Arrow–Debreu theory. I need it as a starting and reference point for what follows. I assume that much of this is known and I omit lengthy proofs which can readily be found in textbooks.

The theory takes the number of goods (the commodity space) as exogenously given. From our point of view the definition of goods is of particular importance. Goods are distinguished by (i) their physical characteristics, (ii) their location, (iii) the date of their availability and (iv) the state of nature. By this last we mean the state of the environment at a particular date. This is not quite the proper definition, but since I shall make the drastic simplification of a two-period economy ($t = 0, 1$) it will not lead to confusion if I speak of the present and future state. The reason for the fourfold distinction of characteristics of goods is of course that this distinction is both relevant in preferences and production: ice-cream tomorrow when the weather is hot is not generally equivalent in preferences to ice-cream tomorrow when the weather is cold.

It will be assumed that there are l different physical characteristics of goods and that they are all available at the same location. The state of nature at $t = 0$ is given and known. There are S possible states at $t = 1$. Hence there are $l(S + 1)$ distinct goods. (S is taken to be finite.)

A fundamental assumption of Arrow–Debreu theory is that each of the $l(S + 1)$ goods has a price at $t = 0$ at which agents can trade. This is equivalent to assuming that all goods have present markets. Hence there is a price today ($t = 0$) for the delivery of ice-cream at $t = 1$ if the weather is hot (and nothing if it is not). Agents can thus insure themselves today to have ice-cream tomorrow if it turns out to be hot. Let $p \in \mathbb{R}_+^{l(S+1)}$ be the price vector.

Several remarks are in order. The following is assumed: (i) every agent knows which state obtains tomorrow when it occurs; (ii) there is complete trust—a contingent promise is always fulfilled; (iii) every agent knows p; and (iv) exchange is costless.

Let $X^h \in \mathbb{R}_+^{l(S+1)}$ be household h's ($h = 1 \dots H$) vector of demand for goods, and let $e^h \in \mathbb{R}_+^{l(S+1)}$ be its endowment. The term $x^h = X^h - e^h \in \mathbb{R}_+^{l(S+1)}$ is h's vector of net demands and supplies: $x_i^h > 0$ denotes net demand and

$x_i^h < 0$ denotes net supply. If for the present we concentrate on a pure exchange economy so that households receive no profits, the constraint set of the household is given by:[2]

$$B^h(p) = \{x^h \mid p \cdot x^h \leqslant 0, e^h + x^h \geqslant 0\} \tag{2.1}$$

where I take a household's consumption set to be $\mathbb{R}_+^{l(S+1)}$.

It is assumed that the household maximizes a monotonic quasi-concave utility function

$$u^h = u^h(x^h) \tag{2.2}$$

subject to (2.1).

An *equilibrium* of the economy is p^* and (x^{h*}) such that

$$\text{(i)} \quad \sum_h x^{h*} = 0 \tag{2.3}$$

$$\text{(ii)} \quad \text{For all } h \text{ and } x^h \in B^h(p^*): u^h(x^h) \leqslant u^h(x^{h*}) \tag{2.4}$$

Proposition 2.1 (Existence)

If for all $p \in \mathbb{R}_+^{l(S+1)}$, $B^h(p)$ has a non-empty interior, then given the assumption on u^h all h, an equilibrium exists.

Proof: See Arrow–Hahn (1971, chapters 2 and 5) or Hildenbrand and Kirman (1976) or Mas-Colell (1985). The proof relies (i) on the continuity in p of the constraints, (ii) boundedness of excess demands below and an upper boundary condition, and (iii) on the continuity of excess demands on a compact domain.

We notice that the above economy is defined once we are given the commodity space, endowments and preferences. So if ε is a description of an economy we can write:

$$\varepsilon = (\mathbb{R}_+^{l(S+1)}, (u^h)_H, (e^h)_H).$$

We say that the economy is defined by its *fundamentals*. We shall see that such a description is not always possible. Let $\hat{\varepsilon}$ be the set of economies that could be generated for a given commodity space by postulating different quasi-concave monotonic utility functions and different non-negative endowments.

---

[2] In what follows, row and column vectors are to be distinguished by context.

Proposition 2.2 (Regularity—Debreu, 1970)

The set of economies with equilibria none of which for some $\epsilon > 0$ have an equilibrium in their ϵ-neighbourhood, is open-dense in $\hat{\mathcal{E}}$. (For almost all economies equilibria are isolated.)

Proof: See Debreu (1970).

Thus almost all economies have a countable (in distinction to a continuum) number of equilibria. We shall see that even this weak result may not survive in sequence economies.

I conclude this section with the two fundamental theorems of welfare economics. Readers familiar with the proofs should go on to the next section. The reason for this account is that it will be desirable that there is an understanding of the importance of a single budget constraint for the validity of these theorems.

Proposition 2.3

The equilibrium defined by (2.3) and (2.4) is Pareto-efficient.

Proof: If not, then there is $(x^h)_H \neq (x^{h*})_H$ with $\Sigma_h x^h = 0$ such that $u^h(x^h) \geq u^h(x^{h*})$ all h and $u^h(x^h) > u^h(x^{h*})$ some h. But then by rationality

$$p^* x^h \geq p^* x^{h*} \text{ all } h$$
$$p^* x^h > p^* x^{h*} \text{ some } h$$

From this, $p^* \Sigma x^h > 0$ since $p^* \Sigma x^{h*} = 0$ by assumption of equilibrium. Hence $\Sigma x^h > 0$, contrary to hypothesis $((x^h)_H$ is not feasible).

Proposition 2.4

Let $x = \Sigma_h x^h$ and assume $x^* = 0$ and $(x^{h*})_H$ is Pareto-efficient. Then there exists $p^* > 0$ and $(\hat{e}^h)_H$ such that p^* and $(x^{h*})_H$ is an equilibrium for the economy with endowments $(\hat{e}^h)_H$.

Proof:

$$\text{Let } F = \{x \mid x = \Sigma x^h, x \leq 0\} \text{ and let}$$
$$H^*(x^*) = \{x \mid x = \Sigma x^h, u^h(x^h) \geq u^h(x^{h*}) \text{ all } h\}$$

(i)   Then by the assumption that $(x^{h*})_H$ is Pareto-efficient,

$$H^*(x^*) \cap F = \phi \tag{2.5}$$

But F is a convex set and since utility functions are quasi-concave, so is $H^*(x^*)$. By a separation theorem for convex sets, there exists $a \in \mathbb{R}^{l(S+1)}$, $a \neq 0$ and a scalar c such that

$$a.x \geqslant c \text{ all } x \in H^*(x^*) \qquad (2.6)$$

$$a.x \leqslant c \text{ all } x \in F \qquad (2.7)$$

(That is, the hyperplane $a.x = c$ separates the two sets.)

(ii) $a > 0$. Suppose not, e.g. $a_k < 0$. Let $x \in H^*(x^*)$ and let

$$x'(v) = x + ve(k), \; v > 0, \; e(k) = k^* \text{ unit vector}$$

By monotoneity $x'(v) \in H^*(x^*)$ all $v > 0$. Then as $v \to \infty$ we contradict (2.6).

(iii) $a.x^* \geqslant c$. Let $x^\mu \to x^*$ with $x^\mu \in H^*(x^*)$ all μ. Then by (2.6), $ax^\mu \geqslant c$ all μ and so $\lim_{\mu \to \infty} ax^\mu = ax^* \geqslant c$.

(iv) $ax^* = c = 0$. Since $x^* \in F$, $a.x^* \leqslant c$. By (iii), $a.x^* \geqslant c$ so $ax^* = c$. But $x^* = 0$.

(v)   Interpret a as a price vector, i.e. $a = p^*$. Then by (iv) there is an allocation of endowment such that $p^*x^{h*} = 0$ all h. It remains to show that h chooses x^{h*}. Suppose not, and that for some preferred x^h one has $p^*x^h < p^*x^{h*} = 0$. Then consider $x(h) = \Sigma_{k \neq h} x^{k*} + x^h$ and note that $x(h) \in H^*(x^*)$, but $p^*x(h) < 0$, a contradiction of (2.6). Suppose lastly that $p^*x^h = p^*x^{h*}$ with x^h preferred to x^{h*}. Let $\bar{x}^h$ be such that $p^*\bar{x}^h < 0$ and

$$x^h(\alpha) = \alpha\bar{x}^h + (1 - \alpha)x^h, \qquad \alpha \in (0, 1)$$

Then for some α close to (1), $x^h(\alpha)$ is preferred to x^{h*} and $p^*x^h(\alpha) < 0$, which case we know to lead to a contradiction.

The reader will note that both theorems make extensive use of the hypothesis that households face a single budget constraint.

Production can now be easily added to the description of this economy. One assumes there to be F firms with production sets $Y_f \subset \mathbb{R}^{l(S+1)}$. One calls $y_f \in Y_f$ an activity of firm f ($y_{fi} > 0$ means i is an output, $y_{fi} < 0$ means i is an input). To avoid complications, we assume that for all f, Y_f is closed and bounded, that $0 \in Y_f$, that $y_f > 0$ implies $y_f \notin Y_f$ and if $y_f \in Y_f$ then y_f' with $y_f' < y_f$ also belongs to Y_f. (Boundedness of Y_f is a bad assumption—it excludes constant returns, for instance. Consult, say, Arrow–Hahn (1971, chapter 3) for better assumptions.)

It is assumed that each f chooses y_f^*, which solves $\max_{y_f} p.y_f$. Recall the definition of goods when interpreting this assumption. Firms are agents of households who own them. Let $0 \leqslant \theta_{hf} \leqslant 1$, $\Sigma_h \theta_{hf} = 1$ represent h's share entitlement to f's profits. Then the budget constraint of h is $p.x^h \leqslant \Sigma_f \theta_{hf}(p.y_f)$.

The reader should now define equilibrium. To prove that an equilibrium exists and to prove the second welfare theorem, we now need: Y_f is convex all f.

3. Introduction to Incomplete Markets

The assumption which has been maintained so far, that all the goods which we have distinguished have markets, is falsified by a cursory glance at the world. After all, if it were true, we would carry out all transactions we would ever want to make at $t = 0$. There would be no further market transactions subsequently. This of course is contradicted by the facts. In addition one notices that if the world were indeed like that, no one would ever hold fiat money, so that it could not exist. (You should prove this assertion.) There are economists (e.g. Friedman) who are not worried by radically false assumptions—indeed they almost welcome them. But we need not enter into methodological disputes here, since the predictions of the theory, e.g. that there is trade only at one date and that fiat money cannot exist, are false.

Now the concept of 'market' employed by the theory is simply that a good has a known price at which it can be traded. But in fact what is traded at $t = 0$ are not only goods, but promises or contracts. Consider a contract at $t = 0$ for the delivery of a certain amount of good i at $t = 1$ if the state is s. Such a contract has two sources of moral hazard: the promise may not be kept, and if the two parties are differently informed about s, one of them may claim 's' or 'not s' without the other being able to verify the claim. Let us consider this second source.

A partition $\mathfrak{p}$ of S is a family of subsets $A_i \subset S$ such that $A_i \cap A_j = \phi$ for every i and j and $\cup A_i = S$. These subsets are taken to represent information concerning S in the following sense: an agent can only distinguish between two states, s_1 and s_2, if they belong to different subsets. If s_1 and s_2 both belong to, say, A_i, then the agent cannot distinguish between them and so his actions will be the same for both states. A partition $\mathfrak{p}$ with subsets $A_i \ldots$ is *finer* than a partition $\mathfrak{p}'$ with subsets $B_i \ldots$ if for all j and i either $A_i \cap B_j = \phi$ or $A_i \subset B_j$. We can also say that $\mathfrak{p}'$ is *coarser* than $\mathfrak{p}$.

Radner (1968) used this formalism to describe agents' information concerning the states of the world. He then noted that the second source of moral hazard can only be avoided by trades conditioned on the common coarsest partition. For instance if one agent has information represented by $\mathfrak{p}$ and the other by $\mathfrak{p}'$ then a contract between them can only be conditioned by the states represented by the sets B_i. From this he concluded that asymmetric information sets a natural limit on the contingent forward contracts which could be made at $t = 0$.

When Radner wrote, contract theory was not much developed and so it was natural that he should have ignored the possibility of writing contracts which ensured incentive compatibility between the differently informed parties (but see Radner (1982)). That is, there may be contracts which ensure that the better informed party reveals the true state because it is in that party's interest to do so. His conclusion may therefore have been too hasty. But from our present point of view this is not very important because we can be sure that an incentive compatible contract will not take the simple form postulated by the Arrow–Debreu model. For now we may take Radner as having shown that at any rate Arrow–Debreu type markets may not be possible.

The other source of moral hazard applies to all intertemporal contracts. These may be self-enforcing if it is in the interest of the parties concerned to abide by them. Often that can only be ensured, if at all, by legal punishments for default. For that to be possible the enforcing agency must have at least as fine a partition as the parties concerned, and the punishments must be large enough to deter violations. None of these conditions are formally taken notice of in Arrow–Debreu. Since I am here only interested to explain why some markets may be absent, it suffices for us to note that enforcing authorities in fact often have poorer information than do the parties. That is one of the reasons why also central planners have enforcement difficulties.

A rather different but related reason for incomplete markets turns on transaction costs (Hahn, 1971). In the elementary theory of exchange we are taught the difficulties of barter. That is, the difficulty of finding a partner with whom to undertake a Pareto-improving exchange. We know that the device of money here provides savings in search time. Even so, in the absence of middlemen, considerable information costs in the form of search would be required. A middleman willing to buy and sell a given good provides informational services which agents would be willing to pay for. Where there are middlemen we may speak of 'organized markets'. Since they are costly to establish, the prospective return needs to be high enough to induce mediation. In many cases this may not be the case, in particular since one suspects that mediation is carried on under strongly increasing returns. Where organized markets are absent, exchange may still be possible, but it will not be easily captured in formal models. We shall ignore such 'informal' opportunities for exchange, but the reader should bear in mind that we are doing so.

In any case, moral hazard and transaction costs suffice for an understanding of incomplete (organized) markets. Nonetheless it has proved hard to make the number of markets endogenous to the theory. I return to this matter again later, but for the present I shall treat the number of markets as exogenous.

4. A Simple Sequence Economy

Definition 4.1

A sequence economy is one in which there is trading at every date

(Radner, 1972). It is taken for granted that there are insufficient markets for agents to carry out all the trades they will ever wish to make at the initial date.

Strictly speaking, asymmetric information and/or transaction costs should be elements of a sequence economy model, since they are responsible for the sequential structure in the first place. For instance, contingent forward contracts may be conditioned not on a single state but on all states falling into the same partition of the state span which is common to all transactions in a particular good. That would take account of Radner's argument and, indeed, he has shown how to proceed in this manner (1968). But it needs a great deal of notation, and in an expository piece like this we are after insights which survive simplification.

So let us assume that everyone has complete information concerning states (the information of every agent can be represented as the finest partition of S) and that there are no transaction costs. However, only some goods can be traded contingently on some states of nature. There are spot markets at each date and state.

This now means that agents must not only have beliefs concerning the occurrence of states of nature, but also beliefs as to what spot prices will be for each such state. This is an important difference from the Arrow–Debreu economy which could be described by the 'fundamentals' of the economy. Now in order to describe the economy we must add price-expectations to the fundamentals. This opens the door to possible equilibria which do no 'reflect' fundamentals, e.g. 'sunspot equilibria'. But in any case the model differs fundamentally from Arrow–Debreu where the future is collapsed into the present. Now future actions of other agents are relevant to price expectations and to current actions.

The manner in which expectations enter into the description of the economy partly depends on our theoretical intentions. If we are only interested to study certain long-run equilibria it may be legitimate to equip all agents with the same 'correct' price-expectations. I shall later argue that there is a difficulty with this procedure, but for the moment let us accept it as a possible one. On the other hand for other (more interesting) purposes we may endow agents with expectation functions. Typically they will map past experience (history) into probability distributions of future spot prices. So the description of an economy would now need to include its history. As the economy evolves through time there is 'more history' and we need to specify how this is reflected in price expectations. We must specify how agents learn. All of this is not only well beyond the scope of this essay, but also pretty well beyond our present knowledge. We shall therefore (except for some remarks) confine the analysis to long-run equilibria. That is, situations in which there is nothing that agents can learn from history.

For the present we shall assume that all agents have identical single valued price expectations.

Assumption 4.1

For every $s \in S$ there is a price vector $p(s) \in \mathbb{R}_t^l$ which is expected with certainty for $t = 1$ and s by every h at $t = 0$. We further assume that $p(s)$ is the price vector in fact faced by all agents at $(s, t = 1)$. Call this the assumption of 'perfect foresight'.

In the simple case now to be considered, we shall suppose that there are contingent futures markets for every $s \in S$ for good 1, while no other good has a futures market at all.

Let $y^h(s) > 0$ be a demand by h for delivery of good 1 at $t = 1$ if the state is s, and interpret $y^h(s) < 0$ as a similar conditional supply. Let $q(s)$ be the price at $t = 0$ of a unit contract of this kind, and $q \in \mathbb{R}_+^S$ the corresponding vector. Then if the agent has $y^h(s) > 0$ at $t = 0$ the agent receives $p_1(s)y^h(s)$, at $t = 1$ and at state s, i.e. his wealth is increased by this amount while in other states it is unaffected. Accordingly since there are S markets of this type we may define a return matrix $\mathbf{R}$ which is $S \times S$ and given by

$$\mathbf{R} = \mathrm{diag}(p_1(1) \ldots p_1(S))$$

In particular if $y^h \in \mathbb{R}^S$ is the vector of forward contracts, $w^h(s)$ the wealth due to the sth contract in state s at $t = 1$ and $w^h \in \mathbb{R}^S$, the vector of these, we have

$$w^h = \mathbf{R}y^h \tag{4.1}$$

Let $x^h(0) \in \mathbb{R}^l$ and $x^h(s) \in \mathbb{R}^l$ to be the net demand (or trade) vectors of h at $t = 0$ and at $t = 1$ and s respectively. Also $p(0) \in \mathbb{R}_t^l$ is the price vector at $t = 0$. Lastly $[p(s)x^h(s)]$ denotes the S-column vector with elements $p(s)x^h(s)$, $(s = 1 \ldots S)$. The agent is taken to maximize $u^h(x^h)$ subject to

$$p(0)x^h(0) + qy^h = 0 \tag{4.2}$$

$$[p(s)x^h(s)] = \mathbf{R}y^h \tag{4.3}$$

$$p(s)e^h(s) \geqslant -p_1(s)y^h(s) \text{ all } s \tag{4.4}$$

The constraints (4.2) and (4.3) require no comment. In (4.4), $e^h(s)$ is the endowment vector at s. The constraint demands that the agent does not promise to deliver more of good 1 in state s than his endowment of that good then, plus what he can buy on the spot market if he sold all of his endowment of other goods. So h is assumed honest (or frightened sufficiently by legal penalties). This constraint will cause considerable difficulties if we attempt to prove the existence of the equilibrium which I now define. (Note that we do not need a constraint like this for the Arrow–Debreu economy, since there are spot markets only at $t = 0$.)

Definition 4.2

We say that $(x^{h*})_H$, $(y^{h*})_H$, $p^* \in \mathbb{R}_+^{l(S+1)}$, $q^* \in \mathbb{R}_+^S$ is an equilibrium if:

$$\sum_h x^{h*} = 0 \text{ and } \sum_h y^{h*} = 0 \tag{4.5}$$

$$(4.4) \text{ is satisfied for } p^*(s), y^{h*}(s) \text{ all } h \text{ and } s \tag{4.6}$$

$$x^{h*} \text{ maximizes } u^h(x^h) \text{ subject to } (4.2)-(4.4) \tag{4.7}$$

I shall not discuss the special cases where such an equilibrium exists. Instead I shall take it that it does, in order to gain one particular insight. To do so we must assume a little more than is required by (4.6). We shall assume that in equilibrium (4.4) is slack (strict inequality) for all h and s. This means that all agents will satisfy the following first-order conditions for utility maximization:

$$q^*(s) = \mu^h(s)p_1^*(s) \text{ all } s \tag{4.8}$$

where $\mu^h(s)$ is the marginal rate of substitution for h of wealth at $t = 1$ state s for wealth at $t = 0$. (Recall that $y^h(s)$ is unrestricted in sign.) So from (4.8) we have:

$$q^* = \mu^h \mathbf{R}^* \tag{4.9}$$

where $\mu^h \in \mathbb{R}_+^S$ is the vector with components $\mu^h(s)$. If $\mathbf{R}^*$ is of full rank (S) in equilibrium (recall that it depends on prices $p_1^*(s)$), then (4.9) has a unique solution. Moreover, (4.9) must hold for all h, and so:

$$\mu^h = \mu^* \text{ all } h \tag{4.10}$$

This gives the clue to the next step. Since marginal rates of substitution are equalized between agents, this particular equilibrium is also likely to be an Arrow–Debreu equilibrium. That this is so can be seen as follows. Since from (4.9) and (4.10)

$$qy^h = \mu^* \mathbf{R} y^h = \mu[p(s)x^h(s)] \text{ by (4.3)},$$

we can see that the equilibrium we are considering would also be an equilibrium for the Arrow–Debreu economy with prices $p^*(0)$, $\pi^*(s) = \mu^*(s)p(s)$ all s. For any agent faced with the single budget constraint

$$p^*(0)x^h(0) + \sum_s \pi^*(s)x^h(s) = 0 \tag{4.11}$$

would have exactly the same choices as were available in the simple sequence economy. Therefore the particular incompleteness of markets here considered is *inessential* for at least one equilibrium. In particular this equilibrium is Pareto-efficient.

It is easy to see how this comes about, even without algebra. Suppose agent h in the sequence equilibrium would like to ensure that he has one unit of good i at $t = 1$, state s, but there is no forward market in that good. What he can do at $t = 0$ is to buy $p_i(s)/p_1(s)$ extra units of good 1 for delivery at s. The cost is $q_i(s)p_i(s)/p_1(s) = \mu(s)p_i(s) = \pi_i(s)$. So $\pi_i(s)$ is the implicit Arrow–Debreu price for the contingent demand for good i.

But this simple example, while it illustrates the important point that what is needed for inessentiality is the possibility of trading wealth and not goods across states, also gives rise to existence problems. In the next section we shall follow the much more satisfactory route through Arrow-securities. But before we leave the present case, confirm that you have understood the importance of the assumptions concerning (4.4) and of course the importance of **R** having full rank.

5. Arrow-Securities

The first person to understand the lesson expressed in the previous section was Arrow (1953). He argued that even when there are no contingent forward markets in goods, Arrow–Debreu equilibria would result, provided there was a sufficiently rich array of securities to allow all agents to trade wealth across all states.

A security is defined by its vector of returns in different states. Let us write $r_j = (r_j(1) \ldots r_j(S)) \in \mathbb{R}^S$ as the return vector of the jth security. (Arrow in fact took each security as paying a return in only one state.) We shall have to decide in what units these returns are denominated. Three cases can be distinguished:

(i) r_j is denominated in unit of account. By this we mean that there is no good entering the utility function which corresponds to this unit—it is an accounting unit only.

(ii) r_j is denominated in terms of some particular good to be called the numeraire. If money enters agents' utility function directly or indirectly, then the numeraire could be taken to be money.

(iii) Each element of r_j, e.g. $r_j(s)$, is the value at s prices of a predetermined bundle of goods. For instance in state s, the security may promise to pay the bundle $z_j(s) = \{z_{j1}, (s) \ldots z_{jl}(s)\}$, where $r_j(s) = p(s)z_{j1}(s)$. One may think of such securities as claims to the outputs of a production process.

Each of these specifications gives rise to special problems. Since it is the simplest, start with the case where securities are denominated in numeraire. In that case we can repeat the analysis of the previous section with only small modifications. But we shall need the following mathematical concept.

Definition

Let $\mathbf{A}$ be an $S \times B$ matrix. Then the span of $\mathbf{A}$ (written sp.$\mathbf{A}$) is the smallest subspace of $\mathbb{R}^S_+$ containing the columns of $\mathbf{A}$. Or equivalently it is the intersection of all the subspaces containing these columns. Or, again equivalently, it is the space generated by linear combinations of these columns.

Now suppose that there are $B \leqslant S$ securities with numeraire return vectors $r_1 \ldots r_B$. The $\mathbf{R}$, an $S \times B$ matrix consisting of the columns r_j, can be called the returns matrix. Let $q \in \mathbb{R}^B_+$ be the price vector of securities at $t = 0$, and let agent h choose the portfolio $a^h \in \mathbb{R}^B$ where $a^h_j > 0$ means that the jth security is bought and $a^h_j < 0$ means that it is sold. (One calls the case $a^h_j < 0$ a *shortsale* of j.)

Assumption 5.1

There is no restriction on the extent to which any security can be sold forward. (That is, a^h_j may be any negative scalar for all j.)

This is a pretty bad assumption. It suggests that there is no limit on the amount that can be borrowed at $t = 0$. But that is not quite correct, since for any s we want $x^h(s) + e^h(s) \geqslant 0$, which becomes impossible if the debt at the beginning of $t = 1$ is large enough and must be repaid. Yet there is a real difficulty nonetheless, because lenders do not necessarily know borrowers' endowments and have to rely on their unexplained honesty. Nonetheless we adopt this assumption for the moment and note that it allows us to dispense with a constraint like (4.4) which awkwardly depends on prices. But a difficulty remains (see below).

The assumption also allows us to make use of a fundamental proposition which I now state and prove.

Proposition 5.1 (No Arbitrage)

Given an $S \times B$ returns matrix $\mathbf{R}$ there exists (for any equilibrium) a vector $\beta \in \mathbb{R}^S_+$ such that

$$q = \beta \mathbf{R} \tag{5.1}$$

Proof: Note that it is claimed that in any equilibrium the asset price vector q must belong to the cone C where

$$C = \{ y \mid y = \beta \mathbf{R} \text{ for some } \beta \in \mathbb{R}^S_+ \}$$

Evidently C is convex. So if, contrary to Proposition 5.1, $q \notin C$, there must be a hyperplane $q'b = 0$ (with $b \in \mathbb{R}^B$, $b \neq 0$) through q such that

$$yb > 0 \qquad \text{all } y' \in C.$$

(As in Proposition 2.2, we are using the separation theorem.) Consider $\beta = (1\ 0\ 0\ 0\ )$ so that $\{r_1(s_1), r_2(s_1) \ldots r_B(s_1)\} = y \in C$. Interpret b as the portfolio a. Then at $t = 0$ the portfolio is self-financing ($qa = 0$) but makes a positive profit at $s = s_1$. By letting $\beta = (0\ 1\ 0\ 0\ )$ etc. successively we see that this self-financing portfolio makes a positive profit at every $s \in S$. But then the desired trade in assets at $t = 0$ will be unboundedly large. (Note that $q'ak = 0$ also for every $k > 0$.) No equilibrium would be possible.

Now (5.1) is very much like (4.9), except that we do not now appeal directly to utility maximization. Notice also that the non-arbitrage proposition was not available when we were dealing with contingent forward trades in good 1, because 4.4 restricted the forward sale of good 1. In any case we have the budget constraints (with p in terms of numeraire),

$$p(0)x^h(0) + qa^h = 0 \tag{5.2}$$

$$[p(s)x^h(s)]\,S = \mathbf{R}a^h \tag{5.3}$$

Letting $\bar{p}(s) = \beta(s)p(s)$ we find that on pre-multiplying (5.3) by β', and using (5.1) to substitute into (5.2) we obtain the single budget constraint

$$p(0)x^h(0) + \Sigma\,\bar{p}(s)x^h(s) = 0 \tag{5.4}$$

(Compare this with (4.11).) But we must remember that the agent is constrained to wealth profiles over S which are available through trade in securities. This constraint is captured by

$$[p(s)x^h(s)] \in sp\mathbf{R} \tag{5.5}$$

Evidently this constraint will be slack if $\mathbf{R}$ is of full rank (there are as many independent securities as states). In that case we say that securities markets are *complete*. Notice that it is only in this case that we can be sure that the marginal rates of substitution ($\mu^h(s)$) are equalized over agents.

Let $\bar{B}^h(\bar{p})$ be the set of x^h which satisfy (5.4) and (5.5) and $B^h(p, q)$ be the set of x^h and a^h which satisfy (5.2) and (5.3). Then there are two equivalent definitions of equilibrium:

(i) $\bar{E}$: is the set of $\bar{p}^*, (x^{h*})_H$ such that

$$\sum_h x^{h*} = 0 \tag{5.6}$$

$$x^{h*} \in \arg\max_{\bar{B}^h(\bar{p}^*)}\ U^h(x^h)\ \text{all}\ h \tag{5.7}$$

(ii) E: is the set of $p^*, (x^{h*})_H, (a^{h*})_H, q^*$ such that

$$\sum_h x^{h*} = 0 \text{ and } \sum_h a^{h*} = 0 \tag{5.8}$$

$$x^{h*} \in \arg\max_{B^h(p^*, q^*)} U^h(x^h) \tag{5.9}$$

It is not hard to see that as far as equilibrium net trade in goods is concerned, both definitions are equivalent. This is a good exercise which is left to the reader. But notice that when $(\bar{x}^{h*})_H \in \bar{E}$ that the spanning condition (5.5) holds for all h so that (5.3) can be satisfied for $\bar{x}^{h*}$ all h. Notice also that using Walras' Law will show that the a^h thus derived satisfy $\Sigma a^h = 0$. The fact that we have these alternative definitions of equilibrium is very useful. The definition of E, for instance, tells us at once (by condition (5.5)) why incomplete markets are likely to lead to departures from Arrow–Debreu equilibrium. On the other hand, E emphasizes the sequential structure of the economy.

A further advantage of the formulation $\bar{E}$ is that it provides an immediate understanding of the Modigliani–Miller theorem (1958). Suppose there is a firm—its actions need not now be specified—which has issued a number of bonds paying r_b in all s and a number of shares which pay dividends depending on s. It is clear that so long as a firm is financed by a different mixture of bonds and shares which leaves $sp\mathbf{R}$ unchanged, it will also leave the real equilibrium of the economy unchanged. That is the theorem. If the firm operates under limited liability then the return on bonds may become state-dependent. For one now has $r_b(s) = \min(r, \pi(s))$, where $\pi(s)$ is the firm's profit at s per unit bond. As long as profits suffice for the payment of r_b, our previous conclusion stands. But as more bonds are issued, $\pi(s)$ becomes smaller so the return on bonds may become state-dependent. This can change the span of $\mathbf{R}$, since $\mathbf{R}$ now depends on spot prices, since $\pi(s)$ does. Hence the theorem may not hold.

Returning to the main theme, if we now consider the case where securities are denominated in unit of account, we see from (5.3) where the elements of $\mathbf{R}$ are all in unit of account that each of the budget constraints are homogeneous of degree zero in prices in unit of account. We can therefore choose a numeraire for each s without affecting the set of feasible choices. For instance, we could choose the first good as numeraire for all s, i.e. express all prices *and* $\mathbf{R}$ in terms of this numeraire. We would then be back in the case which we have already studied. However, notice that the choice of numeraire for each s is arbitrary and this will be of importance later. In particular, $\mathbf{R}$ will depend on this choice. Here we note simply that a security denominated in unit of account is not really fully defined for the agent until he knows what can be obtained with the payment the security offers.

Lastly, when securities pay in bundles of goods, clearly $\mathbf{R}$ will depend on prices in each state. For instance, let $\bar{r}_j(s) \in \mathbb{R}^l$ be the bundle promised by security j for state s. Then $r_j(s) = p(s)\bar{r}_{js}$ so the r.h.s. of (5.3) as well as the l.h.s. depends on $(p(s))S$. That too has some interesting consequences, but not for the definitions of equilibrium.

6. Existence of Equilibrium

If one wants to discuss properties of equilibria, it is not unimportant to check that the concept is not vacuous i.e. that equilibrium is not logically impossible, or that it is not at risk, i.e. that there may not be some range of values of parameters for which equilibrium is impossible. It turns out that proving that an equilibrium exists for the economies which we are now considering is not always straightforward. Indeed, it sometimes requires techniques which few economists know, and I shall in these cases refer the reader to the literature which allows him or her to learn these techniques.

It turns out that it is only in economies where securities pay in bundles of goods that new techniques are required for an existence proof. Such proofs, for instance for Arrow–Debreu economies, have made use of fixed point theorems which rely on some form of continuity and boundedness of excess demands, and so on the continuity of a map from convex compact sets into themselves. Now if we stick to securities which have returns denominated in numeraire, or equivalently if we choose a numeraire for financial securities, continuity is not a problem when utility functions are 'well-behaved'. In both these cases, **R** is given independently of what happens to prices, and the constraints in $\bar{B}^h(p)$ have the usual continuity properties in p provided we make the customary assumption that at all relevant p each agent can participate in exchange. (See Arrow and Hahn (1971) for this last.) The endowments also provide lower bounds for x^h. Only one matter causes a problem.

Think of excess demand functions rather than correspondences for the sake of simplicity. They are homogeneous of degree zero in prices. But when the price of a good is zero, the excess demand is not well defined. Indeed if we let, say, two prices tend to zero, the limiting excess demand might depend on the sequence chosen. Accordingly, one has utilized an extended notion of continuity which requires $\Sigma_h \parallel x_i^h \parallel$ to go to infinity as $p_i \to 0$. (See Arrow and Hahn, pp. 29–33.) But this requirement cannot be met in the present case because of (5.5).

The solution to this conundrum has, in an elegant way, been provided by Cass (1984). Consider a fictional economy in which one agent, say $h = 1$, lives in a full Arrow–Debreu economy, that is, he is not constrained by (5.5). All the other agents are so constrained. The boundary condition in question is met by this economy and so, taking account of what has already been said, an equilibrium exists. But that means that (5.5) holds for all $h \neq 1$ and of course $\Sigma_{h \neq 1} x^h(s) + x^1(s) = 0$. But then evidently $x^1(s)$ also satisfies (5.5) and we have found an equilibrium for the actual economy. A simple and ingenious argument!

This leaves the awkward case of securities that pay in bundles of goods. Hart (1975) noted the following possibility. Since **R** depends on $(p(s))_S$, it is pretty clear that the span of **R** depends on these prices as well. As we search amongst prices for an equilibrium—in the usual case, proceed with a mapping whose fixed point is to be the equilibrium—the span may change. (Hart (1975) gave an example.) When it does, the excess demands can be discontinuous at a point of change. In particular if the rank drops below the number of securities, then from the non-arbitrage proposition we deduce that the forward sale of some asset j will be unboundedly large ($a_j = -\infty$). That is because when the returns evaluated at these critical prices of securities become linearly dependent, infinite purchases can be financed by infinite sales.

The problem of unbounded forward transactions was first noticed by Radner (1972) who dealt with it by imposing an arbitrary bound. Later Hart (1975) showed that the equilibrium obtained may crucially depend on this arbitrary bound, which is clearly unsatisfactory.

It may be helpful if I transcribe an example given by Geanakoplos (1990) and which is based on Hart's (1975) famous example.

There are two agents (types) A and B, and there are two states of nature. At the initial date (0) and in state (2) there is one good and in state (1) there are two goods. In obvious notation let

$$U^A(x_0, x_1, y_1, x_2) = \log x_1 + 2 \log y_1 + \log x_2$$

$$U^B(x_0, x_1, y_1, x_2) = \log x_1 + \log y_1 + 2 \log x_2$$

Endowments are given by: $e^A = (0, 1, 1, 2)$ and $e^B = (0, 1, 2, 1)$.

There are two assets. Asset 1 pays one unit of the x good in both states and the other pays one unit of the y good in state 1 and one unit of the x good in the second state. So if we write p_x^s and p_y^s as the spot prices of x and y in state s, the pay-off matrix is

$$\mathbf{R} = \begin{bmatrix} p_x^1 & p_y^1 \\ p_x^2 & p_y^2 \end{bmatrix}$$

If **R** has full rank then we know that the sequence is inessential and we obtain Arrow–Debreu prices $p = (0, 1, 1, 1)$. But at these prices **R**'s columns are colinear and the rank is not full. But then the assets will not be traded and we obtain the spot price vector $p = (0, 1, 7/8, 1)$. But at these prices **R** has full rank and assets will be traded. So no equilibrium exists.

The following points are worth noting. As long as $p_y^1 \neq 1$, **R** has full rank. It is only at $p_y^1 = 1$ that the drop in span occurs. This will be associated with a change in the demand for y_1 from $2/p_y^1 + 1$ to 17/16, i.e. a discontinuity. But it occurs only 'rarely', in the sense that for a slightly different choice of parameters it would be removable—rendered innocuous for existence, for instance a small change in the endowment of the y good in state one. This, however, is not at all obviously the case when the number of securities never span S. Lastly note that from the non-arbitrage theorem, as in the above we let $p_y^1 \to 1$ the supply of some asset (short sales) approaches $-\infty$ since the non-arbitrage condition cannot be fulfilled.

Now in some sense we would expect that as we search amongst the set of conditional prices for an equilibrium, that a change in the span of $\mathbf{R}$ would occur only 'rarely'. Put differently, if there is a change of rank at $\bar{p}$ we would expect a small change in the endowments and underlying returns matrix would remove it. That is, the Hart discontinuity is not 'generic'. By this we mean that the set of economies which we can generate by changes in endowment and in $\mathbf{R}$ and which possess an equilibrium is open dense in the set of economies.

It is a plausible argument, but to prove it is quite hard. A number of authors have done so (Duffie and Shafer, 1985 and 1986; Geanakoplos and Shafer, 1990; Werner 1990; Husseini, Lasry and Magill, 1990; Hirsch, Magill and Mas-Colell, 1990). They have not all used the same technique, but they have it in common that the techniques are all 'advanced'. There is no possibility of giving an account of these proofs here and the reader who is interested and able is referred to these authors.

It is possible to give some intuition of the method of proof using 'Grassmanians' which is a collection of open subspaces of Euclidean space. (See Geanakoplos, 1990, whom I follow.) Consider such a subspace say in $\mathbb{R}^S$, say L and pretend that it has the full dimension of the number of securities. Replace (5.5) by the requirement

$$[p(s)x^h(s)] S \in L$$

Since L is now given and since it can be shown that x^h is continuous, an equilibrium relatively to L can be shown to exist. But we cannot be sure that $L = sp[\mathbf{R}(p)]$ where $\mathbf{R}(p)$ is the notation which reminds us that returns are here price dependent. But suppose we only require that $L \supset sp[\mathbf{R}(p)]$. Then it can be shown that if along a price sequence $sp[\mathbf{R}(p^\mu)] \to L$ as $p^\mu \to p$, then if the span of $\mathbf{R}(p^\mu)$ drops dimension it is still in L. One then shows that an equilibrium exists for the economy (p, L), i.e. one can find L and p such that the usual equilibrium conditions hold. Such an equilibrium is called a 'pseudo-equilibrium'. One then establishes the central result that for generic $\mathbf{R}$ and endowments all pseudo-equilibria are full equilibria. The reader will not need reminding that these remarks do not constitute a proof. What may be gleaned is that by looking at a fictional or pseudo economy in which changes in the span of $\mathbf{R}$ cannot matter, one shows that generically such changes in span do not matter. My guess is that there will shortly become available much simpler proofs, but until then. ...

Lastly we should note a case in which no tricks will save an existence proof (Gottardi, 1990; Polemarchakis and Ku, 1990). This occurs when some of the securities are options. The return of an option for a particular state is max [p-call price, 0]. This is not linear in prices and so there may be large ranges of p for which the return is zero and large ranges for which it is positive. But that means that our plausible earlier argument for supposing that changes in the span of **R** are rare does not apply here, and so one cannot expect genericity of existence.

7. Welfare Economics

When we claim that some allocation is Pareto-inefficient we surely have it in mind that it is feasible to bring about a Pareto-improvement. In the usual Arrow–Debreu theory this means only that any Pareto-improving reallocation should be physically feasible. In a pure exchange economy, for instance it must not require more of any one good than is available as the economy's endowment. (See our earlier discussion in 2.3 and 2.4.) But suppose that the number of independent Arrow-securities is regarded as part of the fundamental description of an economy. (Of course it is not, but in the absence of a persuasive theory that is how we have treated it.) In that case we can only consider reallocations which can be achieved given the number of securities available (and assuming that there are no direct contingent forward markets in goods).

So suppose that we can, in a pure exchange economy, only reallocate first-period endowments and holdings of securities amongst agents. We can then ask: is the equilibrium of the economy with $B < S$ securities Pareto-efficient with respect to these feasible reallocations? If yes, then we say that it is *constrained* Pareto-efficient. Of course, if $B = S$, constrained and ordinary Pareto-efficiency coincide.

Now to evaluate the welfare consequences of a redistribution of securities, since they do not directly enter agents' utility functions, we must look at the consequences for the equilibrium allocation which we are testing for constrained efficiency. This is equivalent, once we recall the indirect utility function, to looking at the consequence of the reallocation of securities for equilibrium prices. In this section I shall only consider the case where equilibria are isolated. (See Proposition 2.1, which, however, applied to Arrow–Debreu economies—here regularity may, in certain cases, fail. I return to these later.)

Before I proceed, a simple intuitive argument is worth making. We know that when $B = S$ the equilibrium marginal rates of substitution of wealth over different states are the same for all agents. If then in an equilibrium there is a small reallocation of securities between, say, two agents which keeps their first period wealth the same, we would expect no change at all in equilibrium prices. That is because locally the individuals are identical (because of the equalized marginal rates of substitution) so that any change in the consumption of one of them in state s due to the change in wealth there is exactly offset by the opposite change in consumption by the other agent. Put differently: the agents can locally be aggregated into a 'representative' agent. When $B \neq S$, the marginal rates of substitution will generally differ over agents and so the redistribution will affect equilibrium prices. This is the clue to the conclusion that in this case the equilibrium can be constrained Pareto-inefficient. Indeed (see below) a stronger conclusion can be reached. We must now make this intuitive argument more precise.

Define by $V^h(p, \mathbf{R}a^h)$ the maximum utility attainable by h given the price p, his portfolio of securities a^h. That is, it is the maximum utility subject to (5.2) and (5.3), given a^h. So if p^* are the equilibrium prices and a^{h*} the equilibrium portfolio, and if $\mathbf{R}$ is independent of prices, then $V^h(p^*, \mathbf{R}a^{h*})$ is the utility of h in equilibrium.

Let $a = (a^1 \dots a^H)$ and consider first the case where $B = S$, that is, where security markets are complete and where we know that an Arrow–Debreu equilibrium is attained and which therefore is Pareto-efficient. Then if

$$W(p, a, \alpha) = \Sigma \, \alpha_h V^h(p, \mathbf{R}a^h); \qquad \alpha_h > 0, \alpha = (\alpha_1 \dots \alpha_H) \qquad (7.1)$$

is a social welfare function there must be a choice of α such that no permitted redistribution of a can improve W. That is, p^*, a^* the equilibrium prices and portfolios must for some α solve

$$\max_{\Sigma a^h = 0} \; W(p^*, a, \alpha) \qquad (7.2)$$

Let us assume that p^* is differentiable in a. (This is not necessarily true, but eases exposition; recall that the economy is regular by assumption.) First-order necessary conditions for (7.2) using well-known duality results are of the form:

$$\sum_i \sum_h \alpha_h \omega^h(0) x_i^h(0) \cdot \frac{dp_i^*(0)}{da_j^h} + \sum_i \sum_s \sum_h \alpha_h \omega^h(s) x_i^h(s) \, \frac{dp_i^*(s)}{da_j^h}$$

$$+ \, q_j - \alpha_h \Sigma \, \omega^h(s) r_j(s) = 0 \quad (7.3)$$

where q_j is the Lagrangean multiplier for the constraint $\Sigma a_j^h = 0$ which is here interpreted as the utility price of security j, and $\omega^h(\cdot)$ is h's marginal utility of wealth in the indicated states.

It is clear that if we choose α_h so that it satisfies

$$\alpha_h \omega^h(0) = 1 \text{ all } h \qquad (7.4)$$

that we obtain in the notation of (4.8),

$$\sum_i \sum_h x_i^h(0) \cdot \frac{dp_i^*(0)}{da_j^h} + \sum_i \sum_s \sum_h \mu^h(s) x_i^h(s) \, \frac{dp_i^*(s)}{da_j^h} + q_j - \sum_s \mu^h(s) r_j(s) = 0$$

$$(7.3')$$

Since we are in equilibrium the first term is zero. Since $\mu^h(s) = \mu(s)$ all h, the second term is also zero, and so of course is the difference between the last two terms. (See 4.9, for instance.) So indeed the equilibrium is Pareto-efficient and maximizes social welfare for this choice of α.

It is easy to see that α will have to satisfy (7.4) if any equilibrium is to be efficient. That is, the social planner will have to choose this α if at the resulting shadow prices of securities the analogue to (4.8) is to hold for an equilibrium. But if we now drop the assumption that $B = S$ and revert to incomplete security markets, it will, as we know, no longer be the case that $\mu^h(s) = \mu(s)$ all h. Hence there is no guarantee that the second term in (7.3′) will vanish in equilibrium. But for the equilibrium to be constrained Pareto-efficient, each agent h in his choice of security j would need to take account of the 'externality' of changed relative prices. That is, one needs

$$q_j = \sum_s \mu^h(s) r_j(s) - \sum_i \sum_s \sum_h \mu^h(s) x_i^h(s) \frac{dp_i^*(s)}{da_j^h} \qquad (7.5)$$

and of course in fact the last term on the r.h.s. of (7.5) will be ignored by a private agent.

Now we can think of cases where the externality does not occur, in spite of $B < S$. For instance, if all agents are identical in all respects, or if they have special preferences so that $\omega(\cdot)$ is independent of wealth so that $\mu^h(s) = 1$ all h, or indeed if there is only one good. These are plainly special cases. One can now go to work to prove that in fact the externality is generic.

Proposition 7.1

The set of economies generated by different utilities and endowments and which is constrained Pareto-inefficient is open dense in the set of economies, provided $l > 1$ (Geanakoplos and Polemarchakis, 1986).

These co-authors assumed that transfers were not permitted and so required a large enough number of households to make budget-balance preserving reallocations of securities possible. I have allowed transfers. The genericity proof is not too hard for those who are familiar with that branch of mathematics. But I do not give it here: the result is sufficiently intuitive to allow the reader to put his simple faith in the correctness of the proposition.

As a matter of fact, a very analogous result is available for a two-period economy with transaction costs and *complete* asset markets (no uncertainty). (Hahn (1973) and Starrett (1973) got some of the way.) The point here is that in models with transaction costs, buying and selling prices will differ. By an allocation being constrained Pareto-efficient we mean that no Pareto-improvement is possible by a reallocation after taking account of the resources that need to be used to bring it about. It is easiest to establish this if we assume that trade in goods uses no transaction resources, while trade in securities does. For the latter, assume that every unit sale or purchase of one unit of security j requires a vector of T_j of inputs. So to buy one unit of a_j adds $p(0)\,T_j$ to its price, and when one unit is sold one receives $p(0)\,T_j$ less than its price. The reader is invited to use what he or she has learned so far to establish the possibility of a constrained-inefficient equilibrium for this economy. Unless it is a familiar technique, genericity should be ignored.

There are two more comments. The generic inefficiency result has been extended to a production economy by Geanakoplos, Magill, Quinzii and Dreze (1990). That that can be done should occasion no surprise. Indeed one finds that the intuition gets stronger once production is included.

The second comment concerns models in macroeconomics which make use of a representative agent. In a complete market economy with no transaction costs we can think of the representative agent as having utility function $W(\cdot)$ for the appropriate weights α. (Recall Negishi's (1960) and Arrow and Hahn's (1971) proof of the existence of equilibrium.) We have seen that with incomplete markets this is not possible (generically). This is not a trivial point. For instance both in growth and business cycle theory it has become popular to proceed with a representative 'Ramsey agent'. That is a representative agent who maximizes over integral of expected felicities, possibly discounted, over the infinite future. This procedure (for a certain range of discount rates) rules out for well-known technical reasons all sorts of dynamic possibilities. But once the aggregation over agents is seen to be illegitimate (because of incomplete markets) these restrictions are artefacts and a full range of dynamics becomes possible. But notice also that all these models of a representative agent assume a sequence economy and so *ipso-facto* incomplete markets. Much may be claimed for 'simple' models, but not when they are as logically flawed as these are.

8. Indeterminacy

Those who are familiar with general equilibrium analysis are also familiar with the possibility of multiple equilibria. Such multiplicity, of course, is a kind of indeterminacy in the sense that from the data used it is not possible to predict which equilibrium would be the true state. Indeed the problem has no meaning without a process being modelled as well. But until recently we could rely on Proposition 2.2, which predicts generically that equilibria will be isolated and countable. That result at least holds out the promise of meaningful comparative statics. But the study of economies with an incomplete set of Arrow-securities has shown that we cannot always rely on this proposition.

This new work is not yet completed and I shall concentrate on the case where S is finite and securities pay in unit of account—financial securities. Before proceeding, a rather important point should be clearly understood. In the literature the unit of account is identified as 'money' which is not in the domain of preferences. However the manner in which this 'money' is introduced into the model, its real value would be indeterminate whether markets are complete or not. That is because there is only inside 'money' so that in the complete asset economy the excess demands for money at $t = 0$ would be homogeneous of degree zero in prices alone. This is just the situation Patinkin (1965) discussed very many years ago to show that the 'classical dichotomy' leaves the price level indeterminate. For these reasons I am reluctant to refer to 'money' in what follows, and stick to unit of account.

The result which we are about to discuss is this. If $B < S$ then (under some conditions) there is an $(S - 1)$ dimensional indeterminacy of 'real' equilibria (i.e. allocation of goods). Moreover this result is generic for the set of economies generated by different assignments of endowments. This is a truly remarkable result, in particular in that the dimension of indeterminacy does not depend on the extent to which securities fail to be complete. (Note an $(S - 1)$ dimensional indeterminacy means that there is a C^1 function on $\mathbb{R}^{S-1}$ which generates the set of equilibrium allocations.)

The intuition for this result (now that it has been proved) is relatively straightforward. Call a 'numeraire economy' one which has security returns denominated in numeraire, and call a 'nominal economy' one which has security returns denominated in unit of account. Let $\mathbf{R}$ be the return matrix for the latter and $\bar{\mathbf{R}}$ a return matrix for the former. Let $(\bar{x}^h, \bar{a}^h)_H$ be an equilibrium for the numeraire economy when, say, the numeraire is good 1. That is, one can set $\bar{p}_1(s) = 1$ all s. We have as usual

$$[\bar{p}(s)\bar{x}^h(s)] = \bar{\mathbf{R}}\bar{a}^h \tag{8.1}$$

(Note that $\bar{p}_i(s) = p_i(s)/p_1(s)$ where p is the price vector in unit of account.) If we multiply each row of (8.1) by the appropriate $p_1(s)$ we obtain

$$[p(s)\bar{x}^h(s)] = \operatorname{diag}(p_1(1) \ldots p_1(s))\bar{\mathbf{R}}\bar{a}^h = \mathbf{R}\bar{a}^h \tag{8.2}$$

No real constraint is changed and so $(\bar{x}^h, \bar{a}^h)$ is still an equilibrium. But given $\mathbf{R}$, there are many possible numeraires. In fact, given $\mathbf{R}$ let Λ be an $S \times S$ diagonal matrix with elements λ_s. Then for all $\bar{\mathbf{R}}$ which satisfy

$$\Lambda \mathbf{R} = \bar{\mathbf{R}} \tag{8.3}$$

there will be an equilibrium in the numeraire economy which is also an equilibrium in the nominal economy with return $\mathbf{R}$. (Notice, from (8.2), $\lambda_s = 1/p_1(s)$). If we fix, say, $\lambda_1 = 1$ then we can vary Λ over an open subset of $\mathbb{R}_{++}^{S-1}$. That is, we can generate a set of equilibria in the nominal economy (each of which corresponds to some numeraire equilibrium) by a choice of Λ in $\mathbb{R}_{++}^{S-1}$.

At first sight this may seem trivial. Nominal securities are only defined from the point of view of the utility maximizer when the price level in each state is known. So from a given $\mathbf{R}$ we can generate many 'real' returns profiles and we know that for each of these (when expressed in numeraire) an equilibrium exists which must then also be an equilibrium for the nominal economy. But that is not yet what is being claimed. That is that each of these equilibria differ in $(x^h)_H$: differences between them are real, and not just confined to differences in portfolios.

We take it for granted now that $B < S$ and that all utility functions are smooth. We shall further assume that $\mathbf{R}$ is in 'general position', which means that every sub-matrix of $\mathbf{R}$ of B rows is of full rank. This excludes the specification of securities first suggested by Arrow where each security has a non-zero return in only one state. In that case $\mathbf{R}$ is diagonal and violates the assumption of general position.

What we want to do is this. Suppose we consider two equilibria for the numeraire economy generated by $\Lambda \mathbf{R}$ and $\Lambda^0 \mathbf{R}$. If $\bar{a}^h$ and $\bar{a}^{0h}$ are h's portfolio choices, then if for some h we have $\Lambda \mathbf{R} a^h \neq \Lambda^0 \mathbf{R} \bar{a}^{0h}$ we are 'home'. That is because if it were the case that $\bar{x}^h = \bar{x}^{0h}$ there would be the same marginal rates of substitution between goods, and so price would have to be the same in the two economies. But then from the budget constraints we would have the contradiction $\Lambda \mathbf{R} \bar{a}^h = \Lambda^0 \mathbf{R} \bar{a}^{0h}$.

This suggests the next step. We must show that for 'genuinely different' numeraire systems, $\Lambda \mathbf{R} \bar{a}^h \neq \Lambda^0 \mathbf{R} \bar{a}^{0h}$ some h. By 'genuinely different' we mean that there is no scalar $\alpha > 0$ such that $\Lambda^0 = \alpha \Lambda$. It can, however, be shown that this arises when $sp(\Lambda \mathbf{R}) = sp(\Lambda^0 \mathbf{R})$, and this is the clue we are looking for. More formally:

Proposition 8.1 (Geanakoplos and Mas-Colell, 1989)

Let $\mathbf{R}$ be $S \times B$ with $B < S$ and such that every set of B rows of $\mathbf{R}$ is linearly independent ('general position'). Then if $sp(\Lambda_1 \mathbf{R}) = sp(\Lambda_2 \mathbf{R})$ there is $\alpha > 0$ such that $\Lambda_1 = \alpha \Lambda_2$.

Proof: Since $sp(\Lambda_2^{-1} \Lambda_1 \mathbf{R}) = sp(\mathbf{R})$ under the hypothesis of P.8.1, we may just as well take $\Lambda_1 = \Lambda$ as $\Lambda_2 = \text{diag}(1 \ldots 1)$.

Now suppose $sp(\Lambda \mathbf{R}) \subset sp(\mathbf{R})$, then this is equivalent to asserting that there is $B \times B$ matrix $\mathbf{Y}$ such that

$$\Lambda \mathbf{R} = \mathbf{RY} \tag{8.3'}$$

Hence the sth row of $\mathbf{R}$ is an eigen vector of $\mathbf{Y}$ with eigen value λ_s.

If we let $\mathbf{R}_j$ be the jth row of $\mathbf{R}$, then by the assumption that $\mathbf{R}$ is in general position there must be $\mu_j(s) \neq 0, \mu_j = 1 \ldots B$, such that

$$\mathbf{R}_s = \sum_1^B \mu_j(s) \mathbf{R}_j \tag{8.4}$$

So from 8.3′,

$$\mathbf{R}_s \mathbf{Y} = \lambda_s \left(\sum_1^B \mu_j \mathbf{R}_j \right)$$

and

$$\left(\sum_1^B \mu_j \mathbf{R}_j \right) \mathbf{Y} = \sum_1^B \lambda_j \mu_j \mathbf{R}_j$$

Taking these together yields

$$\sum \mu_j (\lambda_s - \lambda_j) \mathbf{R}_j = 0 \tag{8.5}$$

but since $\mathbf{R}$ is in general position this is only possible if $\lambda_j = \lambda_s$ all $j = 1 \dots B$.

To complete the argument, all we need to suppose is that the $\dim sp(\bar{a}^1 \dots \bar{a}^H) = \dim sp(\bar{a}^{01} \dots \bar{a}^{0H})$ and that $\Lambda^0 \neq \alpha \Lambda$. Then it must be that for some h,

$$\Lambda \mathbf{R} \bar{a}^h \neq \Lambda^0 \mathbf{R} \bar{a}^{0h}$$

or else we would have a relation like (8.3′) (with a matrix $(\bar{a}^h)$) contradicting that $\Lambda^0 \neq \alpha \Lambda$. But that is where we came in. (This proof is by the authors of the theorem.)

The only argument remaining is one to show that the main result which we are discussing is generic in endowments. As usual with genericity arguments we refer the reader to the literature (e.g. Geanakoplos and Mas-Colell, 1989). For now we conclude with a formal statement of the main result.

Proposition 8.2 (Geanakoplos and Mas-Colell)

Let $\mathbf{R}$ be in unit of account and $B < S$ and in general position. Assume that $H > B$. Then generically there are $S - 1$ dimensions of real indeterminacy. (All equilibria differ in x^h for at least one h.)

It is interesting to note that this result can be extended to an economy with a mixture of nominal and numeraire assets. If there are B of the former and A of the latter then one needs to assume that $B \geqslant 2$ and $S > 2(A + B)$ and $H > (A + B)$. The proof of this is on the same lines as before. (See Geanakoplos and Mas-Colell (1989).)

Let us take stock. As I have already noted, the result is rather closely related to that of Patinkin (1965). He showed that with purely inside money the price level is indeterminate. But he neglected uncertainty and therefore different price levels in different states of the world. Since the marginal rate of substitution between wealth in any two states must in equilibrium equal its marginal rate of transformation which, with nominal assets, depends on the price levels in the two states, we are not surprised that these price levels have real effects. But we cannot 'determine' them, since the inside money hypothesis still leaves us with the Patinkin kind of indeterminacy.

A two-period economy is not helpful for an account of outside money. But any model which accounts for outside money being viable will also have to be one in which the price level is not indeterminate in the sense of Patinkin. To that extent the indeterminacy results which we have discussed are perhaps of relatively small economic interest. However, to this conclusion there is a caveat. Mas-Colell (1989) has shown that the indeterminacy (in the sense of violating 'regularity') can also arise with numeraire securities, provided that S is infinite. The argument here turns on the multiplicity of spot equilibria for each state. For instance, if there are no securities, there are as many equilibria for the economy as we can select from amongst a combination of spot equilibria. If S is a continuum then one will also have the indeterminacy we are interested in. (For further details see Mas-Colell (1989).) But while it is easy to agree that there is a continuum of states (think of temperature), it is hard to believe that there is a continuum of states relevant to preferences and so relevant to excess demands.

References

Arrow, K.J. (1953): 'Le role des valeurs boursieres pour la repartition la meilleure des risques', *Econometrie*, Colloques Internationaux du Centre National de la Recherche Scientifique 11, 41–7. English translation, *Review of Economic Studies*, **31** (1964), 91–6.

Arrow, K.J. and Hahn, F.H. (1971): *General Competitive Analysis*, North Holland.

Cass, D. (1984): 'Competitive Equilibrium with Incomplete Financial Markets', CARESS Working Paper No. 85–16, University of Pennsylvania.

Debreu, G. (1970): 'Economies with a Finite Set of Equilibria', *Econometrica*, **38**, 387–92.

Duffie, D. and Shafer, W. (1985): 'Equilibrium in Incomplete Markets, I', *Journal of Mathematical Economics*, **14**, 285–300.

Duffie, D. and Shafer, W. (1986): 'Equilibrium in Incomplete Markets, II', *Journal of Mathematical Economics*, **15**, 199–216.

Geanakoplos, J. (1990): 'An Introduction to General Equilibrium with Incomplete Asset Markets', *Journal of Mathematical Economics*.

Geanakoplos, J., Magill, M., Quinzii, M. and Dreze, J. (1990): 'Generic Inefficiency of Stock Market Equilibrium when Markets are Incomplete', *Journal of Mathematical Economics*.

Geanakoplos, J. and Mas-Colell, A. (1989): 'Real Indeterminacy with Financial Assets', *Journal of Economic Theory*, **47**(1), 22–38.

Geanakoplos, J. and Polemarchakis, H. (1986): 'Existence, Regularity, and Constrained Suboptimality of Competitive Allocations when Markets are Incomplete', in W. Heller, R. Starr, and D. Starrett (eds), *Essays in Honor of Kenneth Arrow*, Volume 3, Cambridge University Press, Cambridge.

Geanakoplos, J. and Shafer, W. (1990): 'Solving Systems of Simultaneous Equations in Economics', *Journal of Mathematical Economics*.

Gottardi, P. (1990): 'Essays on Financial Policy with Incomplete Markets', Ph.D. dissertation for Cambridge University.

Hahn, F.H. (1971): 'Equilibrium with Transaction Costs', *Econometrica*, **39**, 417–39.

Hahn, F.H. (1973): 'On Transaction Costs, Inessential Sequence Economies and Money', *Review of Economic Studies*, **XL**(4), 124, 449–62.

Hart, O. (1975): 'On the Optimality of Equilibrium When the Market Structure is Incomplete', *Journal of Economic Theory*, **11**(3), 418–43.

Hildenbrand, W. and Kirman, A. (1976): *Introduction to Equilibrium Analysis*, North Holland.

Hirsch, W., Magill, M. and Mas-Colell, A. (1990): 'A Geometric Approach to a Class of Equilibrium Existence Theorems', *Journal of Mathematical Economics*.

Husseini, S.Y., Lasry, J.M. and Magill, M. (1990): 'Existence of Equilibrium with Incomplete Markets', *Journal of Mathematical Economics*.

Mas-Colell, A. (1985): *The Theory of General Economic Equilibrium*, Cambridge University Press, Cambridge.

Mas-Colell, A. (1989): 'Indeterminacy in Incomplete Market Economies', mimeo.

Modigliani, F. and Miller, M. (1958): 'The Cost of Capital, Corporation Finance, and the Theory of Investment', *American Economic Review*, **48**, 261–97.

Negishi, T. (1960): 'Welfare Economics and the Existence of an Equilibrium for a Competitive Economy', *Metro-economica*, **5**, 92–7.

Newbery, D.M. and Stiglitz, J. (1982): 'The Choice of Techniques and the Optimality of Market Equilibrium with Rational Expectations', *Journal of Political Economy*, **90**, 2, 223–46.

Patinkin, D. (1965): *Money, Interest and Prices* (2nd edn), Harper and Row, New York.

Polemarchakis, H.M. and Ku, B. (1990): 'Options and Equilibrium', *Journal of Mathematical Economics*.

Radner, R. (1968): 'Competitive Equilibrium under Uncertainty', *Econometrica*, **36**, 31–58.

Radner, R. (1972): 'Existence of Equilibrium of Plan, Prices and Price Expectations', *Econometrica*, **40**, 2, 289–303.

Radner, R. (1982): 'Competitive Equilibrium under Uncertainty', in K. J. Arrow and M. D. Intriligator (eds), *Handbook of Mathematical Economics*, Volume II, North Holland.

Starrett, D. (1973): 'Inefficiency and the Demand for "Money" in a Sequence Economy', *Review of Economic Studies*, **XL**(4), 124, 437–48.

Werner, J. (1985): 'Equilibrium in Economies with Incomplete Financial Markets', *Journal of Economic Theory*, **36**, 110–19.

PART II:
Macroeconomics

3

Government Policy and Economic Growth

Charles R. Bean

London School of Economics

1. Introduction

What determines the Wealth of Nations? This is a fundamental question which taxed the Classical economists from Adam Smith onwards, but one that largely disappeared from the macroeconomic agenda during the post-war heyday of the Keynesian–Neoclassical synthesis. However, the last few years have seen a resurgence of interest in questions such as: What makes a country rich or poor? What makes a country grow fast or slowly? and What role does government policy play in the growth process? In this chapter I shall try to outline what modern macroeconomics has to say about these issues.

It is as well to start any discussion of long-run growth with a few facts. Conventionally, growth economics is organized around Kaldor's (1961) 'stylized facts'. Among these are the observation that while both output per head and capital per head tend to grow over time, the capital/output ratio is relatively constant. Figure 1 exhibits this 'fact' for the United Kingdom since the middle of the nineteenth century (total work hours rather than heads are used as the measure of labour input). While there are certainly important fluctuations around the trends of the three series, the picture is generally one of an economy on some sort of equilibrium, or balanced, growth path. (I shall be more precise about what we mean by these terms below.)

A second 'fact' is that both the return on capital and the share of profit in income is relatively constant. Figure 2 documents this for the United Kingdom since the middle of the last century. Thus, despite the fact that both capital and capital per head have been rising steadily, there is little evidence of diminishing returns to capital setting in, at least so long as we are willing to assume that the rate of return on capital tells us something about its marginal product.

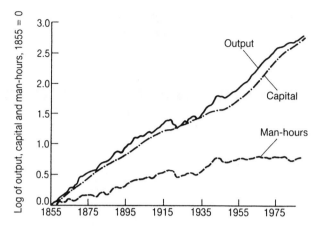

Figure 1.   Output, capital and manhours in the UK,
1856–1987.

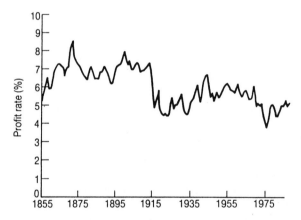

Figure 2.   Profit rate in the UK, 1856–1987.

A third 'fact' is that growth rates differ widely across countries. Yet an interesting question is whether growth rates are systematically related to initial conditions. Figure 3 plots the level of real output per capita for the G-7 countries in the post-war period (in order to render the series comparable across countries, the output series for the non-US economies have been converted to constant price US dollars using OECD estimates for purchasing power exchange rates, rather than actual rates). This figure shows a marked tendency for countries with low initial output per head, e.g. Japan, to grow systematically faster and 'converge' on the leading country, the United States. But even here there is evidence that countries do not necessarily converge to identical levels of output per head: the United Kingdom appears to be converging to a level some 30 per cent lower than the United States. When we

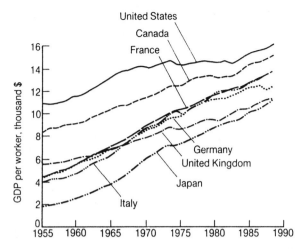

*Figure 3. Output per worker in G-7, 1987, PPP
exchange rates.*

look at a wider and more heterogeneous group of countries, the evidence for
convergence is weak or even non-existent. Figure 4 plots the average growth
rate of output per head over the period 1960–85 for nearly a hundred countries
against initial levels of output per head, together with a regression line. The
correlation between the two is minimal (indeed the correlation is marginally

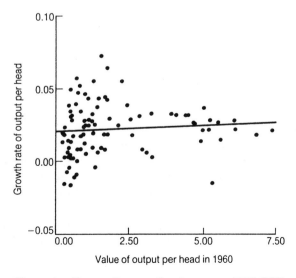

*Figure 4. Per capita growth rate versus 1960 GDP
per capita.*

perverse). While there is a growing literature[1] concerned with testing the hypothesis of convergence, for my purposes it is enough to note that any tendency to convergence is very much weaker in some samples, and across some periods, than others.

What does growth theory have to say by way of explanation of these facts? Most of the analysis in the body of this chapter will be concerned with economies peopled by optimizing households. However, a number of key points can be made in the context of a simple Solovian, closed economy growth model (Solow, 1956) in which households save a constant fraction, s, of their current disposable income:

$$S = s(Y - T) \qquad (1.1)$$

where S = savings; Y = income and all income in the economy accrues to households; and T = taxes. Output, Y, is given by a well-behaved, constant returns to scale technology

$$Y = F(K, L) = Lf(k) \qquad (1.2)$$

where $k \equiv K/L$. Population grows exogenously at rate n, and there is continuous market clearing in factor and goods markets. For simplicity also assume that the government budget is continuously balanced with $G = T$, where G is the level of government spending. This spending is useless, e.g. ICBMs, and the share of government spending in output, τ, is given exogenously. Using the goods market identity that gross investment, I, equals savings, it then follows that

$$\dot{k} = \frac{\dot{K}}{L} - \frac{K}{L} \cdot \frac{\dot{L}}{L} = \frac{(I - \delta K)}{L} - \frac{K}{L} \cdot \frac{\dot{L}}{L}$$

$$\qquad (1.3)$$

$$= s(1 - \tau)f(k) - (\delta + n)k$$

where δ is the rate of (exponential) depreciation.

The evolution of the economy is depicted in Fig. 5, which plots output per head, $f(k)$; national savings per head, $s(1 - \tau)f(k)$; and the investment level required simply to maintain the capital–labour ratio in the face of depreciation and population growth, $(\delta + n)k$. The first two are concave, while the latter is just a ray through the origin. Provided the production function satisfies the Inada conditions, the national savings per head schedule intersects

---

[1] Contributions to this literature include: Barro and Sala-i-Martin (1991a, 1991b), Baumol (1986), Bernard and Durlauf (1991), Dowrick and Nguyen (1989), Quah (1990).

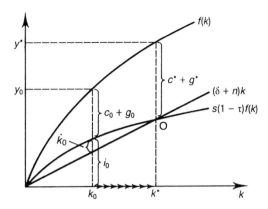

Figure 5. Solow growth model.

the constant capital–labour ratio schedule once and only once. There is thus a unique equilibrium capital–labour ratio, k^*, which satisfies the equation:

$$g(k^*) = (\delta + n)/s(1 - \tau) \qquad (1.4)$$

where $g(k)$ ($\equiv f(k)/k$) is the output–capital ratio. Note that $g'(k) < 0$ and also that $g(k) \rightarrow \infty$ (0) as $k \rightarrow 0$ (∞) if the technology satisfies the Inada conditions. Thus the equilibrium level of capital per head, and therefore also the equilibrium level of output per head, is increasing in the private savings rate, s, and decreasing in the rate of depreciation, δ, the rate of population growth, n, and the share of taxes/government spending in output, τ. Furthermore, since to the left (right) of k^* savings exceeds (falls short of) that level required simply to maintain the capital–labour ratio at existing levels, this equilibrium is stable, so that starting from an arbitrary initial capital–labour ratio, k_0, the economy converges over time to k^*.

When the economy reaches this 'balanced growth' equilibrium, both the output–capital ratio and capital–labour ratio will be constant, and all quantities in the economy are growing at rate n; growth depends on neither savings behaviour nor government policy. A constant output–capital ratio is obviously consistent with Fig. 1, but a constant capital–labour ratio clearly is not. We can explain the rising capital–labour ratio exhibited in Fig. 1 (and with it continuously rising real per capita incomes) by introducing labour-augmenting technical progress,[2] so that the technology becomes $Y = F(K, AL)$ where A is an index of technical progress. All the previous analysis goes through, except that k must now be interpreted as the ratio of capital to the

---

[2] Both output-augmenting technical progress, $Y = AF(K, L)$, and capital-augmenting technical progress, $Y = F(AK, L)$, are inconsistent with the stylized facts. The former implies a constant capital–labour ratio and a rising output–capital ratio along an equilibrium growth path, while the latter implies a constant output–labour ratio and a rising output–capital ratio.

effective labour force, i.e. $k \equiv K/AL$, and n is now the sum of the rate of growth of population and the rate of growth of technical progress. Equilibrium output per head (rather than per effective worker) now grows at the rate of technical progress.

How much of the growth in UK output since 1855 can be attributed to growth in factor inputs and how much to technical progress? Following Solow (1956), we can conduct a 'growth-accounting' exercise by differentiating the production technology with respect to time:

$$\frac{\dot{Y}}{Y} = \frac{F_1}{Y} \dot{K} + \frac{F_2}{Y} (A\dot{L} + \dot{A}L)$$

$$= S_K \frac{\dot{K}}{K} + S_L \frac{\dot{L}}{L} + S_L \frac{\dot{A}}{A}$$

(1.5)

where $S_K \equiv qK/Y$ is the capital share, $S_L \equiv WL/Y$ is the labour share, q is the user cost of capital,[3] W is the real wage, and I have assumed competitive markets so that factors receive their marginal product. Using the conventional national accounts definitions of the labour and capital share, we obtain the decomposition of output growth given in Fig. 6. This shows that something approaching a half of the growth in output is attributed to technical progress, leaving only a relatively small part explained within the model via factor accumulation. Indeed, looking at Fig. 1, we see that factor accumulation could only account for the bulk of output growth if the capital share were close to unity. So at a minimum this sort of model seems unsatisfyingly incomplete in leaving a large part of the growth in output to be explained by other unspecified forces.

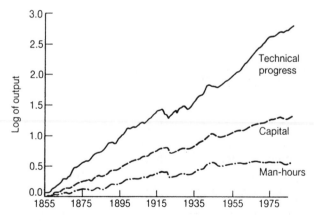

Figure 6.   *Sources of growth in the UK, 1856–1987.*

---

[3] $q = r + \delta$, where r is the real interest rate.

At this juncture it is useful to note that Fig. 5 can also be used to derive the 'Golden Rule' savings rate which maximizes consumption including government spending (current expenditure) per head in the steady state, $c^* + g^*$. Current expenditure per head is just the vertical distance between the output per head and gross investment per head schedules. If the latter is under the control of the authorities, i.e. they vary $s(1 - \tau)$, this gap will be maximized when the national savings rate, $s(1 - \tau)$, is such that $f'(k^{**}) = \delta + n$, where k^{**} solves equation (1.4) for this value of $s(1 - \tau)$. Since $r = f'(k) - \delta$ in competitive markets, it follows that current expenditure per head is maximized when $r = n$. If the national savings rate, and capital–labour ratio, are higher than this, then the economy is said to be 'dynamically inefficient'. Current expenditure per head can be raised at *all* dates simply by eating some of the existing capital *and* saving less in the future. In this region there is no intertemporal trade-off facing the government. This is no longer true if $k^* < k^{**}$, since higher steady state current expenditure can only be bought at the cost of lower current expenditure today.

In order to make sense of the comparative data presented in Figs 3 and 4, it is useful to consider a slight transformation of equation (1.3) in which the rate of growth of the capital–labour ratio appears on the left-hand side:

$$\dot{k}/k = s(1 - \tau)g(k) - (\delta + n) \qquad (1.3')$$

Because the rate of growth of output per head (or output per effective worker in the presence of labour-augmenting technical progress) is just the marginal product of capital times the rate of growth of the capital–(effective) labour ratio, equation (1.3') enables us to directly compare growth rates across economies (assuming, of course, they are all subject to the same rate of exogenous technical progress). Figure 7(a) plots the gross investment rate, $s(1 - \tau)g(k)$, against the level of capital per head; this is downward-sloping. The steady state is obtained where it intersects the horizontal line describing the gross investment rate necessary to maintain the capital–labour ratio, $(\delta + n)$. This diagram shows clearly that if two countries are identical in all respects, except for their initial conditions, then the country with the lower level of capital per head should grow faster and asymptotically catch up with the initially capital-rich country. This is what is exhibited in Fig. 3—the UK aside—and is referred to as 'unconditional convergence'.

How can the model explain the behaviour of the UK in Fig. 3, as well as the diversity in growth experience exhibited in Fig. 4? Here we need to invoke differences in technology, savings rates, etc., as well. Thus Fig. 7(b) portrays the growth experience of two economies, one of which has e.g. a higher savings rate than the other (s_R and s_P respectively). Even though this country also starts out with a higher initial level of capital, it is still capable of exhibiting higher growth along the transition path than the poor country. However, asymptotically, output per head can only grow as fast as the exogenous rate of labour-augmenting technical progress. Thus countries

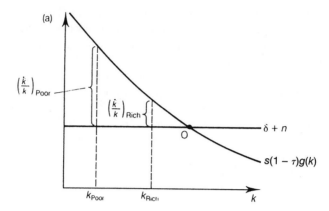

Figure 7(a). *Unconditional convergence.*

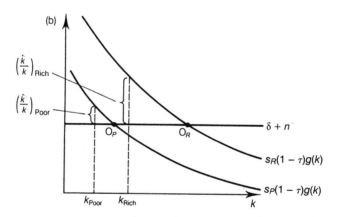

Figure 7(b). *Conditional convergence.*

should converge in growth rates, but not necessarily in absolute standards of living. This is sometimes referred to as 'conditional convergence'.

An obvious question to ask is at what sort of rate can we expect two other-wise identical economies to converge? Linearizing equation (1.3) around the equilibrium, k^*, and using equation (1.4) gives:

$$\dot{k} = [s(1-\tau)f'(k^*) - (\delta + n)]\,(k - k^*)$$
$$= -(\delta + n)S_L^*(k - k^*) \tag{1.6}$$

where S_L^* is the steady-state labour share. The 'half-life' for this economy is then just $ln2/(\delta + n)S_L^*$; setting $(\delta + n)$ to 10 per cent per annum and S_L^* to 0.7 thus implies that it takes around ten years for half of any initial divergence in living standards to be eliminated. This is clearly much faster than is exhibited even in Fig. 3, let alone Fig. 4. Furthermore, models incorporating permanent income consumers imply even more rapid convergence. Clearly there is something lacking in the basic story.

The recent 'endogenous growth' literature, due to Romer (1986, 1987, 1990), Lucas (1988), and Grossman and Helpman (1990, 1991a, 1991b) seeks to generate unbounded growth in output per head without relying on exogenous labour-augmenting technical progress. Although the details of the various models differ, they all have the feature of endogenizing the process by which the efficiency of labour is enhanced over time, either through the expansion of knowledge, or else through investment in human, rather than purely physical, capital. Whilst all of these models contain important externalities, they are in fact not essential to generating unbounded growth endogenously, as a number of authors have emphasized; see e.g. King, Plosser and Rebelo (1988), and Jones and Manuelli (1991). In fact, as a glance at either Fig. 5 or Figs 7(a)/(b) reveals, all we need to generate continued growth in output per head endogenously is that the national savings/gross investment schedules should not intersect the corresponding constant capital–labour ratio lines. In that case net investment per capita will always be positive and output per head will keep on growing indefinitely. It therefore follows that asymptotically we must have $s(1 - \tau)f'(k) \geqslant (\delta + n)$, i.e. the marginal product of capital is bounded below. In turn this implies that asymptotically we must have constant (or increasing) returns to scale in reproducible factors. In essence, all of the endogenous growth models cited above have this feature.

Thus a simple way of generating endogenous growth is simply to posit a technology $Y = AK$, where A $(> (\delta + n)/s(1 - \tau))$ is a constant. The output–capital ratio is then just A and equation (1.3′) gives the growth rate of capital per head as

$$\dot{k}/k = s(1 - \tau)A - (\delta + n) \qquad (1.3'')$$

By virtue of the absence of diminishing returns to capital, this is also the rate of growth of output per head, which now depends on the national savings rate, including government policy. This is in stark contrast to the classical growth model considered above in which the growth rate along the balanced growth path was exogenously given, and independent of policy. A second feature to note of this model is that there is no tendency to convergence, even across economies with similar technologies and national savings rates. Initial differences in capital–labour ratios and output per capita will persist indefinitely. This feature is clearly potentially useful in helping to explain the apparent lack of convergence exhibited in Fig. 4.

But isn't this example with constant returns to scale in capital somewhat strained? After all, the share of capital income is of the order of only a third, with the implication in Fig. 6 that capital has only a modest role to play. The answer is that such a model is really quite reasonable if we interpret it broadly as including human as well as physical capital. Then much of the income accruing to labour can be interpreted as a return to human capital, rather than raw labour power. We can extend the classical Solovian growth model quite simply to incorporate two sorts of capital, by writing the technology as $Y = F(K, HL)$, where H is human capital, and there are constant returns to scale in K and HL (and therefore *increasing* returns if K, H, and L are raised by the same proportion). For simplicity, let us also assume the population is fixed, with L normalized to unity.[4] Now all we need to do is append an equation for the accumulation of human capital. One possibility is a straight-forward analogue of equation (1.1), in which a constant proportion of after-tax income is allocated to (gross) human capital accumulation. To make it slightly more interesting, however, let us assume that the government expenditure is actually used for the purposes of human capital accumulation, i.e.

$$\dot{H} = eG - \delta H \tag{1.7}$$

where e is an efficiency parameter for the 'education' sector, and for simplicity the rate of depreciation is the same for human as for physical capital. The rate of growth of human capital is then

$$\dot{H}/H = e\tau f(Z) - \delta \tag{1.8}$$

where $Z \equiv K/H$ and $f(Z) \equiv F(K/H, 1)$. The growth rate of physical capital is

$$\dot{K}/K = s(1 - \tau)f(Z)/Z - \delta \tag{1.9}$$

Balanced growth is therefore characterized by a ratio of physical to human capital, Z^*, given by

$$Z^* = s(1 - \tau)/e\tau \tag{1.10}$$

while the associated growth rate, γ^*, is

$$\gamma^* = e\tau f[s(1 - \tau)/e\tau] - \delta \tag{1.11}$$

Assuming the technology satisfies the Inada conditions, equation (1.11) describes a sort of Laffer curve between the share of government spending and the growth rate, with γ^* initially increasing as τ rises above zero, and then ultimately declining as high values of τ hit physical capital accumulation. We shall meet such a 'growth Laffer curve' below in the context of Barro's (1990) model.

This two-capital-good model has a similar feature to the one-capital-good model considered above, namely that if we take two economies with similar

---

[4] If $n \neq 0$ then the growth rate depends on the size of the labour force, L, and thus varies with the scale of the economy.

characteristics that both start off on the balanced growth path with $Z = Z^*$, the economy with lower levels of physical and human capital will never catch up with the richer economy. Models with multiple capital goods are, however, potentially useful for rationalizing the apparent convergence on the United States and Canada exhibited in Fig. 3 by the other G-7 countries in the post-war period. These economies suffered significant destruction of their physical capital during World War II and so found themselves with $Z < Z^*$. Relatively rapid growth in output per head can then be attributed to temporarily high levels of physical capital formation reflecting the high marginal product of capital. However, to capture this phenomenon one needs a model with rather more sophisticated savings behaviour than that considered here.[5]

The introduction of more sophisticated savings behaviour is, in fact, our next objective. How is the growth process affected when consumers are forward-looking and are free to borrow and lend on the capital market? Can we expect competitive markets to lead to 'good' outcomes, and how do government spending and borrowing policies affect the transition path and equilibrium of the economy in such circumstances?

2. Growth with Infinitely-Lived Consumers

We shall begin by introducing sophisticated consumers into the basic Solovian growth model, with diminishing returns to reproducible factors. This is the Ramsey–Cass–Koopmans growth model, which forms the starting point for much of modern macroeconomics (Ramsey, 1928; Cass, 1965; Koopmans, 1965). There is a large, but fixed, number of identical households; without loss of generality, normalize the mass of these households to unity. The number of household members grows at rate n and each household member is endowed with one unit of labour which it supplies inelastically in return for income w_t and on which it pays lump-sum taxes t_t. The household can borrow and lend freely at rate r_t. Household preferences are characterized by the felicity function $u(c_t)$ and a discount factor $(1 - \theta)$, with $0 < \theta < 1$. Then in discrete time the household's problem is

$$\underset{\{c_s, a_s\}}{Max} \sum_{s=t}^{\infty} (1 - \theta)^{s-t} u(c_s) \qquad (2.1)$$

subject to

$$a_s = [(1 + r_s)/(1 + n)] a_{s-1} + w_s - c_s - t_s \text{ (for all } s \geqslant t), \qquad (2.2)$$

where a_s is end-of-period non-human wealth per household member. In

---

[5] In fact it is not difficult to show that the growth rate of output in the model considered here is, to a first approximation, independent of the initial physical/human capital ratio.

addition to (2.2) we also need a boundary condition that prevents the household financing high levels of consumption by running up ever higher levels of debt in relation to its capacity to pay. The condition we need is therefore that

$$\lim_{T \to \infty} a_T \bigg/ \prod_{s=t}^{T} [(1 + r_s)/(1 + n)] = 0 \qquad (2.3)$$

i.e. that debt grows more slowly than the growth-corrected rate of interest. The first-order conditions for this problem imply that, for $s \geq t$

$$u'(c_s)/(1 - \theta)u'(c_{s+1}) = (1 + r_{s+1})/(1 + n) \qquad (2.4)$$

The left-hand side is the marginal rate of substitution between consumption at dates s and $s + 1$, while the right-hand side is the intertemporal relative price of per capita consumption in the household. This set of equations describe the 'tilt' of the household's consumption path over time. In addition the boundary condition (2.3) in conjunction with equation (2.2) gives an intertemporal budget constraint for the household relating the present discounted value of expenditure to the present discounted value of resources; the consumption path given by (2.4) must also satisfy this.

In practice it will be more convenient to work in continuous time. By the mean value theorem there exists a $c_s^* \in [c_s, c_{s+1}]$ such that $u'(c_{s+1}) = u'(c_s) + u''(c_s^*)(c_{s+1} - c_s)$. Substituting into equation (2.4), and letting the length of the time period go to zero gives:

$$\dot{c}_s/c_s = \sigma(r_s - n - \theta) \qquad (2.4')$$

where $\sigma \equiv -u'(c_s)/c_s u''(c_s)$. $\sigma(>0)$ is the intertemporal elasticity of substitution[6] and, for this intertemporally separable preference structure, is just the inverse of the coefficient of relative risk aversion for the felicity function $u(c)$. Henceforth we shall assume σ is a constant, i.e. $u(c) = (c^{1-1/\sigma} - 1)/(1 - 1/\sigma)$ with $u(c) = lnc$ when $\sigma = 1$. Equation (2.4') holds along the optimal path, but will cease to hold at the instant when there is 'news' about income prospects, etc.

---

[6] To see this most simply, first take logarithms of equation (2.4) and then differentiate, holding c_{s+1} constant, to give:

$$u''(c_s)dc_s/u'(c_s) = dr_{s+1}/(1 + r_{s+1})$$

The intertemporal elasticity of substitution is given by

$$\sigma \equiv -dln(c_s/c_{s+1})/dln(1 + r_{s+1})$$
$$= -(1 + r_{s+1}) \, dc_s/c_s dr_{s+1}$$
$$= -u'(c_s)/c_s u''(c_s)$$

by the first expression.

We next need to describe the evolution of interest rates. If the production structure is as for the Solovian model of the Introduction, with output per head given by $f(k)$ and competitive goods and factor markets, we have that the user cost of capital, $r + \delta$, is equal to the marginal product of capital, $f'(k)$. Omitting subscripts for brevity, equation (2.4') then becomes

$$\dot{c}/c = \sigma[f'(k) - \delta - n - \theta] \tag{2.5}$$

The model is completed with the goods market identity, written in per capita terms as:

$$\dot{k} = f(k) - c - g - (\delta + n)k \tag{2.6}$$

where g is per capita government expenditure. In addition there is the government (flow) budget identity,[7] also written in per capita terms,

$$\dot{b} = (r - n)b + g - t \tag{2.7}$$

where b is the per capita stock of government debt and $a \equiv b + k$.

This economy contains three state variables: c, k and b. However, for any given sequence of government spending, the evolution of the economy can be described in terms of just two variables: c and k. The phase-plane diagram corresponding to equations (2.5) and (2.6) is given in Fig. 8. Per capita

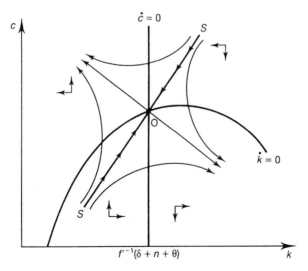

Figure 8.   The Ramsey–Cass–Koopmans model.

---

[7] In addition there is a boundary condition requiring that government debt per capita grows no faster than the growth-corrected real interest rate.

consumption is stationary if and only if the growth-corrected rate of interest, $r - n$, is exactly equal to the rate of time preference, θ (the 'Modified Golden Rule'), and the consumption stationary is thus a vertical line in (k, c) space. To the right (left) of the stationary the growth-corrected real interest rate is less (greater) than the rate of time preference and consumption is falling (rising) over time. The capital stationary is concave with a maximum at $r = n$ (the usual, unmodified, Golden Rule); above (below) this stationary net investment per head is negative (positive) and capital per head is falling (rising). Approach to the equilibrium, O, is along the saddlepath SS.[8]

Now suppose the economy is initially in equilibrium and there is an unanticipated permanent increase in government spending. The capital stationary will shift downwards, as in Fig. 9. The decline in household permanent income is exactly equal to the increase in government spending, so per capita consumption falls one-for-one with the increase in government expenditure, and the economy jumps from O to O': there is thus full crowding out of current consumption, with no effect on capital accumulation or output per head. This result is in stark contrast to what is predicted by the simple Solovian model; there an increase in government spending necessarily leads to capital decumulation and a lower level of output.

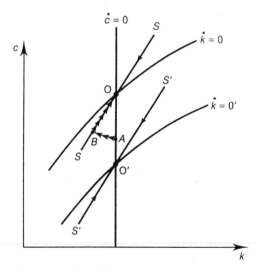

Figure 9.   Increased government spending.

[8] To see that the saddlepath must be the solution, suppose we start above SS. Then eventually capital decumulation must occur and the economy hits $k = 0$ in finite time. At this point, assuming the Inada conditions are satisfied, consumption must fall discretely to zero. This is clearly inconsistent with the intertemporal optimality condition (2.5). Conversely suppose we start below SS. Then the economy converges (asymptotically) to the capital level $\bar{k}$ satisfying $f(\bar{k}) - (\delta + n)\bar{k} = g$ with $c = 0$. Although such paths are not inconsistent with (2.5), they are eventually dynamically inefficient and so again violate optimality.

Things are rather different with an unanticipated temporary increase in government spending. Now the decline in household permanent income will be rather less than the increase in government expenditure, so per capita consumption also declines less. As a consequence there is an excess demand for goods which is eliminated by an increase in interest rates, prompting higher household savings,[9] as well as discouraging investment. The economy jumps from O to A, travels along the unstable path AB during the period of high government expenditure, and then from B back to O after government spending has returned to its level *ab initio*.

Note that we have so far said nothing about how these increases in government spending were financed. *Any* time profile of taxes that is consistent with the government's intertemporal budget constraint will do. This is a striking result and implies that the decision to finance the increased spending through current taxes or borrowing, i.e. future taxes, is irrelevant. This proposition is variously referred to as 'Debt Neutrality', 'Ultrarationality' or 'Ricardean Equivalence'. We shall be interested in seeing how robust a property it is. One obvious way it could fail is if taxes were distortionary, rather than lump-sum; in the present model this would be the case if taxes were paid on interest income. There would then be a wedge between pre- and post-tax real interest rates, and variations in the tax rate would shift the intertemporal optimality condition (2.5). Further consideration of the effect of distortionary taxes will be postponed until the discussion of Barro's (1991) model, which also incorporates useful public spending.

An important question that can be addressed in this present framework is whether competitive markets lead to socially efficient outcomes. We can answer this by comparing a competitive economy with a hypothetical one administered by an all-powerful benevolent social planner. This social planner maximizes the same objective function (2.1), except subject to the budget constraint for the economy, equation (2.6), rather than for the individual household. It is straightforward to show that this procedure yields an identical optimality condition (2.5), and hence that the allocations are the same. A competitive economy of this sort is thus Pareto efficient. This is hardly surprising since there are no distortions, missing markets, etc., present.

To conclude this section, let us briefly note how the analysis must be modified in an endogenous growth setting. Take the simple one-capital-good model with $Y = AK$ and $A > \delta + n + \theta$.[10] Then the marginal product of capital is just A, and from equation (2.5) the growth rate of consumption per head is

$$\dot{c}/c = \sigma(A - \delta - n - \theta) \equiv \gamma \tag{2.5'}$$

which is constant. The dynamics of capital, and hence also of output, are then

---

[9] There is no income effect from the change in interest rates because near the equilibrium consumption is exactly equal to income. Hence the sign of the effect on consumption of a change in interest rates is unambiguous.

[10] Strictly speaking we also need $(A - \delta - n)(1 - 1/\sigma) < \theta$ to ensure utility is bounded.

given by the counterpart of equation (2.6):

$$\dot{k} = (A - \delta - n)k - c - g \qquad (2.6')$$

Consequently along a balanced growth path we have output and capital per head also growing at a rate γ. An unanticipated permanent increase in government spending once again leads to the complete crowding-out of consumption, with no effect on the path of capital or output. However, a temporary increase in government spending has more interesting effects. Now there is partial crowding-out of capital accumulation as well, so that output growth falls below γ for the duration of the spending increase. When the fiscal stimulus is removed, capital accumulation and output growth recover to the original rate, γ, except that the levels of the output and capital paths are *permanently* lower than they would have otherwise been; transitory fiscal impulses thus have permanent adverse effects on output per head. (See Bean, 1990, for an empirical test of this proposition.)

3. Growth with Finitely-Lived Consumers

I now want to consider the model of Blanchard (1985) which introduces death—or rather birth—into the analysis;[11] because this constitutes the creation of a missing market it leads to significant changes to the conclusions of the preceding section. Suppose that the number of household members remains constant ($n = 0$), but that each household has a constant probability per unit time, p, of dying. Dying households are continuously replaced by new ones. These new households come into the world with nothing, and furthermore inherit nothing from the households that they replace. Without loss of generality, let us normalize the population size at unity. Households can (and will) purchase annuities from an insurance company by pledging their assets to the insurance company in the event of their death; financial intermediation by insurers is costless. Surviving households thus receive a dividend per unit time of p guilders for each guilder invested; effectively the wealth of dying households is shared out among the survivors according to their stake in the fund. Finally household preferences are assumed to be logarithmic (i.e. $\sigma = 1$; this makes aggregation easier to handle). Consumers then maximize expected utility, conditional on being alive to enjoy it, i.e.

$$\underset{\{c_s, a_s\}}{Max} \sum_{s=t}^{\infty} (1 - \theta - p)^{s-t} \, lnc_s \qquad (2.1')$$

---

[11] There is, of course, continued birth in the Ramsey–Cass–Koopmans model. The key difference is that new births here occur outside the household, whereas before they occurred within the household.

subject to

$$a_s = (1 + r_s + p)a_{s-1} + w_s - c_s - t_s \text{ (for all } s \geqslant t) \tag{2.2'}$$

plus a suitable boundary condition to prevent households from financing consumption by running up ever higher levels of debt relative to their capacity to pay. Here the p in (2.1') reflects the probability of death, while the p in (2.2') reflects the 'survival dividend'. Repeating the analysis of section 2 gives the continuous time intertemporal optimality condition for an individual household as (for all $s \geqslant t$)

$$\dot{c}_s/c_s = (r_s + p) - (p + \theta) = r_s - \theta \tag{2.4''}$$

i.e. exactly as before, but with $\sigma = 1$ and $n = 0$. Combining this with the household's intertemporal budget constraint (obtained from (2.2') and the boundary condition) it is straightforward to show that

$$c_t = (\theta + p)(a_t + h_t) \tag{3.1}$$

where h_t is the present discounted value of labour income net of taxes, $w_s - t_s$, discounted at rate $r_s + p$. This equation just says that consumption is proportional to the sum of non-human and human wealth where the latter includes a risk premium in the discount factor to reflect the positive probability of not being around to receive the future income. Aggregating across cohorts then gives aggregate consumption as

$$C_t = (\theta + p)(A_t + H_t) \tag{3.2}$$

where upper-case letters are used to denote corresponding aggregate quantities. Since all households receive the same wage, pay the same taxes, and have the same probability of survival independent of their present age,

$$\dot{H}_t = (r_t + p)H_t - W_t + T_t \tag{3.3}$$

However, the accumulation of non-human wealth is *not* given simply by the analogue of (2.2'), which only describes the evolution of non-human wealth for surviving households. At an aggregate level the 'survival dividend' is simply a redistribution, and aggregate non-human wealth evolves according to

$$\dot{A}_t = r_t A_t + W_t - T_t - C_t \tag{3.4}$$

Now differentiate equation (3.2) with respect to time and subtract $(r_t + p)C_t$ from both sides:

$$\dot{C}_t - (r_t + p)C_t = (\theta + p)[\dot{A}_t + \dot{H}_t - (r_t + p)(A_t + H_t)] \tag{3.5}$$

Using equations (3.3) and (3.4), together with the identity $A_t \equiv B_t + K_t$, and rearranging then gives

$$\dot{C}_t/C_t = (r_t - \theta) - p(\theta + p)(B_t + K_t)/C_t \tag{3.6}$$

Comparing this with equations (2.4′) and (2.4″) we see that the important difference is in the appearance of the non-human wealth to consumption ratio in the equation describing the evolution of aggregate (or average per capita) consumption, a term which disappears with infinitely-lived households ($p = 0$).

The rest of the model is essentially as before. Remembering that the total population of households is normalized to unity (so that the aggregates are also average per capita quantities), we have that the marginal product of capital, $f'(K_t)$, is equal to the user cost of capital, $r_t + \delta$, while capital accumulation is given through the goods market identity,

$$\dot{K}_t = F(K_t) - C_t - G_t - \delta K_t \tag{2.6″}$$

The new phase-plane diagram is given in Fig. 10. The important modification introduced by finite lives is that the consumption stationary is now positively sloped, asymptoting to the Modified Golden Rule where $r = \theta$ (remember $n = 0$). As well as the saddlepoint O, there is also a low-level unstable equilibrium, but this is of little interest.

What is of interest is the change in the comparative dynamics with respect to changes in government spending. Suppose first that these are tax-financed so that the bond stock, B, remains unchanged. An unanticipated permanent increase in government spending shifts the capital stationary downwards as

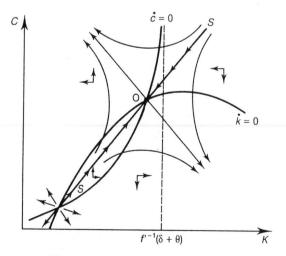

Figure 10.   The Blanchard model.

before (see Fig. 11). However, because the consumption stationary is no longer vertical there is an effect on the capital stock as well as on consumption; the economy jumps from O to *A* on impact, and then converges to O' along the saddlepath as capital and output fall. The crowding out of consumption in the short run is thus incomplete and there is now also some crowding out of investment. In the long run, however, this capital decumulation is associated with a fall in consumption that is even greater than the original increase in government spending.

Now consider a bond-financed tax cut with government spending held fixed; taxes are cut today and raised in the future by just enough to cover the cost of the increase debt interest, so that there is a once-off increase in the stock of public debt, *B*. The effect is to shift the consumption stationary upwards (see Fig. 12). Consumption initially rises as the economy jumps from O to *A*, but then ultimately declines as capital decumulation drives the economy to the new equilibrium O'. Thus the current generation of consumers benefit at the expense of future generations; government debt is not neutral in its effects. The key feature that leads to this breakdown in the Ricardean Equivalence proposition is the continued appearance of new generations whose welfare does not figure in the preferences of those who are alive today. Note that finite lives *per se* will not do the trick, for I can escape higher future taxes only by dying; if I live I have an even higher future tax burden because I also inherit the burden of those who have passed away. By contrast with the continued birth of new households, there is the possibility of future generations bearing some of the burden of the debt; by surviving I do not increase my expected tax burden per unit time.

This feature is also responsible for the breakdown of social efficiency in this

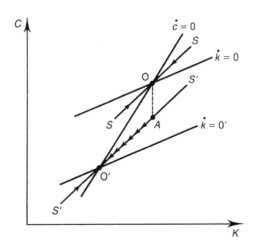

Figure 11. Tax financed increase in government spending.

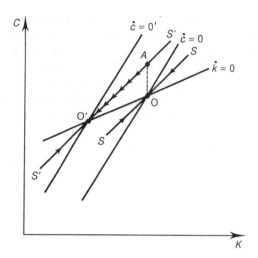

Figure 12.   Bond financed tax cut.

model. It is not difficult to demonstrate that a benevolent social planner who cares about the welfare of all generations and tries to maximize expected utility would still pick a level of capital corresponding to the Modified Golden Rule. By contrast, a competitive equilibrium produces a lower level of capital, output and consumption. The reason for the breakdown in the usual theorem concerning the efficiency of competitive markets is that unborn generations are unable to trade in current markets. In principle they would like to be able to persuade the current generation to save more by trading in today's market for savings; unfortunately, this possibility is not open to them. However, the government can in principle operate on these future generations' behalf by saving on their behalf i.e. building up a *positive* asset position.

At first glance it may seem natural to adopt the model of this section, rather than the Ramsey–Cass–Koopmans set-up, for positive and normative analysis; after all people and households do not live forever. But we have seen that the key difference is that completely new households are continually being created out of nowhere in the Blanchard model. In reality these new households are somebody's offspring. Barro's celebrated (1974) article shows that provided parents care about the utility of their offspring, then a series of finitely-lived households are equivalent to a single infinitely-lived dynasty as in the Ramsey–Cass–Koopmans structure, with bequests and/or gifts *inter vivos* being used to transfer purchasing power across generations.

There is a large literature, both theoretical and empirical, on the Ricardean Equivalence Proposition, to which it is impossible to do justice here. At a theoretical level it turns out to be rather difficult to dispose of the Equivalence

Proposition.[12] It might be thought that imperfect capital markets which prevent consumers freely redistributing expenditure over time would be enough to disrupt it. However, one also needs to explain the nature of the capital market imperfection, and how it is affected by government policy action. It turns out that plausible stories of credit rationing also produce debt neutrality once the endogeneity of the capital market imperfection is recognized (Yotsuzuka, 1987). At an empirical level a variety of approaches have been taken to test the proposition, ranging from: microeconometric studies of bequest behaviour; quasi-reduced form consumption functions relating aggregate consumption expenditure to disposable income, the budget deficit, and measures of wealth (the Ricardean Equivalence Proposition predicts that it is $Y - G$ rather than $Y - T$ that matters, and that government debt should not be considered part of net wealth by consumers e.g. Buiter and Tobin, 1981; Bean, 1987; Kormendi, 1983); structural consumption studies based on the aggregate intertemporal optimality condition (equation (3.6)) (Evans, 1988); event studies of particular instances of bond-financed tax cuts (Blinder and Deaton, 1985); and analysis of the effects of government debt on variables such as interest rates (Evans, 1985, 1987). All of these approaches have their shortcomings, and as ever econometric studies do not give a clear answer, being plagued by problems of lack of power and uncertainty as to the correct specification. To my mind the most convincing approach is that of the event study. Thus Blinder and Deaton show that the debt-financed tax cuts of the Reagan years were not accompanied by a surge in saving as predicted by the Ricardean Equivalence Proposition; instead, consumption and the US economy boomed. However, a die-hard believer in debt neutrality could argue that this reflected the beneficial supply-side effects of the reduction in tax rates, so even here the evidence is not conclusive. It seems likely, therefore, that this debate will run and run; for further discussion, both at a theoretical and empirical level, see the survey by Bernheim (1987), and the interchange between Barro and Bernheim in the *Journal of Economic Perspectives* (1989).

The final task in this section is to consider the implications of death and birth for endogenous growth models. As before, let us take the simple one-capital-good model with gross output, $Y = AK$. Then from equation (3.6) we have

$$\dot{C}_t/C_t = (A - \delta - \theta) - p(\theta + p)(B_t + K_t)/C_t \qquad (3.6')$$

---

[12] Bernheim and Bagwell (1986) in fact go to the other extreme and argue that since (asymptotically) all dynasties are interrelated by marriage, it is as if there were but one, rather than many, dynasties in the world. In that case the economy will always replicate the social planner's solution, even when only distortionary taxes are available. Consequently 'everything' is neutral! They regard this as a case of *reductio ad absurdam*, arguing that we should not take the basic Ricardean Equivalence Proposition seriously for a similar reason.

while the goods market identity (2.6″) gives

$$\dot{K}_t/K_t = (A - \delta) - (C_t + G_t)/K_t \qquad (2.6''')$$

Hence along a balanced growth path with $\gamma = \dot{C}_t/C_t = \dot{K}_t/K_t$ we have [13]

$$\gamma = (A - \delta) - (\theta + Ag)/2 - [(\theta - Ag)^2 + 4p(\theta + p)/(1 - \beta)]^{1/2}/2 \quad (3.7)$$

where $g(\equiv G/Y)$ is the share of government spending in output, and $\beta(\equiv B/(B + K))$ is the share of government debt in household wealth. Thus an increase in the share of government debt, with spending held constant, will tend to reduce the growth rate, because a switch of taxes from the present to the future raises consumption and crowds out capital accumulation. Similarly a tax-financed increase in the share of government spending reduces the growth rate because consumption is crowded out less than one-for-one. (Endogenous growth models with Blanchard-style consumers are further investigated by Alogoskoufis and Van der Ploeg, 1990, and Buiter, 1991.)

4. Growth with a Useful Public Good and Distortionary Taxes

So far we have assumed that government spending is intrinsically useless. This is not a very satisfactory state of affairs, since even the most ardent free marketeer would allow for the possibility of public goods, both in consumption and production. Following Barro (1990), I therefore now want to introduce public goods into the analysis. At the same time I also want to allow for the fact that in practice taxes are usually distortionary rather than lump sum in nature. Because labour is still supplied inelastically, a proportional tax on labour will not affect the equilibrium allocation. However, a proportional tax on interest income will drive a wedge between the pre- and post-tax interest rate and thus potentially affect savings and capital accumulation.

Let us begin by considering the case where the public good facilitates production e.g. infrastructure spending. To keep things short I will only consider the endogenous growth case; the interested reader can work through the details of the classical growth case for himself. We assume then that the technology of the economy takes the form $Y = AK^{1-\alpha}G^\alpha$ with $0 < \alpha < 1$; for simplicity we also assume that there is no depreciation, i.e. $\delta = 0$. Then the *pre-tax* private marginal product of capital is just $(1 - \alpha)A(G/K)^\alpha$. There is

---

[13] We need the negative root in the solution to the quadratic equation for γ to ensure that equation (3.7) yields (2.5′) when $p = n = 0$ and $\sigma = 1$.

no borrowing, so that government spending is financed entirely by current income taxes; hence the proportional tax rate, τ, is just

$$\tau = G/AK^{1-\alpha}G^{\alpha} \qquad (4.1)$$

Finally we assume that consumers are infinitely lived with isoelastic preferences, as in section 2. For simplicity, let us also assume a constant population. Then the intertemporal optimality condition (2.4′) still holds (with $n = 0$), where r is to be interpreted as the *post-tax* return to saving, i.e. $(1 - \tau)(1 - \alpha)(G/K)^{\alpha}$. Using equation (4.1) to eliminate G/K it then follows that the growth rate of consumption, γ, is given by

$$\gamma = \sigma[(1 - \alpha)\phi(\tau) - \theta] \qquad (4.2)$$

where $\phi(\tau) \equiv (1 - \tau)\tau^{\alpha/(1-\alpha)}A^{1/(1-\alpha)}$. There are no transition dynamics in this one-good world, so equation (4.2) also gives the growth rate of output and capital. The equation gives a Laffer-curve relationship between the growth rate and the tax rate. This is plotted in Fig. 13, and there is a unique maximum at $\tau = \alpha$. Interestingly this is also the share of government spending that would materialize if it was supplied competitively.

Of course growth maximization is not an appropriate objective in general. Rather we are interested in maximizing utility. Using equation (4.2)

$$U = \int_0^{\infty} \frac{(C_t^{1-1/\sigma} - 1)}{(1 - 1/\sigma)} e^{-\theta t} \, dt = \frac{1}{(1 - 1/\sigma)} \left[\frac{C_0^{1-1/\sigma}}{\theta - \gamma(1 - 1/\sigma)} - \frac{1}{\theta} \right] \qquad (4.3)$$

where from the goods market identity we know that

$$C_0/K_0 = \phi(\tau) - \gamma \qquad (4.4)$$

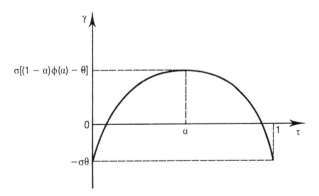

Figure 13.   The growth Laffer curve.

Combining equations (4.2), (4.3) and (4.4) then gives

$$U = \frac{1}{(1 - 1/\sigma)} \left[\frac{K_0^{1-1/\sigma} \{ \phi(\tau)[1 - \sigma(1 - \alpha)] + \sigma\theta \}^{1-1/\sigma}}{\phi(\tau)(1 - \alpha)(1 - \sigma) + \sigma\theta} - \frac{1}{\theta} \right] \qquad (4.5)$$

Tedious but straightforward algebra then establishes that U is increasing in $\phi(\tau)$. Hence utility is also maximized when $\tau = \alpha$. This result is not general, however, and merely occurs here because of the particular functional forms chosen—for instance, it would not hold for an arbitrary CES production function. Thus generally speaking, the growth-maximizing and utility-maximizing shares of government spending will not coincide.

Is the competitive equilibrium efficient? Using equation (4.1) we can write the production technology as $Y = \tau^{\alpha/(1-\alpha)} A^{1/(1-\alpha)} K$. However each extra unit of output only yields $(1 - \tau)$ units for private use in consumption or capital accumulation, the other τ units being used to maintain the share of government spending as input to production. So the social marginal product of capital is $(1 - \tau)\tau^{\alpha/(1-\alpha)} A^{1/(1-\alpha)} = \phi(\tau)$. Consequently the socially efficient growth rate, γ^*, is

$$\gamma^* = \sigma[\phi(\tau) - \theta] \qquad (4.6)$$

Comparing this with equation (4.2) we see that growth in the competitive case is too low by a factor $\sigma\alpha\phi(\tau)$. Essentially competitive producers ignore the fact that higher output and higher taxes generate more spending on the useful public good.

How can we implement the social optimum? Suppose the government has access to lump-sum taxes. Then there is no wedge between the pre-tax and post-tax interest rates in the competitive equilibrium. The return to saving is thus $(1 - \alpha)A(G/K)^{\alpha} = (1 - \alpha)\phi(\tau)/(1 - \tau)$, and the growth rate, γ^L, is given by

$$\gamma^L = \sigma[(1 - \alpha)\phi(\tau)/(1 - \tau) - \theta] \qquad (4.7)$$

Hence if the share of government spending is set at its optimal level with $\tau = \alpha$ we have $\gamma^L = \gamma^*$, so that lump-sum taxes implement the first best.

Suppose now that we also have public goods that enter into consumer utility, as well as public goods that affect production possibilities. Denote the two sorts of public spending as G_c and G_p respectively. As before, (net) output is given by $Y = AK^{1-\alpha}G_p^{\alpha}$, while the representative consumer's instantaneous utility function is now $U(C, G_c) = [(C^{1-\beta}G_c^{\beta})^{1-1/\sigma} - 1]/(1 - 1/\sigma)$, i.e. preferences are isoelastic in a Cobb–Douglas mix of private and public consumption goods. Define $\tau_c \equiv G_c/Y$ and $\tau_p \equiv G_p/Y$, so that $\tau = \tau_c + \tau_p$ is the overall government spending share/income tax rate (once again we rule out lump-sum taxes). Then the private pre-tax marginal product of capital is $(1 - \alpha)A(G_p/K)^{\alpha} = (1 - \alpha)A^{1/(1-\alpha)}\tau_p^{\alpha/(1-\alpha)}$, while the post-tax return on saving is just $(1 - \tau)$ times this quantity. Despite the introduction of public consumption goods, the particular form of preferences ensures that the relevant intertemporal optimality condition for private consumption is still equation (2.4'). Thus the growth rate in competitive equilibrium now becomes

$$\gamma = \sigma[(1 - \tau_p - \tau_c)(1 - \alpha)A^{1/(1-\alpha)}\tau_p^{\alpha/(1-\alpha)} - \theta] \qquad (4.8)$$

Once again there is a Laffer-curve type relationship between the growth rate, γ, and the share of public production goods, τ_p, with a maximum at $\tau_p = \alpha(1 - \tau_c)$. Tedious algebra shows that $\tau_p = \alpha$ is still, however, the utility-maximizing choice. By contrast the growth rate is monotonically declining in the share of public consumption goods, τ_c. Thus if we look at differences in growth rates across countries we might expect to see little systematic relationship with the share of public production goods (if τ_p is set randomly) or else an inverse relationship (if τ_p is set approximately optimally so that countries are generally on the downward-sloping portion of the growth Laffer curve). By contrast there should be an unambiguous inverse relationship with the share of public consumption goods. Barro (1990) finds that there is indeed a statistically significant inverse relationship between the growth rate and the share of public consumption goods across the countries in the Summers–Heston data set, but that there is little evidence of any link with the share of public production goods.

5. Knowledge, Externalities and Growth

Many of the recent endogenous growth models are characterized by the presence of increasing returns and externalities. Although this is by no means necessary to obtain unbounded endogenous growth, the presence of fixed factors, such as labour[14] and natural resources, implies that if there are constant returns to scale in reproducible inputs (physical and human capital) then there must be increasing returns in fixed and reproducible factors taken together. But the presence of increasing returns immediately poses problems for the existence of a competitive equilibrium. There are two possible ways out: either assume imperfect competition, or else introduce some positive externality so that while there may be increasing returns at the level of the whole economy, there are constant or decreasing returns at the level of the firm.

However, the introduction of externalities is not just a technical trick to ensure that a competitive equilibrium still exists. Rather the very nature of the process of knowledge accumulation is likely to create potential positive externalities, because a key feature of knowledge is that it is 'non-rivalrous';

---

[14] This could be made into a reproducible factor by introducing a suitable fertility mechanism into the model, see e.g. Barro and Becker (1989) and Becker and Barro (1988).

once the knowledge, e.g. the laws of mechanics, has been acquired for one use it can be reapplied elsewhere indefinitely without compromising the efficacy of its use in the line of work for which it was originally developed. There is also a second distinction between whether a good is 'excludable' or not; an excludable good is one where the supplier can prevent anyone other than the purchaser from consuming the good. Goods supplied by the market are generally both 'rivalrous' and 'excludable', because my purchase and consumption of a commodity, e.g. a hamburger, precludes someone else from consuming it. Many public goods are by contrast 'non-rivalrous' and 'non-excludable'. Knowledge could be either excludable or non-excludable. The former would arise if application for the knowledge could be patented, in which case private enterprise will invest in creating knowledge but, because of the barriers to entry and resultant imperfect competition created by the patents, at possibly sub-optimal levels. The latter would be more appropriate for fundamental knowledge and research—one cannot really envisage Einstein patenting his Theory of Relativity—and direct public action is called for.

There are endogenous growth models focusing on both types of knowledge. In this final section I want to develop a model due to Romer (1987, 1990) where knowledge is excludable by patent. His model captures the idea that growth proceeds not simply by accumulating more capital, but also through the development of new varieties of capital goods as well. There is a potentially infinite set of varieties of capital goods, ordered from 1 to N. Research and development then allows N to expand over time (at a cost). The technology for the (net) output of final goods is assumed to take the form

$$Y = AL^\alpha \sum_{i=1}^{N} K_i^{1-\alpha} \tag{5.1}$$

This technology has constant returns in $\{L, K_1, ..., K_N\}$ but increasing returns in $\{L, K_1, ..., K_N, N\}$. For simplicity I shall keep the labour force, L, fixed throughout at unity. The product market for final goods is competitive, so the demand for capital inputs by final goods producers take the form

$$(1 - \alpha)AK_i^{-\alpha} = R_i \tag{5.2}$$

where R_i is the user cost of capital for the ith variety. The associated marginal productivity condition for labour simply determines the wage in general equilibrium and is omitted, since it is not essential to what follows.

We now turn to the capital goods industry. A capital goods producer can develop a new variety of capital by expending β units of final output. Thereafter he can produce as many units as he likes of the new capital good at a constant marginal cost of η units of final output. The producer can also acquire, without cost, an infinitely-lived patent giving a monopoly in the supply of the new capital good. Now it turns out that with this structure, the rental rate that a given capital goods producer receives, R_i, will be independent of time, as is also both the demand for the ith capital good forthcoming at that rental rate, and the interest rate, r, on financial assets in the economy. In that case it will be optimal for the capital goods supplier to produce all the capital he intends to lease out as soon as it has been developed. The profit, Π_i, from the innovation of a new variety of capital is therefore

$$\Pi_i = R_i K_i / r - (\beta + \eta K_i) \qquad (5.3)$$

where the demand for capital good i with user cost R_i is given by (5.2). The first term on the right-hand side of (5.3) is the annuity value of the infinite flow of revenues, while the second term is the cost of innovation and production for the new capital good. Maximizing equation (5.3) subject to equation (5.2) gives the profit maximizing rental rate as

$$R_i = r\eta / (1 - \alpha) \qquad (5.4)$$

while (5.2) gives the associated production level for K_i. If there is free entry into research and development of new capital goods then we also have that $\Pi_i = 0$ and hence from (5.3) that

$$K_i = \beta (1 - \alpha) / \alpha \eta \qquad (5.5)$$

Combining equations (5.2), (5.4) and (5.5), it follows that the interest rate must satisfy

$$r = A (1 - \alpha)^{2 - \alpha} (\alpha / \beta)^{\alpha} \eta^{\alpha - 1} \qquad (5.6)$$

Equations (5.4), (5.5) and (5.6) confirm our conjecture above that the levels of K_i, R_i and r are all time invariant.

To find the growth rate of consumption, γ, all we need to do is combine equation (5.6) with the usual intertemporal optimality condition for an infinitely-lived consumer, equation (2.4′) with $n = 0$, to give

$$\gamma = \sigma [A (1 - \alpha)^{2 - \alpha} (\alpha / \beta)^{\alpha} \eta^{\alpha - 1} - \theta] \qquad (5.7)$$

where I have assumed any government spending is financed via lump-sum taxes. Thus the growth rate is decreasing in both the cost of innovation, β, and the cost of capital goods production, η.

This relationship prompts the question as to how growth takes place if the stock of each variety of capital goods remains constant, as in equation (5.5). The answer follows immediately by substituting (5.5) into the technology (5.1) to give

$$Y = NA [\beta (1 - \alpha) / \alpha \eta]^{1 - \alpha} \qquad (5.8)$$

Thus the engine of growth in this model is the expansion of varieties through *N*, which grows at the same rate as consumption.

Is this growth rate socially efficient? The answer, not surprisingly, is 'No'. However, things are more subtle than they at first appear. It might be thought that the problem arises because the capital is not priced at its social marginal cost, $r\eta$, but rather at $r\eta/(1 - \alpha)$, i.e. incorporating a monopoly mark-up which *ex post* just covers the additional cost of innovation. However the interest rate, *r*, also differs between the decentralized and centralized economies. In fact it can be shown that the quantity of each variety of capital that is produced is the same in both economies, i.e. as in equation (5.5).[15] It follows that the interest rate must be higher in the centralized economy by a factor $1/(1 - \alpha)$. The growth rate under a benevolent social planner, γ^*, is thus

$$\gamma^* = \sigma[A(1 - \alpha)^{1-\alpha}(\alpha/\beta)^{\alpha}\eta^{\alpha-1} - \theta] \qquad (5.9)$$

It follows therefore that the rate of innovation is too low in the decentralized economy. However, note that this cannot be corrected simply by introducing a subsidy to research (β), because this will also affect the volume of each capital good that is produced via equation (5.5). What is needed instead is a subsidy to capital goods users that lowers the cost of capital by α per cent. The effect of this subsidy is, in general equilibrium, to draw more resources into the development of new capital goods and to drive up the interest rate. This is rather a neat example of the old adage that he who pays the tax (here a subsidy) does not necessarily bear the burden (here a bonus).

While Romer's model is neat, it does have some unsatisfactory features. In particular, capital goods, once invented, will continue to be used for ever more. Yet clearly we no longer use flint axes to fashion wood, nor chariots to get around. Authors such as Grossman and Helpman (1990, l991a, l991b) and Aghion and Howitt (1990) have developed models with quality 'ladders' in which new goods completely supersede older varieties, before ultimately being replaced themselves. Nevertheless many of the insights of the Romer model carry over to models with such obsolescence.

6. Concluding Remarks

There are many issues I have not addressed in this chapter, including the links between income distribution and growth, international trade and growth, and business cycles and growth. There is already much work in the 'new' growth literature on these themes, and there will surely be even more by the time this book has been published. However, let me conclude by noting that while there has been an explosion in the theory of endogenous growth, empirical work, with the exception of that on the convergence issue, is as yet rather thin on

---

[15] See Romer (1987) for further details.

the ground. Yet empirical work is urgently needed to sort out which are the most important endogenous growth mechanisms. Without this knowledge, policy prescriptions based on the new growth theory will remain on somewhat shaky foundations. Hopefully the next decade will see substantive progress on this as well as the other issues raised above.

References

Aghion, P. and Howitt, P. (1990): 'Growth through Creative Destruction', *Econometrica*, (forthcoming).

Alogoskoufis, G. and Van der Ploeg, F. (1990): 'On Budgetary Policies and Economic Growth', Centre for Economic Policy Research, London, mimeo.

Barro, R. (1974): 'Are Government Bonds Net Wealth?' *Journal of Political Economy*, **82**, 1095–1117.

Barro, R. (1987): 'The Ricardean Approach to Budget Deficits', *Journal of Economic Perspectives*, **3**, 2, 37–54.

Barro, R. (1990): 'Government Spending in a Simple Model of Endogenous Growth', *Journal of Political Economy*, **98**, 5, S102–25.

Barro, R., and Becker, G. (1989): 'Fertility Choice in a Model of Economic Growth', *Econometrica*, **57**, 2, 481–502.

Barro, R. and Sala-i-Martin, X. (1991): 'Convergence across States and Regions', *Brookings Papers on Economic Activity*, **1**, 107–82.

Baumol, W.J. (1986): 'Productivity Growth, Convergence, and Welfare: What the Long Run Data Show', *American Economic Review*, **76**, 1072–85.

Bean, C.R. (1987): 'The Impact of North Sea Oil', in R. Dornbusch and R. Layard (eds), *Britain's Economic Performance*, Oxford.

Bean, C.R. (1990): 'Endogenous Growth and the Procyclical Behaviour of Productivity', *European Economic Review*, **34**, 355–63.

Becker, G. and Barro, R. (1988): 'A Reformulation of the Economic Theory of Fertility', *Quarterly Journal of Economics*, **103**, 1–25.

Bernard, A. and Durlauf, S. (1991): 'Interpreting Tests of the Convergence Hypothesis', Stanford University, mimeo.

Bernheim, B.D. (1987): 'A Neo Classical Perspective on Budget Deficits', *Journal of Economic Perspectives*, **3**, 2, 55–72.

Bernheim, B.D. (1987): 'Ricardian Equivalence: An Evaluation of Theory and Evidence', *NBER Macroeconomics Annual*, 263–315.

Bernheim, B.D. and Bagwell, K. (1988): 'Is Everything Neutral?', *Journal of Political Economy*, **96**, 2, 308–38.

Blanchard, O.J. (1985): 'Debt, Deficits and Finite Horizons', *Journal of Political Economy*, **93**, 2, 223–47.

Blinder, A. and Deaton, A. (1985): 'The Time Series Consumption Function Revisited', *Brookings Papers on Economic Activity*, 2, 465–511.

Buiter, W.H. (1991): 'Saving and Endogenous Growth: A Survey of Theory and Policy', Centre for Economic Policy Research, London, mimeo.

Buiter, W.H. and Tobin, J. (1981): 'Debt Neutrality: A Brief Review of Doctrine and Evidence', in G. von Furstenberg (ed.), *Social Security and Private Saving*.

Cass, D. (1965): 'Optimum Growth in an Aggregative Model of Capital Accumulation', *Review of Economic Studies*, **32**, 233–40.

DeLong, J.B. (1988): 'Productivity Growth, Convergence, and Welfare: Comment', *American Economic Review*, **78**, 1138–54.

Dowrick, S. and Nguyen, D. (1989): 'OECD Comparative Economic Growth 1950–85: Catch-Up and Convergence', *American Economic Review*, **79**, 1010–30.

Evans, P. (1985): 'Do Large Deficits Produce High Interest Rates?', *American Economic Review*, **75**, 1, 68–87.

Evans, P. (1987): 'Interest Rates and Expected Future Budget Deficits in the United States', *Journal of Political Economy*, **95**, 2, 34–58.

Evans, P. (1988): 'Are Consumers Ricardean? Evidence for the United States', *Journal of Political Economy*, **96**, 5, 983–1004.

Grossman, G. and Helpman, E. (1990): 'Comparative Advantage and Long-Run Growth', *American Economic Review*, **80**, 4, 796–815.

Grossman, G. and Helpman, E. (1991a): 'Quality Ladders in the Theory of Growth', *Review of Economic Studies*, **58**, 43–61.

Grossman, G. and Helpman, E. (1991b): 'Quality Ladders and Product Cycles', *Quarterly Journal of Economics*, **106**, 557–86.

Jones, L.E. and Manuelli, R. (1990): 'A Convex Model of Equilibrium Growth: Theory and Policy Implications', *Journal of Political Economy*, **98**, 1008–38.

Kaldor, N. (1961): 'Capital Accumulation and Economic Growth', in F. Lutz and D. Hague (eds), *The Theory of Capital*, Macmillan, London.

King, R., Plosser, C.I. and Rebelo, S. (1988): 'Production, Growth and Business Cycles: II New Directions', *Journal of Monetary Economics*, **21**, 309–42.

Koopmans, T.C. (1965): 'On the Concept of Optimal Economic Growth', in *The Econometric Approach to Development Planning*, North Holland, Amsterdam.

Kormendi, R.C. (1983): 'Government Debt, Government Spending, and Private Sector Behaviour', *American Economic Review*, **73**, 994–1010.

Lucas, R.E. (1988): 'On the Mechanics of Economic Development', *Journal of Monetary Economics*, **22**, 3–42.

Quah, D. (1990): 'Galton's Fallacy and Tests of the Convergence Hypothesis', MIT, mimeo.

Ramsey, F.P. (1928): 'A Mathematical Theory of Saving', *Economic Journal*, **38**, 543–59.

Romer, P. (1986): 'Increasing Returns and Long-Run Growth', *Journal of Political Economy*, **94**, 1002–37.

Romer, P. (1987): 'Growth Based on Increasing Returns due to Specialisation', *American Economic Review*, **77**, (*Papers and Proceedings*), 56–62.

Romer, P. (1990): 'Endogenous Technical Change'. *Journal of Political Economy*, **98**, S71–102.

Solow, R.M. (1956): 'A Contribution to the Theory of Economic Growth', *Quarterly Journal of Economics*, **70**, 65–94.

Yotsuzuka, T. (1987): 'Ricardean Equivalence in the Presence of Capital Market Imperfections', *Journal of Monetary Economics*, **20**, 411–36.

4

The Intertemporal Optimizing Approach to International Macroeconomics*

Stephen J. Turnovsky

University of Washington

1. Introduction and Overview

The dynamic international macroeconomic models of the 1970s emphasized the dynamic interaction between exchange rates, prices, and asset accumulation. Typically, these were extensions of the traditional Keynesian *IS–LM*–Phillips Curve framework and were arbitrarily specified, as a result of which, they were frequently criticized as being *ad hoc*. Recent work in macroeconomics in general, and in international macroeconomics in particular, has emphasized the need to base such models on firm microeconomic underpinnings. Essentially, this has come to mean that the underlying behavioural relationships should be derived from some form of intertemporal optimization by representative agents, with particular attention being devoted to ensuring that the equilibrium is consistent with the intertemporal resource constraints facing the individual and the economy. While it is fair to say that macroeconomic theory is being increasingly carried out within this type of framework, nevertheless there are eminent economists who remain sceptical of what this approach has to offer. This view is expressed most forcibly by Dornbusch (1988), who in the introduction to his collection of essays writes:

> Although much of policy-oriented open-economy macroeconomics stands unproved, I am impressed with the near-complete sterility of the intertemporal

---

* Material from this chapter formed the basis for an invited presentation to the 1989 Australasian meetings of the Econometric Society, held at the University of New England, Armidale NSW, Australia.

approach in the face of actual policy issues. Perhaps as it matures in the hands of some of the excellent scholars now working in that mode, it will come to yield a richer harvest.

This chapter discusses the basic procedures and some of the issues involved in the intertemporal approach to international macroeconomics. There are two features to this approach which practitioners of this framework find to be attractive. First, by deriving the model from underlying microeconomic principles, much of the arbitrariness associated with macroeconomic modelling is eliminated. But at the same time, the extent to which this is accomplished should not be overstated, since a good deal of arbitrariness still remains. The nature of the objective function, the range of decision variables, the specification of the constraints, all typically remain subject to choice. The arbitrariness that all this entails remains inevitable. Secondly, by explicitly introducing some intertemporal measure of welfare, the intertemporal approach provides a natural framework for performing macroeconomic welfare analysis and for discussing optimal macroeconomic policy-making.

One cannot hope to do justice in a single chapter to the vast literature which has been evolving over the last decade or so, and our treatment is therefore necessarily selective. Our objective is primarily to present an exposition of the intertemporal optimizing method, rather than to attempt to provide a comprehensive survey.

To this end, section 2 begins with what would seem to be a natural extension of a simple, but standard, monetary model of the 1970s. It consists of a single good produced by a single factor of production, labour, and two assets, domestic money and traded bonds. The main point we make here is that in this simple model the dynamics degenerates, unless some form of sluggishness is introduced into the evolution of the economy. There are various ways that this may be accomplished, some of which are discussed. These include: (i) the introduction of a variable rate of time preference; (ii) the introduction of imperfections in the bond market; (iii) a growing population of infinitely lived households.

But the most important source of sluggishness introduced into the recent intertemporal optimizing model is the accumulation of capital, which is assumed to take place subject to convex costs of adjustment. Such a model is set out in detail in section 3, which constitutes the core of this chapter. The model is illustrated by analysing the dynamic response to increases in government expenditure on both domestic and imported goods. But we should stress that the objective here is largely illustrative and the approach can be readily adapted to the analysis of other forms of disturbance to the economy. We should add that while the discussion is primarily on the positive aspects, describing how the economy responds to the various shocks, we also include a brief discussion of the effects on the welfare of the representative agent, as reflected by his intertemporal utility function. This forms the basis for conducting normative analysis, although this is not pursued here.

Section 4 indicates some of the directions in which the type of model developed in detail in section 3 has been extended. These include: (i) relaxing the assumption of perfect capital markets; (ii) the introduction of two or more production sectors; and (iii) two-country models. Our objective here is modest: it is simply to point out some of the issues involved. The extension to two countries opens up a whole range of issues relating to strategic behaviour, formation of unions, etc., which are at the forefront of current research. These topics are not discussed at all, although they would seem to be directions in which the intertemporal optimizing model is headed.

2. Basic Monetary Model

The model we shall consider contains three sectors: (i) consumers, (ii) firms, and (iii) the government. To preserve analytical tractability we assume that all consumers and firms are identical, enabling us to focus on the representative agent in each group. Perfect foresight is assumed to hold throughout.

2.1. Structure of Economy

We assume that the domestic economy is small. It produces a single traded good, the foreign price of which is given in the world market. In the absence of any impediments to trade, purchasing power parity (PPP) holds, which expressed in percentage change terms implies

$$p = q + e \tag{2.1.1}$$

where:

p = rate of inflation of the good in domestic currency,
q = rate of inflation of the good in foreign currency,
e = rate of exchange depreciation.

We assume that the domestic residents may hold two assets. The first is domestic money, which is not held by foreigners. Secondly, we assume that there is a traded world bond, with uncovered interest parity (UIP) holding at all times:

$$i = i^* + e \tag{2.1.2}$$

where

i = domestic nominal interest rate,
i^* = foreign nominal interest rate, assumed to be given,
e = expected rate of exchange depreciation, which assuming perfect foresight is equal to the actual rate of exchange depreciation.

For the present, we abstract from physical capital.

The representative consumer is assumed to choose his level of consumption, labour supply, real money balances, holdings of the traded bond, by solving the following intertemporal optimization problem: [1]

$$\max \int_0^\infty [U(c, l) + V(m)] \, e^{-\beta t} \qquad U_c > 0, U_l < 0, V' > 0 \qquad (2.1.3)$$

subject to the budget constraint:

$$c + \dot{m} + \dot{b} = wl + \pi + (r^* - q)b - (q + e)m - T \qquad (2.1.4)$$

and initial conditions:

$$m(0) = \frac{M_0}{P(0)}; \qquad b(0) = \frac{E(0)B_0}{P(0)} = \frac{B_0}{Q_0} \qquad (2.1.5)$$

where:

c = real consumption,
m = real money balances; M = nominal money balances,
b = real stock of traded bonds; B = nominal stock of traded bonds,
l = supply of labour,
w = real wage rate,
π = real profit, paid out to consumers,
β = rate of time preference, taken to be constant,
P = domestic price level,
Q = foreign price level,
E = nominal exchange rate,
T = real lump-sum taxes.

The utility function is assumed to be concave in its arguments c, l, and m. The separability of the utility function into a function of c and l, on the one hand, and m on the other, is made primarily for expositional simplicity. It leads to a separation of the real part of the system from the nominal. The budget constraint is straightforward, the only point requiring comment is that, given the assumptions of PPP and UIP, the real rates of return on holding bonds and money are $(i - q)$, and $-p = -(q + e)$, respectively.

In determining his optimal plans for c, l, m, and b, the consumer is assumed to take e, q, π, w, i, i^*, T, the price level P, and the exchange rate E, as parametrically given. The initial conditions in (2.1.5) relate to the initial stocks of real bonds and real stock of money balances held by consumers. By definition, these are the corresponding initial nominal stocks divided by the initial price level.

---

[1] We shall adopt the following notation: where appropriate, primes shall denote derivatives, subscripts shall denote partial derivatives, and a dot shall denote a derivative with respect to time.

The first-order optimality conditions for consumers are described by:

$$U_c(c, l) = \lambda \tag{2.1.6}$$

$$U_l(c, l) = -w\lambda \tag{2.1.7}$$

$$V'(m) = r\lambda \tag{2.1.8}$$

$$\dot{\lambda} = \lambda[\beta - (i^* - q)] \tag{2.1.9}$$

together with the transversality conditions:

$$\lim_{t \to \infty} \lambda m e^{-\beta t} = \lim_{t \to \infty} \lambda b e^{-\beta t} = 0 \tag{2.1.10}$$

where λ, the Lagrange multiplier associated with the accumulation equation (2.1.4), is the shadow value of wealth.

Taken in pairs, the first three equations describe the static marginal rate of substitution conditions necessary for consumer optimality. The marginal rate of substitution between consumption and labour supply must equal the real wage; the marginal rate of substitution between consumption and real money balances must equal the nominal interest rate. Equation (2.1.9), rewritten as:

$$\beta - \frac{\dot{\lambda}}{\lambda} = i^* - q \tag{2.1.9'}$$

is the usual Keynes–Ramsey rule, describing the optimal intertemporal allocation of consumption. The marginal utility loss from giving up a unit of consumption equals the real rate of return on a unit of saving. With β, and $i^* - q$, being exogenously given constant, in order for (2.1.9') to imply a non-degenerate steady state value for λ, we require $\beta = i^* - q$; that the rate of time preference must equal the world real interest rate. But this implies $\dot{\lambda} = 0$, for all t, so that the marginal utility is constant over time; i.e., $\lambda = \bar{\lambda}$. This is important and imposes severe restrictions on the dynamics consistent with the attainment of a finite steady state.

In the absence of physical capital, the firm's optimization problem is very simple. It just hires labour to maximize real profit:

$$\pi = F(l) - wl \qquad F' > 0, F'' < 0 \tag{2.1.11}$$

where $F(l)$, the firm's production function, is assumed to possess the usual property of positive, but diminishing, marginal physical product of labour. The optimality condition is the usual marginal condition:

$$F'(l) = w \tag{2.1.12}$$

The final agent, the domestic government, operates in accordance with its budget constraint:

$$\dot{m} + \dot{a} = g + (r^* - q)a - (q + e)m - T \qquad (2.1.13)$$

where

$a =$ stock of traded bonds issued by the domestic government,
$g =$ real government expenditure.

In addition, government policy needs to be specified. As an example, we shall assume that the government allows the domestic nominal money supply to grow at the fixed rate θ, and continually balances its budget with lump-sum taxes. These policies are specified by:

$$\dot{m} = (\theta - q - e)m \qquad (2.1.14)$$

$$T = g + (r^* - q)\bar{a} - \theta m \qquad (2.1.15)$$

where the bar denotes the fact that a remains fixed. Note that summing the constraints (2.1.4), (2.1.11), and (2.1.13), leads to:

$$\dot{n} = F(l) - c - g + (r^* - q)n \qquad (2.1.16)$$

where $n \equiv b - a$ is the net stock of traded bonds (i.e., net credit) of the domestic economy. This equation simply confirms that the current account equals the trade surplus (output less domestic absorption) plus the real interest earned on foreign bond holdings. There is nothing to rule out $n < 0$, in which case the country is a debtor, rather than a creditor, nation.

2.2. Macroeconomic Equilibrium

The macroeconomic equilibrium to this model is attained when the planned demand and supply functions, that solve the optimization problems, consistent with the accumulation equations, clear all markets at all points of time. Combining the optimality conditions (2.1.6)–(2.1.9), (2.1.12), together with the accumulation equation (2.1.13), policy specifications (2.1.14), (2.1.15) and current account relationship (2.1.16), this is described by the set of relationships:

$$U_c(c, l) = \bar{\lambda} \qquad (2.2.1)$$

$$U_l(c, l) = -F'(l)\bar{\lambda} \qquad (2.2.2)$$

$$V'(m) = (i^* + e)\bar{\lambda} \qquad (2.2.3)$$

$$\dot{m} = (\theta - q - e)m \tag{2.2.4}$$

$$\dot{n} = F(l) - c - g + (i^* - q)n \tag{2.2.5}$$

$$T = g + (i^* - q)\bar{a} - \theta m \tag{2.2.6}$$

as well as the transversality conditions.

Unfortunately, the dynamics of this macroeconomic equilibrium degenerate. This can be seen as follows. With the shadow value of wealth remaining constant over time, the marginal conditions (2.2.1), (2.2.2) imply that both c and l must also remain constant over time. Extreme consumption smoothing is optimal. Next, (2.2.3) can be solved for the rate of exchange depreciation as a function $e = e(m)$, with $e'(m) < 0$. Substituting this into (2.2.4) yields the differential equation in m:

$$\dot{m} = [\theta - q - e(m)]m \tag{2.2.7}$$

This implies a finite steady-state stock of real money balances if and only if:[2]

$$\theta = q + e(m) \tag{2.2.8}$$

which implies that both m and e remain constant over time. With c and l being constant, the equation (2.2.5) describing the accumulation of bonds can be easily solved. It can be verified that the country's intertemporal budget constraint will be met if and only if:

$$F(l) - c - g + (i^* - q)n_0 = 0 \tag{2.2.9}$$

where n_0 is the initial stock of bonds held by the economy. No accumulation of bonds in fact occurs. The economy is always in steady state. Equations (2.2.1)–(2.2.3), (2.2.8), (2.2.9) determine these stationary solutions to c, l, e, m, and $\bar{\lambda}$. Once these values are known, (2.2.6) determines the lump-sum taxes required to maintain the government budget balance.

Despite the rigour with which the underlying equilibrium is derived, it is not very interesting. Basically what happens is that any shock to the system generates an instantaneous jump in the nominal exchange rate, E, causing the real money balances to jump such that $e(m) = \theta - q$. The fundamental problem is that there is no sluggishness in the system. Nothing prevents it from fully adjusting to any shock instantaneously. Sluggish adjustment can be introduced in various ways. One key way is through the accumulation of physical capital, and this will be discussed at length in section 3 below. Within the context of a simple model such as this, sluggishness can be conveniently

---

[2] This condition is stronger than the transversality condition on money contained in (2.1.10). That is, it is sufficient, but not necessary, for that condition to hold.

introduced by modifying the assumptions relating to time preference and capital mobility. These shall be briefly discussed.

2.3. Sluggish Adjustment in Basic Monetary Model

The key feature of the model giving rise to the degeneracy of the dynamics is the condition:

$$\beta = i^* - q \tag{2.3.1}$$

The earliest monetary model restored non-degenerate dynamics to this model by in effect modifying this relationship. Obstfeld (1981) does so by endogenizing the consumer rate of time preference β, through the introduction of Uzawa (1968) preferences, postulating:

$$B(t) = \int_0^t \beta(s)\,ds, \qquad \beta(s) = \beta[U(c(s), m(s))] \tag{2.3.2}$$

The instantaneous rate of discount is thus a function of the level of utility at time t. The marginal utility λ is no longer constant, and the condition:

$$\beta[U(c, m)] = i^* - q \tag{2.3.3}$$

now holds only in steady-state equilibrium. In effect the exogenously given world real interest rate $i^* - q$ now determines the equilibrium level of instantaneous utility, which will equilibrate the domestic rate of time preference to the world real interest rate. By assuming that the function β is positive and satisfies $\beta'(U) > 0$, $\beta''(U) > 0$, $\beta(U) - U\beta'(U) > 0$, one can show that the dynamics of λ and m will have a saddlepoint property, thereby giving rise to non-degenerate dynamics. The problem with this approach is that the rationale for the restrictions on the function β are not particularly compelling.

Turnovsky (1985) adopts a somewhat different approach. He introduces non-traded bonds, which are imperfect substitutes for traded bonds. He does so by introducing quadratic costs on holding foreign bonds. This is meant to capture, in a certainty equivalent framework, the imperfect substitutability between domestic and foreign bonds. In a stochastic model, the cost parameter would be a function of the degree of exchange risk and the degree of risk aversion of domestic investors. This procedure also gives rise to a saddlepoint property. However, it suffers from two drawbacks. First, while it does generate a perfectly plausible demand function for foreign bonds, dependent upon the uncovered interest differential, the fact is that this formulation does represent a short cut. It is preferable to model imperfect capital mobility within an explicit stochastic framework. Secondly, dynamic responses to shocks may, or may not, degenerate, depending upon the shocks, and the precise formulation of these costs. In fact, this procedure tends to highlight the arbitrariness which remains even when the model is grounded in intertemporal optimization.

Alternatively, non-degenerate dynamics can be restored by introducing the uncertain lifetime assumption of Blanchard (1985) or a growing population of infinitely-lived households, as in Weil (1989). In either case, for specific forms of the utility function, for example if it is logarithmic, an aggregate consumption function of the form:

$$\dot{c} = (i^* - q - \beta)c - \eta(m + b) \qquad (2.3.1')$$

is obtained. In effect, this equation replaces the condition (2.3.1) and is a source of sluggishness, which may give rise to saddlepoint behaviour.[3]

3. Real Models of Capital Accumulation

The recent literature based on optimizing models of small open economies has introduced capital accumulation, and the models have generally been real. Non-degenerate dynamics have typically been introduced by imposing convex costs of adjustment on the rate of investment. The shocks that are usually studied include:

- *Fiscal disturbances* (government expenditure); see e.g., Frenkel and Razin (1987), Buiter (1987), Brock (1988), Obstfeld (1989);
- *Tariffs*; see e.g., Edwards (1987), Sen and Turnovsky (1989b), Engel and Kletzer (1990), Gavin (1991), Turnovsky (1991);
- *Relative price shocks*; see e.g., Svensson and Razin (1983), Persson and Svensson (1985), Matsuyama (1988), Sen and Turnovsky (1989b);
- *Productivity shocks*; see e.g., Murphy (1986), Matsuyama (1987).

Not all of the above models incorporate capital, but they are all based on the intertemporal optimizing approach being emphasized here.

In this section of the chapter we develop a model of capital accumulation and intertemporal optimization and use it to discuss various aspects related to fiscal shocks. Our discussion draws heavily on the recent paper by Turnovsky and Sen (1991) which addresses this issue. While the analysis of fiscal policy serves as a useful vehicle for displaying the model, it is very adaptable, and essentially the same structure can be applied to the analysis of other disturbances; see e.g., Sen and Turnovsky (1989a, 1989b, 1990).

The present section discusses the effects of government expenditure policy using a two-good model of a semi-small open economy.[4] Since we wish to

---

[3] A further possible way to generate dynamics in this model is through the introduction of nominal price or wage rigidity; see e.g., van de Klundert and van der Ploeg (1989) for an example of such an analysis.

[4] By semi-small we mean that the economy is able to influence the price of its export goods.

focus on expenditure, rather than on the details of government finance, we assume the existence of infinitely-lived private agents, when, with competitive markets, the conditions of Ricardian equivalence are known to prevail. Investment behaviour is generated by a Tobin q-theoretic function, first developed within an intertemporal optimizing framework by Hayashi (1982), Abel (1982), and others.[5] The convex installation costs ensure that the rate of investment remains finite at all times. As will become evident in due course, the endogeneity of employment is crucial to the dynamics of the entire system. Without it, the dynamics would degenerate; a fiscal expansion would give rise to an instantaneous adjustment in the relative price, with no change in the capital stock.

Using this framework, we analyse the effects of changes in government expenditure on both a domestically produced good and an imported good on a number of key macroeconomic variables. These include the rate of capital accumulation, employment, output, the current account deficit, the real interest rate, and the real exchange rate. The model is sufficiently tractable to enable us to characterize in detail the dynamic adjustment of the economy and to highlight the critical role played by the accumulating capital stock in this process. In particular, the evolution of the current account is seen to mirror that of capital. But, as well as describing the responses of the variables enumerated above, our approach provides a natural framework for assessing the effects of such policy shocks on the welfare of the representative agent, as measured by his utility along the entire adjustment path.[6]

For both forms of government expenditure, two types of changes are analysed: namely an unanticipated permanent, and an unanticipated temporary expansion. A striking feature of the latter is that a temporary fiscal shock has a permanent effect on the economy. The reason for this is that, as we shall demonstrate below, the steady state corresponding to some sustained policy depends upon the initial conditions of the economy prevailing at the time this policy is introduced. The adjustment which occurs during some temporary policy change will have an important bearing on the initial conditions in existence at the time the temporary policy is permanently revoked.

The fact that the steady state may depend upon initial conditions in models with infinitely lived maximizing agents, having a constant rate of time discount and facing perfect capital markets (assumptions to be made below), has been previously discussed by Giavazzi and Wyplosz (1984). However, its significance for the implications of temporary shocks has only recently begun to

---

[5] This approach to investment is also adopted by Buiter (1987). His analysis of the semi-small economy is based on numerical simulations; the model developed in this chapter is investigated entirely analytically. For other recent applications of the cost of adjustment approach to investment to the analysis of alternative macro disturbances in open economies see e.g., Matsuyama (1987), Brock (1988), Sen and Turnovsky (1989).

[6] This is in contrast to a consideration of steady-state utility, which neglects welfare along the transitional adjustment path.

receive consideration.[7] Yet this is a crucial issue, especially in the light of the recent interest pertaining to hysteresis and the random walk behaviour of real variables such as output and employment. The present framework provides a plausible framework for generating this type of behaviour.

In characterizing the dynamic adjustment paths generated by these fiscal disturbances, the analysis identifies several channels through which they are transmitted to the rest of the economy. First, there is the usual direct effect. This is simply the channel whereby a fiscal expansion on the domestic good impinges directly on the domestic output market, while a fiscal expansion on the imported good impacts directly on the trade balance. Secondly, a fiscal expansion induces a short-run change in the price of capital (the Tobin q), which in turn determines the transitional adjustment in the capital stock over time. The model is forward-looking and as a consequence of this, the short-run adjustment depends upon the long-run response of the capital stock. As we will show below, this in turn depends upon the form of fiscal expansion. While government expenditure on the domestic good is unambiguously expansionary, government expenditure on the imported good is not. Thirdly, a fiscal expansion generates a wealth effect, which with perfect capital markets, remains constant over time. Moreover, because the economy changes its stock of wealth while a temporary policy is in effect, thereby determining the initial conditions in existence when the policy ceases, this wealth effect provides the channel whereby the temporary policy has a permanent effect. It is the essential source of the hysteresis generated by the model.

3.1. The Macroeconomic Framework

For present purposes the household and production sectors of the economy may be consolidated. The economy we consider is inhabited by a single infinitely-lived representative agent who accumulates capital (k) for rental at its competitively determined rental rate and supplies labour (l) at its competitive wage. The agent is specialized in the production of a single commodity, using the stock of capital and labour by means of a neoclassical production function $F(k, l)$. Expenditure on any given increase in the capital stock is an increasing function of the rate of capital accumulation. That is, there are increasing costs associated with investment (I), which we represent by the convex function $C(I)$: $C' > 0, C'' > 0$.[8] By choice of units, we assume

---

[7] A detailed discussion of this issue is presented by Sen and Turnovsky (1990).

[8] This formulation of the installation function follows the original specification of adjustment costs introduced by Lucas (1967) and Gould (1968). More recent work by Hayashi (1982) and others postulates an installation function which depends upon k as well as I. This modification makes little difference to our analysis and for simplicity we retain the simpler specification.

$C(0) = 0, C'(0) = 1$, so that the total cost of zero investment is zero and the marginal cost of the initial installation is unity.[9]

Domestic output is used in part for investment, in part as a domestic consumption good (x), with the rest being exported. In addition to consuming part of this output, the agent also consumes another good (y), which is imported from abroad. While the price of this latter good is taken as given, the economy is large enough in the production of the domestic good to affect its relative price and therefore the terms of trade.

The agent can also accumulate net foreign bonds (b) that pay an exogenously given world interest rate (i^*). Equation (3.1.1) describes the agent's instantaneous budget constraint

$$\dot{b} = \frac{1}{\sigma} [F(k, l) - C(I) - x - \sigma y + \sigma i^* b - T] \tag{3.1.1}$$

where:

σ = relative price of the foreign good in terms of the domestic good,
T = lump-sum taxes.

In addition, the rate of capital accumulation and investment are related by the constraint

$$\dot{k} = I \tag{3.1.2}$$

where for simplicity we abstract from depreciation.

The agent's decisions are to choose consumption levels x, y, labour supply l, the rate of investment I, and the rates of asset accumulation $\dot{b}, \dot{k}$ to

$$\text{Maximize} \int_0^\infty [U(x, y) + V(l) + W(g_x, g_y)] e^{-\beta t} \, dt \tag{3.1.3}$$

$$U_x > 0, U_y > 0, V' > 0, W_{g_x} > 0, W_{g_y} > 0$$

where g_x, g_y denote real domestic government expenditure on the domestic good and the import good, respectively. The optimization is subject to the constraints (3.1.1), (3.1.2), and the given initial conditions $K(0) = K_0, b(0) = b_0$. For simplicity, the instantaneous utility function is assumed to be additively separable in the private consumption goods, x and y, labour, l, and the public expenditures g_x and g_y. We also assume that the utility function is increasing in the consumption of both private and public goods, but decreasing in labour,

---

[9] Note that this specification implies that in the case where disinvestment may occur $I < 0, C(I) < 0$ for low rates of disinvestment. This may be interpreted as reflecting the revenue obtained as capital is sold off. The possibility that all changes in capital are costly can be incorporated by introducing sufficiently large fixed costs, so that $C(0) > 0$. This does not alter our analysis in any substantive way.

and that it is strictly concave. Finally, the two private goods are taken to be Edgeworth complementary, so that $U_{xy} > 0$.

The current-value Hamiltonian for this optimization is expressed by:

$$H \equiv U(x, y) + V(l) + W(g_x, g_y)$$

$$+ \frac{\lambda}{\sigma} [F(k, l) - C(I) - x - \sigma y + \sigma i^* b - T] + q^* I \quad (3.1.4)$$

where λ is the shadow value (marginal utility) of wealth in the form of internationally traded bonds and q^* is the shadow value of the agent's capital stock. Exposition of the model is simplified by using the shadow value of wealth as numeraire. Consequently, $q \equiv \sigma q^*/\lambda$ is defined to be the market price of capital in terms of the (unitary) price of foreign bonds.

The first order optimality conditions with respect to x, y, l, and I are respectively:

$$U_x(x, y) = \frac{\lambda}{\sigma} \quad (3.1.5)$$

$$U_y(x, y) = \lambda \quad (3.1.6)$$

$$V'(l) = -\frac{\lambda}{\sigma} F_l(k, l) \quad (3.1.7)$$

$$C'(I) = q \quad (3.1.8)$$

Pairwise the first three equations describe the usual marginal rate of substitution conditions for consumers. Equation (3.1.8) equates the marginal cost of investment to the market value of capital, which is essentially a Tobin q theory of investment.[10]

In addition, the shadow value of wealth and the market value of capital evolve in accordance with:

$$\dot{\lambda} = \lambda(\beta - i^*) \quad (3.1.9)$$

$$\dot{q} = \left(i^* + \frac{\dot{\sigma}}{\sigma}\right)q - F_k(k, l) \quad (3.1.10)$$

Since β and i^* are both fixed, the ultimate attainment of a steady state is

---

[10] In the case where the installation cost function is homogeneous of degree 1 in I and k, the investment function implied by (3.1.8) is modified to

$$\frac{I}{k} = G(q)$$

possible if and only if $\beta = i^*$, and henceforth we assume this to be the case. This implies $\dot{\lambda} = 0$ everywhere, so that λ is always at its steady-state value $\bar{\lambda}$ (to be determined below). Given the assumption of interest rate parity, the domestic interest rate $i(t)$ is related to the world interest rate by:

$$i(t) = i^* + \frac{\dot{\sigma}}{\sigma} \tag{3.1.11}$$

Equation (3.1.10) is therefore an arbitrage condition equating the rate of return on capital, $(F_k + \dot{q})/q$, to the domestic interest rate, $i(t)$.

Finally, in order to ensure that the private agent satisfies his intertemporal budget constraint, we need to impose the transversality conditions

$$\lim_{t \to \infty} \lambda b e^{-i^*t} = \lim_{t \to \infty} qke^{-i^*b} = 0 \tag{3.1.12}$$

Turning to the domestic government, its budget constraint, expressed in terms of the foreign good, is described by the equation

$$\dot{a} = \frac{1}{\sigma} \left[g_x + \sigma g_y + \sigma i^* a - T \right] \tag{3.1.13}$$

where a is the stock of (traded) bonds issued by the domestic government. This equation is perfectly straightforward and requires no further comment.

Subtracting (3.1.13) from (3.1.1) yields the national budget constraint:

$$\dot{n} = \frac{1}{\sigma} \left[F(k, l) - (x + g_x) - \sigma(y + g_y) - C(I) + \sigma i^* n \right] \tag{3.1.14}$$

where $n \equiv b - a = $ stock of net credit of the domestic economy. That is, the rate of change of net credit of the domestic economy equals the balance of payments on current account, which in turn equals the balance of trade plus the net interest earned on the traded bonds. To rule out the possibility that the country can run up infinite debt or credit with the rest of the world, we impose the following intertemporal budget constraint:

$$\lim_{t \to \infty} ne^{-i^*t} = 0 \tag{3.1.15}$$

This relationship, together with the transversality condition (3.1.12), imposes a corresponding constraint on the domestic government, namely:

$$\lim_{t \to \infty} ae^{-i^*t} = 0 \tag{3.1.16}$$

The complete macroeconomic equilibrium can now be described as follows.

First, there are the static optimality conditions (3.1.5)–(3.1.8), with $\lambda = \bar{\lambda}$, together with the domestic output market clearing condition,

$$F(k, l) = x + Z(\sigma) + C(I) + g_x \tag{3.1.17}$$

where $Z(\cdot)$ is the amount of the domestic good exported, with $Z'(\cdot) > 0$. Secondly, there are the dynamic equations (3.1.2), (3.1.10), (3.1.13), (3.1.14), together with the transversality conditions (3.1.12), (3.1.15), (3.1.16).

The five static equations may be solved for x, y, l, I, and σ, in terms of $\bar{\lambda}$, k, q, and g_x, as follows:

$$x = x(\bar{\lambda}, k, q, g_x) \qquad x_{\bar{\lambda}} < 0, \, x_k > 0, \, x_q < 0, \, x_{g_x} < 0 \tag{3.1.18}$$

$$y = y(\bar{\lambda}, k, q, g_x) \qquad y_{\bar{\lambda}} < 0, \, y_k > 0, \, y_q < 0, \, y_{g_x} < 0 \tag{3.1.19}$$

$$l = l(\bar{\lambda}, k, q, g_x) \qquad l_{\bar{\lambda}} \gtreqless 0, \, l_k \gtreqless 0, \, l_q > 0, \, l_{g_x} > 0 \tag{3.1.20}$$

$$\sigma = \sigma(\bar{\lambda}, k, q, g_x) \qquad \sigma_{\bar{\lambda}} > 0, \, \sigma_k > 0, \, \sigma_q < 0, \, \sigma_{g_x} < 0 \tag{3.1.21}$$

$$I = I(q) \qquad I' > 0 \tag{3.1.22}$$

The following explanation of these partial derivatives may be given. An increase in the marginal utility of wealth leads to a reduction in the domestic consumption of both goods. The reduction in the demand for the domestic good causes its relative price to fall, i.e., σ rises, thereby stimulating exports. The overall effect on the demand for domestic output depends upon whether or not this exceeds the reduction in x. If so, domestic output and employment both rise, if not, both fall. An increase in the stock of capital raises output and the real wage. The higher domestic income stimulates the consumption of x, though by a lesser amount, and the relative price σ rises. With the two private goods being complementary in utility ($U_{xy} > 0$), the increase in the consumption of the domestic good increases the demand for the import good as well. While the rise in the real wage rate tends to decrease V', thereby stimulating employment, the rise in σ has the opposite effect; the net effect on employment depends upon which influence dominates. An increase in q stimulates investment. This increases the demand for the domestic good and its relative price rises; i.e., σ falls. This in turn raises the marginal utility of the domestic good, implying that the consumption of x must fall, and with $U_{xy} > 0$, y falls as well. On balance, the increase in investment exceeds the fall in demand stemming from the reduction in x and lower exports, so that domestic output and employment rises.

An increase in government expenditure on domestic output raises the demand for that good, thereby raising its relative price (lowering σ). Employment and domestic output are therefore stimulated. However, the increased output, together with the reduced exports stemming from the fall in σ, is smaller than the increase in demand generated by the additional government expenditure, so that x must fall in order for domestic goods market equilibrium to prevail. With $U_{xy} > 0$, the reduced demand for the domestic good spills over to the import good. All this describes only the partial effects of a short-run change in government expenditure on good x. In addition, such an expenditure generates jumps in $\bar{\lambda}$ and q, thereby inducing further responses. The complete short-run response consists of a combination of these effects and will be discussed in section 5 below. Finally, we may note that given the separability of the utility function in private and public goods, the short-run equilibrium does not depend directly upon g_y. However, as we shall see in section 3.4, g_y has an indirect effect through its impacts on $\bar{\lambda}$ and q.

The evolution of the system is determined by substituting the short-run equilibrium into the dynamic equations and ensuring that the transversality conditions are met. It is readily apparent that in fact the dynamics can be determined sequentially. Equations (3.1.2) and (3.1.10) can be reduced to a pair of autonomous differential equations in q and k and these constitute the core of the dynamics. This is achieved by first differentiating (3.1.21) with respect to t:

$$\dot{\sigma} = \sigma_k \dot{k} + \sigma_q \dot{q} \qquad (3.1.21')$$

and then substituting this equation, together with (3.1.20) and (3.1.21), into (3.1.2) and (3.1.10). Next (3.1.14) equates the accumulation of foreign assets by the economy to its current account surplus. Using the domestic goods market clearing condition (3.1.17), this may be expressed equivalently in terms of exports minus imports plus the interest service account:

$$\dot{n} = \frac{1}{\sigma} \left[Z(\sigma) - \sigma(y + g_y) + \sigma i^* n \right] \qquad (3.1.14')$$

This equation may in turn be reduced to an autonomous differential equation in n, after substituting the solutions for q and k. The same applies to the government budget constraint (3.1.13).

3.2. Equilibrium Dynamics

Carrying out the procedure outlined above, (3.1.10) and (3.1.2) may be reduced to the following pair of linearized differential equations around the steady state:[11]

$$\begin{bmatrix} \dot{q} \\ \dot{k} \end{bmatrix} = \begin{bmatrix} i^* & -\theta[F_{kk} + F_{kl}l_k] \\ \dfrac{1}{C''} & 0 \end{bmatrix} \begin{bmatrix} q - \tilde{q} \\ k - \tilde{k} \end{bmatrix} \qquad (3.2.1)$$

where $\theta \equiv \sigma/(\sigma - q\sigma_q) > 0$, and $\tilde{}$ denotes steady-state values.

The determinant of the coefficient matrix in (3.2.1) can be shown to be negative, and therefore the long-run equilibrium is a saddlepoint with eigen values $\mu_1 < 0, \mu_2 > 0$. It is clear that while the capital stock always evolves continuously, the shadow price of capital, q, may jump instantaneously in response to new information. Along the stable arm, therefore, k and q follow the paths

$$k = \tilde{k} + (k_0 - \tilde{k})e^{\mu_1 t} \tag{3.2.2}$$

$$q = \tilde{q} + \left(\frac{\mu_1}{I'}\right)(k - \tilde{k}) \tag{3.2.3}$$

To determine the dynamics of the current account, we consider (3.1.14′) in the form:

$$\dot{n} = \frac{Z[\sigma(\bar{\lambda}, k, q, g_x)]}{\sigma(\bar{\lambda}, k, q, g_x)} - y(\bar{\lambda}, k, q, g_x) + i^* n \tag{3.2.4}$$

Linearizing this equation around steady state yields:

$$\dot{n} = \frac{1}{\tilde{\sigma}} \left[(\delta\sigma_k - \sigma y_k)(k - \tilde{k}) + (\delta\sigma_q - \sigma y_q)(q - \tilde{q}) \right] + i^*(n - \tilde{n})$$

where $\delta \equiv Z' - Z/\sigma$. Using (3.2.2), (3.2.3), this equation may be written as:

$$\dot{n} = \Omega(k_0 - \tilde{k})e^{\mu_1 t} + i^*(n - \tilde{n}) \tag{3.2.5}$$

where:

$$\Omega \equiv \frac{1}{\tilde{\sigma}} \left[\delta\left(\sigma_k + \sigma_q \frac{\mu_1}{I'}\right) - \sigma\left(y_k + y_q \frac{\mu_1}{I'}\right) \right]$$

Assuming that the economy starts out with an initial stock of traded bonds $n(0) = n_0$, the solution to (3.2.5) is:

$$n(t) = \tilde{n} + \frac{\Omega(k_0 - \tilde{k})}{\mu_1 - i^*} e^{\mu_1 t} + \left[n_0 - \tilde{n} - \frac{\Omega}{\mu_1 - i^*}(k_0 - \tilde{k}) \right] e^{i^* t}$$

---

[11] Note, the (1-1) element in the matrix (3.2.1) is obtained as follows. In general, following the procedure outlined it is equal to $\theta[i^* + \sigma_k I'/\sigma - F_{kl}l_q]$. Evaluating the derivatives σ_k, I', l_q and noting the steady-state conditions given in (3.2.11)–(3.2.20), this expression evaluated at steady state reduces to i^*.

Invoking the intertemporal budget constraint for the economy, (3.1.15), implies:

$$n_0 = \tilde{n} + \frac{\Omega}{\mu_1 - i^*} (k_0 - \tilde{k}) \qquad (3.2.6)$$

so that the solution for $n(t)$ consistent with long-run solvency is:

$$n(t) = \tilde{n} + \frac{\Omega}{\mu_1 - i^*} (k_0 - \tilde{k}) e^{\mu_1 t} \qquad (3.2.7)$$

Equation (3.2.7) describes the relationship between the accumulation of capital and the accumulation of traded bonds. Of particular significance is the sign of this relationship.

The definition of Ω given in (3.2.5) emphasizes that capital exercises two channels of influence on the current account. First, an increase in k raises the relative price σ, both directly, but also through the accompanying fall in q, as seen in (3.2.3). What this does to the trade balance depends upon δ. From the above definition of δ, $\delta > 0$ if and only if the relative price elasticity of the foreign demand for exports exceeds unity. At the same time, the increase in k increases imports both directly, and again through the fall in q, and this reduces the trade balance. While either case is possible, we shall assume that the relative price effect dominates, so that $\Omega > 0$.

Performing the same procedure for government debt, one can obtain an analogous set of equations to (3.2.5)–(3.2.7), namely:

$$a(t) = \tilde{a} + \frac{\Phi}{\mu_1 - i^*} (k_0 - \tilde{k}) e^{\mu_1 t} \qquad (3.2.8)$$

where

$$a_0 - \tilde{a} = \frac{\Phi}{\mu_1 - i^*} (k_0 - \tilde{k}) \qquad (3.2.9)$$

$$\Phi \equiv \left(\frac{g_y + i^* a}{\sigma} \right) \left(\sigma_k + \frac{\sigma_q \mu_1}{I'} \right) > 0 \qquad (3.2.10)$$

The steady state of the economy is obtained when $\dot{k} = \dot{q} = \dot{n} = \dot{a} = 0$ and is given by the following set of equations:

$$U_x(\tilde{x}, \tilde{y}) = \frac{\overline{\lambda}}{\tilde{\sigma}} \qquad (3.2.11)$$

$$U_y(\tilde{x}, \tilde{y}) = \overline{\lambda} \qquad (3.2.12)$$

$$V'(\tilde{l}) = -F_l(\tilde{k}, \tilde{l})\,\frac{\bar{\lambda}}{\tilde{\sigma}} \tag{3.2.13}$$

$$\tilde{q} = 1 \tag{3.2.14}$$

$$F(\tilde{k}, \tilde{l}) = \tilde{x} + Z(\tilde{\sigma}) + g_x \tag{3.2.15}$$

$$F_k(\tilde{k}, \tilde{l}) = i^* \tag{3.2.16}$$

$$F(\tilde{k}, \tilde{l}) = \tilde{x} + g_x + \tilde{\sigma}(\tilde{y} + g_y) - \tilde{\sigma}i^*\tilde{n} \tag{3.2.17}$$

$$n_0 - \tilde{n} = \frac{-\Omega}{\mu_1 - i^*}\,(k_0 - \tilde{k}) \tag{3.2.18}$$

$$a_0 - \tilde{a} = \frac{\Phi}{\mu_1 - i^*}\,(k_0 - \tilde{k}) \tag{3.2.19}$$

$$T = g_x + \tilde{\sigma}g_y + \tilde{\sigma}i^*\tilde{a} \tag{3.2.20}$$

These equations jointly determine the steady-state equilibrium values of $\tilde{x}$, $\tilde{y}$, $\tilde{k}$, $\tilde{l}$, $\tilde{\sigma}$, $\tilde{q}$, $\tilde{n}$, $\tilde{a}$, and T.

Several aspects of this steady state merit comment. First, the steady-state value of q is unity, consistent with the Tobin q theory of investment. Secondly, the steady-state marginal physical product of capital is equated to the exogenously given foreign interest rate, thereby determining the capital–labour ratio. Thirdly, equation (3.2.17) implies that in steady-state equilibrium, the current account balance must be zero. Combined with (3.2.15), we see that this requires the trade balance to offset the interest earnings on traded bonds. Equation (3.2.18) describes the equilibrium relationship between the change in the stock of capital and the change in the net credit of the economy. Equation (3.2.19) describes an analogous relationship between the stock of capital and the level of government debt, while (3.2.20) determines the required lump-sum tax, which will ensure that the steady-state government budget remains in balance. [12] Finally, the steady state depends upon the initial stocks of assets k_0, n_0, and a_0. It is this dependence upon initial conditions which is the source of the *temporary* fiscal (or other) shocks having *permanent* effects.

3.3. Long-Run Effects of Fiscal Expansions

The long-run effects of fiscal expansions, taking the form of increases in

---

[12] We should note that the adjustment of some form of tax is necessary in order for the steady-state equilibrium to be sustainable. If instead of being lump sum, taxes were distortionary, then the appropriate rate consistent with (3.2.20) would need to be set. This chosen rate would of course impact on the decisions of the representative agent.

government expenditure on domestic goods and on import goods respectively, are set out in the Appendix, and shall be discussed in turn.

Increase in Government Expenditure on Domestic Good

First, since the world interest rate i^* remains fixed, the marginal product condition (3.2.16) implies that the long-run capital–labour ratio is a constant, independent of either g_x or g_y. Capital and labour therefore change in the same proportion, so that the marginal physical product of labour and hence the real wage rate also remain constant. An increase in g_x stimulates domestic output, thereby increasing employment and capital. The stimulus in demand through government expenditure may, or may not, exceed the addition to output and the relative price of the import good σ may either rise or fall. At the same time, the increase in the steady-state stock of capital leads to a decline in the steady-state stock of traded bonds held by the domestic economy. The increase in taxes necessary to finance the additional government expenditure, coupled with the reduction in net interest earnings by the economy, means a reduction in real disposable income. As a consequence, the private consumption of the two goods, $\tilde{x}$ and $\tilde{y}$, both decline. While the reduction in $\tilde{y}$ tends to raise the marginal utility $\bar{\lambda}$, the reduction in $\tilde{x}$ tends to lower it (since $U_{xy} > 0$). In general, the overall effect is unclear, although $\bar{\lambda}$ will certainly be increased if the utility function is additively separable in the two goods. Finally, we see from (3.2.19) that the long-run increase in $\tilde{k}$ must lead to a steady-state increase in the stock of government debt.

Substituting (3.2.15) into (3.2.17), the equilibrium trade balance is given by:

$$Z(\tilde{\sigma}) - \tilde{\sigma}(\tilde{y} + g_y) = -\tilde{\sigma}i^*\tilde{n} \qquad (3.3.1)$$

The fiscal expansion on the domestic good raises the equilibrium trade balance, when measured in terms of the foreign good $(-i^*\tilde{n})$. It will do the same, even more strongly, in terms of the domestic good, as long as the domestic economy is a net creditor nation $(\tilde{n} > 0)$. However, for a debtor country, the trade balance in terms of domestic goods may fall, if the relative price effect is sufficiently strong.

Increase in Government Expenditure on Import Good

The long-run effects on domestic activity, as measured by employment, capital, and output, may all be either expansionary or contractionary. What is going on is the following. The increase in government expenditure on the import good raises its relative price, thereby stimulating the demand for the domestic good, and this is expansionary. But at the same time, the increase in lump-sum taxes necessary to finance the additional expenditure reduces disposable income, reducing private expenditure on the domestic good (without any corresponding increase in public expenditure on that good), and this is contractionary. The net impact on domestic activity depends upon which effect dominates. In addition, the reduction in disposable income lowers the private consumption of the import good as well. The response of the marginal utility $\bar{\lambda}$ is an unambiguous increase. This is because the government expenditure impacts more on the private consumption of the import good $\bar{y}$ than on the domestic good $\bar{x}$, with the result that the increase in the marginal utility resulting from the fall in the former outweighs the decrease stemming from the fall in the latter.

The response of the equilibrium level of national credit $\bar{n}$ and the equilibrium level of government debt $\bar{a}$, both depend upon whether the long-run effect of this form of fiscal expansion is expansionary or contractionary. In the former case, $\bar{n}$ will fall and $\bar{a}$ will rise; in the latter case the reverse occurs. What happens to the trade balance as measured in terms of the foreign good, depends upon what happens to $\bar{n}$. In the expansionary case it will rise, while in the contractionary case it will fall. In terms of the domestic good, the relative price effect also needs to be taken into account.

3.4. Transitional Dynamics

As discussed in section 3.2, the dynamics of k and q are described by a saddle-point in $k - q$ space. The stable arm XX (see Fig. 1(a)) is given by:

$$q = 1 + \frac{\mu_1}{I'} (k - \tilde{k}) \qquad (3.4.1)$$

and is negatively sloped; the unstable arm (not illustrated), is described by:

$$q = 1 + \frac{\mu_2}{I'} (k - \tilde{k}) \qquad (3.4.2)$$

and is positively sloped. The effects of the two types of fiscal expenditure shall be considered in turn.

Government Expenditure on Domestic Good

As long as no future change is anticipated, the economy must lie on the stable locus XX. The initial jump in $q(0)$, following an unanticipated permanent increase in g_x is:

$$\frac{dq(0)}{dg_x} = \frac{-\mu_1}{I'} \frac{d\tilde{k}}{dg_x} > 0 \qquad (3.4.3)$$

The long-run increase in the capital stock thus gives rise to a short-run increase in the shadow price $q(0)$.

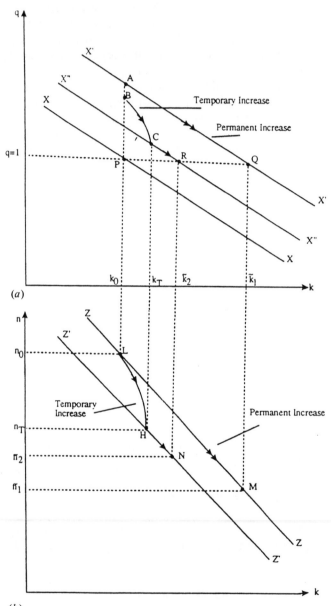

(a)

(b)

Figure 1.   Increase in government expenditure on export good.

The dynamics following an unanticipated permanent increase in g_x is illustrated in Fig. 1(a) and 1(b). Figure 1(a) describes the adjustment in q and k, while Fig. 1(b) describes the evolution of net credit. Suppose that the economy starts in steady-state equilibrium at the point P on the stable arm XX and that there is a permanent increase in g_x. The new steady state is at the point Q, with the higher equilibrium capital stock $\tilde{k}$, and an unchanged shadow price of capital $\tilde{q} = 1$. In the short run, q jumps from P to A on the new stable locus $X'X'$. From (3.1.8) it is seen that the increase in q has an immediate expansionary effect on investment, and capital begins to accumulate.

The initial responses of other key variables are:

$$\frac{dl(0)}{dg_x} = \frac{\partial l}{\partial g_x} + \frac{\partial l}{\partial \bar{\lambda}} \frac{\partial \bar{\lambda}}{\partial g_x} + \frac{\partial l}{\partial q} \frac{dq(0)}{dg_x} > 0 \tag{3.4.4}$$

$$\frac{d\sigma(0)}{dg_x} = \frac{\partial \sigma}{\partial g_x} + \frac{\partial \sigma}{\partial \bar{\lambda}} \frac{\partial \bar{\lambda}}{\partial g_x} + \frac{\partial \sigma}{\partial q} \frac{dq(0)}{dg_x} < 0 \tag{3.4.5}$$

$$\frac{dx(0)}{dg_x} = \frac{\partial x}{\partial g_x} + \frac{\partial x}{\partial \bar{\lambda}} \frac{\partial \bar{\lambda}}{\partial g_x} + \frac{\partial x}{\partial q} \frac{dq(0)}{dg_x} < 0 \tag{3.4.6}$$

$$\frac{dy(0)}{dg_x} = \frac{\partial y}{\partial g_x} + \frac{\partial y}{\partial \bar{\lambda}} \frac{\partial \bar{\lambda}}{\partial g_x} + \frac{\partial y}{\partial q} \frac{dq(0)}{dg_x} < 0 \tag{3.4.7}$$

which consist of two channels of influence. First, there are the direct effects, consisting of the partial derivatives such as $\partial l/\partial g_x$ and discussed in section 3.2. Secondly, there are the indirect effects, which operate through induced jumps in $\bar{\lambda}$ and q.

Despite the fact that the various effects may, or may not, work in the same direction (and in fact the effects through $\bar{\lambda}$ are ambiguous), we are able to establish that overall a permanent increase in g_x will have the same qualitative effects on employment and consumption in the short run as it does in the steady state. Namely it will raise employment, while reducing the consumption of the two goods. In addition it will lower the relative price σ. How the magnitudes of these short-run responses compare with the long run depends upon whether the short-run effects resulting from the rise in the shadow price of investment $q(0)$ dominates the long-run effects stemming from the eventual increase in the capital stock.

From equation (3.1.21′) and the fact that upon reaching the point A in Fig. 1(a) on the new stable locus, $\dot{q} < 0, \dot{k} > 0$, we can infer that in the short run and during the subsequent transition, $\dot{\sigma} > 0$, i.e. that the relative price of the import good must be increasing. This means that the short-run fall in the relative price overshoots its long-run response. At the same time, the fact that

$\dot{\sigma} > 0$ means that the fiscal expansion initially raises the domestic interest rate above the fixed real world rate. [13]

Differentiating (3.1.18), (3.1.19) analogously with respect to t, one can show using a similar argument that during the transition $\dot{x} > 0$, $\dot{y} > 0$, so that these consumptions also overreact in the short run. In both cases, the shadow price of investment effect dominates. In the case of employment, however, we are unable to determine the relative sizes of the short-run and long-run adjustments.

Critical to these adjustments is the endogeneity of employment. To see this, consider the steady-state relationships (3.2.11)–(3.2.20) and assume instead that employment is fixed, so that the optimality condition (3.2.13) is no longer applicable. The marginal productivity condition (3.2.16) now implies that the equilibrium stock of capital (rather than the capital–labour ratio) is determined exogenously by i^* and is independent of g_x. It therefore follows from (3.2.2), (3.2.3) that the capital stock and the shadow price of investment remain constant at all points of time. Output is therefore unchanged. There are no dynamics, and all that happens is that the fiscal expansion leads to a once-and-for-all decline in the relative price σ and the private consumptions x, and y. [14]

Figure 1(b) illustrates the relationship between n and k, which combining (3.2.2) and (3.2.7) is

$$n(t) - \tilde{n} = \frac{-\Omega}{i^* - \mu_1} (k(t) - \tilde{k}) \qquad (3.4.8)$$

This is a negatively sloped line, denoted by ZZ. Since $d\tilde{n}/dg_x = - [\Omega/(i^* - \mu_1)]$ $d\tilde{k}/dg_x$, this line remains fixed. The movement along A to Q in Fig. 1(a) corresponds to a movement along LM in Fig. 1(b). From this figure we see that an increase in government expenditure on the domestic good leads to an immediate decumulation of foreign bonds. This is brought about by the fact that the increase in g_x leads to an immediate reduction in the relative price σ, which with $\Omega > 0$ creates an immediate current account deficit. With the stock of traded bonds being predetermined, the trade balance, measured in terms of the foreign good also falls, and with the fall in σ, the trade balance in terms of domestic goods falls even more. Over time, the initial decumulation of

---

[13] These results imply that in spite of a higher (but declining) interest rate, crowding in of investment occurs.

[14] Actually it is the assumption of endogeneity of employment in conjunction with infinitely-lived agents that is critical. This is because this gives rise to short-run dynamics which are driven by long-run changes in the capital stock alone; see equations (3.1.18)–(3.1.22), (3.2.2) and (3.2.3). This may be compared to the Buiter (1987) model, for example, where employment is fixed, but consumers have finite lives. In this case, the long-run capital stock is also independent of everything other than the foreign interest rate, and is therefore also independent of domestic fiscal policy. However, in contrast to the present analysis, temporary changes in the capital stock may still occur. This is due to the fact that the short-run dynamics are also driven by long-run changes in other forms of financial wealth which may be generated by changes in fiscal policy.

foreign bonds is reversed. This occurs through the rising relative price σ, which causes the trade deficit to decline over time.

Consider now a temporary increase in g_x. Specifically, suppose that at time 0 the government increases its expenditure on the domestic good, but is expected to restore its expenditure to its original level at time T. The transitional adjustment is now as follows. As soon as the increase in g_x occurs, the stable arm XX will shift up instantaneously (and temporarily) to $X'X'$, while the shadow price q increases to the point B, which lies below $X'X'$, at which point the initial rate of capital accumulation is moderated. The same is true of employment. As is the case for a permanent expansion, the initial increase in (iq) is less than the increase in the marginal physical product of capital resulting from the additional employment, so that q begins to fall; see (3.1.10). Moreover, the accumulation of capital is accompanied by a decumulation of traded bonds. Hence immediately following the initial jump, q and k follow the path BC in Fig. 1(a), while k and n follow the corresponding path LH in Fig. 1(b). At time T, when the level of government expenditure is restored to its original level, the stock of capital and traded bonds will have reached a point such as H in Fig. 1(b). The accumulated stocks of these assets, denoted by k_T and n_T respectively, will now serve as initial conditions for the dynamics beyond time T when g_x reverts permanently to its original level. As noted in section 3.2, they will therefore in part determine the new steady-state equilibrium. With no new information being received at time T (since the temporary nature of the fiscal expansion was announced at the outset), and no further jumps, the stable locus relevant for subsequent adjustments in q and k beyond time T is the locus $X''X''$, parallel to XX which passes through the point $k = k_T$. Likewise, the relevant locus linking the accumulation of capital and traded bonds is now $Z'Z'$.

After time T, q and k follow the stable locus CR in Fig. 1(a) to the new steady-state equilibrium at R, while correspondingly k and n follow the locus HN in Fig. 1(b) to the new equilibrium point N. One can establish formally that $X''X''$ lies above the original stable locus XX, while $Z'Z'$ lies below ZZ, as these curves have been drawn. In the new steady state, the shadow price q reverts to 1, but with a higher stock of capital and a lower stock of traded bonds than originally. The striking feature of the adjustment is that the temporary increase in government expenditure leads to a permanent increase in the stock of capital, accompanied by a lower stock of traded bonds. This is because during the transitional adjustment period, during which the fiscal expansion is in effect, the accumulation of capital and bonds will influence subsequent initial conditions, which in turn will affect the subsequent steady state.[15]

---

[15] As the figures are drawn, C lies above R and H lies above N, respectively. The complete adjustment paths BCR and LHN are therefore monotonic. We are unable to rule out the possibility of C lying below R and H lying above N, in which case the accumulation of capital and decumulation of bonds would be reversed at some point during the transition. In any event, the temporary increase in the relative price of domestic goods generates an initial current account deficit, which continues as long as capital is being accumulated.

Government Expenditure on Import Good

The initial response of $q(0)$ to a fiscal expansion taking the form of an increase in government expenditure on the import good g_y is given by

$$\frac{dq(0)}{dg_y} = -\frac{\mu_1}{I'}\frac{d\tilde{k}}{dg_y} \gtrless 0 \qquad (3.4.9)$$

and depends upon whether the long-run effect on the capital stock is expansionary or contractionary. In the former case, the dynamics are essentially as illustrated in Fig. 1. There is an initial stimulus to investment, leading to a long-run accumulation of capital, and decumulation of traded bonds. In the latter case, the adjustment paths are as depicted in Fig. 2(a) and (b). The fiscal expansion now generates an initial drop in the shadow price $q(0)$, leading to a long-run decumulation of capital, accompanied by an accumulation of traded bonds.

The initial responses of l, σ, x, and y are given by:

$$\frac{d\theta(0)}{dg_y} = \frac{\partial\theta}{\partial\bar{\lambda}} + \frac{\partial\theta}{\partial q}\frac{dq(0)}{dg_y} \qquad \theta \equiv l, \sigma, x, y \qquad (3.4.10)$$

In contrast to g_x, there is no direct effect: government expenditure on the import good operates entirely through $\bar{\lambda}$ and q. This is a consequence of our assumption of additive separability of utility in private and public consumption.

By a parallel argument to that given above, we can show the short-run response of the relative price, σ, over-adjusts in the direction of the long-run response. In the case that the long-run effect of the fiscal expansion is expansionary, the initial fall in $\sigma(0)$ exceeds the corresponding long-run reduction in $\tilde{\sigma}$. On the other hand, if the long-run effect of g_y is contractionary, σ over-increases in the short run. In this case, the fact that $\dot{\sigma} < 0$ over time as the capital stock falls and the shadow price of investment increases, means that the domestic interest rate falls below the world rate during the transition. The over-response of x and y is also true when g_y is expansionary, but in the contractionary case this is not necessarily so—in this case, x and y may actually increase on impact, though they will thereafter fall continuously to their lower equilibrium levels. Finally, the short-run employment effect is unclear. This is in part due to the fact that one effect of the higher g_y is to raise the marginal utility $\bar{\lambda}$, the effects of which on employment are ambiguous.

The relationship between the current account and the accumulation of traded bonds is analogous to that already given and requires no further discussion. The same applies with respect to the analysis of temporary increases. This is illustrated in Fig. 2 and should be self-explanatory.

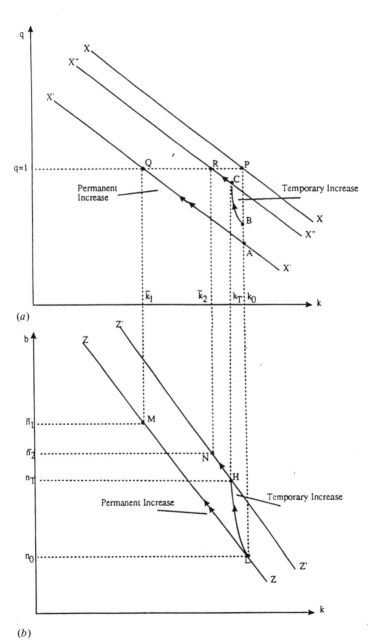

Figure 2.   Increase in government expenditure on import good: contractionary case.

3.5. Welfare Effects

Thus far, we have been describing the adjustment of the economy to the various fiscal expansions. Of particular relevance is the impact of such shocks on the welfare of the representative agent in the economy. This can be conveniently analysed by considering the effect on the intertemporal utility function (with $\beta = i^*$):

$$\Psi \equiv \int_0^\infty [U(x, y) + V(l) + W(g_x, g_y)] e^{-i^* t} \, dt \qquad (3.5.1)$$

In this section we briefly consider the welfare effects of permanent fiscal expansions, when consumptions x, y and employment l follow the solutions given by (3.1.18)–(3.1.20), where k and q evolve in accordance with the dynamic paths (3.2.2), (3.2.3).[16]

The evaluation is based on a linear approximation to Ω. To obtain this we first linearize the instantaneous utility function $U(\cdot) + V(\cdot)$ about steady state

$$U(x, y) + V(l) \cong U(\tilde{x}, \tilde{y}) + V(\tilde{l}) + U_x(x - \tilde{x}) + U_y(y - \tilde{y}) + V'(l - \tilde{l})$$

where the marginal utilities U_x, U_y, V' are all evaluated at steady state. The transitional paths followed by consumption and employment may be linearly approximated by

$$x(t) \cong \tilde{x} + (x(0) - \tilde{x})e^{\mu_1 t} \qquad (3.5.2)$$

$$y(t) \cong \tilde{y} + (y(0) - \tilde{y})e^{\mu_1 t} \qquad (3.5.3)$$

$$l(t) \cong \tilde{l} + (l(0) - \tilde{l})e^{\mu_1 t} \qquad (3.5.4)$$

With g_x, g_y constant, one can then readily show that welfare Ψ may be linearly approximated by:

$$\Psi \cong \frac{1}{i^*} [U(\tilde{x}, \tilde{y}) + V(\tilde{l}) + W(g_x, g_y)] + \frac{U_x[x(0) - \tilde{x}]}{i^* - \mu_1}$$

$$+ \frac{U_y[y(0) - \tilde{y}]}{i^* - \mu_1} + V' \frac{[l(0) - \tilde{l}]}{i^* - \mu_1} \qquad (3.5.5)$$

The first term in (3.5.5) represents the level of welfare, if the steady state were attained instantaneously. The remaining terms reflect adjustments to this, due

---

[16] The welfare effects of temporary shocks can be analysed similarly. They are a little more complicated, due to the fact that part of the transition is along an unstable path of higher dimension.

to the fact that the steady state is reached only gradually along the transitional paths followed by consumption and employment. It is possible to express this linearized solution in terms of the time path of the capital stock but for present purposes this is not necessary.

Using the equilibrium conditions (3.1.5)–(3.1.7), the effect of an increase in government expenditure on good i $(i = x,y)$ on total welfare is given by:

$$\frac{d\Psi}{dg_i} = \frac{1}{i^*}\frac{\partial W}{\partial g_i} - \frac{\mu_1 U_x}{i^*(i^* - \mu_1)}\left[\frac{d\tilde{x}}{dg_i} + \sigma\frac{d\tilde{y}}{dg_i} - F_l\frac{d\tilde{l}}{dg_i}\right]$$

$$+ \frac{U_x}{i^* - \mu_1}\left[\frac{dx(0)}{dg_i} + \sigma\frac{dy(0)}{dg_i} - F_l\frac{dl(0)}{dg_i}\right] \qquad i = x, y \quad (3.5.6)$$

This is seen to consist of two types of effect. The first is the direct effect, $\partial W/\partial g_i$, which being permanent, is capitalized at the constant rate i^*. This effect is welfare improving. The second are indirect effects which operate through private consumption and employment. These in turn comprise the steady-state effects and those along the transitional path. Because the adjustment path can be characterized in terms of the initial points and steady state (see (3.5.2)–(3.5.4)), these effects can be expressed in terms of changes in the initial consumptions $x(0)$, $y(0)$, and employment $l(0)$, and the corresponding steady-state quantities $\tilde{x}$, $\tilde{y}$, and $\tilde{l}$.[17]

Since an increase in government expenditure on the domestic good g_x lowers the consumption of both goods and raises employment (lowers leisure), both initially and in the steady state (and therefore along the entire adjustment path), we can see from (3.5.6) that what we have called the indirect effects are negative. Thus whether an increase in g_x is welfare improving or not depends upon whether these dominate the positive direct effects. The optimal level of government expenditure on the domestic good is obtained by equating the discounted direct marginal gains to the marginal losses resulting from the crowding out of private consumption and leisure.

The welfare effects of an increase in g_y are generally similar. Even in the case where increased expenditure on the import good is contractionary, so that employment declines, the welfare-improving increase in leisure is dominated by the welfare-deteriorating reduction in private consumption. This net welfare loss must then be weighed up against the positive direct effect, as before.

4. Some Extensions

The models discussed in the previous sections have three characteristics. They

---

[17] It is possible to express all the changes in consumption and employment appearing in (3.5.6) in terms of changes in the long-run equilibrium capital stock. However, this does not turn out to be particularly illuminating.

are (i) based on perfect markets; (ii) they are aggregate (single-sector) models; (iii) they are small economies, which take the rest of the world as given. Current research in progress is directed at relaxing these and other assumptions. In this section, we briefly discuss some of this work.

4.1. Upward-Sloping Supply Schedule for Debt

Most of the literature is restricted to small open economies and assumes that such economies face a perfect capital market for debt and are free to borrow or lend as much as desired at the given world rate of interest. As we have seen, in this case, the dynamic adjustment has a simple recursive structure. On the one hand, the dynamic adjustment within the economy is driven by the accumulation of capital and does not depend directly upon the stock of foreign asset holdings (or debt). On the other hand, the current account and the stock of foreign assets itself mirror the stable adjustment path of the capital stock.

While for many countries the assumption of perfect capital markets may not be too bad, for small developing countries the assumption of a perfectly elastic supply of debt is clearly unrealistic. Experience with external borrowing in such economies has shown that debt repayments are not always made on time, and sometimes with difficulties. International capital markets are likely to react to their perception of a country's ability to repay, with lenders requiring a risk premium on the rate at which they are willing to lend to such economies.

A recent paper by Bhandari, Haque, and Turnovsky (1990) incorporates this idea into a macrodynamic model, such as that developed in section 2, by assuming that the small economy faces an upward-sloping supply schedule for debt, which embodies the risk premium associated with lending to the sovereign borrower. This is formalized by postulating:

$$i(z) = i^* + i_1 w(z) \tag{4.1}$$

where i^* is the interest rate prevailing internationally and $i_1 w(z)$ is the country-specific risk premium, which varies with the stock of debt z say, held by the country. Carrying out the intertemporal optimization, as in section 3, one can show that if the representative agent treats the country-specific risk premium as parametrically given, the shadow value of wealth, λ, now evolves in accordance with

$$\dot{\lambda} = \lambda [\beta - i(z)] \tag{4.2}$$

With the domestic interest rate now being a function of debt, z, λ need no longer be constant. As a result, the simple recursive dynamic structure associated with a perfectly elastic supply of debt breaks down. This is because the marginal cost of capital facing firms, and therefore determining their investment decisions, is dependent upon the outstanding stock of national debt. Conditions in the international capital market therefore become important in determining the growth of capital in the domestic economy. Bhandari, Haque, and Turnovsky show how analytically this causes the dynamics involving (i) the stock of capital k, (ii) the marginal utility of wealth λ, (iii) the shadow price of capital q, (iv) the stock of national credit n, and (v) the stock of government debt a, all to become interdependent, giving rise to a high order system. Formal analytical solutions become harder to derive, although not impossible. Bhandari, Haque, and Turnovsky are able to conduct a fairly explicit analysis of the dynamic adjustment of the system in response to a variety of disturbances.

4.2. Sectoral Models

The dependent economy model of Salter (1959) and Swan (1960) has played an important role in international macroeconomics. By distinguishing between traded and non-traded goods, it provides a convenient framework for analysing the behaviour of the real exchange rate, both in a static and in a dynamic context. Recently, several authors have begun to incorporate capital formation into this framework: see e.g., Razin (1984), Murphy (1986), Brock (1988, 1992), Obstfeld (1989), Engel and Kletzer (1989), Turnovsky (1991), Turnovsky and Sen (1992), van Wincoop (1993).

Once the distinction between traded and non-traded goods is introduced, how investment is to be classified becomes important. At an intuitive level, investment can reasonably fall in either category. Capital goods, taking the form of infrastructure and construction, are presumably non-traded; investments in the form of machinery or inventories are obviously potentially tradable. Different treatments of investment, reflecting these different possibilities, can be found in the literature. For example, Obstfeld (1989), while allowing for capital to be instantaneously movable between sectors, assumes that only the traded good is used for investment. He therefore allows the capital stock to be instantaneously augmented at any point in time by an exchange of traded financial assets for capital. Brock (1988) also treats capital as being traded, though the investment process involves convex costs of adjustment, thereby constraining the rate of investment at any point in time to remain constant. By contrast, other authors such as Murphy (1986), Brock (1992), and Turnovsky and Sen (1992), treat investment as being non-traded.

The nature of investment is crucial for the dynamics. If the investment good is traded, then in the absence of any installation costs, it is easily shown that the adjustment of the capital stock occurs instantaneously. Convex costs of adjustment are necessary in order for interesting dynamics to obtain. The same applied to the aggregate model of section 2, which was also based on the assumption of the investment good being traded.

By contrast, if the capital accumulation is in the form of the non-traded good, then even in the absence of adjustment costs associated with investment non-degenerate dynamics are obtained. The rate of investment remains finite due to the fact that the supply of traded goods is subject to increasing marginal costs. In other words, these increasing marginal costs play the same role as do adjustment costs in the traded case. The dynamics are shown to involve a saddlepoint structure in terms of (i) the aggregate capital stock and (ii) the relative price of the non-traded good, i.e., the real exchange rate. The nature of this turns out to depend critically upon the relative capital intensities of the two sectors. First, if the traded sector is the more capital intensive, the complete adjustment of the real exchange rate to any unanticipated permanent shock occurs immediately. The subsequent accumulation, or decumulation of capital, in response to such a shock takes place with no concurrent change in the real exchange rate. By contrast, if the non-traded sector is the more capital intensive, then any initial adjustment in the real exchange rate is only partial. The transitional adjustment in the capital stock is accompanied by a further continuously changing real exchange rate. The responses of this model to (i) permanent demand shocks taking the form of fiscal expenditures on the traded and non-traded goods, respectively; and (ii) productivity disturbances in the two sectors, are discussed at length by Turnovsky and Sen (1992).

4.3. Two-Country Models

Most of the literature deals with small open economies, which may take the behaviour in the rest of the world as given. But there is a growing recognition of the interdependence of the world economy and the need to extend the intertemporally optimizing framework to two (or more) economies. Needless to say, such a task is analytically difficult, in effect doubling the dimensions of the dynamics. But some interesting work is being done and progress is being made. Probably the most comprehensive treatment of two-country models is provided by Frenkel and Razin (1987), who focus primarily on the transmission of fiscal shocks. However, their analysis abstracts from physical capital accumulation, and by making appropriate assumptions, they are able in effect to collapse much of their analysis into a two-period framework, consisting of the present and the future. Perhaps the closest two-country analogue to the type of model developed in section 2 is Devereux and Shi (1991), who analyse the determination of debt and the accumulation over time.

One emerging issue in the development of the two-country model is the international harmonization of taxes. With perfectly integrated financial markets, arbitrage conditions, as reflected by appropriate optimality conditions, are shown to impose constraints on the tax rates on capital income, which may be set by the two countries. Different principles of tax collection may, or may not, be consistent with these constraints; see e.g., Sinn (1990), and Razin and Sadka (1991). An interesting research programme would be to focus on the dynamics of the international transmission of tax shocks under these alternative principles of taxation.

Appendix: Long-Run Effects of Increase in Government Expenditures

A1. Domestic Good g_x

(i)   *Capital–labour ratio:*

$$\frac{d(k/l)}{dg_x} = 0$$

(ii)   *Capital, employment and output:*

$$\frac{1}{k}\frac{d\tilde{k}}{dg_x} = \frac{1}{l}\frac{d\tilde{l}}{dg_x} = \frac{1}{z}\frac{d\tilde{z}}{dg_x} = \frac{F_l}{\sigma l D}\left[\delta\Delta - \lambda U_{xx}\right] > 0$$

(iii)   *Relative price:*

$$\frac{d\tilde{\sigma}}{dg_x} = \frac{1}{D}\left[V''\left[U_{xy} - \sigma U_{xx}\right] - \frac{\Delta\psi F_l}{\sigma}\right] \gtreqless 0$$

(iv)   *Consumption of domestic good:*

$$\frac{d\tilde{x}}{dg_x} = \frac{1}{D}\left[\frac{V''\delta}{\sigma}\left[\sigma U_{xy} - U_{yy}\right] + \frac{\lambda}{\sigma}\left[V'' + U_{xy}\frac{F_l\psi}{\sigma}\right]\right] < 0$$

(v)   *Consumption of imported good:*

$$\frac{d\tilde{y}}{dg_x} = \frac{1}{D}\left[\frac{V''\delta}{\sigma}\left[U_{xy} - \sigma U_{xx}\right] - \frac{\lambda}{\sigma^2} U_{xx}F_l\psi\right] < 0$$

(vi)   *Marginal utility:*

$$\frac{d\bar{\lambda}}{dg_x} = \frac{1}{D}\left[U_{xy}V''\frac{\bar{\lambda}}{\sigma} - \Delta\left(\delta V'' + \psi F_l\frac{\bar{\lambda}}{\sigma^2}\right)\right] \gtreqless 0$$

(vii)   *Net credit:*

$$\frac{d\tilde{n}}{dg_x} = \frac{-\Omega}{i^* - \mu_1}\left(\frac{d\tilde{k}}{dg_x}\right) < 0$$

(viii)   *Net government debt:*

$$\frac{d\tilde{a}}{dg_x} = \frac{\Phi}{i^* - \mu_1} \left(\frac{d\tilde{k}}{dg_x} \right) > 0$$

where:

$$\psi \equiv \frac{-\sigma i^* \Omega}{i^* - \mu_1} \left(\frac{\tilde{k}}{\tilde{l}} \right) < 0; \quad \delta \equiv Z' - \frac{Z}{\sigma} > 0; \quad \Delta \equiv U_{xx} U_{yy} - U_{xy}^2 > 0$$

$$D \equiv -V'' \left[U_{xy} Z' + \frac{\bar{\lambda}}{\sigma} - Z' U_{xx} \sigma \right] - V'' \delta \left[U_{xy} - \frac{1}{\sigma} U_{yy} \right]$$

$$- F_l \psi U_{xy} \frac{\bar{\lambda}}{\sigma^2} - F_l \frac{F}{l} U_{xx} \frac{\bar{\lambda}}{\sigma} + \Delta \frac{F_l}{\sigma} \left(\frac{F\delta}{l} + \psi Z' \right) > 0$$

A2.   Import Good g_y

(i)   *Capital–labour ratio:*

$$\frac{d(\tilde{k}/l)}{dg_y} = 0$$

(ii)   *Capital, employment, and output:*

$$\frac{1}{k} \frac{d\tilde{k}}{dg_y} = \frac{1}{l} \frac{d\tilde{l}}{dg_y} = \frac{1}{z} \frac{d\tilde{z}}{dg_y} = \frac{F_l}{\sigma l D} [Z' \Delta - \bar{\lambda} U_{xy}] \gtrless 0$$

(iii)   *Relative price:*

$$\frac{d\tilde{\sigma}}{dg_y} = \frac{1}{D} \left[V'' (U_{yy} - \sigma U_{xy}) + \Delta F \frac{F_l}{l} \right] > 0$$

(iv)   *Consumption of domestic good:*

$$\frac{d\tilde{x}}{dg_y} = \frac{1}{D} \left[V'' Z' [\sigma U_{xy} - U_{yy}] - \frac{\bar{\lambda}}{\sigma} U_{xy} F \frac{F_l}{l} \right] < 0$$

(v)   *Consumption of imported good:*

$$\frac{d\tilde{y}}{dg_y} = \frac{1}{D} \left[V'' Z' [U_{xy} - \sigma U_{xx}] + \frac{\bar{\lambda}}{\sigma} \left[V'' + F \frac{F_l}{l} \frac{\bar{\lambda}}{\sigma} U_{xx} \right] \right] < 0$$

(vi)   *Marginal utility:*

$$\frac{d\bar{\lambda}}{dg_y} = \frac{1}{D}\left[U_{yy}V''\frac{\lambda}{\sigma} + \Delta\left[\frac{F}{l}F_l\frac{\lambda}{\sigma} - V''Z'\sigma\right]\right] > 0$$

(vii)   *Net credit:*

$$\frac{d\tilde{n}}{dg_y} = \frac{-\Omega}{i^* - \mu_1}\left(\frac{d\tilde{k}}{dg_y}\right) \gtreqless 0$$

(viii)   *Net government debt:*

$$\frac{d\tilde{a}}{dg_y} = \frac{\Phi}{i^* - \mu_1}\left(\frac{d\tilde{k}}{dg_y}\right) \gtreqless 0$$

References

Abel, A.B. (1982): 'Dynamic Effects of Permanent and Temporary Tax Policies in a *q* Model of Investment', *Journal of Monetary Economics*, **9**, 353–73.

Bhandari, J.S., Haque, N. and Turnovsky, S.J. (1990): 'Growth, External Debt, and Sovereign Risk in a Small Open Economy', *IMF Staff Papers*, **37**, 388–417.

Blanchard, O.J. (1985): 'Debt, Inflation, and Finite Horizons', *Journal of Political Economy*, **83**, 223–47.

Brock, P.L. (1988): 'Investment, the Current Account and the Relative Price of Nontraded Goods in a Small Open Economy', *Journal of International Economics*, **24**, 235–53.

Brock, P.L. (1992): 'International Transfers and the Current Account', University of Washington, Working Paper.

Buiter, W.H. (1987): 'Fiscal Policy in Open Interdependent Economies', in A. Razin and E. Sadka (eds), *Economic Policy in Theory and Practice*, St Martins Press, New York.

Devereux, M.B. and Shi, S. (1991): 'Capital Accumulation and the Current Account in a Two-Country Model', *Journal of International Economics*, **30**, 1–25.

Dornbusch, R. (1988): *Exchange Rates and Inflation*, MIT Press, Cambridge, MA.

Edwards, S. (1987): 'Tariffs, Terms of Trade, and the Real Exchange Rate in an Intertemporal Optimizing Model of the Current Account', Working paper No. 2175, National Bureau of Economic Research.

Engel, C. and Kletzer, K. (1989): 'Saving and Investment in an Open Economy with Nontraded Goods', *International Economic Review*, **30**, 735–52.

Engel, C. and Kletzer, K. (1990): 'Tariffs and Saving in a Model with New Generations', *Journal of International Economics*, **28**, 71–91.

Frenkel. J.A. and Razin, A. (1987): *Fiscal Policies and the World Economy*, MIT Press, Cambridge, MA.

Gavin, M. (1991): 'Tariffs and the Current Account: On the Macroeconomics of Commercial Policy', *Journal of Economic Dynamics and Control*, **15**, 27–52.

Giavazzi, F. and Wyplosz, C. (1984): 'The Real Exchange Rate, the Current Account, and the Speed of Adjustment', in J. Bilson and R. Marston (eds), *Exchange Rate Theory and Practice*, University of Chicago Press.

Gould, J.P. (1968): 'Adjustment Costs in the Theory of Investment of the Firm', *Review of Economic Studies*, **35**, 47–56.

Hayashi, F. (1982): 'Tobin's *q*, Rational Expectations and Optimal Investment Rules', *Econometrica*, **50**, 213–24.

Klundert, Th. van de and Ploeg, F. van der (1989): 'Wage Rigidity and Capital Mobility in an Optimizing Model of a Small Open Economy', *De Economist*, **137**, 47–75.

Lucas, R.E. (1967): 'Adjustment Costs and the Theory of Supply', *Journal of Political Economy*, **75**, 321–34.

Matsuyama, K. (1988): 'Terms of Trade, Factor Intensities, and the Current Account in a Life-Cycle Model', *Review of Economic Studies*, **55**, 247–62.

Murphy, R.G. (1986): 'Productivity Shocks, Nontraded Goods and Optimal Capital Accumulation', *European Economic Review*, **30**, 1081–95.

Obstfeld, M. (1981): 'Macroeconomic Policy, Exchange Rate Dynamics, and Optimal Asset Accumulation', *Journal of Political Economy*, **89**, 1142–61.

Obstfeld, M. (1989): 'Fiscal Deficits and Relative Prices in a Growing World Economy', *Journal of Monetary Economics*, **23**, 461–84.

Persson, T. and Svensson, L.E.O. (1985): 'Current Account Dynamics and the Terms of Trade: Harberger–Laursen–Metzler Two Generations Later', *Journal of Political Economy*, **93**, 43–65.

Razin, A. (1984): 'Capital Movements, Intersectoral Resource Shifts and the Trade Balance', *European Economic Review*, **26**, 135–52.

Razin, A. and Sadka, E. (1991): 'Capital Market Integration: Issues of International Taxation', in H. Siebert (ed.), *Reforming Capital Income Taxation*, J.C.B. Mohr, Tubingen.

Salter, W. (1959): 'Internal and External Balance: The Role of Price and Expenditure Effects', *Economic Record*, **35**, 226–38.

Sen P. and Turnovsky, S.J. (1989a): 'Deterioration of the Terms of Trade and Capital Accumulation: A Re-examination of the Laursen–Metzler Effect', *Journal of International Economics*, **26**, 27–250.

Sen, P. and Turnovsky, S.J. (1989b): 'Tariffs, Capital Accumulation and the Current Account in a Small Open Economy', *International Economic Review*, **30**, 811–31.

Sen, P. and Turnovsky, S.J. (1990): 'Investment Tax Credit in an Open Economy', *Journal of Public Economics*, **42**, 277–99.

Sinn, H.W. (1990): 'Tax Harmonization and Tax Competition in Europe', *European Economic Review*, **34**, 489–504.

Svensson, L.E.O. and Razin, A. (1983): 'The Terms of Trade and the Current Account: The Harberger–Laursen–Metzler Effect', *Journal of Political Economy*, **91**, 97–125.

Swan, T.W. (1960): 'Economic Control in a Dependent Economy', *Economic Record*, **36**, 51–66.

Turnovsky, S.J. (1985): 'Domestic and Foreign Disturbances in an Optimizing Model of Exchange Rate Determination', *Journal of International Money and Finance*, **4**, 151–71.

Turnovsky, S.J. (1991): 'Tariffs and Sectoral Adjustments in an Open Economy', *Journal of Economic Dynamics and Control*, **15**, 53–89.

Turnovsky, S.J. and Sen, P. (1991): 'Fiscal Policy, Capital Accumulation, and Debt in an Open Economy', *Oxford Economic Papers*, **43**, 1–24.

Turnovsky, S.J. and Sen, P. (1992): 'Investment in a Two-Sector Dependent Economy', University of Washington Working Paper.

Uzawa, H. (1968): 'Time Preference, the Consumption Function, and Optimum Asset Holdings', in J.N. Wolfe (ed.), *Value, Capital and Growth: Papers in Honour of Sir John Hicks*, Aldine, Chicago.

van Wincoop, E. (1993): 'Structural Adjustment and the Construction Sector', *European Economic Review*, **37**, 177–206.

Weil, P. (1989): 'Overlapping Families of Infinitely-Lived Agents', *Journal of Public Economics*, **38**, 183–98.

PART III:
Econometrics

5

GARCH Modelling of Volatility: An Introduction to Theory and Applications

Theo E. Nijman and Franz C. Palm[*]

Tilburg University and Limburg University

1. Introduction

The objective of this chapter is to introduce GARCH models of volatility in financial series, discussing the properties of these models and showing how they have been applied in finance and international economics. Rather than presenting a complete survey of this rapidly expanding literature, as provided by Bollerslev, Chou and Kroner (1992), we discuss a limited number of applications in detail.

This chapter is organized as follows. The relevance of econometric models of volatility for modern finance will be illustrated in section 2. In section 3, the autoregressive conditional heteroskedastic (ARCH) model put forward by Engle (1982), and extensions such as GARCH, ARCH-M and EGARCH will be presented. Their properties will be discussed in section 4. Methods to estimate these models will be presented and tests for the presence of ARCH will be discussed. Alternative approaches to modelling volatility and issues of temporal aggregation will be discussed as well. Sections 5 and 6 will be devoted to the use of ARCH- and GARCH-type models to describe the time variation of the risk premia in the forward foreign exchange market and in returns on stocks and bonds respectively. Section 7 concludes this chapter.

---

[*] The authors thank Frank de Jong and Peter Schotman for helpful comments on an earlier version of this chapter.

2. Volatility in Economic Models

In this section two models in which volatility plays a crucial role will be discussed. Section 2.1 deals with risk premia in forward foreign exchange. We discuss a simple example of the models for risk premia which have been developed building on Lucas (1982). Section 2.2 treats a capital asset pricing model with time-varying second moments.

2.1. Risk Premia in Foreign Exchange

Consider a model for two countries, A and B, and two non-storable commodities, X and Y. The endowments of the consumers of the countries A and B are $2X_t$ units of X and zero units of Y, and $2Y_t$ units of Y and zero units of X respectively. Each consumer maximizes the expected time-additive utility over an infinite horizon:

$$E_0 \sum_{t=0}^{\infty} \beta^t U(X_t, Y_t) \qquad (2.1.1)$$

where β $(0 < \beta < 1)$ is the time discount factor, and the subscript 0 indicates that the expectation is conditional on the information available in time period t $(t = 0)$. We assume a cash in advance economy. At the beginning of each period, per capita money balances in countries A and B are M_t and N_t respectively. Agents are assumed to engage in trade and to invest in assets after the uncertainty about the present state of the economy has been resolved.

We are interested in solving the model for the exchange rate S_t, the forward rate F_t, the forward risk premium and the interest rates R_t^A and R_t^B given the processes for the exogenous variables X_t, Y_t, M_t and N_t.

Given the above endowments, prices of goods expressed in domestic currencies are $p_t^{XA} = 0.5\, M_t/X_t$ and $p_t^{YB} = 0.5\, N_t/Y_t$. The first-order conditions for expected utility maximization imply, for instance, for country A that:

$$p_t^{YA}/p_t^{XA} = (\partial U_t/\partial Y_t)/(\partial U_t/\partial X_t) \qquad (2.1.2)$$

where the r.h.s. is the marginal rate of substitution with $\partial U_t/\partial X_t = \partial U(X_t, Y_t)/\partial X_t$. The exchange rate S_t expressing the value of the currency in B in terms of that of A can be written as $p_t^{YA} = p_t^{YB} \cdot S_t$. Substitution of this expression in (2.1.2) yields:

$$S_t = (p_t^{XA}\, \partial U_t/\partial Y_t)/(p_t^{YB}\, \partial U_t/\partial X_t) \qquad (2.1.3)$$

Each unit of domestic currency which is saved has a yield after one period of R_t^A and R_t^B respectively.

The equilibrium conditions for postponed consumption are given by the following first-order condition for expected utility maximization:

$$R_t^A = \partial U_t/\partial X_t(p_t^{XA})^{-1}/E_t[\beta\ \partial U_{t+1}/\partial X_{t+1}(p_{t+1}^{XA})^{-1}] \tag{2.1.4}$$

and an analogous expression for R_t^B. Finally, if there are no restrictions on the capital market, the covered interest rate parity leads to:

$$F_t = S_t R_t^A/R_t^B \tag{2.1.5}$$

Along with Domowitz and Hakkio (1985), we assume that the utility function is of the Cobb–Douglas form:

$$U(X_t, Y_t) = X_t^\alpha Y_t^{1-\alpha} \qquad (0 < \alpha < 1) \tag{2.1.6}$$

and that the logarithm of the endowments with goods and money, denoted by the corresponding lower-case letters, are potentially conditionally hetero-skedastic and generated by independent AR(1) processes. The autocorrelation coefficients are denoted by ρ_x, ρ_y, ρ_m and ρ_n respectively. The innovations in the log endowments, denoted by u_{xt}, u_{yt}, u_{mt} and u_{nt} are serially independent, normally distributed with mean vector zero and diagonal covariance matrix with diagonal elements h_{xt}, h_{yt}, h_{mt} and h_{nt}. Substituting the expressions for the prices of goods and the marginal rate of substitution corresponding to (2.1.6) into (2.1.2) yields:

$$S_t = cM_t/N_t \tag{2.1.7}$$

with $c = (1 - \alpha)/\alpha$. In order to find an expression for R_t^A, we write:

$$E_t[\partial U_{t+1}/\partial X_{t+1}(p_{t+1}^{XA})^{-1}] = 2\alpha E_t[X_{t+1}^\alpha M_{t+1}^{-1} Y_{t+1}^{1-\alpha}]$$

$$= 2\alpha\ \exp[\alpha\rho_x x_t - \rho_m m_t + (1 - \alpha)\rho_y y_t$$

$$+ 0.5(\alpha^2 h_{xt} + h_{mt} + (1 - \alpha)^2 h_{yt})] \tag{2.1.8}$$

Notice that we use the property that $E[\exp(x)] = \exp(\mu + 0.5\sigma^2)$ if $x \sim N(\mu, \sigma^2)$. Substituting (2.1.8) into (2.1.4) leads to:

$$R_t^A = \beta^{-1}\ \exp[\alpha(1 - \rho_x)x_t - (1 - \rho_m)m_t + (1 - \alpha)(1 - \rho_y)y_t$$

$$- 0.5\alpha^2 h_{xt} - 0.5h_{mt} - 0.5(1 - \alpha)^2 h_{yt}] \tag{2.1.9}$$

For R_t^B, the same expression as (2.1.9) can be obtained with the exception that ρ_m, m_t and h_{mt} have to be replaced by ρ_n, n_t and h_{nt} respectively. Substituting the expression for R_t^A and R_t^B into (2.1.5), the logarithm of the forward rate, f_t, can be expressed as:

$$f_t = \ln c + \rho_m m_t - \rho_n n_t - 0.5 h_{mt} + 0.5 h_{nt} \qquad (2.1.10)$$

If similarly s_t denotes the log spot rate, (2.1.7) yields:

$$E_t s_{t+1} = \ln c + \rho_m m_t - \rho_n n_t \qquad (2.1.11)$$

so that the forward risk premium defined as $E_t s_{t+1} - f_t$ becomes:

$$E_t s_{t+1} - f_t = 0.5(h_{mt} - h_{nt}) \qquad (2.1.12)$$

The forward risk premium depends on the difference between the conditional variances of the money balances in the two countries. If the uncertainty about money balances is the same in both countries, the risk premium is zero, i.e. the forward rate is an unbiased forecast of the future spot rate, and uncovered interest rate parity will hold as well.

Most importantly, the simple model shows that conditional variances of economic variables play a crucial role in economic models that take uncertainty into account. If these variances vary through time, it will be crucial to appropriately model the time dependence of h_{mt} and h_{nt} in order to explain the behaviour of the forward premium. Along the same lines the more sophisticated model of Hodrick (1989) leads to an expression in which the variances of income and the shares of government expenditures become additional determinants of the risk premium.

2.2. The Static Capital Asset Pricing Model

In this subsection we consider a second example of a model in which volatility plays a crucial role. We postulate a representative investor, maximizing a utility function defined over the expected value and the variance of end-of-period wealth W_{t+1}:

$$\max U[E_t(W_{t+1}), \sigma_t^2(W_{t+1})] \qquad (2.2.1)$$

where

$$E_t(W_{t+1}) = W_t x_t' E_t(R_{t+1}) + W_t(1 - x_t' \iota) R_t^f \qquad (2.2.2)$$

$$\sigma_t^2(W_{t+1}) = W_t^2 x_t' \Sigma_t \, x_t \qquad (2.2.3)$$

where W_t represents the investor's wealth and x_t is an $n \times 1$ vector of investment shares in risky assets whose rates of return have conditional means and covariances denoted by $E_t(R_{t+1})$ and Σ_t respectively. R_t^f is the rate of return on a risk-free asset, and ι is a unit vector.

The first-order conditions for the maximization problem (2.2.1) yield:

$$x_t = (\rho_t \, \Sigma_t)^{-1}(E_t(R_{t+1}) - \iota R_t^f) \qquad (2.2.4)$$

where ρ_t is the relative risk aversion coefficient, $\rho_t = -2W_t U_2/U_1$, and U_1 and U_2 are the partial derivatives of U with respect to the first and second argument in (2.2.1) respectively (assumed to be $U_1 > 0$, $U_2 < 0$). Equation (2.2.4) determines the optimal composition of the portfolio of the investor, the determinants of which are ρ_t, R_t^f and the expected returns and the covariance matrix of the risky assets. Equation (2.2.4) can also be solved for the equilibrium expected returns:

$$E_t(R_{t+1}) - \iota R_t^f = \rho_t \, \Sigma_t \, x_t = (-2U_2/U_1) \, \Sigma_t \, W_t x_t \qquad (2.2.5)$$

where $W_t x_t$ is the actual value which in equilibrium is equal to demand and supply. Since the expectation of R_{t+1} equals its realization minus the forecast error ξ_{t+1}, we have:

$$R_{t+1} = \iota R_t^f + \rho_t \, \Sigma_t \, x_t + \xi_{t+1} \qquad (2.2.6)$$

where ξ_{t+1} has conditional mean zero and conditional covariance matrix Σ_t. Model (2.2.6) has the property that there are restrictions between the conditional mean of future returns and their conditional covariance matrix. Notice that (2.2.5) can also be expressed in terms of the familiar β coefficients. From (2.2.5), the expected excess return of the portfolio with shares x_t is given by $\rho_t x_t' \, \Sigma_t \, x_t$. Therefore when we substitute this expression into (2.2.5), we get the capital asset pricing model (CAPM),

$$E_t R_{t+1} - \iota R_t^f = \beta_t (E_t R_{t+1}^p - R_t^f) \qquad (2.2.7)$$

where $\beta_t = \Sigma_t \, x_t / x_t' \, \Sigma_t \, x_t = \mathrm{cov}_t(R_{t+1}, R_{t+1}^p)/\mathrm{var}_t(R_{t+1}^p)$ and R_t^p denotes the return on the portfolio. Note that β_t is not assumed to be time-invariant.

As in the previous subsection, the covariance matrix Σ_t plays a central role in the model. If Σ_t is time-dependent, it will be crucial for the analysis of the CAPM (2.2.6) to get a good specification for this time variation.

2.3. Concluding Remarks

The two examples have a basic feature in common. Volatility of the series measured by the conditional variances plays an important role in the economic explanation of the level (or the conditional mean) of variables such as the forward risk premium in exchange markets and expected future returns in asset markets. In other words, the conditional mean is linearly related to the conditional variance. Similar models have also been used in modelling the pricing of futures. For a recent application, we refer to Nijman and Beetsma (1991) and Baillie and Myers (1991). Any time-dependence of the conditional variance therefore has direct implications for the time-dependence of the conditional mean. In the next section, we shall present models which are designed to describe the time-variation of conditional variances.

3. Models for Conditional Heteroskedasticity

Econometric models with time-varying conditional variances have recently received much attention in the literature. In a seminal paper, Engle (1982) introduced stochastic models of the form:

$$y_t = \varepsilon_t h_t^{1/2} \tag{3.1}$$

$$h_t = \alpha_0 + \alpha_1 y_{t-1}^2 + \cdots \alpha_q y_{t-q}^2, \qquad \alpha_0 > 0, \alpha_i \geqslant 0, \sum_{i=1}^{q} \alpha_i < 1 \tag{3.2}$$

where the ε_t are i.i.d. with $E(\varepsilon_t) = 0$ and $\mathrm{var}(\varepsilon_t) = 1$. This is a qth order autoregressive conditional heteroskedasticity (ARCH) model. Adding the assumption of conditional normality, the model can be written as:

$$y_t \mid \Phi_{t-1} \sim N(0, h_t) \tag{3.3}$$

with h_t being given by (3.2) and Φ_{t-1} being the set of information available at time $t - 1$. The non-negativity of the α_is is required for the variance to be non-negative, whereas the requirement that the α_is sum to less than one is needed for y_t to be wide sense stationary (see Engle (1982)). In the first order ARCH-model, the conditional variance of y_t will increase when y_{t-1}^2 increases and decrease as y_{t-1}^2 decreases. The ARCH-model is a generalization of linear models with homoskedastic disturbances in which the conditional mean varies with the variables in Φ_{t-1} (such as ARMA-models or linear regression models), for which the conditional variance is constant across time. It is closely related to the bilinear models introduced by Granger and Andersen (1978) (see also Weiss (1986a)), an example of which is of the form $y_t = \varepsilon_t y_{t-1}$, with conditional variance $\sigma^2 y_{t-1}^2$ so that the unconditional variance becomes zero, one or infinity, depending on the value of σ^2.

A generalization proposed by Bollerslev (1986) is the GARCH model. For the GARCH(1, 1) model, the conditional variance is given by:

$$h_t = \alpha_0 + \alpha_1 y_{t-1}^2 + \beta h_{t-1} \tag{3.4}$$

with $\alpha_0, \alpha_1, \beta > 0, \alpha_1 + \beta < 1$. Equation (3.4) can be written as

$$h_t = \sigma^2 + \alpha_1 \sum_{i=0}^{\infty} \beta^i (y_{t-i-1}^2 - \sigma^2) \tag{3.5}$$

with $\sigma^2 = \alpha_0 / (1 - \alpha_1 - \beta)$. According to the assumption made in (3.4) (or (3.5)), the conditional variance of y_t will be large if the weighted average of past y_t^2 with geometrically declining weights is large. When y_t is stationary, $Ey_t^2 = Ey_{t-k}^2$, (3.5) implies that $Ey_t^2 = E(E(y_t^2 \mid \Phi_{t-1})) = Eh_t^2 = \sigma^2$ so that the conditional variance (3.5) can become larger than the unconditional variance if past realizations of y_t^2 have been larger than σ^2. The realizations of a GARCH(1, 1) model exhibit clusters of large values. A comparison of the GARCH(1, 1) model (3.4) with the ARCH(q) model (3.3) indicates that the former one may be seen as a parsimonious parametrization with features similar to those of the ARCH(q) models with exponentially declining coefficients α_i. Notice the similarity between the ARMA(1, 1) model and a high order MA(q) process.

Of course, along with Bollerslev (1986), one can also consider the extension of (3.4) to the GARCH(p, q) model for the conditional variance of (3.1):

$$h_t = \alpha_0 + \sum_{i=1}^{p} \beta_i h_{t-i} + \sum_{i=1}^{q} \alpha_i y_{t-i}^2 \tag{3.6}$$

with $\alpha_0, \beta_i, \alpha_i > 0, \Sigma_i \beta_i + \Sigma_i \alpha_i < 1$. Again, the non-negativity conditions imply a non-negative variance, while the condition that the sum of the α_is and β_is is smaller than one is required for wide sense stationarity of y_t (see Bollerslev (1986)).

When $\Sigma_i \beta_i + \Sigma_i \alpha_i = 1$, the integrated GARCH (IGARCH) model arises (see Engle and Bollerslev (1986)). It has a unit root in the autoregressive polynomial of the variance function. For instance, for the simple IGARCH(1, 1) model with $\alpha + \beta = 1$, the minimum mean square error forecast for the conditional variance s steps ahead, h_{t+s}, is equal to $\alpha_0(s - 1) + h_{t+1}$. As for the random walk model for the series itself, current information remains important for forecasts of the conditional variance for all horizons in the IGARCH(1, 1) model. Although there are similarities with the model that is integrated in the mean, the problems which arise if one estimates a model with unit roots in the conditional mean do not arise in this case (see e.g. Lumsdaine (1990)).

In the empirical analysis of economic data, higher-order GARCH models do not generally yield a better representation of the features of the data than the

GARCH(1, 1) or the GARCH(1, 2) models. A similar finding holds for the choice of the order of ARMA models to describe the serial correlation of many univariate macroeconomic series.

For all the models introduced above, the reaction of the conditional variance is symmetric for increases as well as decreases of the same size of the variables in Φ_{t-1}. A specification which allows for asymmetric reactions of the conditional variance is the exponential GARCH (EGARCH) model put forward by Nelson (1991):

$$\ln h_t = \alpha_0 + \sum_{i=1}^{p} \beta_i \ln h_{t-i} + \sum_{i=1}^{q} \alpha_i(\varphi \varepsilon_{t-i} + \gamma \, | \, \varepsilon_{t-i} | - \gamma E \, | \, \varepsilon_{t-i} |) \quad (3.7)$$

where the parameters α_0, β_i and α_i are not restricted to being non-negative. An asymmetric reaction in the variance of the return of stocks can be expected as a result of the so-called leverage effect. A negative shock to the returns increases the debt-equity ratio and therefore increases uncertainty of future returns. In the EGARCH(1, 1) model, this could occur when $\alpha_1 > 0$ and $\varphi < 0$.

Engle, Lilien and Robins (1987) introduced the ARCH-M model in which the conditional mean is a function of the conditional variance of the process

$$y_t = g(x_{t-1}, h_t) + \varepsilon_t h_t^{1/2} \quad (3.8)$$

where x_{t-1} is a vector of predetermined variables, g is some function of x_{t-1} and h_t, and h_t is generated by an ARCH(q) process. The most common ARCH-M model simply has $g(x_{t-1}, h_t) = \delta h_t$. As the examples presented in section 2 show, many theories in finance involve an explicit trade-off between risk and expected return, leading to models in which the conditional mean depends on the conditional variance.

The models presented until now have all been univariate. As indicated by the theoretical model in section 2.2, the analysis of many issues of asset pricing and portfolio allocation requires a multivariate framework. Extensions of the models presented in this section to a multivariate setting will be considered in sections 5 and 6.

Measures of volatility which are not based on ARCH-type models have also been put forward in the literature. For instance, French *et al*. (1987) construct monthly stock return variance estimates by taking the average of the squared daily returns. To assess the temporal dependence, standard time series models are subsequently estimated for these variance estimates. This procedure does not make efficient use of all the data. Another drawback of this approach is that it does not yield the high frequency variance forecasts which are required in many models originating in financial theory. Furthermore, the conventional standard errors from the second-stage estimation may not be appropriate. Nevertheless, the computational simplicity of this procedure and a related model put forward by Schwert (1989), in which the conditional standard deviation is measured by the absolute value of the residuals from a first step estimate of the conditional mean, makes them appealing alternatives to more complicated ARCH type models for preliminary data analysis.

4. Some Statistical Properties of Models for Conditional Heteroskedasticity

In this section, we shall summarize the main results about the statistical properties of the models presented in the preceding section and we shall present estimation and testing procedures for these models. Finally, we shall discuss some issues related to temporal aggregation of ARCH and GARCH models.

4.1. Moments and Stationarity

Bollerslev (1986) has shown that under normality the GARCH process defined in (3.6) is wide sense stationary with $E(y_t) = 0$ and $\mathrm{var}(y_t) = \alpha_0 [1 - \alpha(1) - \beta(1)]^{-1}$ and $\mathrm{cov}(y_t y_s) = 0$ for $t \neq s$, if and only if $\alpha(1) + \beta(1) < 1$. For the GARCH(1, 1) model given by (3.6) when $p = q = 1$, a necessary and sufficient condition for the existence of the $2m$th moment is $\sum_{j=0}^{m} \binom{m}{j} a_j \alpha_1^j \beta_1^{m-j} < 1$, when $a_0 = 1$ and $a_j = \Pi_{i=1}^{j} (2i - 1)$, $j = 1, 2, \ldots$. Finally, Bollerslev (1986) has given a recursive formula for the even moments of y_t when $p = q = 1$. The fourth moment of a conditionally normal GARCH(1, 1) variable e.g. will be $Ey_t^4 = 3(Ey_t^2)^2 [1 - (\beta + \alpha_1)^2] / [1 - (\beta + \alpha_1)^2 - 2\alpha_1^2]$ if this moment exists. As a result of the symmetry of the normal distribution, the odd moments are all zero if they exist.

4.2. Estimation of GARCH Models

The parameters of the models described here can be estimated by the maximum likelihood (ML) method. For simplicity, we discuss estimation of the parameters of the GARCH(1, 1) model under the assumption that $\varepsilon_t \sim IN(0, 1)$. The log-likelihood function for a sample of T observations $y_1, y_2, \ldots y_T$, can be written as

$$L(y_1, y_2, \ldots y_T \mid \vartheta) = \sum_{t=1}^{T} \{c - \tfrac{1}{2} \ln h_t(\vartheta) - \tfrac{1}{2} y_t^2 / h_t(\vartheta)\} \qquad (4.2.1)$$

where $\vartheta = (\alpha_0, \alpha_1, \beta)$, $h_1(\vartheta) = \sigma^2 = \alpha_0 / (1 - \alpha_1 - \beta)$ and $h_t(\vartheta) = \alpha_0 + \beta h_{t-1}(\vartheta) + \alpha_1 y_{t-1}^2$ ($t > 1$). Given (initial) values of the parameters ϑ, the value of the log-likelihood function (4.2.1) can be recursively evaluated. Compute $h_1(\vartheta)$, then get $h_2(\vartheta)$ etc. and substitute the values into (4.2.1) to get the value of L. Standard numerical procedures can be used to compute the maximum of L in (4.2.1).

Under regularity conditions which are given in e.g. Crowder (1976), the value of which ϑ maximizes L, $\hat{\vartheta}_{ML}$, is consistent, asymptotically normally distributed and efficient,

$$\sqrt{T}(\hat{\vartheta}_{ML} - \vartheta) \overset{d}{\sim} N(0, \text{var}(\hat{\vartheta}_{ML})) \qquad (4.2.2)$$

with $\text{var}(\hat{\vartheta}_{ML}) = [E(T^{-1}\partial^2 L/\partial\vartheta\,\partial\vartheta')]^{-1}$. The asymptotic covariance matrix of $\hat{\vartheta}_{ML}$ can be consistently estimated by computing the inverse of the Hessian matrix associated with the log-likelihood function (4.2.1) evaluated at $\hat{\vartheta}_{ML}$. Most authors assume that the fourth moment of the data exists. Conditions for the existence of Ey_t^4 have been discussed in section 4.1. Under that assumption the proof of consistency of the estimators is greatly simplified. We note that Lumsdaine (1990) proves consistency without requiring fourth moments to exist.

The estimation of the ARCH-M model poses no extra problems. However, as shown by Engle (1982), in absence of ARCH-M effects, the information matrix for the model under conditional normality is block-diagonal between the parameters in the conditional mean and the variance functions. This is no longer true for the ARCH-M model. Thus unlike the ARCH model where consistent estimates of the parameters in the conditional mean, $g(x_{t-1})$, can be obtained even if h_t is misspecified, consistent estimation in the ARCH-M model requires the full model to be correctly specified.

Finally, if the parameters of the conditional variance in a regression model are nuisance parameters only, one can of course simply estimate the parameters in the conditional mean by ordinary least squares if the conditional variance does not affect the conditional mean. Note, however, that one has to use heteroskedasticity consistent standard errors, as proposed by White (1980), to conduct valid inference. Suppose e.g. that ρ is the parameter of interest in the regression $y_t = \rho y_{t-1} + u_t$ where u_t is uncorrelated with mean zero and conditional variance $\alpha_0 + \alpha_1 u_{t-1}^2$, i.e. the error is ARCH(1). The ordinary least squares estimator of ρ is a pseudo maximum likelihood estimator and its large sample distribution is given by $\sqrt{T}(\hat{\rho}_{OLS} - \rho) \sim N(0, \mathbf{A}^{-1}\mathbf{B}\mathbf{A}^{-1})$ where $\mathbf{A} = E[-T^{-1}\partial^2 C/\partial\rho^2]$ and $\mathbf{B} = E[T^{-1}\{\partial C/\partial\rho\}^2]$ and C is the pseudo log likelihood $C = -\Sigma_{t=1}^T (y_t - \rho y_{t-1})^2$, see e.g. Gouriéroux *et al.* (1984). The matrices $\mathbf{A}$ and $\mathbf{B}$ can easily be estimated consistently.

One of the implications of the need to correct the standard errors of estimators of parameters in the conditional mean is that in the presence of ARCH, standard tests for serial correlation in y_t will be upward biased, thus leading to over-rejections. Consider e.g. a test for first-order autocorrelation if the data are in fact generated by an ARCH(1) model and assume conditional normality. The standard estimate of the first-order autocorrelation coefficient coincides with the ordinary least squares estimator in a first-order autoregressive model. From the results above it is easily checked that under the null hypothesis that $\rho = 0$ the large sample variance of $\hat{\rho}_{OLS}$ will be $T^{-1}\{\alpha_0 Ey_{t-1}^2 + \alpha_1 Ey_{t-1}^4\}/\{Ey_{t-1}^2\}^2$ if fourth moments exist. From section 4.1

this can be rewritten as $T^{-1}(1 + 2\alpha_1 - 3\alpha_1^2)(1 - 3\alpha_1^2)^{-1}$, when $\alpha_1 < 1/\sqrt{3}$. For $\alpha_1 = 0.5$, this large sample variance exceeds the conventional asymptotic variance, $1/T$, by a factor of five (see e.g. Diebold (1987) for further discussion).

4.3. Testing for Conditional Heteroskedasticity

The likelihood ratio (LR) criterion can be used to test the hypothesis of conditional homoskedasticity e.g. against the GARCH(1, 1) alternative in (3.4). The LR-statistic associated with H_0: $\alpha_1 = 0$ and $\beta = 0$ does not have a χ^2-distribution with two degrees of freedom in this case, as the alternative hypothesis is H_1: $\alpha_1 \geqslant 0$ and $\beta \geqslant 0$. The standard assumption that the true parameter value under H_0 does not lie on the border of the parameter space under H_1 does not hold. An LR test which uses a χ^2-distribution with two degrees of freedom can be shown to be conservative (see e.g. Kodde and Palm (1986)), that is if it rejects the null hypothesis, then the LR-test which uses the correct distribution will certainly reject the null hypothesis. Demos and Sentana (1990) present critical values for the LR and Wald tests for testing ARCH effects versus constancy of the variance of a series. A second problem arises as the parameter β is not identified if $\alpha_1 = 0$. Therefore a test of H_0: $\alpha_1 = 0$ could yield misleading results. Engle (1984) shows how to carry out a test if some nuisance parameters are not identified under the null hypothesis.

A simple and frequently used test for conditional heteroskedasticity is the LM test of the hypothesis H_0: $\alpha_1 = \alpha_2 = \cdots \alpha_q = 0$ in the ARCH(q) model in (3.2). It has the form:

$$\text{LM} = (\partial L / \partial \alpha')(\partial^2 L / \partial \alpha \, \partial \alpha')^{-1}(\partial L / \partial \alpha) \, |_{\alpha = \hat{\alpha}} \qquad (4.3.1)$$

where $\hat{\alpha}$ denotes the ML estimate of α under H_0. For the ARCH(q) model, $h_t = z_t' \alpha$ and

$$(\partial L / \partial \alpha)_{\alpha = \hat{\alpha}} = (1/2\hat{\alpha}_0) \sum_t z_t (y_t^2 / \hat{\alpha}_0 - 1) = (1/2\hat{\alpha}_0) z' f_0 \qquad (4.3.2)$$

where $z_t' = (1, y_{t-1}^2, ..., y_{t-q}^2)$ and $z = (z_1, z_2, ..., z_T)$ and f_0 is the column vector of $(y_t^2 / \hat{\alpha}_0 - 1)$.

The Hessian matrix can be written as:

$$J_{\alpha\alpha} \, |_{\alpha = \hat{\alpha}} = (1/2\hat{\alpha}_0^2) z' z \qquad (4.3.3)$$

and therefore the LM test statistic can be written as:

$$\text{LM} = 1/2 f_0' z (z' z)^{-1} z' f_0 \qquad (4.3.4)$$

Notice that plim $f_0'f_0/T = 2$, because normality has been assumed. Therefore, an asymptotically equivalent statistic would be:

$$\text{LM} = Tf_0'z(z'z)^{-1}zf_0/f_0'f_0 = TR^2 \qquad (4.3.5)$$

where R^2 is the squared multiple correlation between f_0 and z. Since adding a constant and multiplying by a scalar will not change the R^2 of a regression, this is also the R^2 of a regression of y_t^2 on an intercept and q lagged values of y_t^2. Demos and Sentana (1990) propose a simple one-sided version of the TR^2-type LM test for ARCH in (4.3.5), which is computed from the same auxiliary regression of the squares of the residuals on a constant and its lags. They report critical values for the one-sided LM test. These critical values are robust to non-normality.

4.4.   Non-Normality of the Conditional Density of ε_t

As discussed above, financial return series often exhibit volatility clustering, and their unconditional distribution tends to have fatter tails than the normal distribution. Moreover, the conditional distribution of the standardized variable $y_t/\sqrt{h_t}$ often appears to be leptokurtic.

Bollerslev (1987) suggests use of the standardized Student-t distribution with the degrees of freedom ν being estimated. The log-likelihood of this model is:

$$L = T \ln k(\nu) - \sum_{t=1}^{T} 0.5(\nu + 1)\ln [1 + (\nu - 2)^{-1}\varepsilon_t^2/h_t] \qquad (4.4.1)$$

with $k(\nu) = \Gamma((\nu + 1)/2)\Gamma(\nu/2)^{-1}(\pi(\nu - 2))^{-1/2}$. The t-distribution has fatter tails than the normal distribution. As ν increases, it converges to the normal distribution. Other densities that have been used in the estimation of ARCH models are the normal-Poisson mixture distribution (see e.g. Jorion (1988), Nieuwland *et al.* (1991)) and the normal-lognormal mixture distribution (see e.g. Hsieh (1989)). An alternative to parametric ML estimation is the use of a semi-parametric density estimation technique which approximates the density function (see e.g. Gallant and Tauchen (1989) or Engle and Gonzalez-Rivera (1991)). Notice that semi-parametric and non-parametric methods can also be used to approximate an unknown conditional variance function (see Gallant and Tauchen (1989) and Pagan and Ullah (1988)).

In applications, the distribution of the disturbance is often unknown. Weiss (1986b) and Bollerslev and Wooldridge (1990) have shown that quasi-maximum likelihood estimators which are based on a normality assumption are consistent under weak assumptions even if the normality assumption does not hold. Moreover they show how asymptotic standard errors for the parameters in the conditional mean and variance functions that are robust to departures from normality can be obtained.

4.5.   Temporal Aggregation of ARCH Processes

Issues of temporal aggregation play an important role in time series modelling, in particular when the investigator has the choice between using data observed with a high frequency (e.g. daily observations) or using observations (e.g. monthly) sampled less frequently.

In this section, we illustrate how temporal aggregation affects the structure of the model in the case where the high frequency data are generated by an ARCH(1) model. This section draws on Drost and Nijman (1990) who also consider more general cases. Diebold (1988) has shown that the conditional heteroskedasticity disappears in the limit if the sampling frequency decreases and that in case of flow variables the implied marginal low frequency distribution converges to the normal distribution. Nelson (1990) considered the case of an increasing sampling frequency and derived the limiting continuous time model.

We consider an ARCH(1) model for a stock variable y_t which is observed every second period ($t = 2, 4, \ldots T$), with, for simplicity reason, T being assumed to be even. Along with Drost and Nijman (1990) we distinguish between three forms of ARCH models. We say that $y_t = \varepsilon_t h_t^{1/2}$ is generated by a semi-strong ARCH(1) model if:

$$E(y_t \mid y_{t-1}, y_{t-2}, \ldots) = 0 \qquad (4.5.1)$$

$$E(y_t^2 \mid y_{t-1}, y_{t-2}, \ldots) = h_t \qquad (4.5.2)$$

and h_t is generated by (3.2) with $q = 1$. The strong form corresponds to the case where the disturbance is assumed to be identically distributed with mean zero and variance equal to one, while for the weak form, condition (4.5.1) holds but condition (4.5.2) is replaced by the condition that the projection of y_t^2 on the space generated by $y_{t-1}, y_{t-2}, \ldots$ and its squares is equal to h_t. Integrating expressions (4.5.1) and (4.5.2) with respect to $y_{t-1}, y_{t-3}, \ldots$ we get for the low frequency model:

$$E(y_t \mid y_{t-2}, y_{t-4}, \ldots) = 0 \qquad (4.5.3)$$

$$E(y_t^2 \mid y_{t-2}, y_{t-4}, \ldots) = \tilde{\alpha}_0 + \tilde{\alpha}_1 y_{t-2}^2 = \tilde{h}_t \qquad (4.5.4)$$

with $\tilde{\alpha}_0 = \alpha_0(1 + \alpha_1)$ and $\tilde{\alpha}_1 = \alpha_1^2$. The low-frequency model is semi-strong ARCH(1) as well, with parameters $\tilde{\alpha}_0$ and $\tilde{\alpha}_1$ replacing the high frequency parameters α_0 and α_1.

A natural question to consider is whether the class of strong ARCH(1) models for stock variables is closed under temporal aggregation as well.

Assuming that ε_t is i.i.d. with distribution $D(0, 1)$, the rescaled disturbances in the low-frequency model are defined by

$$\nu_t = y_t / \tilde{h}_t^{1/2} \tag{4.5.5}$$

Rewriting (4.5.5), one can easily show that:

$$\nu_t = \varepsilon_t [\lambda_t + (1 - \lambda_t)\varepsilon_{t-1}^2]^{1/2} \text{ with } \lambda_t = \tilde{\alpha}_0 \tilde{h}_t^{1/2} \tag{4.5.6}$$

According to (4.5.6) the rescaled disturbances in the low-frequency model depend on past observations, even if the rescaled disturbances in the high frequency model are i.i.d. From (4.5.6), one can show that:

$$E(\nu_t^4 \mid y_{t-2}, y_{t-4}, \ldots) = \varkappa(\varkappa - 1)(\lambda_t - 1)^2 + \varkappa \tag{4.5.7}$$

where $\varkappa = E\varepsilon_t^4$ which implies that the fourth moment of the low-frequency conditional distribution of the rescaled disturbances will depend on the information set in a way similar to the dependence of the second moments on the past in the GARCH model. The low-frequency model that is implied by a high-frequency strong ARCH(1) process is no longer strong ARCH(1), although it still satisfies the assumptions of semi-strong ARCH(1) as shown above. Therefore, the assumption that rescaled disturbances are i.i.d. at the frequency at which the data happen to be available is arbitrary. More detailed results for higher-order ARCH and for GARCH models for stock and flow variables can be found in Drost and Nijman (1990). In general, it can be said that aggregating strong GARCH processes does not lead to a strong GARCH model. Weak GARCH(1, 1), defined above, generally leads to weak GARCH in the temporally aggregated data.

4.6. Concluding Remarks

In this section we have discussed statistical procedures that can be used to handle GARCH models. Conditional heteroskedasticity of high-frequency financial series is by now a well-established stylized fact. Fama (1965) already observed that price changes tended to be dependent over time and characterized by tranquil and volatile periods, and that the unconditional distributions of the price changes were typically fat-tailed and leptokurtic. Recently, Baillie and Bollerslev (1989) and Hsieh (1989) carried out an extensive study of the time series properties of exchange rates. They show that the first differences of the logarithms of the daily rates are approximately uncorrelated through time, and a GARCH(1, 1) model with near unit roots and conditionally t-distributed errors is found to be a good representation to the leptokurtosis and time-dependent conditional heteroskedasticity. The parameter estimates are similar for the different currencies. The results carry over to weekly and monthly data in which, in line with the results in section 4.5, the degree of time-dependent heteroskedasticity is reduced if the length of the sampling interval increases. Related stylized facts for stock returns and interest rates can be found in Bollerslev *et al.* (1992).

5. Econometric Models of Time-Varying Risk Premia in Foreign Exchange

5.1. Introduction

As shown in section 2.1, Domowitz and Hakkio (1985) (DH85 from now on) have developed a simple model for the risk premium component in forward foreign exchange rates, using the general set-up in Lucas (1982). In this section various ways of testing their model will be described. In section 5.2 we will describe the empirical results in DH85 which are based on a univariate ARCH-M model and monthly data. Section 5.3 will be devoted to Baillie and Bollerslev (1990) where results from a multivariate GARCH-M and weekly overlapping data are provided. Finally section 5.4 is devoted to non-parametric estimation of the variance functions as proposed by Pagan and Ullah (1988). Before we start the discussion of direct tests of the model, it is worthwhile to refer to some related work which is available in the literature.

The existence of a risk premium in forward foreign exchange has been claimed by many authors (see e.g. Baillie, Lippens and McMahon (1983) and Hansen and Hodrick (1980)) who tested the unbiasedness of the forward rate. In a second line of research several authors have tried to assess the importance of time variation in risk premia, without making the strong structural assumptions in DH85. Fama (1984) and Hodrick and Srivastava (1986) have shown that the unconditional variance of the risk premium is greater than the unconditional variance of the expected rate of depreciation. Similarly Wolff (1987) and Nijman, Palm and Wolff (1991) have presented evidence on the conditional variances of the risk premia and expected rate of depreciation using weak structural assumptions only. Wolff (1987) has moreover shown how estimates of the premium can be obtained under similar assumptions. Finally, in a third line of research, Hansen and Hodrick (1983) and Hodrick and Srivastava (1984) have tested the validity of the Euler equation (2.1.4). Evidently the results from these lines of research are taken as starting points in the literature on structural models for the risk premium to be discussed in sections 5.2 to 5.4. An excellent discussion of the literature on these issues which was available about five years ago is provided in Hodrick (1987).

5.2. The Monthly Univariate ARCH-M Model for the Risk Premium in Domowitz and Hakkio (1985)

In section 2.1 we outlined how DH85 derive the model

$$s_{t+1} - f_t = \delta\{h_{mt+1} - h_{nt+1}\} + u_{mt+1} - u_{nt+1}$$

$$u_{mt+1} \mid I_t \sim N(0, h_{mt+1}), \qquad u_{nt+1} \mid I_t \sim N(0, h_{nt+1})$$

(5.2.1)

where $\delta = 0.5$. Equation (5.2.1) can be estimated jointly with the two money supply equations, and along these lines the hypothesis $\delta = 0.5$ can be tested. This approach will be discussed in section 5.4. Instead, DH85 approximated (5.2.1) by:

$$s_{t+1} - f_t = \mu + \delta h_{t+1} + e_{t+1}$$

$$e_{t+1} \mid I_t \sim N(0, h_{t+1})$$

(5.2.2)

where h_{t+1} is assumed to be ARCH(4).

Estimation of the model in (5.2.2) only requires spot and forward exchange rate data and is more straightforward than the multivariate approach which models the money supplies as well. On the other hand, (5.2.2) is only implied by (5.2.1) in special cases such as when one of the two money supplies is conditionally homoskedastic and an ARCH(4) model holds for the conditional variance of the money supply in the other country. Nevertheless, one might expect some impact of h_t on $s_{t+1} - f_t$ in more general cases as well. Note that the estimated risk premium can change sign because of the presence of the constant term.

No doubt motivated by the literature on testing for unbiasedness of the forward rate, which suggested a relation between $s_{t+1} - s_t$ and $f_t - s_t$, DH85 finally include the forward premium $f_t - s_t$ as a regressor by adding $f_t - s_t$ to both sides of the equality which yields their final specification:

$$s_{t+1} - s_t = \mu + \gamma(f_t - s_t) + \delta h_{t+1} + e_{t+1}$$

$$e_{t+1} \mid I_t \sim N(0, h_{t+1})$$

(5.2.3)

DH85 have estimated (5.2.3) by maximum likelihood, assuming that h_{t+1} is generated by an ARCH(4) process, as has been discussed in (4.2.1) for a related case. The standard errors of the estimators have been obtained using a variant of (4.2.2). For monthly data on exchange rates of the pound sterling, the French franc, the German mark and the Swiss franc against the US dollar from June 1973 to September 1982 the results indicate that all four series show very little conditional heteroskedasticity, which with hindsight is not so surprising, given the results in Baillie and Bollerslev (1989) and Drost and

Nijman (1990). The hypothesis that $\mu = 0$, $\gamma = 1$ and $\delta = 0$ can be rejected for the pound sterling, but could not be rejected for the other three currencies. DH85 therefore conclude that 'there is little support for the conditional variance of the exchange rate forecast error being an important sole determinant of the risk premium'.

5.3. The Weekly Multivariate GARCH-M Model for the Risk Premium in Baillie and Bollerslev (1990)

Baillie and Bollerslev (1990) (BB90 from now on) have extended the work of DH85 in at least three ways. First of all they analyse exchange rates of a number of currencies against the dollar in a multivariate setting, thereby avoiding the approximation of (5.2.1) by (5.2.2). Second, they replace the ARCH(4) assumption on the variances by a GARCH(1, 1) assumption, which is more parsimonious and is less likely to yield *a priori* implausible parameter estimates. Finally BB90 analyse weekly data, which contain much more conditional heteroskedasticity than the monthly data used in DH85 and are therefore more likely to reveal a relation between time-varying variances and time-varying risk premia. As no weekly forward contracts are traded, however, they have to stick to monthly forward rates, which creates the problem of overlapping samples discussed before, e.g. in Hansen and Hodrick (1980). In this section the three extensions referred to above will be added to the model one after another, and some of the empirical results in BB90 will be discussed.

Starting with the extension to exchange rates of a number of currencies against the dollar, note that DH85 assume that the model which has been derived holds for all bilateral exchange rates. Note, however, that the underlying model describes a two-country world. Extension to a multi-country setting without affecting the results appears to require extreme separation assumptions, a topic that will not be pursued here. Consider an $N + 1$ country world ($i = 0, ..., N$) where the money stocks are denoted by $m_{i,t}$ and where all exchange rates $s_{i,t}$ ($i = 1, ..., N$) are denominated in the currency of the first country ($i = 0$). Equation (2.1.7) of the DH85 model implies that

$$\text{var}_t[s_{i,t+1}] = \text{var}_t[m_{0,t+1}] + \text{var}_t[m_{i,t+1}] \tag{5.3.1}$$

and

$$\text{cov}_t[s_{i,t+1}, s_{j,t+1}] = \text{var}_t[m_{0,t+1}], \qquad i \neq j \tag{5.3.2}$$

because of the assumed independence of the AR(1) processes which generate the money supplies. Substitution of (5.3.1) and (5.3.2) in (2.1.12) yields:

$$E_t[s_{i,t+1}] - f_{i,t} = \text{cov}_t[s_{i,t+1}, s_{j,t+1}] - 0.5 \, \text{var}_t[s_{i,t+1}] \tag{5.3.3}$$

which is an expression for the risk premium which avoids the use of money supply data and which can be tested in the context of a multivariate GARCH-M model. The model which BB90 propose for an $N + 1$ currency world is:

$$s_{i,t+1} - f_{i,t} = \mu_i + \sum_{j=1}^{N} \delta_{ij} \operatorname{cov}_t[s_{i,t+1}, s_{j,t+1}] + e_{i,t+1} \qquad (5.3.4)$$

for $i = 1, ..., N$, where $s_{i,t}$ stands for the exchange rate of the ith currency against the $N + 1$st and where $e_t' = (e_{1t}, ..., e_{Nt})$ is i.i.d. normal with mean zero and time-varying variance-covariance matrix $\mathbf{H}_t$. Alternatively (5.3.4) can be derived as an approximation to more general models of the risk premium.

The second extension of the work by DH85 which BB90 consider consists in replacing the ARCH specification in DH85 by a multivariate GARCH(1, 1) model with constant conditional correlations:

$$
\begin{aligned}
h_{ii,t} &= \psi_i + \beta_i h_{ii,t-1} + \alpha_i e_{i,t-1}^2 && \text{if } i = j \\
h_{ij,t} &= \rho_{ij}\sqrt{h_{ii,t}}\sqrt{h_{jj,t}} && \text{if } i \neq j
\end{aligned}
\qquad (5.3.5)
$$

where $h_{ij,t} = \{\mathbf{H}_t\}_{ij}$. This specification avoids the implausible lag patterns in DH85 and has the advantage over alternative parametrizations of multivariate GARCH that consistent parameter estimates can be easily obtained under the assumption that the impact of the conditional covariances on the conditional mean can be ignored. If $\delta_{ij} = 0$ ($\forall \, i, j$) univariate GARCH(1, 1) models can be estimated for all bilateral exchange rates separately and subsequently the conditional correlation parameters ρ_{ij} can be estimated as the correlations of the rescaled disturbances $e_{i,t}/\sqrt{h_{ii,t}}$. In this way suitable starting values for the computationally demanding full numerical optimization of the likelihood function can be obtained as long as the GARCH-M effect is not too dominant.

The third extension in BB90 is their use of weekly instead of monthly data. If it is assumed that a month consists of four weeks, the model proposed for weekly data can be written as:

$$s_{i,t+4} - f_{i,t}^{(4)} = \mu_i + \sum_{j=1}^{N} \delta_{ij} \operatorname{cov}_t[s_{i,t+1}, s_{j,t+1}] + \varepsilon_{i,t+4} \qquad (5.3.6)$$

where $f_{i,t}^{(4)}$ is the monthly forward rate in week t of currency i. As by definition $\varepsilon_{i,t+4} = s_{i,t+4} - E_t[s_{i,t+4}]$, $\varepsilon_{i,t}$ is generated by a third-order moving average process, because both $E_{t-k}[s_{i,t}]$ and $s_{i,t}$ are included in the information set at period t if $k > 3$. If weekly exchange rate changes are uncorrelated, which is well known to be approximately true, the first three autocorrelations of $\varepsilon_{i,t}$ will be 0.75, 0.50 and 0.25 respectively. In fact a month contains more than four weeks, which yields a MA(4) process and slightly different autocorrelations (see BB90). BB90 impose orthogonality of the spot rate innovations in the various currencies ($Ee_{i,t}e_{j,s} = 0$ ($\forall\, t, s, i, j$)) and write:

$$\varepsilon_{i,t+4} = e_{i,t+4} + \sum_{k=1}^{4} \vartheta_k e_{i,t+4-k} \qquad (5.3.7)$$

where the ϑ_k are the moving average coefficients which yield the autocorrelations referred to above. These values of ϑ_k are imposed throughout the numerical maximization of the likelihood function corresponding to (5.3.5), (5.3.6) and (5.3.7).

In the empirical section of the paper BB90 restricted themselves to four major European currencies, the pound sterling, the German mark, the Swiss franc and the French franc, all against the US dollar. They consider 462 weekly opening prices from the New York Foreign Exchange Market between March 1, 1980 and February 2, 1989. Imposing $\delta_{ij} = 0$ initially, the authors compute Ljung–Box tests for autocorrelation in the residuals and find no evidence of autocorrelation in the residuals in addition to the imposed MA(4) process. Remember that, as discussed in section 4.3, the presence of conditional heteroskedasticity generally induces an upward bias in the traditional test statistics for the absence of autocorrelation. Estimation of the model while retaining the restriction that $\delta_{ij} = 0$ reveals significant conditional heteroskedasticity.

Instead of estimating all parameters in (5.3.5), (5.3.6) and (5.3.7) simultaneously, BB90 restrict themselves to the computation of Lagrange Multiplier tests for the hypothesis H_0: $\delta_{ij} = 0$. One of the tests carried out by BB90 is a currency-by-currency test of the joint significance of the own conditional variance and the conditional covariances with the other currencies. Again, the results are somewhat disappointing. The four test statistics do not lend much support to the idea that the risk premium is a simple linear function of the corresponding covariances as specified in (5.3.4). Only for the UK is there some evidence that the conditional covariances explain part of the risk premium in addition to the own conditional variances.

5.4. The Monthly Non-Parametric GARCH-M Model for the Risk Premium

The disappointing empirical results in DH85 and BB90 could be due to the fact that the underlying model is an insufficiently accurate description of reality. Several other explanations of the empirical results are possible, however, such as the limited sample size in BB90 and the assumed conditional normality of the disturbances in both papers. In this section we will discuss yet another potential cause of the failure to find empirical results in line with the theory: misspecification of the conditional variance equation, which is based on an auxiliary assumption that is not derived from theory. In section 4.2 we have already referred to the fact that in GARCH-M models incorrect specification of the variance equation will lead to inconsistent estimates of the mean parameters. Fortunately, however, Pagan and Ullah (1988) have suggested tests for the specification of the conditional variance and have proposed estimation strategies which are more robust to the specification of the variance equation.

Let us start the discussion of Pagan and Ullah (1988) (PU88 from now on) by reconsidering equation (5.2.1) assuming that n_t is non-stochastic. If n_t is non-stochastic, (5.2.1) can be written as:

$$s_{t+1} - f_t = \mu + \delta \ \text{var}_t[m_{t+1}] + e_{t+1} \tag{5.4.1}$$

where e_{t+1} is a zero mean, uncorrelated but possibly conditionally heteroskedastic error term. It is important to note that in (5.4.1) the conditional variance of an exogenous variable appears as a regressor. One possible estimation strategy for (5.4.1) starts off by estimating the AR(1) model which generates m_t by assumption. The resulting error terms will be denoted by $\hat{u}_{mt} = m_t - \hat{\rho}_m m_{t-1}$. The second step in this estimation strategy is to replace $\text{var}_t[m_{t+1}]$ by $\hat{u}_{mt+1}^2$, which yields:

$$s_{t+1} - f_t = \mu + \delta \hat{u}_{mt+1}^2 + e_{t+1} + \delta\{\text{var}_t[m_{t+1}] - \hat{u}_{mt+1}^2\} \tag{5.4.2}$$

Ordinary least squares estimation of (5.4.2) will not in general yield consistent estimates of μ and δ as u_{mt+1}^2 will in non-degenerate cases be correlated with $\{\text{var}_t[m_{t+1}] - u_{mt+1}^2\}$. While OLS is inconsistent, instrumental variables estimators will yield consistent estimates of μ and δ if the instruments are observed at time t, are uncorrelated with e_{t+1} and are correlated with the regressors. Instruments such as a constant term, and present and lagged values of m_t^2, will satisfy these requirements under very general assumptions. In this way consistent estimators of the impact of $\text{var}_t[m_{t+1}]$ on $E_t[s_{t+1} - f_t]$ can be obtained without specifying the functional form of $\text{var}_t[m_{t+1}]$, i.e. without making a choice between an ARCH, GARCH, EGARCH model or any other functional form.

Instrumental variables estimation of (5.4.2) has the advantage of being robust against potential misspecification of the variance equation, but it can be very inefficient if the variance of $\delta\{\text{var}_t[m_{t+1}] - \hat{u}_{mt+1}^2\}$ is large compared to that of e_{t+1}. Similar issues of robustness versus efficiency arise in the literature on the estimation of linear models with unobserved rational expectations; see e.g. Nijman (1990) and Nijman and Palm (1991). This literature suggests that more efficient robust IV estimators can be derived by considering better proxies for $\text{var}_t[m_{t+1}]$, i.e. by adopting the substitution approach to replace unobserved variables instead of the errors in variables approach. One possible proxy for $\text{var}[m_{t+1} \mid I_t]$ is $\text{var}[m_{t+1} \mid H_t]$ where $H_t \subset I_t$ and I_t is the set of all information which is available at time t. Note that $\text{var}_t[m_{t+1}] = \text{var}[m_{t+1} \mid I_t]$ by definition. Substitution of $\text{var}[m_{t+1} \mid H_t]$ in (5.4.1) yields:

$$s_{t+1} - f_t = \mu + \delta \, \text{var}[m_{t+1} \mid H_t] + u_{t+1} \tag{5.4.3}$$

where:

$$u_{t+1} = e_{t+1} + \delta\{\text{var}[m_{t+1} \mid I_t] - \text{var}[m_{t+1} \mid H_t]\} \tag{5.4.4}$$

These equations show that a regression of the forward rate forecast errors on the variance of the money supply conditional on a subset of all information will yield consistent estimates of μ and δ. Non-parametric estimates of this variance which do not depend on arbitrary assumptions on the functional form can be obtained, e.g. using kernel estimators of conditional means by noting that:

$$\text{var}[m_{t+1} \mid H_t] = E[m_{t+1}^2 \mid H_t] - \{E[m_{t+1} \mid H_t]\}^2 \tag{5.4.5}$$

The kernel estimator of a conditional mean with a finite number of conditioning variables reads as:

$$\hat{E}[y_t \mid x_t] = \sum_{s=1}^{T} y_s K\{\gamma \bar{T}^{-1}(x_t - x_s)\} \Big/ \sum_{s=1}^{T} K\{\gamma \bar{T}^{-1}(x_t - x_s)\} \tag{5.4.6}$$

where $K\{\ \}$ is a kernel function that aims to smooth the data and where γ_T is the so-called bandwidth parameter that is typically proportional to $T^{-1/(4+q)}$ and q is the dimension of the conditioning set. Many types of kernel might be employed. A popular one is the multivariate normal kernel. Under various restrictions on the bandwidth parameter γ_T and assumptions on the processes generating (y_t, x_t) it has been shown that $\hat{E}[y_t \mid x_t]$ converges to $E[y_t \mid x_t]$ in probability. Recent applications of kernel estimation to modelling conditional heteroskedasticity include PU88, Pagan and Hong (1990) and Sentana and Wadhwani (1989). A good illustration and comparison of different parametric and non-parametric methods of modelling conditional variances is given in Pagan and Schwert (1990).

The empirical results in PU88 still show little sign of impact of the conditional variance on the conditional mean. One explanation is that their empirical results are obtained from monthly data, which do not show much conditional heteroskedasticity. Obviously, another one is that the underlying model does not hold.

5.5. Concluding Remarks on Risk Premia in Foreign Exchange

In this section we have discussed the estimation of structural econometric models of the risk premium. The models that we considered suggest that the risk premium depends on conditional variances and possibly conditional covariances, either of money supplies, or of spot rates. However, the empirical results in neither of the three papers that we discussed, nor in other papers in this area, support the overly simple models which they tested. More sophisticated models to explain time-varying risk premia are required. In particular models in which the risk premium is a function of the conditional variances of a set of exogenous variables seem promising. Hodrick (1989) provides an example of such a model, showing how the exchange rate is affected by uncertainty in the monetary policy, government expenditures and income growth. Implementation and tests of these models can of course be naturally conducted within the framework described in this chapter.

6. Models of Time-Varying Premia in Stock or Bond Returns

6.1. Introduction

In section 2.2 we introduced a capital asset pricing model (CAPM) which can be used to take portfolio decisions in a world where returns have time-varying first and second conditional moments. In order to test the model, or to use the model to achieve an optimal trade-off between expected returns and unhedged risks, estimates of these time-varying moments are required. In this section several multivariate GARCH models will be considered which can be used to model first and second conditional moments of a vector of returns.

In the model presented in Section 2.2, the conditional mean returns depend on the conditional covariances of the returns as in (2.2.5), which we repeat here for convenience:

$$E_t[r_{t+1}] - r_t^f \iota = \rho_t \, \text{var}_t[r_{t+1}] \, x_t \qquad (6.1.1)$$

where r_{t+1} is an $N \times 1$ vector of returns in period $t + 1$ on the N assets in the economy, r_t^f is the risk-free rate in period $t + 1$ which is known in period t, ι is an N-dimensional vector of ones, x_t is an $N \times 1$ vector of investment shares and ρ_t is the price of risk, which will for simplicity be assumed to be time-invariant: $\rho_t = \rho$. Equation (6.1.1) can be derived under much more general assumptions, as in Campbell (1990).

Premultiplication of (6.1.1) with x_t' yields a univariate relation between the conditional mean and variance of the market portfolio. Several authors (see e.g. French, Schwert and Stambaugh (1987)) have used univariate GARCH-M models to describe excess returns on the market portfolio, and found a significant impact of the conditional variance on the conditional mean in line with the underlying CAPM. We shall test (6.1.1) using multivariate GARCH models. Note also that multivariate GARCH models can be used to derive hedging strategies whether or not (6.1.1) holds, as the optimal portfolio for investors who maximize (2.2.1) will still be given by (2.2.4). Obviously the restriction which was imposed in section 2.2 that the economy consists of representative investors can easily be relaxed by allowing for differences in risk aversion.

In section 6.2 we shall first of all consider the diagonal multivariate GARCH model which Bollerslev, Engle and Wooldridge (1988) (BEW88 from now on) used to describe the returns on the US bills, bonds and stock market. As the number of parameters in unrestricted variance equations of multivariate GARCH models soon gets unmanageable, several authors have tried to find parametrizations which impose *a priori* plausible restrictions. In section 6.3 we shall consider one model in this line of research, the FACTOR-ARCH model which is used by Engle, Ng and Rothschild (1990) to model the term structure of interest rates. Section 6.4 concludes.

6.2. The Diagonal Multivariate GARCH Model for US Bills, Bonds and Stock Returns Used by Bollerslev, Engle and Wooldridge (1988)

The conceptually most straightforward generalization of the analysis of the relation between the conditional mean and variance of the returns on the market portfolio to the multivariate case is to consider the multivariate GARCH(P, Q)-M model

$$r_{t+1} - r^f_t = \mu + \rho \, \mathrm{var}_t[r_{t+1}] x_t + \varepsilon_{t+1} \tag{6.2.1}$$

$$E[\varepsilon^2_{t+1} \mid I_t] = \mathrm{var}_t[r_{t+1}] = \Sigma_t \tag{6.2.2}$$

$$\sigma_t(i, j) = \psi_{ij} + \sum_{r,q=1}^{N} \sum_{k=1}^{P} \beta_k(i, j, r, q)\sigma_{t-k}(r, q)$$

$$+ \sum_{r,q=1}^{N} \sum_{k=1}^{Q} \alpha_k(i, j, r, q)\varepsilon_{r,t-k}\varepsilon_{q,t-k} \tag{6.2.3}$$

where $\varepsilon_{t+1} = r_{t+1} - E_t[r_{t+1}]$ and where $\sigma_t(i, j)$ denotes the (i, j)th element of Σ_t. Sufficient conditions on the αs and βs which ensure that Σ_t will be positive definite have been derived in Baba *et al.* (1989). As x_t is observable, the system in (6.2.1), (6.2.2) and (6.2.3) can be estimated in principle from data on r_{t+1}, r^f_t and x_t for $t = 1, ..., T$. One of the implications of (6.1.1) is that $\mu = 0$, which can be tested. In practice, estimation of the unrestricted model in (6.2.1) to (6.2.3) is impossible, however, unless N is very small, as the number of parameters tends to be extremely large. The symmetry of Σ_t implies that the number of parameters in the variance equation is $0.5N(N + 1) + 0.25N^2(N + 1)^2(P + Q)$ which if $P = Q = 1$ yields a value of 12 if $N = 2$, of 42 if $N = 3$, of 110 if $N = 4$, etc. Obviously restrictions are required to keep the estimation problem manageable.

A drastic simplification of (6.2.3) is obtained if one is willing to assume that $P = Q = 1$ and that $\alpha(i, j, q, r) = 0$ and $\beta(i, j, q, r) = 0$ unless $i = q$ and $j = r$, in which case $\alpha(i, j, q, r) = \alpha_{ij}$ and $\beta(i, j, q, r) = \beta_{ij}$. The model which is obtained if these restrictions are imposed, as in BEW88, is known as the diagonal model. If $P = Q = 1$ the diagonal equivalent of (6.2.3) can be written as:

$$\sigma_t(i, j) = \psi_{ij} + \beta_{ij}\sigma_{t-1}(i, j) + \alpha_{ij}\varepsilon_{i,t-1}\varepsilon_{j,t-1} \tag{6.2.4}$$

which contains $1.5N\,(N+1)$ parameters. If $N = 3$, as in the application in BEW88, the number of parameters in (6.2.4) is 18, as opposed to 42 in (6.2.3). Drawbacks of the diagonal model are that the restrictions are quite arbitrary and that the conditional covariance matrix generated by (6.2.4) is not necessarily positive semi-definite.

In the empirical section of their paper BEW88 consider quarterly returns on six-month Treasury bills, twenty-year Treasury bonds and stocks from 1959-I to 1984-II. The return on three-month Treasury bills is taken to represent the risk-free return. The plots of the three excess holding yields which are given in BEW88 clearly suggest that not only their conditional means but also the conditional variances vary over time, in line with (6.1.1).

The model which is estimated in BEW88 consists of (6.2.1), (6.2.2) and (6.2.4). The estimation results suggest a reasonable and significant estimate of the price of risk parameter ρ as well as a time-varying variance for excess returns on six-month bills, a slightly time-varying variance for excess returns on government bonds, but no time-varying variance for excess returns on stocks. All three intercepts μ_i, which should be insignificant if (6.1.1) holds, are in fact significant. BEW88 explain the negative intercept for bonds and stocks from the fact that capital gains are not as heavily taxed as dividend and interest payments. This provides incentives to hold these assets even at otherwise unfavourable rates of return.

BEW88 test the validity of the CAPM relation in (6.1.1) using Lagrange Multiplier tests for the inclusion of additional regressors in the mean equation (6.2.1). The test for the inclusion of the own conditional variances (6.2.2) as regressors in addition to the intercept and the covariance with the market portfolio does not reject (6.1.1). That is of particular interest, since in tests of the time-invariant CAPM the own variance is often found to be highly significant. Tests for the inclusion in (6.2.1) of lagged excess holding yields on the one hand, or innovations in the logarithm of per capita consumption on the other hand, reject the model in (6.2.1), (6.2.2) and (6.2.4) very clearly. One reason might of course be that (6.1.1) does not hold, but another reason could be that the variance equation (6.2.4), which is not derived from theory, is misspecified. Misspecification of (6.2.4) arises if the restrictions imposed by the diagonal model are not satisfied, but another explanation might be that premia and conditional heteroskedasticity depend on information in addition to past innovations in asset returns. In particular the Lagrange Multiplier tests for omitted variables in (6.2.1) suggest that lagged excess holding yields and innovations in consumption might have some explanatory power when added to (6.2.4). Giovannini and Jorion (1989) have extended the diagonal multivariate GARCH model by including cross products $d_{it-1}d_{jt-1}$ in (6.2.4), where d_{it} is the difference in returns on government debt in country i with the return on government debt in the US.

6.3. The Factor-ARCH Model for the Term Structure of Interest Rates Proposed by Engle, Ng and Rothschild (1990)

From section 6.2 it is evident that the most important difficulty in the extension of univariate models for time-varying risk premia to multivariate models, is the fact that in unrestricted models the number of parameters soon becomes unmanageable. In a recent paper, Engle, Ng and Rothschild (1990) (ENR90 from now on) have proposed FACTOR-ARCH models as a parsimonious structure for the conditional covariance matrix of asset excess returns. FACTOR-ARCH models are appealing because they model the notion that the risk on financial markets can be decomposed into a limited number of factors and an asset specific ('idiosyncratic') error term. A similar model arises from the Arbitrage Pricing Theory (APT) although the APT does not imply that the number of factors is finite. The FACTOR-ARCH model is used to model interest rate risk in ENR90, while a companion paper (Ng, Engle and Rothschild (1992)) considers risk premia and anomalies to the CAPM on the US stock market.

One way to generate the model which is used in ENR90 is to assume that the vector of excess returns, $r_{t+1} - r_t^f \iota$, is generated by a factor structure in which the factors are conditionally heteroskedastic:

$$r_{t+1} - r_t^f \iota = \mu_t + \sum_{k=1}^{K} \beta_k f_{kt} + v_t \tag{6.3.1}$$

where r_{t+1} is an N-dimensional vector and $K < N$ is the number of factors. In (6.3.1) μ_t is an N-dimensional vector of risk premia to be determined and β_k is an N-dimensional vector of coefficients. It is assumed that all factors are independent and have zero mean, that the idiosyncratic errors have zero mean, are potentially correlated but are conditionally homoskedastic. The factors on the other hand are allowed to be conditionally heteroskedastic. Stated formally, the assumptions are:

$$E_{t-1}[v_{kt}] = 0, \qquad E_{t-1}[f_{kt}] = 0,$$

$$\text{var}_{t-1}[v_{kt}] = \Omega_{kk}, \qquad \text{var}_{t-1}[f_{kt}] = \lambda_{kt} \tag{6.3.2}$$

$$\text{cov}_{t-1}[v_{kt}, v_{rt}] = \Omega_{kr}, \qquad \text{cov}_{t-1}[f_{kt}, f_{rt}] = 0 \qquad (k \neq r)$$

ENR90 assume that the return on the market portfolio satisfies (6.3.1) and

(6.3.2) as well, which is the case if the optimal portfolio weights x_t are not time-varying ($x_t = x$ ($\forall$ t)). The risk premium on the market portfolio is referred to as μ_t^m, while the 'beta' of the market with respect to the kth factor is referred to as β_k^m, i.e. as a matter of notation one can write:

$$r_{t+1}^m - r_t^f = \mu_t^m + \sum_{k=1}^{K} \beta_k^m f_{kt} + v_t^m \tag{6.3.3}$$

The assumption on the covariance structure of the asset returns in (6.3.1), (6.3.2) and (6.3.3) can be used to derive an expression for the risk premia in the individual assets in which the portfolio weights no longer occur.

Assuming once more that the price of risk is time-invariant, along the lines of section 2.2, expression (6.1.1) can be written as:

$$E_t[r_{t+1}] - r_t^f\iota = \rho \, \text{cov}_t[r_{t+1}, r_{t+1}^m] \tag{6.3.4}$$

Substituting (6.3.1) and (6.3.3), and assuming that the idiosyncratic disturbance on the market return is negligible ($\text{var}_t[v_{t+1}^m] = 0$) one obtains

$$E_t[r_{t+1}] - r_t^f\iota = \rho \sum_{k=1}^{K} \beta_k^m \, \text{var}_t[f_{kt+1}] \beta_k \tag{6.3.5}$$

which yields a direct expression for the risk premium.

As the factors f_k themselves are not observable, ENR90 subsequently define the concept of a factor-representing portfolio. The portfolio with portfolio weights $\alpha_k = (\alpha_{k1}, ..., \alpha_{kN})$ is referred to as a factor-representing portfolio for factor k if its return is uncorrelated with all factors except factor k, and if the (conditional) covariance with factor k coincides with the (conditional) variance of factor k, i.e.:

$$\text{cov}_t[\alpha_k' r_{t+1}, f_{kt+1}] = \text{var}_t[f_{kt+1}] = \lambda_{kt+1}$$
$$\text{cov}_t[\alpha_k' r_{t+1}, f_{qt+1}] = 0 \qquad (k \neq q) \tag{6.3.6}$$

from which it follows that $\alpha_k' \beta_k = 1$ and $\alpha_k' \beta_l = 0$ ($k \neq l$). ENR90 subsequently show that the risk premium on any asset can be expressed as a linear combination of the premia on the factor representing portfolios, and therefore can be expressed as a linear function of the conditional variances of the factor representing portfolios only

$$E_t[r_{t+1}] - r_t^f\iota = \sum_{k=1}^{K} \{E_t[\alpha_k r_{t+1}] - r_t^f\} \beta_k$$

$$= \sum_{k=1}^{K} \{\gamma_k \, \text{var}_t[\alpha_k r_{t+1}] + c_k\} \beta_k = \mu_t \tag{6.3.7}$$

Comparing (6.1.1) with (6.3.7) it is apparent that the main achievement of the FACTOR-ARCH model is that the risk premium is expressed as a function of the conditional variances of K portfolios rather than as a function of the conditional covariance matrix of all N returns.

In order to complete the model, the factor-representing portfolios and a specification for $\text{var}_t[\alpha_k r_{t+1}]$ $(k = 1, \ldots, K)$ have to be chosen. Although it is in principle possible to choose the factor-representing portfolios by estimating the weights α_k and all other parameters in the model jointly, using a numerical maximization of the likelihood over a large number of parameters, this approach is not taken in ENR90. Instead, *a priori* knowledge of the number of factor-representing portfolios and their weights is assumed, which leaves the specification of $\text{var}_t[\alpha_k r_{t+1}]$ as the final point to consider.

The simplest but most restrictive assumption on the dynamics of the conditional variances of the returns on the factor-representing portfolios is that these returns are not only uncorrelated, $\text{cov}_t[\alpha_k r_{t+1}, \alpha_q' r_{t+1}] = 0$ $(k \neq q)$, but that moreover shocks in one factor do not affect the conditional variance of the other factors in any way, i.e.:

$$\text{var}_t[\alpha_k r_{t+1} \mid r_t, r_{t-1}, \ldots] = \text{var}_t[\alpha_k r_{t+1} \mid \alpha_k r_t, \alpha_k r_{t-1}, \ldots] \qquad (6.3.8)$$

which is referred to by ENR90 as a 'univariate portfolio representation'.

If one is willing to assume that the factor-representing portfolios have a univariate portfolio representation and that the conditional variances of the returns on the factor-generating portfolios are generated by GARCH(1, 1) models, the risk premia on the factor-representing portfolios can be derived by estimating the univariate GARCH-M model:

$$\alpha_k r_{t+1} - r_t^f = c_k + \gamma_k \vartheta_{k,t+1} + e_{k,t+1}$$

$$e_{k,t+1} \sim N(0, \vartheta_{k,t+1}) \qquad (6.3.9)$$

$$\vartheta_{k,t+1} = \psi_k + \varphi_k \vartheta_{k,t} + \omega_k (e_{k,t})^2$$

where we have changed the standard notation of the variance equation to avoid confusion with the β_k and α_k expressions in (6.3.1) to (6.3.7). Adding a normality assumption to (6.3.7) one easily obtains:

$$r_{i,t+1} - r_t^f = \sum_{k=1}^{K} \beta_{ik}(c_k + \gamma_k \vartheta_{k,t+1}) + \varepsilon_{i,t+1}$$

$$\varepsilon_{i,t+1} \sim N\left(0, \sigma_i + \sum_{k=1}^{K} \beta_{ik}^2 \vartheta_{k,t+1}\right) \qquad (6.3.10)$$

A simple way to obtain consistent estimates of the β_{ik} therefore is to maximize the likelihood of the $r_{i,t+1}$ over σ_i and β_{ik} treating the $\hat{c}_k$, $\hat{\gamma}_k$ and $\hat{\vartheta}_{k,t+1}$

expressions as if they coincided with the true values of these parameters. In this way only a small number of relatively simple numerical optimization problems as implied by (6.3.9) and (6.3.10) have to be solved to estimate the full model.

In their empirical application, ENR90 use data on monthly returns on US Treasury bills and on the value-weighted index of NYSE and AMEX stocks from August 1964 to November 1985. The one-month T-bill rate is taken as the riskless return, and the FACTOR-ARCH model is used to model the excess returns on the two- to twelve-month T-bills using an equally weighted portfolio of all T-bills and the stock market portfolio as the *a priori* chosen factor representing portfolios (i.e. $K = 2$). The first portfolio is referred to as EWB (equally-weighted bills), the second one as VWS (value-weighted stocks). The estimates in ENR90 unambiguously reveal that the risk premia and volatilities of T-bills with longer maturities are more sensitive to changes in the conditional variance of the first factor representing portfolio. The βs with respect to the VWS-portfolio tend to be insignificant, suggesting that the data-generating process might in fact be a one-factor model with EWB as the only factor. A battery of tests is used to test the model specification and generally yields results which are supporting for the model.

6.4. Concluding Remarks

Several multivariate GARCH models which can be used to model first- and second-order conditional moments have been discussed in this section. The state of the art model appears to be the FACTOR-ARCH model considered in section 6.3. This model appears to be a powerful but manageable tool. While the models in section 6.2 require high dimensional numerical optimization, the FACTOR-ARCH model can be analysed by estimating a number of relatively simple models only. Note, however, that the important problems of the choice of the number of factors and the weights of the factor-representing portfolios are not addressed by ENR90. Some hints toward possible solutions are given in the companion paper, Ng, Engle, and Rothschild (1992), which contains an application on testing for a firm size anomaly in a conditional CAPM for US stock returns.

7. Conclusions

In this chapter, models for time-varying volatility measures have been presented and their application to and relevance for the analysis of financial series have been illustrated using examples from the finance literature. In a way, GARCH models are natural extensions of ARMA schemes to describe the time dependencies in second moments of many economic series. These non-linear models are fairly easily implemented, estimated and tested. The standard apparatus of autocorrelation function analysis can be applied to the series squared and used to empirically determine the order of the GARCH process. Also these models have been found to be consistent with many stylized facts of financial series, such as fat-tailed marginal distributions and zero serial autocorrelation of a series but dependencies over time characterized by tranquil and volatile periods. Further extensions to non-parametric methods and other functional form specifications for conditional second moments of economic time series are on the research agenda in this area. More applications of the models are expected to contribute to a better understanding of the time series properties of financial and other economic series.

References

Baba, Y., Engle, R.F., Kraft, D.F. and Kroner, K.F. (1989): 'Multivariate Simultaneous Generalized ARCH', unpublished manuscript, Department of Economics, UCSD.

Baillie, R.T. and Bollerslev, T. (1989): 'The Message in Daily Exchange Rates: A Conditional-Variance Tale', *Journal of Business and Economic Statistics*, 7, 297–305.

Baillie, R.T. and Bollerslev, T. (1990): 'A Multivariate GARCH Approach to Modelling Risk Premia in Forward Exchange Rate Markets', *Journal of International Money and Finance*, 9, 309–24.

Baillie, R.T., Lippens, R.E. and McMahon, P.C. (1983): 'Testing Rational Expectations and Efficiency in the Foreign Exchange Market', *Econometrica*, 51, 553–64.

Baillie, R.T. and Myers, R.J. (1991): 'Bivariate GARCH Estimation of the Optimal Commodity Futures Hedge', *Journal of Applied Econometrics*, 6, 109–24.

Bollerslev, T. (1986): 'Generalized Autoregressive Conditional Heteroskedasticity', *Journal of Econometrics*, 31, 307–27.

Bollerslev, T. (1987): 'A Conditional Heteroskedastic Time Series Model for Speculative Prices and Rates of Return', *Review of Economics and Statistics*, 69, 542–7.

Bollerslev, T., Chou, R.Y. and Kroner, K.F. (1992): 'ARCH Modeling in Finance: A Review of the Theory and Empirical Evidence', *Journal of Econometrics*, 52, 5–59.

Bollerslev, T., Engle, R.F. and Wooldridge, J.M. (1988): 'A Capital Asset Pricing Model with Time Varying Covariances', *Journal of Political Economy*, 96, 116–31.

Bollerslev, T. and Wooldridge, J.M. (1990): 'Quasi Maximum Likelihood Estimation and Inference in Dynamic Models with Time-Varying Covariances', Nortwestern University, mimeographed.

Campbell, J.Y. (1990): 'Intertemporal Asset Pricing Without Consumption', London School of Economics, Financial Markets Group, Discussion Paper 107.

Crowder, M.J. (1976): 'Maximum Likelihood Estimation for Dependent Observations', *Journal of the Royal Statistical Society*, Series B, 38, 45–53.

Demos, A. and Sentana, E. (1990): 'Testing for GARCH effects: A One-Sided Approach', London School of Economics, manuscript.

Diebold, F.X. (1987): 'Testing for Serial Correlation in the Presence of ARCH', *Proceedings from the ASA Business and Economic Statistics Section*, 323–8.

Diebold, F.X. (1988): *Empirical Modeling of Exchange Rates*, Springer-Verlag, Berlin.

Domowitz, I. and Hakkio, C.S. (1985): 'Conditional Variance and the Risk Premium in the Foreign Exchange Market', *Journal of International Economics*, 19, 47–66.

Drost, F.C. and Nijman, Th.E. (1990): 'Temporal Aggregation of GARCH Processes', CentER discussion paper 9066, Tilburg University, forthcoming in *Econometrica*.

Engle, R.F. (1982): 'Autoregressive Conditional Heteroscedasticity with Estimates of the Variance of United Kingdom Inflation', *Econometrica*, **50**, 987–1007.

Engle, R.F. (1984): 'Wald, Likelihood Ratio and Lagrange Multiplier Tests in Econometrics', in Z. Griliches and M.D. Intriligator (eds), *Handbook of Econometrics*, North-Holland, Amsterdam.

Engle, R.F. and Bollerslev, T. (1986): 'Modeling the Persistence of Conditional Variances', *Econometric Reviews*, **5**, 1–50, 81–7.

Engle, R.F. and Gonzalez-Rivera, G. (1991): 'Semiparametric ARCH Models', *Journal of Business and Economic Statistics*, **9**, 345–60.

Engle, R.F., Lilien, D.M. and Robins, R.P. (1987): 'Estimating Time Varying Risk Premia in the Term Structure: The ARCH-M model', *Econometrica*, **55**, 391–407.

Engle, R.F., Ng, V. and Rothschild, M. (1990): 'Asset Pricing with a Factor ARCH Covariance Structure: Empirical Estimates of Treasury Bills', *Journal of Econometrics*, **45**, 213–38.

Fama, E. (1965): 'The Behaviour of Stock Market Prices', *Journal of Business*, **38**, 34–105.

Fama, E. (1984): 'Forward and Spot Exchange Rates', *Journal of Monetary Economics*, **14**, 319–38.

French, K.R., Schwert, G.W. and Stambaugh, R.F. (1987): 'Expected Stock Returns and Volatility', *Journal of Financial Economics*, **19**, 3–30.

Gallant, A.R. and Tauchen, G. (1989): 'Semi-Nonparametric Estimation of Conditionally Constrained Heterogeneous Processes: Asset Pricing Applications', *Econometrica*, **57**, 1091–120.

Giovannini, A. and Jorion, P. (1989): 'The Time Variation of Risk and Return in the Foreign Exchange and Stock Markets', *Journal of Finance*, **44**, 307–25.

Gouriéroux, C., Monfort, A. and Trognon, A. (1984): 'Pseudo Maximum Likelihood Methods: Theory', *Econometrica*, **52**, 681–700.

Granger, C.W.J. and Andersen, A. (1978): *An Introduction to Bilinear Time Series Models*, Vandenhoeck and Ruprecht, Göttingen.

Hansen, L.P. and Hodrick, R.J. (1980): 'Forward Exchange Rates as Optimal Predictors of Future Spot Rates: an Econometric Analysis', *Journal of Political Economy*, **88**, 829–53.

Hansen, L.P. and Hodrick, R.J. (1983): 'Risk Averse Speculation in the Forward Foreign Exchange Market: An Econometric Analysis of Linear Models', in J.A. Frenkel (ed.), *Exchange Rates and International Macroeconomics*, University of Chicago Press.

Hodrick, R.J. (1987): *The Empirical Evidence on the Efficiency of Forward and Futures Exchange Markets*, Harwood, London.

Hodrick, R.J. (1989): 'Risk, Uncertainty and Exchange Rates', *Journal of Monetary Economics*, **23**, 433–59.

Hodrick, R.J. and Srivastava, S. (1984): 'An Investigation of Risk and Return in Forward Foreign Exchange', *Journal of International Money and Finance*, **3**, 1–29.

Hodrick, R.J. and Srivastava, S. (1986): 'The Covariation of Risk Premiums and Expected Future Spot Rates', *Journal of International Money and Finance*, **5**, 5–22.

Hsieh, D.A. (1989): 'Modeling Heteroskedasticity in Daily Foreign-Exchange Rates', *Journal of Business and Economic Statistics*, **7**, 307–17.

Jorion, P. (1988): 'On Jump Processes in Foreign Exchange and Stock Markets', *Review of Financial Studies*, **1**, 427–45.

Kodde, D.A. and Palm, F.C. (1986): 'Wald Criteria for Jointly Testing Equality and Inequality Restrictions', *Econometrica*, **54**, 1243–8.

Lucas, R.E. Jr. (1982): 'Interest Rates and Currency Prices in a Two Country World', *Journal of Monetary Economics*, **10**, 335–60.

Lumsdaine, R.L. (1990): 'Asymptotic Properties of the Maximum Likelihood Estimator in GARCH(1, 1) and IGARCH(1, 1) Models', unpublished manuscript, Department of Economics, Harvard University.

Nelson, D.B. (1990): 'ARCH Models as Diffusion Approximations', *Journal of Econometrics*, **45**, 7–38.

Nelson, D.B. (1991): 'Conditional Heteroskedasticity in Asset Returns: a New Approach', *Econometrica*, **59**, 347–70.

Ng, V., Engle, R.F. and Rothschild, M. (1992): 'A Multi-Dynamic-Factor Model for Stock Returns', *Journal of Econometrics*, **52**, 245–66.

Nieuwland, F.G.M.C., Verschoor, W.F.C. and Wolff, C.C.P. (1991): 'EMS Exchange Rates', *Journal of International Financial Markets, Institutions and Money*, **2**, 21–42.

Nijman, Th.E. (1990): 'Estimation of Models Containing Unobserved Rational Expectations', in F. van der Ploeg (ed.), *Advanced Lectures in Quantitative Economics*, Academic Press London, pp. 501–30.

Nijman, Th.E. and Beetsma, R. (1991): 'Empirical Tests of a Simple Pricing Model for Sugar Futures', *Annales d'Economie et de Statistique*, **24**, 121–31.

Nijman, Th.E. and Palm, F.C. (1991): 'Generalized Least Squares Estimation of Linear Models Containing Rational Future Expectations', *International Economic Review*, **32**, 383–90.

Nijman, Th.E., Palm, F.C. and Wolff, C.C.P. (1991): 'Premia in Forward Foreign Exchange as Unobserved Components', CentER discussion paper 9112, Tilburg University, forthcoming in *Journal of Business and Economic Statistics*.

Pagan, A.R. and Ullah, A. (1988): 'The Econometric Analysis of Models with Risk Terms', *Journal of Applied Econometrics*, **3**, 87–105.

Pagan, A.R. and Hong, Y.S. (1990): 'Non-Parametric Estimation and the Risk Premium', in W. Barnett, J. Powell, and G. Tauchen (eds), *Semiparametric Estimation and Nonparametric Methods in Econometrics and Statistics*, Cambridge University Press, Cambridge.

Pagan, A.R. and Schwert, G.W. (1990): 'Alternative Models for Conditional Stock Volatility', *Journal of Econometrics*, **45**, 267–90.

Schwert, G.W. (1989): 'Why Does the Stock Market Volatility Change Over Time', *Journal of Finance*, **44**, 1115–53.

Sentana, E. and Wadhwani, S. (1989): 'Semi-Parametric Estimation and the Predictability of Stock Market Returns: Some Lessons From Japan', *Review of Economic Studies*, **58**, 3, 547–64.

Weiss, A.A. (1986a): 'ARCH and Bilinear Time Series Models: Comparison and Combination', *Journal of Business and Economic Statistics*, **4**, 59–70.

Weiss, A.A. (1986b): 'Asymptotic Theory for ARCH Models: Estimation and Testing', *Econometric Theory*, **2**, 107–31.

White, H. (1980): 'A Heteroskedasticity Consistent Covariance Matrix Estimator and a Direct Test for Heteroskedasticity', *Econometrica*, **48**, 817–38.

Wolff, C.C.P. (1987): 'Forward Foreign Exchange Rates, Expected Spot Rates and Premia: A Signal Extraction Approach', *Journal of Finance*, **42**, 2, 395–406.

6

Empirical Analysis of Time Series: Illustrations with Simulated Data*

Grayham E. Mizon

Southampton University
and
European University Institute

1. Introduction

The theme of the lectures on which this chapter draws was practical econometric modelling with time series data. The aim was to use a mixture of real and simulated data to illustrate some of the difficult problems that face the applied econometrician, and to indicate methods by which they might be overcome. The approach adopted has been made possible by the availability of powerful personal computers, and the development of sophisticated econometric software packages such as *PC GIVE*, *PC FIML*, *PC ASYMP* and *PC NAIVE*. The same approach is adopted in this chapter, and in addition emphasis is placed on the value of simulated data for analysing the relationship between data generation processes (DGPs) and particular models of the data. In particular, knowledge of the DGP enables the derivation of the properties of statistics of interest, such as estimators, and test statistics for specification and misspecification hypotheses (see Mizon (1977)), for any model of the generated data. This argument is then extended to show that a congruent general model of the data available for modelling has an analogous role to that of the unknown DGP. This has implications for the choice of

---

*This chapter is based on material used in lectures presented to the meeting of the Network Quantitative Economics held in Leiden, The Netherlands, February 1989. I am grateful to Aart de Zeeuw for his skill in organizing the Network meeting in Leiden, and for his patience whilst editing this volume. *PC GIVE* (see Hendry (1989)) was used for the econometric analysis of data, and the simulated data were generated using *PC NAIVE* (see Hendry, Neale, and Ericsson (1990)), which was also used for the Monte Carlo analysis reported. The financial support of the ESRC under grant B01250024 is gratefully acknowledged.

modelling strategy, and in particular indicates the importance of congruence and encompassing as critical properties for models to possess. This analysis using simulated data is an illustration of the huge potential value in teaching Monte Carlo simulation which programs such as *PC NAIVE* have.

The next section discusses model congruence, concentrating on the development of models that are data admissible, and in particular consistent with the time series properties of the data. Section 3 uses examples to illustrate that it is possible for a model to be congruent with its own information set, but nonetheless statistically inadequate, in that it cannot encompass rival models. Section 4 contains conclusions.

2. Congruence and the Time Series Properties of Data: Data Admissibility

The importance in econometric modelling of developing models that are congruent with all the available information is now well documented (see, *inter alia*, Hendry and Richard (1982, 1983), Hendry (1987), Hendry and Mizon (1990), Mizon (1989, 1991b), and Spanos (1989)), and so will not be discussed at length here. Briefly, models that are not congruent are by definition failing to exploit available information which would improve their performance, whether this be in their goodness of fit, forecasting ability, *a priori* theory consistency, or policy analysis. Hence, a non-congruent model can be improved from information already available, and a scientific approach to modelling suggests that it should be so improved, rather than left in its present inadequate state. In fact, the value of seeking to develop congruent models has been indicated in many empirical pieces in recent years (e.g. Ahumada (1992), Bårdsen (1992), Clements and Mizon (1991), Hendry and Ericsson (1991a, 1991b), Johansen and Juselius (1990), Nyomen (1992), and Spanos (1990)).

One source of information with which it is important to have models coherent is the measurement system, and in particular the properties of the sample data being used. To use a well known example, the linear regression model $y_t = \beta x_t + u_t$ with u_t assumed to be symmetrically distributed around zero (e.g. $u_t \sim NI(0, \sigma^2)$) is not congruent with a known property of the data when y_t is a probability and thus satisfies $0 \leqslant y_t \leqslant 1$, in that fitted and predicted values of y_t from this model can lie outside this range. Note that the problem arises from specifying the statistical properties of the model via the unknown and unobservable error u_t, rather than specifying an appropriate distribution for the observed regressand y_t. Similar examples arise if the same linear regression model is used for modelling aggregate consumption expenditure ($0 \leqslant y_t$), or the rate of unemployment ($0\% \leqslant y_t \leqslant 100\%$). In the modelling of financial data it is equally important to use models that are capable of capturing the 'stylized facts' of such data, namely unimodal densities with fat tails, and usually a higher mode than that of an ARCH process—see Pagan (1991). When modelling time series variables it is equally important that the class of model chosen for the analysis is capable of being congruent with the time series properties of the data. For example, the above linear regression model would again be non-congruent if y_t was temporally dependent but x_t was not, for in such a case u_t will be serially correlated and this implies that it contains valuable information for the modelling of y_t (namely y_{t-1}, $y_{t-2}, \ldots$) which is being unexploited. Note that in this example even if the parameter of interest is $\partial y_t / \partial x_t = dy_t / dx_t$ in the distribution of y_t conditional only on x_t, OLS estimation of this parameter will be inefficient since it ignores the fact that the variance and autocovariances of u_t depend on this same parameter!

To argue in this case that since the OLS estimator is consistent there is no serious problem arising from ignoring the serial correlation in u_t seems inappropriate as the results set out in Table 1 (which are explained in detail later in the section) using simulated data show. The OLS estimate of β using this simulated data, at 1.0245, is larger than might be expected for an unbiased estimator of the population parameter value of 0.9. However, its standard error at 0.0811 is 84 per cent larger than that associated with the efficient OLS estimator which regresses y_t on x_t and y_{t-1}, and slightly larger than its population value for a sample of size 100 (namely 0.072). Note that in this case reacting to the low Durbin Watson test statistic when y_t is regressed on x_t alone (DW = 0.915), by re-estimating using autoregressive least squares (RALS), is also inappropriate since it yields an inconsistent ($\hat{\beta} = 0.7413$) and imprecise (SE($\hat{\beta}$) = 0.0533) estimate of β. Hence although the non-congruent (u_t is serially correlated) model which regresses y_t on x_t alone yields an unbiased estimator of β (though it is 13.8 per cent above the population value for this particular replication), there is a strong case for correctly identifying the cause of the serial correlation, so that β can be estimated consistently and efficiently by exploiting all the available relevant information. Note that introducing the

Table 1: Results using simulated data from replication 1000.

	DGP value	Inefficient OLS estimate	Efficient OLS estimate	RALS
β	0.9	1.0245	0.9520	0.7413
SE($\hat{\beta}_1$)	0.072	0.0811	na	na
SE($\hat{\beta}_2$)	0.044	na	0.0456	0.0533
α	0.5	0.0	0.5174	0.7069
SE($\hat{\alpha}$)	0.038	na	0.0350	0.0732
DW_1	1.0	0.915	na	na
DW_2	2.0	na	1.80	na
R_1^2	0.6075	0.619	na	na
R_2^2	0.8575	na	0.884	na
σ_u	0.723	0.794	na	na
σ_v	0.436	na	0.444	na
σ_ξ	0.627	na	na	0.6045

(na = not applicable).

assumption that $u_t = \alpha u_{t-1} + \xi_t$ does not yield a congruent model or a good estimator of β, for although ξ_t is white noise it is not an innovation with respect to the information set containing x_t, x_{t-1}, and y_{t-1}. These empirical results using the simulated data from replication 1000, which illustrate the importance of developing models that are congruent with the properties of the data, are shown at the end of this section to be reliable and expected by analysing the results of all 1000 replications in a Monte Carlo study. Mizon (1992) contains more detailed analysis of this example.

If it is important to develop models that are congruent with the properties of the data (data admissible), it is equally important to be able to determine what these properties are. One obvious way to identify the essential characteristics of a time series variable is to inspect its time plot or graph. Figure 1 gives the time plots of 200 realizations, generated by *PC NAIVE*, from nine of the basic time series processes. The first three are stationary processes: white noise ($\epsilon_t \sim NI(0, 1)$, with each of the following ϵ_{it} being independent white noise variables), a first-order moving average ($x_t = \epsilon_{1t} + \theta\epsilon_{1t-1}$, $\theta = 0.9$), a stationary first-order autoregression ($y_t = \rho y_{t-1} + \epsilon_{2t}$, $\rho = 0.9$). The remaining five are non-stationary processes: a random walk ($\Delta w_t = \epsilon_{3t}$), a random walk with drift ($\Delta d_t = \delta_1 + \epsilon_{4t}$, $\delta_1 = 0.1$), a trend stationary process ($z_t = \delta_2 t + \epsilon_{5t}$, $\delta_2 = 0.1$), a second-order autoregressive conditional heteroskedastic process ($a_t \mid \epsilon_{6t-1}, \epsilon_{6t-2} \sim N(0, h_t^2)$ with $h_t^2 = (1 - \alpha)/\sigma + 0.33(2\alpha\epsilon_{6t-1}^2 + \alpha\epsilon_{6t-2}^2)$ when $\alpha = 0.5$ and $\sigma = 1$), and two random walks with trend ($\Delta\tau_{1t} = \delta_3 t + \epsilon_{7t}$, with $\delta_3 = 0.1$ and $\Delta\tau_{2t} = \delta_3 t + \epsilon_{8t}$, with $\delta_3 = 0.005$) respectively. The distinguishing feature of a stationary process is the constancy of its first and second moments over time (weak or wide sense stationarity), whereas non-stationary processes have time-dependent moments. The three stationary processes have zero means and bounded variances, though inspection of the ordinates of the first three graphs in Fig. 1 shows that the variability increases from white noise ($V(\epsilon_t) = 1.0$ so that approximately 95 per cent of the realizations will be within $[-1.96, +1.96]$), to moving average ($V(x_t) = V(\epsilon_{1t}) \times (1 + \theta^2) = 1.81$ so that approximately 95 per cent of the realizations will be within $[-2.64, +2.64]$), and finally the first-order autoregression ($V(y_t) = V(\epsilon_{2t})/(1 - \rho^2) = 5.263$ so that approximately 95 per cent of the realizations will be within $[-4.50, +4.50]$). This is information that the frequency plot option in *PC GIVE* will reveal, as well as indicating the normal kurtosis (i.e. without fat tails or excess concentration of values around the mean) and the symmetrical distribution of each of these variables around their means of zero. The other feature which distinguishes these three stationary processes is their correlograms. Defining the kth order serial correlation coefficient for a stationary random variable η_t as $\rho_k(\eta_t) = \gamma_k(\eta_t)/\gamma_0(\eta_t)$ with $\gamma_k(\eta_t) = E\{(\eta_t - \mu)(\eta_{t-k} - \mu)\}$ and $\mu = E(\eta_t) = E(\eta_{t-k})$, it follows that $\rho_k(\epsilon_t) = 0 \ \forall k$, $\rho_1(x_t) = \theta/(1 + \theta^2) = 0.497$, $\rho_k(x_t) = 0$ for $k > 1$, and $\rho_k(y_t) = \rho^k = 0.9^k \ \forall k$. Hence, inspection of correlograms is a good way to assess whether a stationary time series variable is dependent or not, and if it is dependent whether it is of the moving average or autoregressive type, or combines features of both (ARMA). The Data Description option in

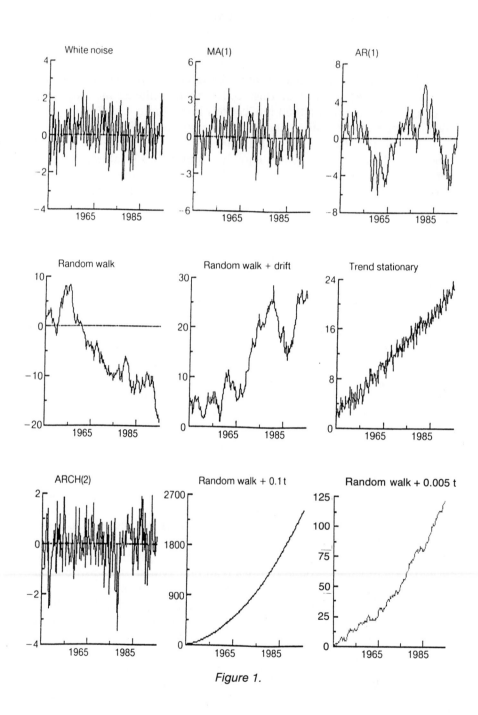

Figure 1.

PC GIVE can be used to inspect the correlograms of the series being analysed in practice.

The moments of non-stationary processes can vary deterministically (e.g. as a function of trend or other deterministic shift variables), or can vary stochastically as in integrated processes which can be differenced to become stationary. Graphs 4, 5, 8 and 9 of Fig. 1 are of variables that have unit roots, and so have 'stochastic trend' or 'trend in variance' which is evident in their time plots. In fact, graph 4 gives the time plot of the random walk $w_t = w_0 + \Sigma^t_{i=1} \epsilon_{3i}$ which is dominated by the partial sum $\Sigma^t_{i=1} \epsilon_{3i}$ that has mean of zero but unconditional variance of $\sigma^2_{\epsilon_3} t$ thus giving rise to the 'erratic' behaviour of w_t. Graph 5 provides the time plot of the random walk with drift variable $d_t = d_0 + \delta_1 t + \Sigma^t_{i=1} \epsilon_{4i}$, which for small enough $\delta_1/\sigma_{\epsilon_4}$ will behave like the random walk w_t, but when $\delta_1/\sigma_{\epsilon_4}$ is large enough, d_t will be dominated by the deterministic trend $\delta_1 t$ and so behave like a trend stationary variable, an example of which is given by the time plot of z_t in graph 6. The importance of the magnitude of $\delta_1/\sigma_{\epsilon_4}$ in determining the distribution of least squares estimators involving variables like d_t is emphasised in Hylleberg and Mizon (1989b). In particular, whilst the limiting distribution of OLS estimators involving variables like d_t is normal (see West (1988)), in small samples the empirical distribution of the OLS estimator can be closer to the Dickey–Fuller distribution than the normal. Each of w_t, d_t, and z_t is $I(0)$ when differenced once, though the non-stationarity in z_t derives from $\delta_1 t$ and so detrending, rather than differencing, is the appropriate transformation of z_t to achieve stationarity. In fact, $\Delta z_t = \delta_2 + \Delta \epsilon_{5t}$ so that the transformed error is a first-order moving average with a unit root, which implies that it cannot be inverted into a finite-order autoregression (non-invertible), and that its serial correlation coefficient (which is also that of Δz_t) is $\theta/(1 + \theta^2) = -0.5$ for the redundant unit root $\theta = -1$. Hence, one way to spot over-differencing is to inspect the correlogram of a variable for a first-order serial correlation coefficient of -0.5 and a flat correlogram otherwise. This latter comment, however, should not be interpreted as implying that it is easy to distinguish between deterministically non-stationary variables (e.g. z_t) and stochastically non-stationary variables (e.g. w_t and d_t)—see Hendry and Neale (1991), Perron (1989), and Rappaport and Reichlin (1989) for more discussion of this point.

Another case in which it can be difficult to distinguish between a stochastically non-stationary variable and a deterministically non-stationary variable is illustrated by the random walks with trend τ_{1t} and τ_{2t} which have the form $\tau_t = \tau_0 + 0.5\delta_3 t(t + 1) + \Sigma^t_{i=1} \epsilon_i$ so that they are dominated by quadratic trend when δ_3/σ_ϵ is sufficiently large. Graph 8 of Fig. 1 shows τ_{1t} dominated by quadratic trend when $\delta_3/\sigma_\epsilon = 0.1$, whereas graph 9 shows τ_{2t} to reflect both the stochastic non-stationarity in the partial sum $\Sigma^t_{i=1} \epsilon_{8i}$ and the deterministic non-stationarity in $\delta_3 t(t + 1)$ when $\delta_3/\sigma_\epsilon = 0.005$. Note that both $\Delta \tau_{1t}$ and $\Delta \tau_{2t}$ are still non-stationary, but that $\Delta^2 \tau_{1t}$ and $\Delta^2 \tau_{2t}$, although being stationary, have been overdifferenced so that they are non-invertible first-order moving averages.

Each of the non-stationary variables that have been considered above have empirical correlograms which reveal the failure of $\rho_k(\eta_t)$ to approach zero as k increases (when $\rho_k(\eta_t) = \gamma_k(\eta_t)/\gamma_0(\eta_t)$ with $\gamma_k(\eta_t) = E\{(\eta_t - E(\eta_t))(\eta_{t-k} - E(\eta_{t-k}))\}$). Indeed, $\rho_k(\eta_t)^2 \simeq (t-k)^2/t(t-k)$ which is close to unity for t large relative to k. Hence the correlogram is useful for distinguishing stationary from non-stationary variables, but other means will have to be used to attempt to distinguish between the different forms of non-stationary process, such as inspection of the correlograms for different orders of differencing applied to the variables, remembering that over-differencing results in a variable with a first-order serial correlation coefficient of -0.5.

Despite the difficulty of distinguishing between deterministic and stochastic non-stationarity, a popular and important way to attempt to determine whether a variable is non-stationary is to use unit root test statistics. Table 2 provides values of some of the commonly used test statistics for the nine 'typical' time series variables and differences of some of them. For the generic time series variable ϕ_t, the particular test statistics reported are:

(i) $DW = \Sigma_{t=2}^{T}(\Delta\phi_t)^2/\Sigma_{t=1}^{T}(\phi_t - \bar{\phi})^2$ which was proposed by Sargan and Bhargava (1983) as a test for a unit root in the $\{\phi_t\}$ process, and takes values close to zero when there is a unit root;

(ii) DF which is the 't' statistic for the hypothesis $\delta = 0$ in the regression $\Delta\phi_t = c_0 + \delta\phi_{t-1} + \zeta_t$ which was shown by Dickey and Fuller (1979, 1981) to have a non-standard distribution when $\delta = 0$, critical values for which they tabulated using simulation. In testing the unit root hypothesis against stationary alternatives, $\delta = 0$ is rejected when the 't' statistic is significantly negative;

Table 2:   Unit root test statistics.

Variable	DW	DF	ADF	DF + t	ADF + t
ϵ_t	1.874*	−13.179*	−9.176*	nc	nc
x_t	0.908*	−7.613*	−9.768*	nc	nc
y_t	0.194	−3.009	−2.733	nc	nc
Δy_t	2.193*	−15.430*	−10.877*	nc	nc
w_t	0.023	−0.143	−0.055	−2.651	−2.548
Δw_t	2.080*	−14.644*	−10.877*	nc	nc
d_t	0.018	−0.586	−0.595	−2.191	−2.229
Δd_t	1.982*	−13.844*	−10.424*	nc	nc
z_t	0.058	−1.630	−0.832	−14.246*	−9.567*
Δz_t	3.054*	−25.145*	−15.838*	−25.080*	−15.798*
τ_{1t}	0.0004	52.290	6.669	0.211	0.212
$\Delta \tau_{1t}$	0.051	−1.650	−1.117	−13.526*	−10.056*
$\Delta^2 \tau_{1t}$	2.912*	−23.189*	−17.235*	−23.126*	−17.187*
τ_{2t}	0.0013	3.347	2.887	−0.671	−0.830
$\Delta \tau_{2t}$	1.681*	−12.050*	−12.206*	−12.726*	−9.285*
a_t	1.660*	−11.805*	7.732*	nc	nc

(nc = not calculated; *indicates rejection of the unit root hypothesis).

(iii) ADF which is an augmented version of the test statistic in (ii), with the augmentation being the inclusion of $\Delta\phi_{t-1}$ in the regression;

(iv) DF + t which is an augmentation of (ii) including a linear trend, and so is based on the regression $\Delta\phi_t = c_0^* + \delta\phi_{t-1} + \lambda t + \zeta_t^*$;

(v) ADF + t which is an augmentation of (iii) to include a linear trend, thus being based on the regression $\Delta\phi_t = c_0^{**} + \delta\phi_{t-1} + \lambda t + \psi\Delta\phi_{t-1} + \zeta_t^{**}$.

The use of these unit root test statistics is intended to be illustrative, and it is noted that there are other test statistics which allow for more general heterogeneous and dependent error processes—see for example Phillips (1987). It is also the case that test statistics for the hypotheses that there is no intercept and/or linear trend in the ADF regressions can reveal important information, and so are potentially of value. However, these test statistics are not reported, in order not to unnecessarily complicate the presentation. For more detailed discussion of these and other tests see, for example, Banerjee *et al.* (1993).

For the three variables ϵ_t, x_t, and a_t the test statistics correctly reject the unit root hypothesis. However, the performance of the test statistics for y_t, which is generated by a first-order autoregressive process with a serial correlation coefficient of 0.9, illustrates the difficulty in discriminating between roots close to unity and unit roots. The hypothesis that y_t has two unit roots reassuringly is rejected decisively by the tests on Δy_t. The results of the DW, DF, and ADF tests for the random walk w_t and the random walk with drift d_t confirm the ability of these unit root tests to work well in situations for which they were designed. For these two variables the trend augmented DF and ADF statistics correctly fail to reject the unit root hypothesis, and correctly reject the presence of a deterministic trend, with the mirror-image property $t_{\lambda=0} = -t_{\delta=0}$ holding approximately for d_t (the DF $t_{\lambda=0} = 2.1597$ and the ADF $t_{\lambda=0} = 2.202$) but not for w_t (the DF $t_{\lambda=0} = -2.848$ and the ADF $t_{\lambda=0} = -2.772$), in accord with the results in Haldrup (1991). The performance of the DW, DF, and ADF test statistics for the trend stationary variable z_t illustrates the difficulty these tests can have in distinguishing between unit roots and deterministic trends, and further highlights the importance of using the trend-augmented ADF test statistics which correctly reject the unit root hypothesis. Note also that the inclusion of the linear trend in DF + t and ADF + t test statistics applied to Δz_t does not adversely affect their performance—they correctly reject the unit root hypothesis and have values almost identical to the corresponding test statistics without trend. It is also worth noting that in the ADF regression for z_t, the estimated coefficient of Δz_{t-1} is -0.522 (with t value of -8.55) and the estimated coefficient of z_{t-1} is -0.0123 (with a t value of -0.832), thus indicating that the differencing of z_t was inappropriate since the transformed variable Δz_t behaves like a non-invertible moving average process with a first-order serial correlation coefficient of -0.5 (NB $\Delta z_t = \delta_2 + \Delta\epsilon_{5t}$). The results of the tests for τ_{1t}, and τ_{2t} illustrate the importance of the magnitude of δ_3/σ_ϵ in determining whether deterministic or stochastic non-stationarity dominate.

For the less extreme variable τ_{2t}, for which $\delta_3/\sigma_\epsilon = 0.005$, the set of unit root test statistics reported in Table 2 correctly indicates the presence of one unit root, whether or not a linear trend is included in DF and ADF regressions. In the case of τ_{1t}, which has $\delta_3/\sigma_\epsilon = 0.1$, it is only the DF $+ t$ and ADF $+ t$ test statistics that correctly indicate the presence of one unit root and a linear trend. Without the inclusion of the linear trend the DF and ADF statistics suggest that τ_{1t} has two unit roots. All the test statistics clearly reject the hypothesis of three unit roots in τ_{1t}, as the test statistics for $\Delta^2\tau_{1t}$ show.

A number of these illustrations of the use and performance of unit root tests suggest that in practice a sensible strategy will be to include a linear trend in the Dickey–Fuller regressions, since this enables the identification of deterministic trend when it is present, and does not adversely affect the performance of the tests otherwise. Another practical suggestion for alleviating an additional problem that can arise in the use of unit root tests, is to compute DF and ADF statistics recursively, in order to check for sensitivity in the results to changes in the sample period. This can be particularly important when the series to be analysed has been affected by regime shifts or structural breaks, as is the case for many macroeconomic time series. Hendry and Mizon (1989) in analysing a small system containing money, inflation, total final expenditure, and an interest rate for the UK during the turbulent 1970s and 1980s demonstrate the value of this suggestion.

The final example of a non-stationary process is a_t, which has a constant conditional mean of zero, but has autoregressive conditional heteroskedasticity. Such processes have become very popular in the modelling of volatile data such as stock prices and other financial data which have fat-tailed distributions. Note that the results in Table 2 show that the unit root hypothesis is rejected for a_t, which is appropriate for a variable generated by an ARCH process, for although it is non-stationary, it is not integrated. These results demonstrate the power of the unit root tests to discriminate in such cases. The graph of a_t shows a number of outliers which will lie in the tails of the empirical frequency distribution, with an especially large one around 1978. In fact, one way of checking for non-constant conditional second moments is to graph the recursive standard deviation (or variance) which should be constant for a stationary series. Mizon (1991a) illustrates the use of recursive means and variances in determining the essential characteristics of data, and Pagan and Schwert (1990a, 1990b) provide more detailed discussion including the proposal of a test for the hypothesis of no change in the conditional variance. Figure 2 provides a graph of the recursive standard deviation of a_t with an initial sample of size fifty, from which it is clear that the second moment of a_t is not constant over time, with a particularly big change around 1978. However, great care needs to be exercised in interpreting such graphs, since even for stationary series there can appear to be 'clear' changes or breaks in the graph. Hence the computation of the bounds test proposed by Pagan and Schwert (1990a) is advisable. It is interesting to note that whilst a_t has a fat-tailed distribution, it does not have the height of mode relative to the range

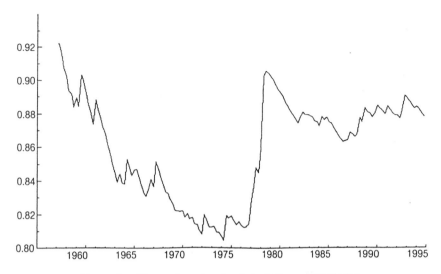

Figure 2.   Recursive standard deviation of ARCH(2).

that is typical of financial data—see Pagan (1991). A transformation of a_t that yields a leptokurtic distribution, but at the expense of introducing a positive skew, is a_t^2. These features of a variable (namely skewness, kurtosis, and the possibility of multimodality) can be examined via its empirical frequency distribution and non-parametric kernel estimates of its density. Figure 3 shows the empirical frequency distribution of a_t^2 together with a non-parametric estimate of its density using a routine of Silverman (1982, 1986). Multimodality in the frequency distribution and density estimate for a variable can result

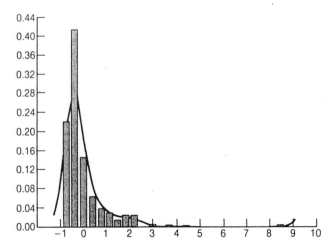

Figure 3.   Empirical frequency plot and non-parametric density estimate for ARCH(2) squared.

from changes in the unconditional mean, such as regime shifts or seasonality. The importance of, and practical difficulty in, distinguishing between stochastic and deterministic shifts in a variable was emphasized above. The fact that many economic time series exhibit seasonal characteristics is also important, and there are many models of seasonality that an investigator needs to be aware of, so that an appropriate choice can be made in the development of an overall congruent model of the variables being analysed. Hylleberg (1992) contains many seminal papers in the analysis of seasonality, and discussion of deterministic models of constant seasonality as well as stochastic seasonality such as seasonal integration and cointegration.

More detailed analysis of the properties of time series processes can be found in texts such as Granger and Newbold (1986), Fuller (1976), and Harvey (1990). Attention here has been concentrated on the use of practical ways to determine the characteristics of time series variables, since such information plays a critical role in the development of models that are congruent with available information.

As a final illustration of the importance of determining the characteristics of data to be modelled, and then ensuring that the chosen class of model is capable of representing these characteristics, consider again the modelling of y_t when the relevant data set consists of x_t and the history of both variables. The behaviour of alternative estimators of β can be assessed via a Monte Carlo study which generates y_t and x_t with the appropriate characteristics, and then computes descriptive statistics for the simulated distributions of these estimators. In fact, the sample means and sample standard deviations of the simulated distributions can be used as estimators of the corresponding population parameters. For example, the simulation sample mean of an econometric estimator of interest (calculated by averaging the value the econometric estimator takes across the Monte Carlo replications), describes the central tendency of the simulated distribution of the estimator, and also provides an estimate of the population mean of the estimator from which its population bias can be calculated. In order that y_t be temporally dependent, but x_t not, the DGP takes the form:

$$y_t = \alpha y_{t-1} + \epsilon_t \text{ with } \begin{pmatrix} \epsilon_t \\ \eta_t \end{pmatrix} \sim \mathbf{NI}\left(\begin{pmatrix} 0 \\ 0 \end{pmatrix}, \begin{pmatrix} \sigma_\epsilon^2 & \rho \\ \rho & \sigma_\eta^2 \end{pmatrix} \right)$$

$$x_t = \eta_t$$

when $\sigma_\epsilon^2 = \sigma_\eta^2 = 1$, $\alpha = 0.5$, $\rho = 0.9$, and the econometric sample size $T = 100$.

This DGP was set up in *PC NAIVE*, and then in three separate runs of *PC NAIVE* (one for each of M_1, M_2 and M_3, with the same seed for the random number generator and 1,000 replications) the results given in Table 3 were obtained. The alternative estimators considered are the OLS estimators of β in

Table 3: *Monte Carlo estimates with 1000 replications.*
(seed = 980, econometric sample size $T = 100$).

	DGP value	M_1	M_2	M_3
$\beta_{1,2,3}$	0.9	0.8996	0.8986	0.8985
$SE(\hat{\beta}_1)$	0.072	0.0723	na	na
$SE(\hat{\beta}_{2,3})$	0.044	na	0.0441	0.0443
$\alpha_{2,3}$	0.5	0.0	0.5015	0.4971
$SE(\hat{\alpha}_2)$	0.038	na	0.0385	na
$SE(\hat{\alpha}_3)$	0.060	na	na	0.0616
γ	0.0	na	na	0.0024
$SE(\hat{\gamma})$	0.070	na	na	0.0709
DW_1	1.0	1.0100	na	na
reject freq		100%	na	na
$DW_{2,3}$	2.0	na	1.9789	1.9771
reject freq		na	5.4%	2.2%
R_1^2	0.6075	0.6097	na	na
$R_{2,3}^2$	0.8575	na	0.8556	0.8570
σ_μ	0.723	0.7228	na	na
σ_ν	0.436	na	0.4366	na
σ_ω	0.436	na	na	0.4365

the following regression models:

M_1: $y_t = \beta_1 x_t + u_t$
M_2: $y_t = \beta_2 x_t + \alpha_2 y_{t-1} + v_t$
M_3: $y_t = \beta_3 x_t + \alpha_3 y_{t-1} + \gamma_3 x_{t-1} + \omega_t$

Model M_1 is non-congruent in that though y_t and x_t are related to each other, x_t (which is serially uncorrelated) cannot explain the temporal dependence in y_t, and as a result the error u_t is serially correlated. In fact, $u_t = \alpha u_{t-1} + \xi_t$ with $V(\xi_t) = \sigma_\epsilon^2 - \beta^2 \sigma_\eta^2 (1 - \alpha^2)$, and although $E(u_t \eta_t) = 0$ there is feedback from x to y in this model since $E(u_t \eta_{t-k}) = \alpha^k \beta \sigma_\eta^2$ for $k > 0$. Hence despite being unbiased, the OLS estimator of β in M_1 is inefficient, and can result in misleading inferences about β. Note in particular, that although there is essentially no bias in the estimators of β from M_1, M_2 or M_3, there is a big difference between the standard errors of the alternative estimators of β. Note also the magnitude of the Durbin Watson test statistics, and the 100 per cent rejection frequency for the null hypothesis of no serial correlation in the errors of the non-congruent model M_1.

It is straightforward in this case to calculate analytically the population parameter values for the three models, by deriving the alternative parameterizations of the DGP which relate directly to the three models:

for M_1:

$$y_t = \beta x_t + u_t \text{ with } u_t = \alpha u_{t-1} + \xi_t, \quad \begin{pmatrix} \xi_t \\ \eta_t \end{pmatrix} \sim \mathbf{NI} \left(\begin{pmatrix} 0 \\ 0 \end{pmatrix}, \begin{pmatrix} \sigma_\xi^2 & 0 \\ 0 & \sigma_\eta^2 \end{pmatrix} \right)$$

$$x_t = \eta_t$$

when $\beta = \rho/\sigma_\eta^2$, $\sigma_\xi^2 = \sigma_\epsilon^2 - \beta^2\sigma_\eta^2(1 - \alpha^2)$ and $E(u_t\eta_{t-k}) = \alpha^k\beta\sigma_\eta^2$ for $k > 0$;

for M_2:

$$y_t = \beta x_t + \alpha y_{t-1} + v_t \text{ with } \begin{pmatrix} v_t \\ \eta_t \end{pmatrix} \sim \text{NI}\left(\begin{pmatrix} 0 \\ 0 \end{pmatrix}, \begin{pmatrix} \sigma_v^2 & 0 \\ 0 & \sigma_\eta^2 \end{pmatrix} \right)$$

$$x_t = \eta_t$$

when $\beta = \rho/\sigma_\eta^2$, and $\sigma_v^2 = \sigma_\epsilon^2 - \beta^2\sigma_\eta^2$;

for M_3:

$$y_t = \beta x_t + \alpha y_{t-1} + \gamma x_{t-1} + \omega_t \text{ with } \begin{pmatrix} \omega_t \\ \eta_t \end{pmatrix} \sim \text{NI}\left(\begin{pmatrix} 0 \\ 0 \end{pmatrix}, \begin{pmatrix} \sigma_\omega^2 & 0 \\ 0 & \sigma_\eta^2 \end{pmatrix} \right)$$

$$x_t = \eta_t$$

when $\beta = \rho/\sigma_\eta^2$, $\gamma = 0$, and $\sigma_\omega^2 = \sigma_\epsilon^2 - \beta^2\sigma_\eta^2$.

However, since the DGP is linear and stationary it is possible to use *PC ASYMP* (a companion program to *PC NAIVE* for calculating the asymptotic moments and population parameters for regression models estimated by OLS or instrumental variables IV) to calculate the values of model parameters implied by the DGP. There was agreement between the analytical derivations and the calculations performed by *PC ASYMP* for these models. Note that all the Monte Carlo estimates, which are averages across the 1,000 replications for each statistic, are extremely close to the population parameter values in all cases.

3. Congruence and Encompassing

It has been argued in the previous section that it is important to develop models that are congruent with available information, otherwise misleading and/or inefficient inferences may be drawn. Of necessity, though, the available information, and especially the sample information, will be determined by choices made by the investigator. As a consequence, a model developed by a particular investigator, even if it is congruent with the information considered by the investigator, may be revealed to be inadequate relative to a larger information set that includes the data of rival models. If this is the case then the investigator's model will not be able to account for, or explain, the results of rival models, and so it will not encompass the rival models. Hence the investigator's model lacks what is an essential property of a good model, namely the ability to explain why previous models were found to perform well, and why they now are inadequate relative to it. That a model can be congruent with respect to a particular information set, and non-congruent when evaluated relative to a larger information set, is not surprising and may be thought to pose no problems since each investigator carefully chooses a relevant information set and thus does not need to consider a larger one. However, this ignores the importance of developing models that encompass rival models, and falls foul of a fundamental flaw in the approach to modelling which uses empirical evidence to confirm or corroborate theories—more than one congruent model can be developed for the same phenomenon when the congruence of each is with respect to its own information set. The disturbing implication of this result for traditional econometric modelling is that the development of a theory-consistent and data-admissible model, which has been subjected to, and has passed, a battery of diagnostic tests, does not guarantee that it is the best model currently available. Further, it makes it abundantly clear that to demonstrate that a model is theory-consistent, data-admissible, and has revealed no evidence of misspecification in diagnostic testing, is not sufficient to establish its credentials, and in particular does not raise the issue of inter-model comparison. Ericsson and Hendry (1989) present an analysis of this issue, and Mizon (1989) illustrates the nature of the problem, and demonstrates that it could occur widely in practice, by generating data so that both a monetarist and a Keynesian model of inflation (which could have very different policy implications) reveal no evidence of misspecification. It is only when each model is evaluated in the context of a larger information set which incorporates the separate information sets supporting each model, that their mutual inadequacy is found. Note also, the fact that both models are inadequate relative to the wider information set needed to support their statistical comparison, implies that the use of a selection criterion to choose one of the models (e.g. minimum mean squared error, Hannan–Quinn (1979), or Schwarz (1978)) is not a sensible way to resolve the problem of having to advise on, or implement, a policy.

To illustrate this point, consider a situation in which a large national food supplier wishes to learn more about the major determinants of the demand for its product. A consultant to the company has provided a model that is based on the premise that demand D_t is best explained in terms of the product's price P_t, and advertising expenditure A_t. The model was estimated using quarterly data on these variables for the period 1960(1) to 1989(4), with the following results:

M_1:   Modelling D_t by OLS

Variable	Coefficient	SE	HCSE	t
A_t	0.76163	0.13388	0.14799	5.6887
P_t	−1.05029	0.15577	0.13823	−6.7424
Constant	−0.05279	0.13514	0.14082	−0.3906

$R^2 = 0.4242$ $\hat{\sigma}_1 = 1.4551$ $F(2,117) = 43.10\,[0.0000]$ $DW = 2.015$
RSS = 247.7158 for 3 variables and 120 observations

Information criteria: SC = 0.844478; HQ = 0.803091; FPE = 2.17
Serial correlation tests: $\chi^2(12) = 9.0261$; $F(12,105) = 0.712\,[0.7371]$
ARCH Test: $F(1,115) = 1.07\,[0.3036]$ Normality Test: $\chi^2(2) = 0.918$
Heteroskedastic Errors Test: $F(4,112) = 1.0892\,[0.3654]$
RESET F-Test for adding $\hat{y}_t^2$: $F(1,116) = 0.713\,[0.4001]$

On the basis of these results, which have estimated coefficients with the signs expected from economic theory ($\partial D_t/\partial A_t > 0$ and $\partial D_t/\partial P_t < 0$), and have none of the diagnostic test statistics indicating any misspecification (for definitions of the test statistics, see Hendry (1989)), this model appears to be congruent and to form an adequate basis for the company to analyse the demand for its product. However, a second consultant has argued that D_t is best explained in terms of P_t, and Total Final Expenditure E_t as a measure of the strength of demand in the economy. The estimates for this model were:

M₂: Modelling D_t by OLS

Variable	Coefficient	SE	HCSE	t
E_t	0.98213	0.12075	0.11440	8.1333
P_t	− 1.07294	0.14021	0.13524	− 7.6521
Constant	− 0.11475	0.12036	0.12066	− 0.9534

$R^2 = 0.5304$ $\hat{\sigma}_2 = 1.31401$ $F(2,117) = 66.09\,[0.0000]$ DW = 1.961
RSS = 202.0145 for 3 variables and 120 observations
Information criteria: SC = 0.640535; HQ = 0.59948; FPE = 1.77
Serial correlation tests: $\chi^2(12) = 10.691$; $F(12,105) = 0.8413\,[0.6081]$
ARCH Test: $F(1,115) = 4.99\,[0.0274]$ Normality Test: $\chi^2(2) = 0.886$
Heteroskedastic Errors Test: $F(4,112) = 0.4766\,[0.7529]$
RESET F-Test for adding $\hat{y}_t^2$: $F(1,116) = 0.250\,[0.6183]$

Again these results have estimated coefficients that are significantly different from zero, and accord with the predictions of economic theory ($\partial D_t/\partial E_t > 0$ and $\partial D_t/\partial P_t < 0$), with only the ARCH diagnostic test statistic indicating the possibility of misspecification. In fact, though not shown, when both of these models are estimated by recursive least squares there is no evidence of parameter non-constancy, and so both models appear to be reasonably congruent with their respective information sets. In this situation it may seem appropriate to use a selection criterion, and on the basis of R^2, the Schwarz criterion SC, the Hannan−Quinn criterion HQ, and the final prediction error FPE, the second model is unanimously 'selected' (the model with the smallest value of the criterion function is chosen) despite the apparent ARCH effects in its residuals. However, to use a selection criterion, even when it is to select amongst models that are congruent with respect to their own information sets, ignores the possibility that there may be a better model than any of those amongst which the selection is being made, which incorporates features of some, or all, of the competing models. One of the properties of encompassing tests, since they require a common statistical distribution within which to compare the rival models, is that they have power against such alternatives. The table below provides the values of the Cox (see Cox (1961, 1962), and Pesaran (1974)) and complete parametric-encompassing CPE (see Mizon and Richard

(1986)) test statistics, from which it is seen that neither M_1 nor M_2 can encompass the other model. Further, note that although $\hat{\sigma}_2 < \hat{\sigma}_1$, there is strong rejection of the hypothesis that $M_2 \mathscr{E} M_1$, thus illustrating directly that variance dominance is necessary but not sufficient for encompassing.

Encompassing test statistics:

$M_1 \mathscr{E} M_2$	Null	Test	Null	$M_2 \mathscr{E} M_1$
− 81.377	N(0, 1)	Cox	N(0, 1)	− 37.799
81.458	F(1, 116)	CPE	F(1, 116)	45.029
[0.0000]				[0.0000]

Hence the use of a selection criterion would result in M_2 being preferred to M_1, whereas the encompassing tests reveal that both models are inadequate, in that though they each capture something of value in explaining the variation in D_t, neither dominates the other in this explanation. Despite the fact that both M_1 and M_2 were congruent with respect to their own information sets, the encompassing comparisons revealed their failure to fully exploit all the available information.

Rather than attempt to modify M_1 and M_2 until the resulting (more general) model is both congruent (with respect to a larger information set implied by the modifications), and can encompass rival models (including M_1 and M_2), it is preferable to start the modelling of D_t again from a general model that nests M_1 and M_2 and includes other potentially relevant variables. This has the advantage of avoiding the dangers of specific-to-general modelling (see, for example, Hendry (1987) and Mizon (1989, 1991b) for amplification of this point), and enables a congruent encompassing model to be found as a series of reductions from a congruent general model. In the present context it seems appropriate to consider linear models for the explanation of D_t which include A_t, E_t, P_t, and a variable C_t which measures the availability of credit, with $\partial D_t / \partial C_t > 0$ expected. The results from estimating this general model M_g are:

M_g: Modelling D_t by OLS

Variable	Coefficient	SE	HCSE	t
E_t	0.9376	0.1028	0.0928	9.118
A_t	0.6969	0.1029	0.1149	6.773
P_t	−0.9988	0.1195	0.1174	−8.357
C_t	0.1376	0.0959	0.1140	1.434
Constant	0.0072	0.1038	0.1082	0.070

$R^2 = 0.6677$ $\hat{\sigma}_g = 1.1149$ $F(4,115) = 55.77\,[0.0000]$ DW $= 2.000$
RSS $= 142.9667$ for 5 variables and 120 observations
Information criteria: SC $= 0.3746$; HQ $= 0.3056$; FPE $= 1.29$
Serial correlation tests: $\chi^2(12) = 6.943$; $F(12,103) = 0.53\,[0.8928]$
ARCH Test: $F(1,113) = 1.29\,[0.2589]$ Normality Test: $\chi^2(2) = 0.589$
Heteroskedastic Errors Test: $F(8,106) = 1.2096\,[0.3005]$
RESET F-Test for adding $\hat{y}_t^2$: $F(1,114) = 0.701\,[0.4044]$

These results for M_g indicate that each of A_t, E_t, and P_t have important roles to play in the explanation of D_t, and their estimated regression coefficients have the theoretically expected signs. Though the estimated coefficient of C_t has the expected sign, it is poorly determined and small. The model as a whole reveals no evidence of misspecification. In view of these results it is appropriate to test for simplifications or reductions of M_g, and bearing in mind the previous interest in M_1 and M_2, an obvious reduction to consider is from M_g to M_c, a completing model which nests both M_1 and M_2, but does not include C_t. When this model was estimated the following results were obtained:

M_c: Modelling D_t by OLS

Variable	Coefficient	SE	HCSE	t
E_t	0.9315	0.1032	0.0900	9.025
A_t	0.6934	0.1033	0.1111	6.710
P_t	-0.9969	0.1201	0.1102	-8.304
Constant	0.0099	0.1043	0.1055	0.095

$R^2 = 0.6618$ $\hat{\sigma}_c = 1.1201$ $F(3,116) = 75.646\,[0.0000]$ DW $= 2.04$
RSS $= 145.5247$ for 4 variables and 120 observations
Information criteria: SC $= 0.352437$; HQ $= 0.297254$; FPE $= 1.296$
Serial correlation tests: $\chi^2(12) = 8.2072$; $F(12,104) = 0.6363\,[0.8069]$
ARCH Test: $F(1,114) = 1.388\,[0.2412]$ Normality Test: $\chi^2(2) = 0.845$
Heteroskedastic Errors Test: $F(6,109) = 0.9713\,[0.4482]$
RESET F-Test for adding $\hat{y}_t^2$: $F(1,115) = 0.713\,[0.4002]$

On the basis of these results M_c is also congruent with respect to an information set which incorporates the information for both M_1 and M_2 and the extra variable C_t. The F-test for the reduction from M_g to M_c is given by $F(1,115) = 2.06\,[0.1542]$, and so the hypothesis that $M_c \, \mathcal{E}_p \, M_g$ having a p-value of 15.4 per cent, appears to be consistent with the evidence. On the other hand the F-test statistics for the reductions from M_g to M_1 ($F(2,115) = 42.13$ $[0.0000]$) and M_g to M_2 ($F(2,115) = 23.75\,[0.0000]$) mean that neither M_1 nor M_2 can parsimoniously encompass the congruent general model M_g. Indeed, the same conclusion is reached if the testing is done incrementally, that is M_c cannot be parsimoniously encompassed by either M_1 or M_2 (NB the relevant test statistics are the CPE F-test statistics reported above). In fact, the data for this example were also generated using $PC\ NAIVE$ (the seed was 282 and the data saved from replication 5), and the DGP defined by:

$$D_t = 0.5A_t + 0.9E_t - 1.0P_t + \epsilon_{1t} \qquad \text{for } t = 1, \ldots, 120$$

$$A_t = \epsilon_{2t}$$

$$E_t = \epsilon_{3t} \qquad\qquad\qquad \text{with } \epsilon_t \sim \mathbf{NI}(0, \mathbf{I}_5)$$

$$P_t = \epsilon_{4t} \qquad\qquad\qquad \text{when } \epsilon_t' = (\epsilon_{1t}, \epsilon_{2t}, \epsilon_{3t}, \epsilon_{4t}, \epsilon_{5t})$$

$$C_t = \epsilon_{5t}$$

Hence M_c corresponds to the DGP for D_t so that in the population M_c has the following properties: (i) it is congruent with respect to the information set that includes all the variables in the DGP (i.e. D_t, A_t, E_t, P_t, and C_t, and their lags); (ii) M_c is a valid reduction of M_g and so $M_c \mathcal{E}_p M_g$; and (iii) M_c automatically encompasses M_1 and M_2 and in particular can explain their misspecifications, since in this case $M_i \mathcal{E}_p M_c$ does *not* hold for $i = 1, 2$. Although these are population properties of M_c, note that in the sample of size 120 obtained from replication 5, none of these three properties was rejected. Further, these properties remained intact on average across 1,000 replications of the simulation experiment—e.g. the hypothesis $M_c \mathcal{E}_p M_g$ was rejected in only 6.5 per cent of the replications when a nominal 5 per cent critical value was used for the test. Also note that since (i) and (ii) are characteristics of the population, the test of (ii) is statistically valid. A further important point is that the Monte Carlo experiment was designed so that C_t, which is redundant for the modelling of D_t, is generated as a temporally independent standard normal variate, since M_g could not otherwise have been a congruent model. As argued in the previous section, potential regressors in a linear time series regression model must have time series properties (in isolation or in combination with other regressors) which are coherent with those of the regressand.

The example above provides a demonstration (albeit in a simple case) of the use of Monte Carlo simulation to illustrate the properties of the DGP, namely its congruence; its ability to detect and explain the misspecifications of models nested within it that are not valid reductions of it (i.e. models that cannot parsimoniously encompass the DGP); its ability to parsimoniously encompass overspecified models which are nonetheless congruent. Knowledge of the DGP, were it available, would endow a modeller with Olympian powers for model evaluation and comparison. Indeed, the DGP is a powerful metric against which to assess the performance of alternative models. Though modellers do not in practice know the DGP, by seeking models that are congruent and encompass rival models, they can hope to develop models that mimic the powerful properties of the DGP. Finally, note that whilst the DGP of a Monte Carlo simulation is fixed once chosen, the process generating observed data in the economy may change. Though this can make it more difficult for the econometrician to develop congruent (particularly with constant parameters) and encompassing models, it also can provide sufficient variability in the data for the econometrician to be able to discriminate between alternative models. For further discussion of the impact of structural change on, and the role of parameter constancy tests in, econometric modelling see *inter alia* Anderson and Mizon (1989), Engle and Hendry (1989), and Favero and Hendry (1992).

4.   Conclusions

Unless a model is congruent with available information (from all sources), the result is likely to be, at worst, that investigators who use it will make invalid or misleading inferences, poor forecasts, and consequently give inappropriate policy advice, and at least the extant potential to improve the quality and performance of the model remains unexploited. It has been argued in this chapter that in modelling it is important to develop models that are congruent and encompass rival models of the same phenomena. In modelling with time series data, an essential requirement is that models are congruent with the temporal characteristics of the data, as well as other properties of the measurement system. In section 2 advantage has been taken of the powerful personal computers and sophisticated econometric software (particularly *PC GIVE*, *PC NAIVE*, and *PC ASYMP*) to illustrate ways in which the properties of time series data can be determined. Though this is much better done in live demonstrations in the lecture hall or class room where interaction is also possible, it is hoped that this text captures some of the essence of the live performance.

By using simulated data, generated by known processes, it was possible to demonstrate the use, and assess the performance, of these methods. The methods used ranged from graphical analysis to the application of unit root tests, and all were seen to have a valuable role as well as weaknesses. It was also possible using simulated data to illustrate the fundamental flaw in using empirical evidence to confirm theories, namely that more than one congruent model can be found. Even if models are subjected to rigorous diagnostic checking with respect to their own information set, they may be unable to account for the behaviour of alternative congruent models of the same phenomena. Hence requiring a model to be congruent and encompass rival models ensures that the model is congruent with respect to an information set larger than the minimum needed to sustain itself, that is with respect to a general model that nests the competing or rival models. Another advantage accruing from the use of simulated data is that it enables a demonstration of the relationship between the DGP and models involving the generated data. In particular, the DGP is by definition congruent, it can be used to detect and explain the deficiencies in misspecified models nested within it, and it can parsimoniously encompass models more general than itself which contain redundant information. Although these are population properties of the DGP, they will also hold with sample data subject to caveats associated with sampling variability and probabilities of Type I error in hypothesis testing. Indeed, provided that the general model which nests the rival models under consideration is congruent, it will be able to mimic these powerful properties of the DGP. Therefore, a modelling strategy that aims to develop data-admissible and coherent models, that are simple and economically interpretable, as well as being able to encompass rival models, has much to recommend it. At the very least it should result in the development of a partial ordering for a set of models relevant for the study of the phenomena of interest, and that are not profligate in their use of information.

Finally, it is important to realize that although the emphasis in this chapter has been on the demonstration of particular properties and results for univariate time series and single equation econometric analysis, most of the analysis extends to multivariate modelling with suitable modification. For example, the discussion of Dickey–Fuller unit root test statistics has its parallel, for multivariate analysis, in the literature on cointegration such as the maximum likelihood analysis of Johansen (1988) and Johansen and Juselius (1990) (see also Phillips and Loretan (1991)). Similarly, the arguments about congruence and encompassing have been extended to systems of non-stationary cointegrated variables by Hendry and Mizon (1989). In addition, although all (or almost all) the properties illustrated in this chapter by using simulation and simulated data can be derived analytically, the purpose of the chapter has been to provide additional insight and understanding of these analytical results.

References

Ahumada, H. (1992): 'A Dynamic Model of the Demand for Currency: Argentina 1977–1988', forthcoming in *The Journal of Policy Modeling*, Special Issue entitled, *Cointegration, Exogeneity, and Policy Analysis*.

Anderson, G.J. and Mizon, G.E. (1989): 'What Can Statistics Contribute to the Analysis of Economic Structural Change?', chapter 1 in P. Hackl (ed.), *Statistical Analysis and Forecasting of Economic Structural Change*, Springer-Verlag, Berlin.

Banerjee, A., Dolado, J., Galbraith, J.W. and Hendry, D.F. (1993): *Equilibrium, Error-Correction and Co-integration in Econometrics*, Oxford University Press, Oxford.

Bårdsen, G. (1992): 'Dynamic Modelling of the Demand for Narrow Money in Norway', forthcoming in *The Journal of Policy Modeling*, Special Issue entitled, *Cointegration, Exogeneity, and Policy Analysis*.

Clements, M.P. and Mizon, G.E. (1991): 'Empirical Analysis of Macroeconomic Time Series: VAR and Structural Models', *European Economic Review*, **35**, 887–932.

Cox, D.R. (1961): 'Tests of Separate Families of Hypotheses', *Proceeding of the Fourth Berkeley Symposium on Mathematical Statistics and Probability*, **1**, 105–23.

Cox, D.R. (1962): 'Further Results on Tests of Separate Families of Hypotheses', *Journal of the Royal Statistical Society*, Series B, **24**, 406–24.

Dickey, D.A. and Fuller, W.A. (1979): 'Distribution of the Estimators for Autoregressive Time Series with a Unit Root', *Journal of American Statistical Association*, **74**, 427–31.

Dickey, D.A. and Fuller, W.A. (1981): 'Likelihood Ratio Statistics for Autoregressive Time Series with a Unit Root', *Econometrica*, **49**, 1057–72.

Engle, R.F. and Hendry, D.F. (1989): 'Testing Super Exogeneity and Invariance in Regression Models', forthcoming, *Journal of Econometrics*.

Ericsson, N.R. and Hendry D.F. (1989): 'Encompassing and Rational Expectations: How Sequential Corroboration Can Imply Refutation', International Finance Discussion Paper No. 354, Board of Governors of the Federal Reserve System, June 1989.

Favero, C. and Hendry, D.F. (1992): 'Testing the Lucas Critique', *Econometric Reviews*, **11**, 265–306.

Fuller, W.A. (1976): *Introduction to Statistical Time Series*, Wiley, New York.

Granger, C.W.J. (ed.) (1990): *Modelling Economic Series. Readings in Econometric Methodology*, Oxford University Press, Oxford.

Granger, C.W.J. and Newbold, P. (1986): *Forecasting Economic Time Series*, second edition, Academic Press, Orlando.

Haldrup, N. (1991): 'A Note on the Dickey–Fuller Regression with a Maintained Trend', Institute of Economics, Aarhus University, Memo No 1991-30.

Hannan, E.J. and Quinn, B.G. (1979): 'The Determination of the Order of an Autoregression', *Journal of the Royal Statistical Society*, Series B, **41**, 190–5.

Harvey, A.C. (1990): *The Econometric Analysis of Time Series*, 2nd edn, Philip Allan, Hemel Hempstead.

Hendry, D.F. (1987): 'Econometric Methodology: A Personal Perspective', Chapter 10 in T.F. Bewley (ed.), *Advances in Econometrics*. Cambridge University Press, Cambridge, pp. 29–48.

Hendry, D.F. (1989): *PC-GIVE: An Interactive Econometric Modelling System*, Oxford Institute of Economics and Statistics, Oxford.

Hendry, D.F. and Ericsson, N.R. (1991a): 'An Econometric Analysis of UK Money Demand in *Monetary Trends in the United States and the United Kingdom* by Milton Friedman and Anna Schwartz', *American Economic Review*, **81**, 8–38.

Hendry, D.F. and Ericsson, N.R. (1991b): 'Modeling the Demand for Narrow Money in the United Kingdom and the United States', *European Economic Review*, **35**, 833–86.

Hendry, D.F. and Mizon, G.E. (1990): 'Procrustean Econometrics: Or Stretching and Squeezing Data', pp. 121–36 in Granger, C.W.J. *op cit*.

Hendry, D.F. and Mizon, G.E. (1989): 'Evaluating Dynamic Econometric Models by Encompassing the VAR', forthcoming in P.C.B. Phillips (ed.), *Models, Methods, and Application of Econometrics. Essays in Honor of Rex Bergstrom*, Basil Blackwell, Oxford.

Hendry, D.F., Neale, A.J. and Ericsson, N.R. (1990): *PC NAIVE: An Interactive Program for Monte Carlo Experimentation in Econometrics*, Oxford Institute of Economics and Statistics, Oxford.

Hendry, D.F. and Neale, A.J. (1991): 'A Monte Carlo Study of the Effects of Structural Breaks on Tests for Unit Roots', in P. Hackl and A. H. Westlund (eds), *Economic Structural Change: Analysis and Forecasting*, Springer Verlag, Berlin, pp. 95–119.

Hendry, D.F. and Richard, J-F. (1982): 'On the Formulation of Empirical Models in Dynamic Econometrics', *Journal of Econometrics*, **20**, 3–33.

Hendry, D.F. and Richard, J-F. (1983): 'The Econometric Analysis of Economic Time Series', *International Statistical Review*, **51**, 111–63.

Hendry, D.F. and Richard, J-F. (1989): 'Recent Developments in the Theory of Encompassing', in B. Cornet and H. Tulkens (eds), *Contributions to Operations Research and Econometrics. The Twentieth Anniversary of CORE*, MIT Press, Cambridge, Mass. pp. 393–440.

Hylleberg, S. (ed.) (1992): *Modelling Seasonality*, Oxford University Press, Oxford.

Hylleberg, S. and Mizon, G.E. (1989a): 'Cointegration and error correction mechanisms', *Economic Journal*, (Conference Supplement), **99**, 113–25.

Hylleberg, S. and Mizon, G.E. (1989b): 'A Note on the Distribution of the Least Squares Estimator of a Random Walk With Drift', *Economics Letters*, **29**, 225–30.

Johansen, S. (1988): 'Statistical Analysis of Cointegration Vectors', *Journal of Economic Dynamics and Control*, **12**, 231–54.

Johansen, S. and Juselius, K. (1990): 'Maximum Likelihood Estimation and Inference on Cointegration—With Applications to the Demand for Money', *Oxford Bulletin of Economics and Statistics*, **52**, 169–210.

Mizon, G.E. (1977): 'Inferential Procedures in Nonlinear Models: An Application in a UK Cross Sectional Study of Factor Substitution and Returns to Scale', *Econometrica*, **45**, 1221–42.

Mizon, G.E. (1984): 'The Encompassing Approach in Econometrics', in D.F. Hendry and K.F. Wallis (eds), *Econometrics and Quantitative Economics*, Basil Blackwell, Oxford, pp. 135–172.

Mizon, G.E. (1989): 'The Role of Econometric Modelling in Economic Analysis', *Revista Espanola de Economia*, **6**, 167–91.

Mizon, G.E. (1991a): 'Modelling Relative Price Variability and Aggregate Inflation in the United Kingdom', *Scandinavian Journal of Economics*, **93**, 189–211.

Mizon, G.E. (1991b): 'The Role of Measurement and Testing in Economics', chapter 28 in D. Greenaway, M. Bleaney and I. Stewart (eds), *Companion to Contemporary Economic Thought*, Routledge, London, pp. 574–92.

Mizon, G.E. (1992): 'A Simple Message for "Autocorrelation-Correctors": Don't', paper presented to the GREQE Workshop on 'Bayesian and Classical Econometric Modelling of Time Series', June 1992.

Mizon, G.E. and Richard, J-F. (1986): 'The Encompassing Principle and its Application to Non-Nested Hypothesis Tests', *Econometrica*, **54**, 657–78.

Nyomen, R. (1992): 'Finnish Manufacturing Wages 1960–1987: Real Wage Flexibility and Hysteresis', forthcoming in *The Journal of Policy Modeling*, Special Issue entitled, *Cointegration, Exogeneity, and Policy Analysis*.

Pagan, A.R. (1991): 'The Econometrics of Financial Markets', CIDE Lecture Notes, Santa Sofia, Italy, June 1991.

Pagan, A.R. and Schwert, G.W. (1990a): 'Alternative Models for Conditional Stock Volatility', *Journal of Econometrics*, **45**, 267–90.

Pagan, A.R. and Schwert, G.W. (1990b): 'Testing for Covariance Stationarity in Stock Market Data', *Economics Letters*, **33**, 165–70.

Perron, P. (1989): 'The Great Crash, the Oil Shock, and the Unit Root Hypothesis', *Econometrica*, **57**, 1361–401.

Pesaran, M.H. (1974): 'On the General Problem of Model Selection', *Review of Economic Studies*, **41**, 153–71.

Phillips, P.C.B. (1987): 'Time Series Regression With a Unit Root', *Econometrica*, **55**, 277–301.

Phillips, P.C.B. and Loretan, M. (1991): 'Estimating Long Run Economic Equilibria', *Review of Economic Studies*, **58**, 407–36.

Rappaport, P. and Reichlin, L. (1989): 'Segmented Trends and Non-Stationary Time Series', *Economic Journal*, (Conference Supplement), **99**, 168–77.

Sargan, J.D. and Bhargava, A. (1983): 'Testing Residuals from Least Squares Regression for Being Generated by the Gaussian Random Walk', *Econometrica*, **51**, 153–174.

Schwarz, G. (1978): 'Estimating the Dimension of a Model', *Annals of Statistics*, **6**, 461–64.

Silverman, B.W. (1982): 'Kernel Density Estimation Using the Fast Fourier Transform', *Applied Statistics*, **31**, 93–9.

Silverman, B.W. (1986): *Density Estimation for Statistics and Data Analysis*, Chapman & Hall, London.

Spanos, A. (1989): 'The Early Empirical Findings on the Consumption Function: Stylized Facts or Fiction?', *Oxford Economic Papers*, **41**, 150–69.

Spanos, A. (1990): 'The Simultaneous Equations Model Revisited: Statistical Adequacy and Identification', *Journal of Econometrics*, **44**, 87–105.

West, K.D. (1988): 'Asymptotic Normality When Regressors Have a Unit Root', *Econometrica*, **56**, 1397–417.

7

Asymptotic Theory for Non-Linear Econometric Models: Estimation[*]

Alberto Holly

University of Lausanne

1. Introduction

The purpose of this chapter is to describe general conditions for the strong consistency of extremum estimators, that is estimators obtained by either maximizing or minimizing a stochastic criterion function defined over the parameter space. In other words, we shall consider estimators obtained as the solution to a stochastic optimization problem of the form

$$\min_{\theta \in \Theta} C_n(y, \theta)$$

The special cases of the maximum likelihood estimator, the so-called M-estimator, and the method of moments estimator will be considered as illustrations of some of the general results.

From a methodological point of view, most of the results derived in the econometric (and statistical) literature may be considered as extension of ideas originated either with Wald's (1949) or Cramér's (1946) proofs of the consistency of the maximum likelihood estimate.[1]

In contrast with Cramér (1946), the approach taken by Wald (see also Doob (1934) and Le Cam (1953)) make no differentiability assumptions. In this chapter, we shall present general results on the strong consistency of

---

[*] I should like to thank an anonymous referee for reading the preliminary version of this chapter and for his helpful comments towards its improvement. All errors remain my responsibility.
[1] Wald's (1949) paper is about 'weak' consistency. Wolfowitz (1949) showed that Wald actually proves strong consistency.

estimators of interest in econometrics obtained in the way described above, whose forms and proofs may be considered as modifications to the Wald (1949) and Wolfowitz (1949) arguments.

As we shall see below, it is useful to make a distinction between the case where $C_n(y, \theta)$ grows to infinity at rate n, and the case where this result does not hold. However, in both cases, there are two questions which need to be addressed for any fixed sample size n: due to the stochastic nature of the optimization problem under consideration, we have to address not only the question of existence, but also that of measurability of the solution. This last property means essentially that the estimator is a random vector, for which it makes sense to make probability statements.

Since we wish to establish properties of estimators obtained as the solution to an abstract optimization problem, it seems natural to investigate this question on the basis of general results derived in the (now extremely vast) literature on the (abstract) optimization theory.[2]

The plan of this chapter is as follows. In the following section we use the linear regression model to outline the main method of proof for non-linear econometric models. Section 3 describes the two main approaches to prove strong consistency of estimators obtained by applying the so-called M-estimation procedure in the context of non-linear models. Section 4 introduces regularity conditions on the exogenous variables. Section 5 examines the maximum likelihood estimation procedure and contains illustrative examples. Section 6 deals with the minimum distance estimation procedure and considers in detail univariate non-linear least-squares. Section 7 describes, in view of efficiency considerations, the asymptotic distribution of the so-called generalized M-estimation procedure. Sections 8 and 9 apply the theory contained in section 7 to the quasi-maximum likelihood and the generalized method of moments respectively.

2. Motivation: the Linear Regression Model

Consider the linear regression model:

$$y = Xa^0 + u^0$$

where $E(u^0) = 0$ and $V(u^0) = \sigma^{0^2} I_T$, T being the number of observations. We assume that a^0 is an element of some compact set $\mathscr{A}$.

Suppose we want to prove that the OLS estimators of a^0 and σ^{0^2} are strongly consistent estimators, without using (or in the belief that we cannot find) their explicit expression.

---

[2] From this vast literature, we made our own selection which includes Aubin (1977), Cea (1978), Ekeland and Temam (1976), Ekeland and Turnbull (1983) and Ioffe and Tihomirov (1979). It is interesting to note that the same results from optimization theory are used in some of the works in economic theory.

Let:

$$S_T(y, a) = (y - Xa)'(y - Xa)$$

The standard approach assumes that y is observed, and we derive an estimate of a^0 by minimizing $S_T(y, a)$. From now on, we shall change this point of view and regard $S_T(y, a)$ as a stochastic criterion function. To be more explicit, write:

$$S_T(y, a) = [u^0 - X(a - a^0)]'[u^0 - X(a - a^0)]$$
$$= u^{0\prime}u^0 - 2(a - a^0)'X'u^0 + (a - a^0)'X'X(a - a^0)$$

It is clear that $S_T(y, a)$, as a function of u^0 is a random variable.

It is natural to divide $S_T(y, a)$ by T and examine whether it converges (in some sense) to a limit. We have:

$$\frac{1}{T}S_T(y, a) = \frac{u^{0\prime}u^0}{T} - 2(a - a^0)'\frac{X'u^0}{T} + (a - a^0)'\frac{X'X}{T}(a - a^0)$$

At this stage, it may be useful to recall a standard Strong Law of Large Numbers (SLLN) in the context of OLS. Assume for simplicity that the u_t^0 expressions are i.i.d. $(0, \sigma^{0^2})$ and that the matrix $X'X/T$ satisfies the following regularity condition:

$$\frac{X'X}{T} \to Q \text{ as } T \to \infty \text{ where } Q \text{ is p.d.}$$

One can show that, under the above regularity conditions, we have:[3]

$$\text{aslim}\left(\frac{X'u^0}{T}\right) = 0$$

and

$$\text{aslim}\left(\frac{u^{0\prime}u^0}{T}\right) = \sigma^{0^2}$$

Note that the above results may be stated differently by saying that for almost every sequence $\{u_t^0\}$, $X'u^0/T$ converges to 0 and $u^{0\prime}u^0/T$ converges to σ^{0^2}.

---

[3] In this chapter we use the notation aslim $X_T = c$ and $X_T \xrightarrow{\text{a.s.}} c$ to mean that X_T converges almost surely (a.s.) to c.

We may now write:

$$\text{aslim}\left[\frac{1}{T} S_T(y, a)\right] = S_\infty(a, a^0)$$

where:

$$S_\infty(a, a^0) = \sigma^{0^2} + (a - a^0)' Q(a - a^0)$$

It is worth noting already at this stage that since $\mathscr{A}$ is compact, the above convergence is uniform in a, as the regularity condition does not depend on this vector. Stated differently, we have shown that $S_T(y, a)/T$ converges almost surely to $S_\infty(a, a^0)$ uniformly for all a in the regression parameters set.

We now note that $S_\infty(a, a^0)$ has a unique minimum at $a = a^0$. Heuristically, because $\hat{a}_T$ minimizes $S_T(y, a)/T$ and because $S_T(y, a)/T$ converges to $S_\infty(a, a^0)$ in the sense given above, one should expect that $\hat{a}_T$ converges almost surely to a^0.

This may be formally proved as follows. We first observe that $S_T(y, a)/T \to \infty$ as $\| a \| \to \infty$. This property of $S_T(y, a)/T$ is known in the theory of optimization as coercivity.[4] This implies that the minimum, if it exists, is not achieved at the infinity. We may therefore assume that the parameter set is a compact subset of $\mathbb{R}^K$ denoted by $\mathscr{A}$. Note that this compactness argument works because of the uniform convergence. Later on, we shall use this property in a more general setting.

Since $\mathscr{A}$ is compact, the sequence $\{\hat{a}_T\}$ has (at least one) limit point, a^l. Let $\{\hat{a}_{T_k}\}$ be any subsequence which converges to a^l. We have:

$$\frac{1}{T_k} S_{T_k}(y, \hat{a}_{T_k}) \leqslant \frac{1}{T_k} S_{T_k}(y, a) \quad \text{for all} \quad a \in \mathscr{A}$$

In particular:

$$\frac{1}{T_k} S_{T_k}(y, \hat{a}_{T_k}) \leqslant \frac{1}{T_k} S_{T_k}(y, a^0)$$

By letting $T_k \to \infty$, it is easy to see, by simple inspection, that:

$$S_\infty(a^l, a^0) \leqslant S_\infty(a^0, a^0)$$

Since a^0 is the unique value which minimizes $S_\infty(a, a^0)$, $a^l = a^0$. This implies that every subsequence $\{\hat{a}_{T_k}\}$ converges to a^0, and thus $\hat{a}_T \to a^0$ as $T \to \infty$. Since this result holds for the convergence of $S_T(y, a)/T$ in the almost sure sense, $\hat{a}_T \to a^0$ almost surely. In other words, we have proved that $\hat{a}_T$ is a strongly consistent estimator of a^0.

---

[4] Later on, we shall use this property in a more general setting.

We also have shown that:

$$\text{aslim}\left[\frac{1}{T} S_T(y, \hat{a}_T)\right] = S_\infty(a^0, a^0)$$

which we may write as:

$$\frac{1}{T} \hat{u}' \hat{u} \xrightarrow{\text{a.s.}} \sigma^{0^2} \quad \text{as} \quad T \to \infty$$

The proof we have just given will be extended later on to estimators obtained as the solution to a stochastic optimization problem, subject to regularity conditions. Before we do so, let us comment on the technical aspects of the proof we have just presented.

(i)   We have assumed that the exogenous variables satisfy the regularity condition $X'X/T \to Q$ d.p. as $T \to \infty$. This does not cover situations such as OLS applied to linear models with a time trend. We shall consider this particular situation later on.

(ii)   The compactness assumption is crucial in the proof of the result. If $\mathscr{A}$ is a closed and unbounded subset of $\mathbb{R}^K$, the coercivity property of the criteria allows us to construct a bounded subset of $\mathscr{A}$ which is now compact.

(iii)   We have used the fact that $(1/T_k)S_T(y, \hat{a}_{T_k})$ converges to $S_\infty(a^l, a^0)$. This may be decomposed as:

$$\begin{cases} \dfrac{1}{T_k} S_{T_k}(y, a) \to S_\infty(a, a^0) \\ \text{and} \\ \hat{a}_{T_k} \to a^l \end{cases} \Rightarrow \frac{1}{T_k} S_{T_k}(y, \hat{a}_{T_k}) \to S_\infty(a^l, a^0)$$

In this situation, the criteria as well as the argument are indexed by T_k. On closer examination, we see that this result is due to the continuity with respect to a of the criteria and the fact that the convergence of $S_T(y, a)/T$ to $S_\infty(a, a^0)$ is uniform with respect to a. This suggests the type of regularity conditions to impose in a more general setting.

(iv)   Finally, this proof shows that it is quite convenient to work with almost sure limit. Since $X'u^0/T$ converges for almost every sequence $\{u_t^0\}$, we first choose such a sequence and apply general properties of sequences of functions. We then conclude that, for such a sequence, $\hat{a}_T$ converges as a numerical sequence, to a^0. The almost sure convergence of $\hat{a}_T$ is due to the fact that this convergence holds for almost all sequences $\{u_t^0\}$.

3. Non-Linear Models: M-Estimation Procedure

This section deals with a general estimation procedure which consists in optimizing a general stochastic criterion function. This is known in the literature as the M-estimation procedure, the M standing for minimizing or maximizing.

Therefore, the class of methods considered in this chapter are of the form:

$$\min_{\theta \in \Theta} C_n(y, \theta)$$

Let us start with some definitions.[5] Let $(\Omega, \mathscr{A}, \mu)$ be a probability space. Any function which assumes its values in the extended domain of real numbers $\bar{R} = R \cup \{\pm \infty\}$ defined on $\Omega \times \mathbb{R}^p$ will be called an integrand. The integrands of interest are of the form $g(\omega, \theta)$ where $g(\omega, \cdot)$ is lower semi-continuous (l.s.c.) and $g(\cdot, \theta)$ is measurable. These integrands will be called 'normal' integrands.[6] A particular case frequently considered is when $g(\omega, \cdot)$ is continuous. Such a normal integrand is known as Carathéodory function.

Now assume θ is a compact subset of $\mathbb{R}^p$ and $C_n(y, \theta)$ is a normal integrand. Theorem VIII 1.2. in Ekeland and Temam (1976) (or Proposition 10 in Ioffe and Tihomirov (1979)) (known as the 'measurable selection theorem') ensures both the existence and the measurability of $\hat{\theta}_n$ (in other words, the existence of a random vector $\hat{\theta}_n$) such that:

$$C_n(y, \hat{\theta}_n) = \min_{\theta \in \Theta} C_n(y, \theta)$$

A similar result is given in Jennrich (1969) for Carathéodory functions.

The same conclusion holds if Θ is an unbounded closed subset of $\mathbb{R}^p$, and $C_n(y, \theta)$ a coercive function, that is if:

$$\lim_{\|\theta\| \to \infty} C_n(y, \theta) = +\infty$$

This can be shown by reducing the problem to the previous case. Let θ^* be an arbitrarily fixed element of Θ, and consider the subset Θ^* of Θ such that:

$$\Theta^* = \{\theta, \theta \in \Theta \quad \text{such that} \quad C_n(y, \theta) \leqslant C_n(y, \theta^*)\}$$

---

[5] The following definitions are taken from the recent literature on optimization theory. They may help the reader making a bridge between this literature and advanced econometric theory. They are also useful in a more general context of semiparametric models where the parameter space is the Cartesian product of a finite dimensional space and an infinite dimensional space.

[6] Convex normal integrands were introduced by Rockafellar (1968, 1971) and the general notion of normal integrands has been introduced by Berliocchi and Lasry (1973). A very useful alternative definition based on the concept of measurable set-valued map is given in Ioffe and Tihomirov (1979). The theory of measurable set-valued map was brought about by the requirement of optimal control theory and mathematical economics (see, for example, Hildenbrand (1974)).

One can easily see that the existence of a minimum in Θ^* is equivalent to that in Θ. The subset Θ^* is bounded. To see this, suppose Θ^* is not bounded. We can find a sequence $\{\theta_k\} \in \Theta^*$ such that $\| \theta_k \| \to \infty$. Then, by the coercivity of $C_n(y, \theta), C_n(y, \theta_k) \to \infty$, which is impossible since $\theta_k \in \Theta^*$ implies that $C_n(y, \theta_k) \leq C_n(y, \theta^*)$.

The above assumptions are in a sense a minimal set of assumptions for proving existence and measurability of estimators obtained as the solution to a stochastic optimization problem. By imposing more conditions on the criteria $C_n(y, \theta)$ we may get interesting properties of $\min_{\theta \in \Theta} C_n(y, \theta)$.

An important case is where y takes its values in a space $\mathcal{Y}$ which is not only measurable, but also a metric space. If $C_n(y, \theta)$ is a real valued function which is lower semi-continuous on the Cartesian product $Y \times \Theta$ and if Θ is a compact subset of $\mathbb{R}^p$ then $\min_{\theta \in \Theta} C_n(y, \theta)$ is a lower semi-continuous function on Y.[7] If we assume that $C_n(y, \theta)$ is continuous on $Y \times \Theta$, then $\min_{\theta \in \Theta} C_n(y, \theta)$ is a continuous function on Y.[8]

Having established existence and measurability of $\hat{\theta}_n$, we now wish to prove strong consistency of $\hat{\theta}_n$. As will be apparent from the discussion below, one has to make a distinction between situations where $C_n(y, \theta)$ grows to infinity at rate n, and the more general situation. For expository purpose we shall first consider the latter.

3.1. Consistency in the General Case

Let θ^0 denote the 'true' parameter which characterizes the probability distribution of y.

The following result which provides a criterion for strong consistency of $\hat{\theta}_n$ is given in Wu (1981). It is closely related to Wald's and Wolfowitz's proof of the strong consistency of maximum likelihood estimators.

Proposition 1

Suppose, for any $\delta > 0$

$$\liminf_{n \to \infty} \left[\inf_{\| \theta - \theta^0 \| \geq \delta} (C_n(y, \theta) - C_n(y, \theta^0)) \right] > 0 \quad \text{a.s.}$$

Then, $\hat{\theta}_n$ is a strongly consistent estimator of θ^0.

Proof:
Suppose $\hat{\theta}_n$ is not a strongly consistent estimator of θ^0 (in other words that $\hat{\theta}_n$ does not converge almost surely to θ^0). Then there exists a $\delta > 0$ such that

---

[7] This follows from a standard result in non-linear optimization theory. See, for example, Aubin (1977).
[8] This result is proved in Jennrich (1969). See also Aubin (1977).

$P\{y: \lim \sup_{n \to \infty} \|\hat{\theta}_n - \theta^0\| \geq \delta\} > 0$. It follows from the definition of $\hat{\theta}_n$ that:

$$P\left\{\lim_{n \to \infty} \inf \left[\inf_{\|\theta - \theta^0\| \geq \delta} (C_n(y, \theta) - C_n(y, \theta^0)) \leq 0\right]\right\} > 0$$

which is a contradiction.   *QED*

In practice, the difficulty in applying Proposition 1 arises from the fact that the condition to be checked does not involve the almost sure limit of $C_n(y, \theta)$ itself. It involves the comparison of $C_n(y, \theta^0)$ with infinitely many functions $C_n(y, \theta)$ in the complement in Θ of all neighbourhoods of θ^0 of the form $\{\theta: \|\theta - \theta^0\| < \delta\}$. This explains why it is important to establish results on the uniform convergence with probability one of a sequence of normal integrands $C_n(y, \theta)$. As we shall see in the next subsection, the method of proof may be much simplified when $(C_n(y, \theta) - C_n(y, \theta^0))$ diverges to infinity at rate n. When the divergence is at a rate slower than n, the method of proof is more elaborate. We shall illustrate this point in section 6 when we consider the non-linear least-squares method.

3.2. The Case of a Criterion Growing to Infinity at a Rate Equal to the Sample Size

In the case where $C_n(y, \theta)$ grows to infinity at rate n, it is possible to spell out more easily verifiable conditions on this criterion which will ensure the strong consistency of $\hat{\theta}_T$.

For simplicity we shall assume that Θ is compact. The following result, which is based on arguments contained in Jennrich, is an extension to the non-linear regression models of the proof of strong consistency for the OLS estimator given in section 1.

Proposition 2

Assume that:

(i) $C_n(y, \theta)$ is a measurable function of y for each θ in Θ and for each y a continuous function of θ (in other words, $C_n(y, \theta)$ is a Carathéodory function).

(ii) $n^{-1} C_n(y, \theta)$ converges almost surely to a limiting function $C_\infty(\theta, \theta^0)$ uniformly for all θ in Θ.

(iii) $C_\infty(\theta, \theta^0)$ has a unique minimum at $\theta = \theta^0$.

Then $\hat{\theta}_T$ is a strongly consistent estimator of θ^0.

Proof:
According to Assumption (ii), $n^{-1} C_n(y, \theta)$ converges to $C_\infty(\theta, \theta^0)$ uniformly for all θ in Θ for almost every y. Choose such a y.

Let θ^l be a limit point of the sequence $\{\hat{\theta}_n\}$, and let $\{\hat{\theta}_{n_k}\}$ be any subsequence which converges to θ^l. By the continuity of $n^{-1}C_n(y, \theta)$ and its uniform convergence to $C_\infty(\theta, \theta^0)$, $n^{-1}C_n(y, \hat{\theta}_n)$ converges to $C_\infty(\theta^l, \theta^0)$ as $n \to \infty$.
By the definition of $\hat{\theta}_{n_k}$,

$$n_k^{-1}C_{n_k}(y, \hat{\theta}_{n_k}) \leqslant n_k^{-1}C_{n_k}(y, \theta^0)$$

It follows, by letting $n_k \to \infty$, that

$$C_\infty(\theta^l, \theta^0) \leqslant C_\infty(\theta^0, \theta^0)$$

Since $C_\infty(\theta, \theta^0)$ has a unique minimum at $\theta = \theta^0$, $\theta^l = \theta^0$. Since every subsequence of $\{\theta_n\}$ converges to θ^0, $\{\hat{\theta}_n\}$ converges to θ^0.

Since this result holds for almost every y, $\theta_n \to \theta^0$ almost surely.   QED

We have already discussed the importance of the compactness assumption and of the properties of the function $C_n(y, \theta)$. Assumption (iii) is crucial in the proof of Proposition 2. We shall call it the *condition for the asymptotic identifiability of* θ^0.

It should be noted that condition (ii) assumes implicitly a stationarity assumption on the data-generating process. Below, we shall make more explicit the stationarity assumption when $C_n(y, \theta)$ depends on exogenous variables.

As will be illustrated in the examples below, verification of Assumption (iii) can be made sometimes by simple inspection of $C_\infty(\theta, \theta^0)$. The main difficulty in applying Proposition 2 is the need to verify Assumption (ii). The uniform convergence of $n^{-1}C_n(y, \theta)$ can be established by using a uniform strong law of large numbers (USLLN).

USLLNs consider sums of the form $n^{-1}\sum_{t=1}^{n}[q_t(z_t, \theta) - Eq_t(z_t, \theta)]$ where $\{z_t\}$ denotes a stochastic data-generating process that takes its values in a space $\mathcal{Z}$. A variety of USLLNs, which provide conditions under which the above sum converges to zero uniformly over the parameter space, is available. Among them, we mention Hoadley (1971), White (1980), Bierens (1981, 1984), Domowitz and White (1982), White and Domowitz (1984), Bates and White (1985), Andrews (1987) and Pötscher and Prucha (1989) (see also Newey (1987)). Choice of the appropriate result depends on assumptions about the functions $q_t(z_t, \theta)$ and on the behaviour assumed for the data process $\{z_t\}$. Specific USLLNs in the presence of exogenous variables and independent random variables have been obtained by Jennrich (1969), Malinvaud (1970), Gallant (1977), Gallant and Holly (1980), Burguete, Gallant and Souza (1982) (see also Gallant (1987)). Below, we shall explain the main ideas behind the USLLNs in the presence of exogenous variables. This may serve as an introduction to USLLNs for stochastic processes $\{z_t\}$ mentioned at the beginning of this paragraph.

4. Regularity Conditions in Presence of Exogenous Variables

In the context of OLS or GLS, the usual regularity conditions on the limiting behaviour of exogenous variables are the convergence of $X'X/T$ or $X'\Sigma^{-1}X/T$. These regularity conditions are sufficient when the exogenous variables enter linearly in $g(x_t, \theta^0)$. In general, however, non-linearity occurs not only in the parameter θ but also in the exogenous variables. The purpose of this section is to introduce a stronger regularity assumption on the exogenous variables.

To understand the regularity conditions on the exogenous variables when they are not stochastic it is useful to first present some results which are valid for i.i.d. variables (or vectors) and then introduce additional concepts which make the exogenous variables behave like i.i.d. variables.

The general results we have in mind for the case of i.i.d. variables is best presented in the framework of probability measures on separable metric spaces. We shall now briefly indicate (without proof!) some of the main concepts and results in this area which are of relevance for the strong consistency proofs. Our presentation is mainly based on the books by Parthasarathy (1967, 1977) (see also Billingsley (1968)). [9]

While doing probability theory in topological spaces in general, it is desirable to include all the topologically important sets (such as open sets, closed sets, compact sets) in the collection of all events. To this end, the definition of Borel σ-algebra of a topological space $\mathscr{X}$ is introduced. Specifically, for any topological space $\mathscr{X}$, the σ-algebra $B_{\mathscr{X}}$ generated by the class of all open subsets of $\mathscr{X}$ is called the Borel σ-algebra of $\mathscr{X}$. Any element of $B_{\mathscr{X}}$ is called a 'Borel set'. It can be shown that measures on the Borel σ-algebra of any metric space is completely determined by its values on the class of all open sets or closed sets.

In what follows, we shall concern ourselves with the properties of weak convergence of measures on separable metric spaces. We shall denote by $C(\mathscr{X})$ the space of all bounded real valued continuous functions on $\mathscr{X}$ and $\mathscr{M}_0(\mathscr{X})$ the space of all probability measures on $\mathscr{X}$.

Let $\mathscr{X}$ be a separable metric space. A sequence $\{\mu_n\}$ in $\mathscr{M}_0(\mathscr{X})$ is said to converge weakly to an element μ in $\mathscr{M}_0(\mathscr{X})$ if

$$\lim_{n \to \infty} \int f \, d\mu_n = \int f \, d\mu \quad \text{for every} \quad f \in C(\mathscr{X})$$

In such a case we write $\mu_n \Rightarrow \mu$ as $n \to \infty$.

To relate the concept of weak convergence of measures and the more familiar concept of convergence in distribution, the following result might be useful. Let μ_n, μ be probability distributions on $\mathbb{R}$ and let F_n, F be their

---

[9] The reader who is not familiar with abstract measure theory for separable metric spaces can assume without any loss that $\mathscr{X}$ is the space $\mathbb{R}$ and the measures as being Lebesgue measures on $\mathbb{R}$.

distribution functions respectively, where $n \geqslant 1$. It can be shown that $\mu_n \Rightarrow \mu$ as $n \to \infty$ if and only if $F_n(x) \to F(x)$ as $n \to \infty$ for every x which is a continuity point of F.

Most of the results presented below may be considered as generalizations of the well-known Glivenko–Cantelli Lemma which deals with so-called empiric distributions in sampling theory. At this stage it may be useful to briefly outline the proof of this Lemma. Let $(\Omega, \mathscr{A}, \mathscr{P})$ be a probability space and $\{X_n, n \geqslant 1\}$ be a sequence of i.i.d. random variables with the common distribution function F. For each n, and each $\omega \in \Omega$, let the n real numbers $\{X_j(\omega), 1 \leqslant j \leqslant n\}$ be arranged in increasing order as:

$$X_{(n1)}(\omega) \leqslant X_{(n2)}(\omega) \leqslant \cdots \leqslant X_{(nn)}(\omega)$$

We now define a discrete distribution function as follows:

$$\begin{cases} F_n(x, \omega) = 0 & \text{if } x \leqslant X_{(n1)}(\omega) \\ F_n(x, \omega) = k/n & \text{if } X_{(nk)}(\omega) < x \leqslant X_{(n,k+1)}(\omega), \qquad 1 \leqslant k \leqslant n-1 \\ F_n(x, \omega) = 1 & \text{if } x > X_{(nn)}(\omega) \end{cases}$$

In other words, for each x, $nF_n(x, \omega)$ is the number of values of j (with $1 \leqslant j \leqslant n$) for which $X_j(\omega) < x$. Again, $F_n(x, \omega)$ is the observed frequency of sample values not exceeding x. The function $F_n(\cdot, \omega)$ is called the empiric distribution function based on n samples from F.

For each x, $F_n(x, \cdot)$ is a random variable. Now, let us introduce the indicator random variables $\{\xi_j(x, \omega), j \geqslant 1\}$ as follows:

$$\xi_j(x, \omega) = \begin{cases} 1 & \text{if } X_j(\omega) < x \\ 0 & \text{if } X_j(\omega) \geqslant x \end{cases}$$

We then have:

$$F_n(x, \omega) = \frac{1}{n} \sum_{j=1}^{n} \xi_j(x, \omega)$$

Since the X_j terms are independent, the ξ_j terms are also independent. Furthermore they have the same Bernouillian distribution, taking the values 1 and 0 with probability $F(x)$ and $1 - F(x)$ respectively. Thus $E(\xi_j(x)) = F(x)$. In addition, the $\xi_j(x, \omega)$ terms are bounded random variables. Hence by Kolmogorov's strong law of large numbers,

$$F_n(x, \omega) \to F(x) \quad \text{a.s.}$$

It is interesting to note that $F_n(x, \omega)$ may be written differently. Let $\mu_n(x, \omega)$ denote the measure which has mass $1/n$ of each of the n points $\xi_j(x, \omega)$, $1 \leqslant j \leqslant n$. We have:

$$\int d\mu_n(x, \omega) = F_n(x, \omega)$$

that is:

$$\int d\mu_n(x, \omega) = \frac{1}{n} \sum_{j=1}^{n} \xi_j(x, \omega)$$

The result we have stated above may be restated as:

$$\int d\mu_n(x, \omega) \to \int d\mu(x) \quad \text{a.s.}$$

Note that this result holds for a particular value of x. Since x ranges over $\mathbb{R}$, it would be interesting to make a global statement about the functions $F_n(\cdot, \omega)$ and $F(\cdot)$. In fact, a theorem due to Glivenko and Cantelli strengthens this result by proving both convergence for all x and uniformity. The Glivenko–Cantelli Theorem may be stated as:

$$\sup_{-\infty < x < +\infty} |F_n(x, \omega) - F(x)| \to 0 \quad \text{a.s. as} \quad n \to \infty$$

The following theorem is important in view of its econometric applications. It is a slightly modified version of Theorem 1 in Jennrich (1969).

Proposition 3

Assume that $\mathscr{X}$ is a separable metric space, Θ is a compact subset of $\mathbb{R}^p$, and g is a continuous and uniformly bounded function on $\mathscr{X} \times \Theta$, i.e. there exists a constant M such that $|g(x, \theta)| \leqslant M$ for all θ in Θ and x in $\mathscr{X}$. Then:

$$\int g(x, \theta) \, d\mu_n(x) \to \int g(x, \theta) \, d\mu(x)$$

uniformly for all θ in Θ and for every sequence of measures $\{\mu_n\}$ on $\mathscr{X}$ that converges weakly to μ.

The uniformly bounded condition on g is restrictive. It is not satisfied, for example, for non-linear models in implicit form which may be written as $g(y_t, x_t, \theta^0, u_t^0) = 0$. The following result assumes a weaker pointwise boundedness condition, and can be proved by using similar arguments as in the proof of Theorem 3.2. in Rao (1962).

Proposition 4

Assume that $\mathscr{X}$ is a separable metric space, Θ is a compact subset of $\mathbb{R}^p$, and g is a continuous and pointwise bounded function on $\mathscr{X} \times \Theta$, i.e. there exists a continuous function $h(x)$ on $\mathscr{X}$ such that $|g(x, \theta)| \leqslant h(x)$ for all θ in Θ and x in $\mathscr{X}$.

Assume that $\{\mu_n\}$ is a sequence of measures on $\mathscr{X}$ such that:

(i)
$$\mu_n \Rightarrow \mu$$

(ii)
$$\int h \, d\mu_n \to \int h \, d\mu$$

Then we have:

$$\int g(x, \theta) \, d\mu_n \to \int g(x, \theta) \, d\mu$$

uniformly for all θ in Θ.

We are now in position to introduce regularity conditions which are useful in the context of non-linear econometric models. Basically, they mean that the sequence of exogenous variables $\{x_t\}$ upon which the results are conditioned behave like observations of random vectors for which Propositions 3 and 4 we have just stated are valid.

A possible approach for the regularity conditions on the exogenous variables is through the concept of Cesaro sum generator which has been introduced by Gallant and Holly (1980). A sequence $\{v_t\}$ of points from a Borel set $\mathscr{V}$ is said to be a Cesaro sum generator with respect to a probability measure ν defined on the Borel subsets of $\mathscr{V}$ and a dominating function $b(v)$ with $\int b \, d\nu < \infty$ if:

$$\frac{1}{n} \sum_{t=1}^{n} f(v_t) \to \int f(v) \, dv \quad \text{as} \quad n \to \infty$$

for every real valued, continuous function f with $|f(v)| \leqslant b(v)$.

Using the concept of a Cesaro sum generator for the sequence $\{x_t\}$, one can prove a uniform strong law of large numbers for sequences of the form $n^{-1} \sum_{t=1}^{n} g(x_t, \theta)$. For more details see Gallant and Holly (1980) and Gallant (1987, pp. 158–62).

Alternatively, one can introduce another form of regularity condition by assuming that $\{x_t\}$ is a sequence of elements of a separable metric space $\mathscr{X}$ whose empiric distribution F_n converges weakly to a distribution function F. This approach has been suggested by Jennrich (1969) and Malinvaud (1970). In that case, proofs of the uniform strong law of large numbers for sequences of the form $n^{-1} \sum_{t=1}^{n} g(x_t, \theta)$ are immediate consequences of Propositions 3 and 4. We shall illustrate this now by presenting a frequently used particular form of a strong law of large numbers for sequences of the form $n^{-1} \sum_{t=1}^{n} g(x_t, \theta) u_t^0$ where the u_t^0 terms are independent identically distributed random variables with zero mean and finite variance σ^{0^2}. The following result is a slightly modified form of Theorem 4 in Jennrich (1969).

Proposition 5

Assume that $\mathscr{X}$ is a separable metric space, Θ is a compact subset of $\mathbb{R}$, and g is a continuous function on $\mathscr{X} \times \Theta$. Assume the u_t^0 terms are independent identically distributed random variables with zero mean and finite variance σ^{0^2}.

If there exists a distribution μ on $\mathscr{X}$ such that:

$$\frac{1}{n} \sum_{t=1}^{n} g(x_t, \alpha) g(x_t, \beta) \to \int g(x, \alpha) g(x, \beta) \, d\mu(x)$$

uniformly for all α and β in Θ, then we have:

$$\frac{1}{n} \sum_{t=1}^{n} g(x_t, \theta) u_t^0 \to 0 \quad \text{a.s.}$$

uniformly for all θ in Θ.

Note that verification of the uniform convergence of $n^{-1} \sum_{t=1}^{n} g(x_t, \alpha) g(x_t, \beta)$ may be achieved through application of Propositions 3 or 4 to the function $g(x_t, \alpha) g(x_t, \beta)$ defined on $\mathscr{X} \times \Theta \times \Theta$.

Proposition 5 will be extremely useful in the context of the several estimation methods that we shall consider in the following sections.

5. Maximum Likelihood Procedure

We assume throughout this section that the observed data $\{y_t, x_t\}$, where y_t is a vector of endogenous variables and x_t a vector of exogenous variables, are generated by a non-linear (possibly linear) model. The sequence $y = \{y_t\}$ is supposed to take its values in a measurable space $\mathscr{Y}$, and the sequence $x = \{x_t\}$ is supposed to take its values in some space denoted as $\mathscr{X}$. It is assumed that we have a family of models giving for a sample size n a log-likelihood $\mathscr{L}_n(\theta)$. To avoid notational burdens, we do not always explicitly write y and x as arguments of $\mathscr{L}_n(\theta)$.

5.1. Consistency in the General Case

Let θ^0 denote the 'true' parameter which characterizes the probability distribution of y.

The following result is the specialization of Proposition 1 to the maximum likelihood procedure:

Corollary 1

Suppose, for any $\eta > 0$

$$\liminf_{n \to \infty} \left[\inf_{\|\theta - \theta^0\| \geqslant \eta} (\mathcal{L}_n(y, \delta) - \mathcal{L}_n(y, \delta^0)) \right] > 0 \quad \text{a.s.}$$

Then, $\hat{\theta}_n$ is a strongly consistent estimator of θ^0.

As already mentioned in section 3, this criterion, although quite general, may be difficult to apply, because verification of the just stated condition may be quite cumbersome.

5.2. The Case of a Criterion Growing to Infinity at a Rate Equal to the Sample Size

In the case where $\mathcal{L}_n(y, \delta)$ grows to infinity at rate n, it is possible to spell out conditions which will ensure the strong consistency of $\hat{\theta}_n$.
    We assume that the following quite general regularity conditions hold:

MLA 1 $\theta \in \Theta$ where Θ is a compact subset of $\mathbb{R}^p$.
MLA 2   For each $(\theta, x) \in \Theta \times \mathcal{X}$, $\mathcal{L}_n(\theta)$ is a measurable function of y, and for each $(y, x) \in \mathcal{Y} \times \mathcal{X}$, $\mathcal{L}_n(\theta)$ is a continuous function of θ.
MLA 3 $n^{-1}\mathcal{L}_n(\theta)$ converges almost surely to a function $\mathcal{L}_\infty(\theta, \theta^0)$ uniformly for all θ in Θ. Moreover, $\mathcal{L}_\infty(\theta, \theta^0)$ has a unique maximum at $\theta = \theta^0$.

The following result is a particular case of Proposition 2.

Corollary 2

Assume that assumptions MLA1 to MLA3 hold. Then $\hat{\theta}_n$ is a strongly consistent estimator of θ^0.

5.3. Examples

It is illuminating to consider the following examples.

Example 1   Linear Regression Model with First-Order Autocorrelated Disturbances

Consider the model:

$$y_t = x_t' a^0 + u_t^0 \qquad (y = X a^0 + u^0)$$

where:

$$u_t^0 = \rho^0 u_{t-1}^0 + v_t^0$$

and the v_t^0 terms are i.i.d. $\mathcal{N}(0, \sigma^{0^2})$.

As is well known, the maximum likelihood procedure consists in maximizing:

$$T^{-1}\mathcal{L}_T(y, a, \sigma^2, \rho) = -\tfrac{1}{2}\log(2\pi) - \tfrac{1}{2}\log \sigma^2 + \tfrac{1}{2}\log(1 - \rho^2)$$

$$-\frac{1}{2\sigma^2} (y - Xa)' V^{-1}(\rho)(y - Xa)$$

By using an appropriate law of large numbers for dependent random variables, one can show (see, for example, Dhrymes (1971, pp. 91–6)) that $T^{-1}\mathcal{L}_T(y, a, \sigma^2, \rho)$ converges almost surely, uniformly in (a, σ^2, ρ) to $\mathcal{L}_\infty$ where:

$$\mathcal{L}_\infty = -\tfrac{1}{2}\log(2\pi) - \tfrac{1}{2}\log \sigma^2 - \frac{1}{2}\frac{\sigma^{0^2}}{\sigma^2} - \frac{1}{2}\frac{\sigma^{0^2}(\rho - \rho^0)^2}{\sigma^2(1 - \rho^2)}$$

$$-\frac{1}{2\sigma^2} (a - a^0)' \left[\lim\left(\frac{1}{T} X'V^{-1}X\right)\right](a - a^0)$$

Assuming that $\lim[X'V^{-1}X/T]$ is non-singular, it is clear that $a = a^0$ and $\rho = \rho^0$ are the unique values which maximize $\mathcal{L}_\infty$. In addition, σ^{0^2} is the unique value which minimizes $\log \sigma^2 + (\sigma^{0^2}/\sigma^2)$. This shows that $\mathcal{L}_\infty$ achieves its maximum at $(a, \sigma^2, \rho) = (a^0, \sigma^{0^2}, \rho^0)$ and the strong consistency of the ML estimators of $(a^0, \sigma^{0^2}, \rho^0)$ is thus proved. A similar proof for the non-linear regression model $y_t = g_t(\theta^0) + u_t^0$ where $u_t^0 = \rho^0 u_{t-1}^0 + v_t^0$ is given in Frydman (1980).

Example 2   Maximum Likelihood Estimation of a Multivariate Non-Linear Regression Model

Consider the same multivariate non-linear model as above. Assume that the u_t^0 terms are i.i.d. $\mathcal{N}(0, \Omega^0)$. The log-likelihood function may be written as:

$$\mathcal{L}_n = -\frac{nG}{2} \log(2\pi) - \frac{n}{2} \log \det \Omega - \tfrac{1}{2} \operatorname{tr} \Omega^{-1} \sum_{t=1}^{n} u_t u_t'$$

where $u_t = y_t - g(x_t, \theta)$.

We may write:

$$\frac{1}{n} \sum_t u_t u_t' = \frac{1}{n} \sum_t u_t^0 u_t^{0\prime} + \frac{1}{n} \sum_t [g(x_t, \theta^0) - g(x_t, \theta)] u_t^{0\prime}$$

$$+ \frac{1}{n} \sum_t u_t^0 [g(x_t, \theta^0) - g(x_t, \theta)]$$

$$+ \frac{1}{n} \sum_t [g(x_t, \theta^0) - g(x_t, \theta)] [g(x_t, \theta^0) - g(x_t, \theta)]'$$

By the strong law of large numbers $n^{-1} \sum u_t^0 u_t^{0\prime}$ converges almost surely to Ω^0. In addition, assume that one is able to show that the matrix

$$\frac{1}{n} \sum_t [g(x_t, \theta^0) - g(x_t, \alpha)] [g(x_t, \theta^0) - g(x_t, \beta)]'$$

converges to the matrix

$$\int [g(x, \theta^0) - g(x, \alpha)] [g(x, \theta^0) - g(x, \beta)]' d\mu(x)$$

uniformly for all α and β in Θ. By an immediate extension to Proposition 5, this would imply that

$$\frac{1}{n} \sum [g(x_t, \theta^0) - g(x_t, \theta)] u_t^{0\prime} \to 0 \quad \text{a.s.}$$

uniformly for all θ in Θ. We thus have:

$$\frac{1}{n} \sum u_t u_t' \to \Omega^0 + \int [g(x, \theta^0) - g(x, \theta)] [g(x, \theta^0) - g(x, \theta)]' d\mu(x) \quad \text{a.s.}$$

uniformly for all θ in Θ.

We have thus shown that $n^{-1} \mathcal{L}_n$ converges almost surely to $\mathcal{L}_\infty$, uniformly for all θ in Θ, where:

$$\mathcal{L}_\infty = -\frac{G}{2} \log 2\pi - \tfrac{1}{2} \log \det \Omega$$

$$- \tfrac{1}{2} \operatorname{tr} \Omega^{-1} \left[\Omega^0 + \int [g(x, \theta^0) - g(x, \theta)] [g(x, \theta^0) - g(x, \theta)]' d\mu(x) \right]$$

If one is able to show that $g(x, \theta) = g(x, \theta^0)$ implies $\theta = \theta^0$, then

$$\operatorname{tr} \Omega^{-1} \int [g(x, \theta^0) - g(x, \theta)] [g(x, \theta^0) - g(x, \theta)]' d\mu(x)$$

has a unique minimum at $\theta = \theta^0$. In addition, one can show that $\log \det \Omega + \operatorname{tr} \Omega^{-1} \Omega^0$ has a unique minimum at $\Omega = \Omega^0$. This shows that the (non-linear) maximum likelihood estimators of θ^0 and Ω^0 are strongly consistent.

It is important to analyse the role of the normality assumption. We used it *only* to write down the expression for the likelihood function. All the statements concerning almost sure convergence were derived by using uniform laws of large numbers which did not rely on the normality assumption. For this reason, the example we have just considered is a good illustration of the quasi-maximum likelihood procedure, which we will consider in more detail in a following section.

Example 3   Simultaneous Equations Models

Consider the following linear simultaneous equation model:

$$A^0 y_t + B^0 x_t = u_t^0$$

where y_t is a G-dimensional vector of endogenous variables, x_t a K-dimensional vector of exogenous variables. The u_t^0 terms are assumed to be i.i.d. as $\mathcal{N}(0, \Sigma^0)$. Assuming that A^{0-1} is non-singular, the reduced form may be written as:

$$y_t = C^0 x_t + v_t^0$$

where v_t^0 are i.i.d. as $\mathcal{N}(0, \Omega^0)$. We have:

$$A^0 C^0 + B^0 = 0$$

$$\Sigma^0 = A^0 \Omega^0 A^{0\prime}$$

We also assume identifying conditions of the form $\Psi(A^0, B^0, \Sigma^0) = 0$.

The Full Information Maximum Likelihood (FIML) estimation procedure consists in finding the estimates of A, B, C, Σ and Ω by solving the following (stochastic) optimization procedure

$$
\left\{
\begin{array}{l}
\text{minimize} \quad \log \det \Omega + \dfrac{1}{T} \operatorname{tr} \Omega^{-1}(Y - XC')'(Y - XC') \\[2ex]
\text{s.t.} \\[2ex]
\qquad\qquad\qquad AC + B = 0 \\[1.5ex]
\qquad\qquad\qquad \Sigma = A\Omega A' \\[1.5ex]
\qquad\qquad\qquad \Psi(A, B, \Sigma) = 0
\end{array}
\right.
$$

We assume that the exogenous variables satisfy the regularity assumption $X'X/T \to Q$ d.p. as $T \to \infty$. The (log-likelihood) criterion of this optimization problem is easily seen to converge to

$$
\log \det \Omega + \operatorname{tr} \Omega^{-1}[\Omega^0 + (C^{0\prime} - C')'Q(C^{0\prime} - C')]
$$

Clearly, C^0 is the unique value of C which minimizes this limiting criterion. Also, one easily verifies that Ω^0 is the unique value which minimizes $\log \det \Omega + \operatorname{tr} \Omega^{-1}\Omega^0$. On the other hand, the identifying conditions ensure that there is a unique solution in A, B and Σ (which is A^0, B^0 and Σ^0) to the system:

$$
\left\{
\begin{array}{l}
AC^0 + B = 0 \\[1.5ex]
\Sigma^0 = A^0 C A^{0\prime} \\[1.5ex]
\Psi(A, B, \Sigma) = 0
\end{array}
\right.
$$

Thus, the true parameters A^0, B^0, Σ^0, C^0 and Ω^0 are the unique solutions to the limiting problem. Therefore the asymptotic identifiability conditions are verified and this proves that FIML estimators are strongly consistent.

Note the importance of the usual identifiability conditions for the proof of strong consistency. These conditions, in conjunction with the asymptotic regularity condition on the exogenous variables, justify the use of the term 'asymptotic identifiability condition' to describe Assumption (iii) of Proposition 2.

6. Minimum Distance Estimation Procedure for Non-Linear Regression

In contrast with the maximum likelihood procedure, the minimum distance estimation procedure does not assume that the distribution of the endogenous variables, conditional on the exogenous variables, is known.

Univariate non-linear least-squares is the first example of the minimum distance estimation procedure. Consider, as in Jennrich (1969) and Malinvaud (1970), the non-linear model:

$$y_t = g_t(\theta^0) + u_t^0 \qquad (t = 1, \dots n)$$

where the g_t are known continuous functions on a compact subset of $\mathbb{R}^p$, and the u_t^0 terms are independent, identically distributed disturbances with zero mean and finite variance σ^{0^2}. The values of θ^0 and σ^{0^2} are unknown.

The non-linear ordinary least squares estimator minimizes the following criterion:

$$C_n(y, \theta) = \sum_{t=1}^{n} (y_t - g_t(\theta))^2$$

In the presence of exogenous variables, the non-linear regression may be written as:

$$y_t = g(x_t, \theta^0) + u_t^0$$

The function g is assumed to be continuous on $\mathscr{X} \times \Theta$, and the u_t^0 terms are assumed to be i.i.d. $(0, \sigma^{0^2})$.

The non-linear least squares estimator of θ^0 minimizes:

$$C_n(y, \theta) = \sum_{t=1}^{n} (y_t - g(x_t, \theta))^2$$

The non-linear least squares may be extended in the multivariate non-linear regression as follows. Consider the multivariate non-linear model:

$$y_t = g(x_t, \theta^0) + u_t^0 \qquad g = 1, \dots, G$$

Define:

$$y_t' = (y_{t1}, \dots, y_{tg}, \dots, y_{tG})$$

$$g(x_t, \theta^0)' = (g_1(x_t, \theta^0), \dots, g_g(x_t, \theta^0), \dots, g_G(x_t, \theta^0))'$$

$$u_t^{0\prime} = (u_{t1}, \dots, u_{tg}, \dots, u_{tG})$$

Let S be any $G \times G$ positive definite matrix. Any vector $\hat{\theta}_n$ in Θ which minimizes

$$C_n(y, \theta) = \text{tr } S^{-1} \sum_{t=1}^{n} [y_t - g(x_t, \theta)] [y_t - g(x_t, \theta)]'$$

will be called a (non-linear) minimum distance estimator of θ^0.

It is sometimes convenient to slightly generalize the method we have just described, by introducing a stochastic matrix S_n which is positive (a.s.) and converges almost surely to a non-stochastic positive definite matrix S. In this framework, any vector $\hat{\theta}_n$ in Θ which minimizes

$$C_n(y, \theta) = \text{tr } S_n^{-1} \sum_{t=1}^{n} [y_t - g(x_t, \theta)] [y_t - g(x_t, \theta)]'$$

will be called a (non-linear) minimum distance estimator of θ^0.

Note that, by stacking the endogenous variables as in the multivariate linear regression model, we may write the minimum distance criterion as:

$$C_n(y, \theta) = [y - g(x, \theta)]'(S_n^{-1} \otimes I_n)[y - g(x, \theta)]$$

As noted earlier, the strong consistency results are immediate consequences of the general exposition contained in section 3. Here again, it is useful to consider separately the case where the criterion grows to infinity at a higher rate than the sample size.

6.1. MDE Criterion Growing to Infinity at a Higher Rate than the Sample Size

In this case, we may apply Proposition 1. However, it is possible to modify this Proposition to deal with the special case of MDE.

To this purpose, let us specialize Proposition 1 to the OLS criterion. By writing that $y_t = g_t(\theta^0) + u_t^0$ and noting that $C_n(y, \theta^0) = \sum_{t=1}^{n} u_t^{0^2}$, we obtain:

$$C_n(y, \theta) - C_n(y, \theta^0) = \sum_{t=1}^{n} (g_t(\theta) - g_t(\theta^0))^2 - 2 \sum_{t=1}^{n} g_t(\theta)u_t^0$$

which we may write as:

$$C_n(y, \theta) - C_n(y, \theta^0) = \left[\sum_{t=1}^{n} (g_t(\theta) - g_t(\theta^0))^2 \right] \left[1 - 2 \frac{\sum\limits_{t=1}^{n} [g_t(\theta) - g_t(\theta^0)] u_t^0}{\sum\limits_{t=1}^{n} (g_t(\theta) - g_t(\theta^0))^2} \right]$$

According to Proposition 1, strong consistency of the OLS estimator is proved if we can show that, for any $\delta > 0$

$$\liminf_{n \to \infty} \left\{ \inf_{\|\theta - \theta^0\| \geq \delta} Q_n(\theta, \theta^0) \left[1 - 2 \frac{\sum_{t=1}^{n} [g_t(\theta) - g_t(\theta^0)] u_t^0}{Q_n(\theta, \theta^0)} \right] \right\} > 0 \quad \text{a.s.}$$

where $Q_n(\theta, \theta^0) = \sum_{t=1}^{n} (g_t(\theta) - g_t(\theta^0))^2$.

Since $Q_T(\theta, \theta^0)$ is not random, the above condition may be separated into the following set of conditions

$$\begin{cases} \text{for any} \quad \delta > 0, \\[2mm] \lim_{n \to \infty} \inf_{\|\theta - \theta^0\| \geq \delta} Q_T(\theta, \theta^0) > 0 \\[4mm] \liminf_{n \to \infty} \left[\sup_{\|\theta - \theta^0\| \geq \delta} \frac{\sum_{t=1}^{n} [g_t(\theta) - g_t(\theta^0)] u_t^0}{Q_T(\theta, \theta^0)} > \frac{1}{2} \right] = 0 \quad \text{a.s.} \end{cases}$$

In a slightly modified form, the conditions we have just written are Malinvaud's (1970) conditions for strong consistency of non-linear OLS estimators.[10]

Despite the generality of the above conditions for strong consistency of the non-linear least squares estimators, they are not very helpful as they stand. Even for relatively simple functions $g_t(\theta^0)$, the above conditions are quite cumbersome to verify.[11]

Of course, one would like to place convenient and primitive conditions on the model which ensure that the condition stated in Proposition 1 is verified. This could be achieved for special criteria such as the non-linear least squares. To understand the technical difficulties involved, let us consider the non-linear least squares procedure. The following discussion is based on Wu (1981).

Assuming that $\lim_{n \to \infty} \inf_{\|\theta - \theta^0\| \geq \delta} Q_T(\theta, \theta^0) \to \infty$ as $n \to \infty$ for any $\delta > 0$, it suffices for the strong consistency of $\hat{\theta}_n$ to prove that:

$$\frac{\sup_{\|\theta - \theta^0\| \geq \delta} \left| \sum_{t=1}^{n} [g_t(\theta) - g_t(\theta^0)] u_t^0 \right|}{\inf_{\|\theta - \theta^0\| \geq \delta} Q_T(\theta, \theta^0)} \to 0 \quad \text{a.s.}$$

---

[10] In Malinvaud (1980) one finds an extension of these conditions to the multivariate non-linear minimum distance procedure.

[11] The reader is strongly recommended to prove the strong consistency of the non-linear least squares estimator of the parameter θ^0 in the model $y_t = \theta^0 + (\exp \theta^0)t + u_t^0$. This is an exercise in Phillips and Wickens (1978).

Assuming further that $g_t(\theta)$ is continuous on the compact subset Θ, it is a bounded function. On the other hand the condition we have just stated involves the almost sure convergence in supreme norm of a sequence of random functions. For these reasons one needs a strong law of large numbers in $C(\Theta)$, the space of continuous function on Θ with supremum norm. The source of the difficulty is that since $C(\Theta)$ is a Banach space, the random values under consideration are Banach space valued. For this reason one needs to resort to the probability theory of Banach valued random variables to prove that, under a set of primitive assumptions, the condition we have just stated is satisfied. Clearly, this theory is far beyond the scope of these lectures on non-linear econometric models! For completeness, however, we shall state below a result proved in Wu (1981).

Assume that:

(i) $Q_T(\theta, \theta^0) \to \infty$ for all $\theta \neq \theta^0$
(ii)   for any $\delta > 0$:

$$\limsup_{n \to \infty} \frac{\left\{ \sum\limits_{t=1}^{n} \sup\limits_{\|\theta - \theta^0\|} (g_t(\theta) - g_t(\theta^0))^2 \right\}^{(1+c)/2}}{\inf\limits_{\|\theta - \theta^0\|} Q_T(\theta, \theta^0)} < \infty$$

for some $c > 0$
(iii) $g_t(\theta)$ are Lipschitz functions on Θ and:

$$\Lambda(g_t) = \sup_{\theta_1 \neq \theta_2} \frac{|g_t(\theta) - g_t(\theta^0)|}{\|\theta_1 - \theta_2\|} \leqslant M \sup_{\|\theta - \theta^0\| \geqslant \bar{\delta}} |g_t(\theta) - g_t(\theta^0)|$$

for some $\bar{\delta} > 0$ and for all t, and where M is independent of t.

Then $\hat{\theta}_n$ converges almost surely to θ^0.

It may be of interest to note that for the linear regression model assumption (ii) reduces to:

$$\limsup_{n \to \infty} \frac{(\text{max eigen value of } X'X)^{(1+c)/2}}{\text{min eigen value of } X'X} < \infty \quad \text{for some } c > 0$$

6.2. MDE Criterion Growing to Infinity at a Rate Equal to the Sample Size

The case of an MDE criterion growing to infinity at a rate equal to the sample size is easier to handle. The consistency result in this case follows from Proposition 2.

To illustrate this point, we observe that $n^{-1}C_n(y,\theta)$ may be written as:

$$\frac{1}{n}C_n(y,\theta) = \frac{1}{n}\sum_{t=1}^{n} u_t^{0^2} + \frac{2}{n}\sum [g(x_t,\theta^0) - g(x_t,\theta)]u_t^0$$

$$+ \frac{1}{n}\sum_{t=1}^{n} [g(x_t,\theta^0) - g(x_t,\theta)]^2$$

By the strong law of large numbers $n^{-1}\sum_{t=1}^{n} u_t^{0^2}$ converges almost surely to σ^{0^2}. Now, assume that, by imposing the appropriate regularity conditions on the sequence $\{x_t\}$ and the function g, one is able to show that:

$$\frac{1}{n}\sum_{t=1}^{n} [g(x_t,\theta^0) - g(x_t,\alpha)]\,[g(x_t,\theta^0) - g(x_t,\beta)]$$

converges to:

$$\int [g(x_t,\theta^0) - g(x_t,\alpha)]\,[g(x_t,\theta^0) - g(x_t,\beta)]\,d\mu(x)$$

uniformly for all α and β in Θ. This would imply, according to Proposition 5, that

$$\frac{1}{n}\sum_{t=1}^{n} [g(x_t,\theta^0) - g(x_t,\theta)]u_t^0 \to 0 \quad \text{a.s.}$$

uniformly for all θ in Θ. Obviously this also implies that:

$$\frac{1}{n}\sum_{t=1}^{n} [g(x_t,\theta^0) - g(x_t,\theta)]^2 \to \int (g(x,\theta^0) - g(x,\theta))^2\,d\mu(x)$$

uniformly for all θ in Θ.
Thus,

$$\frac{1}{n}\sum_{t=1}^{n} (y_t - g(x_t,\theta))^2 \to \sigma^{0^2} + \int (g(x,\theta^0) - g(x,\theta))^2\,d\mu(x) \quad \text{a.s.}$$

uniformly for all θ in Θ. To prove strong consistency of the (non-linear) least squares estimator $\hat{\theta}_n$, it suffices to show that $\int (g(x,\theta^0) - g(x,\theta))^2\,d\mu(x)$ has a unique minimum at $\theta = \theta^0$, i.e. that the asymptotic identifiability condition for θ^0 is satisfied.

It is interesting to note that the same set of conditions imply not only strong consistency of $\hat{\theta}_n$ but also strong consistency of $n^{-1}\sum_{t=1}^{n}\hat{u}_t^2$ where $\hat{u}_t = y_t - g(x_t, \hat{\theta}_n)$. Indeed, since Θ is compact and $n^{-1}\sum_{t=1}^{n}(y_t - g(x, \theta))^2$ converges almost surely and uniformly for all θ in Θ to its limit, we have:

$$\frac{1}{n}\sum(y_t - g(x_t, \hat{\theta}_n))^2 \to \sigma^{0^2} + \int(g(x, \theta^0) - g(x, \theta^0))^2 \, d\mu(x) \quad \text{a.s.}$$

and thus:

$$\frac{1}{n}\sum_{t=1}^{n}\hat{u}_t^2 \to \sigma^{0^2} \quad \text{as} \quad n \to \infty \quad \text{a.s.}$$

The results we have just presented may be extended without difficulty to the multivariate non-linear minimum distance procedure, of which non-linear least squares is a particular case.

7. Generalized M-Estimation Procedure

This section may be considered as a sequel to section 3, since it also deals with a general estimation procedure which consists in optimizing a general stochastic criterion function. The problem of strong consistency has been considered in detail in section 3. Here, we shall be concerned with efficiency considerations, and for this reason also consider asymptotic distribution of estimators.

It is useful, in view of some applications, to extend the M-estimation procedure in the following way.

Suppose one would like to estimate θ efficiently. To this end, it is sometimes possible to make the criterion depend on an additional parameter γ, that is to consider the M-estimation criterion as:

$$\min_{\theta \in \Theta, \gamma \in \Gamma} C_n(y, \theta, \gamma)$$

We assume that $n^{-1}C_n(y, \theta, \gamma)$ converges almost surely, and uniformly in (θ, γ) to $C_\infty(\theta, \theta^0, \gamma, \gamma^0)$. Suppose we are able to obtain, from another estimation method, a strongly consistent preliminary estimator of γ^0, denoted as $\tilde{\gamma}^p$, and consider the estimator of θ obtained as a solution of:

$$\min_{\theta \in \Theta} C_n(y, \theta, \tilde{\gamma}^p)$$

This procedure is what we call a generalized M-estimation procedure. Denote as $\tilde{\theta}$ this estimator. We shall now examine the asymptotic distribution of this estimator. To this purpose, we introduce the following additional assumptions and notation.

We assume that the matrices $n^{-1}(\partial^2 C_n(y, \theta^0, \gamma^0))/\partial\theta\,\partial\theta'$ and $n^{-1}(\partial^2 C_n(y, \theta^0, \gamma^0))/\partial\theta\,\partial\gamma'$ converge in probability, and we denote:

$$\mathcal{J}_{\theta\theta} \stackrel{\text{def}}{=} \text{plim}\left[-n^{-1}\frac{\partial^2 C_n(y, \theta^0, \gamma^0)}{\partial\theta\,\partial\theta'}\right]$$

$$\mathcal{J}_{\theta\gamma} \stackrel{\text{def}}{=} \text{plim}\left[-n^{-1}\frac{\partial^2 C_n(y, \theta^0, \gamma^0)}{\partial\theta\,\partial\gamma'}\right]$$

We also assume that $\mathcal{J}_{\theta\theta}$ is non-singular.

Proposition 6

Suppose that:

$$\mathcal{AD}\begin{pmatrix} n^{-1/2}\,\partial C_n(y, \theta^0, \gamma^0)/\partial\theta \\ n^{1/2}(\tilde{\gamma}^p - \gamma^0) \end{pmatrix} = \mathcal{N}\left[0, \begin{pmatrix} \mathscr{I}_{\theta\theta} & V_{c\gamma} \\ V_{\gamma c} & V_{\gamma\gamma} \end{pmatrix}\right]$$

Then,

$$\mathcal{AD}[n^{1/2}(\tilde{\theta} - \theta^0)] = \mathcal{N}(0, V_a(\tilde{\theta}))$$

where

$$V_a(\tilde{\theta}) = \mathcal{J}_{\theta\theta}^{-1}(I_p: \mathcal{J}_{\theta\gamma})\begin{pmatrix} \mathscr{I}_{\theta\theta} & V_{c\gamma} \\ V_{\gamma c} & V_{\gamma\gamma} \end{pmatrix}(I_p: \mathcal{J}_{\theta\gamma})'\mathcal{J}_{\theta\theta}^{-1}$$

Proof:
See, for example, Gouriéroux and Monfort (1989, pp. 229–31).   *QED*
   The most interesting situation is where $\mathcal{J}_{\gamma\theta} = 0$.

Corollary 3

Suppose $\mathcal{J}_{\gamma\theta} = 0$. Then

$$\mathcal{AD}[n^{1/2}(\tilde{\theta} - \theta^0)] = \mathcal{N}(\beta, \mathcal{J}_{\theta\theta}^{-1}\mathscr{I}_{\theta\theta}\mathcal{J}_{\theta\theta}^{-1})$$

The importance of Corollary 3 lies in the fact that the asymptotic distribution of $n^{1/2}(\tilde{\theta} - \theta^0)$ does not depend on the particular preliminary estimator $\tilde{\gamma}^p$, and is the same as the asymptotic distribution of $n^{1/2}(\hat{\theta} - \theta^0)$.

8. Quasi-Maximum Likelihood (QML)

The following discussion is based on Gouriéroux, Monfort and Trognon (1984a) (see also White (1982) and Trognon (1987)).

Let y be a G-dimensional vector of endogenous variables and x a vector of exogenous variables. The conditional density of the distribution of y given x will be denoted by $l_0(y \mid x)$. In general, we have little information on $l_0(y \mid x)$. However, we are frequently in the position of making assumptions on the first two moments of the distribution of y given x. In other words we assume that:

$$E_0(y \mid x) = \int y l_0(y \mid x) \, dy = g(x, \theta^0)$$

and sometimes that:

$$V_0(y \mid x) = \int (y - E_0(y \mid x))(y - E_0(y \mid x))' l_0(y \mid x) \, dy = h(x, \theta^0, \gamma^0)$$

Putting $u^0 = y - g(x, \theta^0)$, and using the fact that $g(x, \theta^0) = E_0(y \mid x)$ we obtain the following model:

$$\begin{cases} y = g(x, \theta^0) + u^0 \\ E(u^0 \mid x) = 0 \\ V_0(u^0 \mid x) = \Omega_0(x) = h(x, \theta^0, \gamma^0) \end{cases}$$

Since $l_0(y \mid x)$ is unknown, we may think of using any conditional distribution $l(y \mid x)$ provided it is adapted to the first moment or the first two moments. Let us make this concept more precise.

Let us first assume that the only information we would like to use is the conditional first moment. In that case we may consider a class of conditional distributions parametrized by θ, which satisfy the following condition:

$$\int y l(y \mid x, \theta) \, dy = g(x, \theta) \quad \text{for all } x \text{ in } \mathscr{X} \text{ and } \theta \text{ in } \Theta$$

In that case we say that $l(y \mid x, \theta)$ is adapted to the first-order moment.

If we would like to use information about the conditional first and second moments, we may consider a class of conditional distributions parametrized by θ and γ, which satisfy the following conditions:

$$
\begin{cases}
\int yl(y \mid x, \theta, \gamma) = g(x, \theta) \\
\int [y - g(x, \theta)] [y - g(x, \theta)]' l(y \mid x, \theta, \gamma) = h(x, \theta, \gamma) \\
\text{for all } x \text{ in } \mathscr{X}; \theta \text{ in } \Theta, \text{ and } \gamma \in \Gamma
\end{cases}
$$

In that case we say that $l(y \mid x, \theta, \gamma)$ is adapted to the first- and second-order moments.

More generally, suppose the true conditional density of the distribution of y given x depends on a parameter δ^0. We write it as $l_0(y \mid x, \delta^0)$. Suppose one uses an estimation procedure where a conditional density $l(y \mid x, \delta)$ is used in place of $l_0(y \mid x, \delta^0)$. In the following exposition we assume for simplicity that the y_t terms are, conditionally on x, independently and identically distributed (with $l_0(y \mid x, \delta^0)$ as the true conditional density).

The quasi-maximum likelihood procedure consists in maximizing

$$
n^{-1} Q\mathscr{L}_n(y, \delta) = \frac{1}{n} \sum_{t=1}^{n} \log l(y_t \mid x_t, \delta)
$$

Assuming that $\log l(y \mid x, \delta)$ satisfies conditions of the type discussed earlier, we have:

$$
n^{-1} Q\mathscr{L}_n(y, \delta) \to Q\mathscr{L}_\infty(\delta, \delta^0) \quad \text{as} \quad n \to \infty \quad \text{a.s.}
$$

uniformly for δ in Δ, where:

$$
Q\mathscr{L}_\infty(\delta, \delta^0) = \int \left(\int [\log l(y \mid x, \delta)] l_0(y \mid x, \delta^0) \, dy \right) d\mu(x)
$$

Since $l(y \mid x, \delta)$ is not necessarily equal to $l_0(y \mid x, \delta)$, there is no reason to assume that $Q\mathscr{L}_\infty(\delta, \delta^0)$ has a unique maximum at $\delta = \delta^0$. It may well be the case that there is a unique maximum at $\delta = \delta^*$. The pseudo-true parameter is defined to be the value δ^* that minimizes $Q\mathscr{L}_\infty(\delta, \delta^0)$.

By repeating the argument used in the proof of Proposition 2, one can show that the quasi-maximum likelihood estimator (QML) $\tilde{\delta}_n$ which maximizes $n^{-1} Q\mathscr{L}_n(y, \delta)$ converges almost surely to the pseudo-true parameter δ^*. Since, in general $\delta^0 \neq \delta^*$, this implies that in general $\tilde{\delta}_n$ is not a consistent estimator of δ^0.

To illustrate this point suppose we know that:

$$\begin{cases} y = g(x, \theta^0) + u^0 \\ E(u^0 \mid x) = 0 \\ V_0(u^0 \mid x) = \Omega_0(x) = h(x, \theta^0, \gamma^0) \end{cases}$$

We assume that we do not know the expression for the true density of y conditional on x. However, suppose we choose to estimate θ^0 and γ^0 by using the normal density which conditional on x has mean $g(x, \theta)$ and variance $h(x, \theta, \gamma)$. That is to say, we choose to estimate θ^0 and γ^0 by maximizing:

$$n^{-1} Q\mathscr{L}_n(y, \theta, \gamma) = -\tfrac{1}{2} \log 2\pi - \frac{1}{2n} \sum_{t=1}^n \log h(x_t, \theta, \gamma) - \frac{1}{2n} \sum_{t=1}^n \frac{(y_t - g(x_t, \theta))^2}{h(x_t, \theta, \gamma)}$$

Then we have, under appropriate regularity conditions of the type mentioned earlier,

$$n^{-1} Q\mathscr{L}_n(y, \theta, \gamma) \to Q\mathscr{L}_\infty(\theta, \gamma, \theta^0, \gamma^0) \quad \text{a.s.}$$

uniformly for (θ, γ) in $\Theta \times \Gamma$, where:

$$Q\mathscr{L}_\infty(\theta, \gamma, \theta^0, \gamma^0) = -\tfrac{1}{2} \log 2\pi - \frac{1}{2} \int \left[\log h(x, \theta, \gamma) + \frac{h(x, \theta^0, \gamma^0)}{h(x, \theta, \gamma)} \right] d\mu(x)$$

$$- \frac{1}{2} \int \frac{(g(x, \theta^0) - g(x, \theta))^2}{h(x, \theta, \gamma)} d\mu(x)$$

We see in this example that $Q\mathscr{L}_\infty$ does not necessarily have a maximum at $\delta = \delta^0$. This is, however, the case when the conditional variance $h(x, \theta^0, \gamma^0)$ does not actually depend on θ^0. For, in this case, we would have:

$$Q\mathscr{L}_\infty(\theta, \gamma, \theta^0, \gamma^0) = -\tfrac{1}{2} \log 2\pi - \frac{1}{2} \int \left[\log h(x, \gamma) + \frac{h(x, \gamma^0)}{h(x, \gamma)} \right] d\mu(x)$$

$$- \frac{1}{2} \int \frac{(g(x, \theta^0) - g(x, \theta))^2}{h(x, \gamma)} d\mu(x)$$

Now, if the identifiability conditions $[g(x, \theta^0) = g(x, \theta) \Leftrightarrow \theta = \theta^0]$ and $[h(x, \gamma) = h(x, \gamma^0) \Leftrightarrow \gamma = \gamma^0]$ are satisfied, then $Q\mathscr{L}_\infty(\theta, \gamma, \theta^0, \gamma^0)$ has a unique minimum at (θ^0, γ^0). Therefore the QML estimators $\tilde{\theta}_n$ and $\tilde{\gamma}_n$ are strongly consistent estimators of θ^0, γ^0 despite the fact that the true distribution conditional on x may not be the normal distribution.

More generally, it is natural to seek conditions under which the QML estimator is a strongly consistent estimator of the true parameter. This question has been addressed by Gouriéroux, Monfort and Trognon (1984a) for families of likelihoods adapted to the first-order moment, and to the first- and second-order moments. Let us first consider the case where only the information about the first-order moment is used. In that case, it is natural to restrict the class of conditional densities $l^+(y, m)$ to those which are parametrized by their mean, that is such that:

$$\int y l^+(y, m) \, dy = m$$

We would then base the QML procedure on $l(y \mid x, \theta)$ where:

$$l(y \mid x, \theta) = l^+(y, g(x, \theta))$$

We have the following characterization:

Proposition 7 (Gouriéroux, Monfort and Trognon (1984a))

The QML estimator $\tilde{\theta}_n$ is a strongly consistent estimator of θ^0 for all distributions l_0 and all distributions μ if and only if the family $\{l^+(y, m)$ where m is in some set $\mathcal{M}\}$, is a linear exponential family, i.e. a family of the form:

$$l^+(y, m) = \exp[a(m) + b(y) + c'(m)y]$$

where $a(m)$ is an application from $\mathcal{M}$ to $\mathbb{R}$, $b(y)$ an application from $\mathbb{R}^G$ to $\mathbb{R}$, and $c(m)$ an application from $\mathcal{M}$ to $\mathbb{R}^G$.

This exponential linear family contains all the distributions belonging to the so-called exponential family in mathematical statistics.

The asymptotic distribution of the QML estimator $\tilde{\theta}_n$, based on any member of the linear exponential family, may be derived as follows.

Let $\Omega(x)$ be the true conditional variance of y given x, and let $\Sigma(x)$ be the conditional variance of y given x based on a particular member of this family. Then, one can show (see Gouriéroux, Monfort and Trognon (1984a)) that:

$$\mathscr{I}_{\theta\theta} = \int \left(\frac{\partial g(x, \theta^0)}{\partial \theta}\right)' \Sigma(x)^{-1} \Omega(x) \, \Sigma(x)^{-1} \left(\frac{\partial g(x, \theta^0)}{\partial \theta}\right) \, d\mu(x)$$

and:

$$\mathscr{J}_{\theta\theta} = \int \left(\frac{\partial g(x, \theta^0)}{\partial \theta}\right)' \Sigma(x)^{-1} \left(\frac{\partial g(x, \theta^0)}{\partial \theta}\right) \, d\mu(x)$$

The asymptotic distribution of $n^{1/2}(\tilde{\theta} - \theta^0)$ follows from Proposition 6.

The matrix of the asymptotic normal distribution is equal to $\mathcal{J}_{\theta\theta}^{-1}\mathcal{I}_{\theta\theta}\mathcal{J}_{\theta\theta}^{-1}$. It is interesting to note that we obtain a result analogous to the Gauss–Markov Theorem for linear models, which applies to the linear exponential family. In fact, intuition suggests that this variance is minimal when $\mathcal{I}_{\theta\theta} = \mathcal{J}_{\theta\theta}$, that is when $\Sigma(x) = \Omega(x)$. Define $\mathcal{K}_{\theta\theta}$ as:

$$\mathcal{K}_{\theta\theta} = \left[\int \left(\frac{\partial g(x, \theta^0)}{\partial \theta}\right)' \Omega(x)^{-1} \left(\frac{\partial g(x, \theta^0)}{\partial \theta}\right) d\mu(x) \right]^{-1}$$

Proposition 8 (Gouriéroux, Monfort and Trognon (1984a))

Within the linear exponential family, the lower bound of the variance of the asymptotic distribution of $n^{1/2}(\tilde{\theta} - \theta^0)$ is equal to $\mathcal{K}_{\theta\theta}$.

The interesting question is now to describe situations where such a lower bound may be achieved. To this purpose, Gouriéroux, Monfort and Trognon (1984a) extend the linear exponential family by making it depend on an additional parameter, α say, defined as:

$$l^+(y, m, \alpha) = \exp[a(m, \alpha) + b(y, \alpha) + c'(m, \alpha)y]$$

The auxiliary parameter α is, in fact, a function of m and $\Sigma(x)$ such that, for fixed m, the correspondence between α and Σ is one-to-one. Suppose, now, that:

$$V(y \mid x) = \Omega(x, \gamma^0)$$

Suppose we are able to obtain, from another estimation method, a strongly consistent preliminary estimator of δ^0, denoted as $\tilde{\delta}^p$, and consider the estimator of θ obtained as a solution of:

$$\max_{\theta \in \Theta} \frac{1}{n} \sum_{t=1}^n \log f(y_t \mid x_t, g(x_t, \theta), \alpha(g(x_t, \tilde{\theta}^p), \Omega(x, \tilde{\gamma}^p)))$$

This procedure is what we call a generalized QML estimation procedure. Denote as $\tilde{\tilde{\theta}}$ this estimator. The following result is an immediate application of Corollary 3.

Proposition 9 (Gouriéroux, Monfort and Trognon (1984a))

Suppose that $\tilde{\delta}^p$ is a strongly consistent estimator of δ^0, and that $n^{1/2}(\tilde{\delta}^p - \delta^0)$ has an asymptotic normal distribution. Then, the generalized QML estimator $\tilde{\tilde{\theta}}$ is strongly consistent, and

$$\mathcal{AD}[n^{1/2}(\tilde{\tilde{\theta}} - \theta^0)] = \mathcal{N}(\beta, \mathcal{K}_{\theta\theta})$$

This result shows that the generalized QML procedure yields an asymptotic efficient estimator within the linear exponential family, whatever the choice of the preliminary estimator $\tilde{\delta}^p$. Let us now consider the case where informations about the first two conditional moments are used.

It is also natural to restrict the class of conditional densities to those which are characterized by the mean m and the covariance matrix Σ, that is to the class $l^{++}(y, m, \Sigma)$ such that:

$$\int y l^{++}(y, m, \Sigma) \, dy = m$$

and

$$\int (y - m)(y - m)' l^{++}(y, m, \Sigma) = \Sigma$$

We would then base the QML procedure on $l(y \mid x, \theta, \gamma)$ where:

$$l(y \mid x, \theta, \gamma) = l^{++}(y, g(x, \theta), h(x, \theta, \gamma)).$$

Proposition 10   (Gouriéroux, Monfort and Trognon (1984a))

The QML estimator $(\tilde{\theta}_n, \tilde{\gamma}_n)$ is a strongly consistent estimator of (θ^0, γ^0) for all distributions l_0 and all distributions μ, if and only if the family $l^{++}(y, m, \Sigma)$ is a quadratic exponential family, i.e. a family of the form:

$$l^{++}(y, m, \Sigma) = \exp[a(m, \Sigma) + b(y) + c'(m, \Sigma)y + y'D(m, \Sigma)y]$$

For the proofs of Propositions 7 to 10, the reader is referred to Gouriéroux, Monfort and Trognon (1984a), which also contains the derivations of useful properties of linear and quadratic exponential families. Applications of these families to different models are considered in Gouriéroux, Monfort and Trognon (1984b).

9.   Generalized Method of Moments

The generalized method of moments (GMM hereafter) is a generalization of the instrumental variables procedure which has been suggested by Hansen (1982). It consists in estimating the parameter θ^0, which is a solution to the following non-linear system of equations:

$$E[\psi(y, x, \theta^0)] = 0$$

where $\psi(y, x, \theta^0)$ is an m-dimensional vector.

Let S_n be a positive definite matrix. The generalized method of moments consists in estimating the parameter θ^0 by solving the following minimization problem:

$$\min_{\theta \in \Theta} \left(\sum_i^n \psi(y_i, x_i, \theta) \right)' S_n^{-1} \left(\sum_i^n \psi(y_i, x_i, \theta) \right)$$

Let $\tilde{\theta}_n(S_n)$ be the solution to this problem, which we call generalized method of moments (GMM) estimator of θ^0.

Assumptions:

GMMA1 $\theta \in \Theta$, where Θ is compact.
GMMA2 $\psi(y, x, \theta)$ is jointly continuous with respect to (y, x, θ).
GMMA3 (y_i, x_i), $i = 1, \ldots, n$ are i.i.d.
GMMA4 $E[\psi(y, x, \theta)]$ exists for all $\theta \in \Theta$, and $E[\psi(y, x, \theta^0)] = 0$.
GMMA5 S_n converges almost surely to a non-stochastic positive definite matrix S^0.
GMMA6   (asymptotic identifiability):

$$[E[\psi(y, x, \theta^0)]]' S^{0-1} [E[\psi(y, x, \theta^0)]] = 0 \Rightarrow \theta = \theta^0$$

GMMA7 $n^{-1} \sum_i^n \psi(y_i, x_i, \theta)$ converges almost surely, and uniformly with respect to θ to $E[\psi(y, x, \theta)]$.

Using Proposition 2 it is straightforward to show the following result.

Proposition 11

Under assumptions GMMA1 to GMMA7, $\tilde{\theta}_n(S_n)$ is a strongly consistent estimator of θ^0.

To obtain the asymptotic distribution of $n^{1/2}[\tilde{\theta}_n(S_n) - \theta^0]$, we introduce the following assumptions:

GMMA8 θ^0 is an interior point of Θ.
GMMA9 $\psi(y, x, \theta)$ is differentiable with respect to θ.
GMMA10 $n^{-1} \sum_i^n (\partial \psi / \partial \theta')(y_i, x_i, \theta)$ converges almost surely, and uniformly with respect to θ to $E[(\partial \psi / \partial \theta')(y, x, \theta)]$.
GMMA11 $E[\psi(y, x, \theta^0)\psi(y, x, \theta^0)'] = V^0$, where V^0 is a positive definite matrix.
GMMA12

$$\left[E\left[\frac{\partial \psi}{\partial \theta'}(y, x, \theta^0) \right] \right]' S^{0-1} \left[E\left[\frac{\partial \psi}{\partial \theta'}(y, x, \theta^0) \right] \right]$$

is non-singular. This implies that $m \geq p$.

Using Proposition 6 it is an easy exercise to show the following result.

Proposition 12

Under assumptions GMMA1 to GMMA12,

$$\mathscr{AD}[n^{1/2}[\bar{\theta}_n(S_n) - \theta^0]] = \mathscr{N}(0, V_a(\bar{\theta}_n(S_n)))$$

where:

$$V_a(\bar{\theta}_n(S_n)) = \Delta^0 V^0 \Delta^{0\prime}$$

and

$$\Delta^0 = \left\{ \left[E\left[\frac{\partial \psi}{\partial \theta'}(y, x, \theta^0) \right] \right]' S^{0-1} \left[E\left[\frac{\partial \psi}{\partial \theta'}(y, x, \theta^0) \right] \right] \right\}^{-1}$$

$$\times \left[E\left[\frac{\partial \psi}{\partial \theta'}(y, x, \theta^0) \right] \right]' S^{0-1}$$

Finally, one obtains the following result about the optimal GMM estimator. Its proof uses standard arguments and, therefore, is omitted.

Proposition 13

The optimal GMM estimator is obtained for $S^{0-1} = V^0$. In this case:

$$V_a(\bar{\theta}_n(S_n)) = \left\{ \left[E\left[\frac{\partial \psi}{\partial \theta'}(y, x, \theta^0) \right] \right]' S^{0-1} \left[E\left[\frac{\partial \psi}{\partial \theta'}(y, x, \theta^0) \right] \right] \right\}^{-1}$$

To conclude this chapter, we would like to stress the fact that the theory presented in sections 3 and 4 is quite general and powerful. It can be applied to many estimation procedures, as illustrated here with the most classical ones. There are numerous other examples and a few other estimation procedures for which this theory applies, as the reader may easily discover in the econometric literature.

References

Andrews, D.W.K. (1987): 'Consistency in Nonlinear Econometric Models: a Generic Uniform Law of Large Numbers', *Econometrica*, **55**, 1465–71.
Aubin, J.P. (1977): *Applied Abstract Analysis*, J. Wiley & Sons, New York.
Bates, C. and White, H. (1985): 'A Unified Theory of Consistent Estimation for Parametric Models', *Econometric Theory*, **1**, 151–78.

Berliocchi, H. and Lasry, J.M. (1973): 'Intégrandes Normales et Measures Paramètres en Calcul des Variations', *Bulletin de la Société Mathématique de France*.

Bierens, H.J. (1981): 'Robust Methods and Asymptotic Theory in Nonlinear Econometrics', *Lecture Notes in Economics and Mathematical Systems*, vol. 192. Springer Verlag, Berlin.

Bierens, H.J. (1984): 'Model Specification Testing of Times Series Regression', *Journal of Econometrics*, **26**, 323–53.

Billingsley, P. (1968): *Convergence of Probability Measures*, John Wiley, New York.

Burguete, J.F., Gallant, A.R. and Souza, G. (1982): 'On Unification of Asymptotic Theory of Nonlinear Econometric Models', *Econometric Reviews*, **1**, 151–90.

Cea, J. (1978): *Lectures on Optimization-Theory and Algorithms*, Tata Institute of Fundamental Research, Bombay.

Cramér, H. (1946): *Mathematical Methods in Statistics*, Princeton University Press, Princeton.

Dhrymes, P.J. (1971): *Distributed Lags*, Holden-Day, Inc., San Francisco.

Domowitz, I. and White, H. (1982): 'Misspecified Models with Dependent Observations', *Journal of Econometrics*, **20**, 35–58.

Doob, J.L. (1934): 'Probability and Statistics', *Transactions of the American Mathematical Society*, **36**, 759–75.

Ekeland, I. and Temam, R. (1977): *Convex Analysis and Variational Problems*, North-Holland, Amsterdam.

Ekeland, I. and Turnbull, T. (1983): *Infinite-Dimensional Optimization and Convexity*, The University of Chicago Press, Chicago.

Frydman, R. (1980): 'A Proof of Strong Consistency of Maximum Likelihood Estimators of Nonlinear Regression Models with Autocorrelated Errors', *Econometrica*, **48**, 853–60.

Gallant, A.R. (1977): 'Three-Stage Least Squares Estimation for a System of Simultaneous, Nonlinear, Implicit Equations', *Journal of Econometrics*, **5**, 71–88.

Gallant, A.R. (1987): *Nonlinear Statistical Models*, J. Wiley & Sons, Inc., New York.

Gallant, A.R. and Holly, A. (1980): 'Statistical Inference in an Implicit, Nonlinear, Simultaneous Equation Model in the Context of Maximum Likelihood Estimation', *Econometrica*, **48**, 697–720.

Gouriéroux, C. and Monfort, A. (1989): *Statistique et Modèles économétriques*, vol. 1, Economica, Paris.

Gouriéroux, C., Monfort, A. and Trognon, A. (1984a): 'Pseudo Maximum Likelihood Methods: Theory', *Econometrica*, **52**, 681–700.

Gouriéroux, C., Monfort, A. and Trognon, A. (1984b): 'Pseudo Maximum Likelihood Methods: Applications to Poisson Model', *Econometrica*, **52**, 701–20.

Hansen, L.P. (1982): 'Large Sample Properties of Generalized Method of Moments Estimators', *Econometrica*, **50**, 1029–54.

Hildenbrand, W. (1974): *Core and Equilibria of a Large Economy*, Princeton University Press, Princeton, New Jersey.

Hoadley, B. (1971): 'Asymptotic Properties of Maximum Likelihood Estimators for the Independent not Identically Distributed Case', *Annals of Mathematical Statistics*, **42**, 1977–91.

Ioffe, A.D. and Tihomirov, V.M. (1979): *Theory of Extremal Problems*, North-Holland, Amsterdam.

Jennrich, R.I. (1969): 'Asymptotic Properties of Non-Linear Least Squares Estimators', *Annals of Mathematical Statistics*, **40**, 633–43.

Le Cam, L. (1953): 'On Some Asymptotic Properties of Maximum Likelihood Estimates and Related Bayes Estimates', *University of California Publications in Statistics*, **1**, 277–328.

Malinvaud, E. (1970): 'The Consistency of Nonlinear Regressions', *Annals of Mathematical Statistics*, **41**, 956–69.

Malinvaud, E. (1980): *Statistical Methods of Econometrics*, (third revised edition), North-Holland, Amsterdam.

Newey, W.K. (1987): 'Expository Notes on Uniform Laws of Large Numbers', Princeton University, mimeo.

Parthasarathy, K.R. (1967): *Probability Measures on Metric Spaces*, Academic Press, New York.

Parthasarathy, K.R. (1977): *Introduction to Probability and Measure*, The Macmillan Company of India Limited, Dehli.

Phillips, P.C.B. and Wickens, M.R. (1978): *Exercises in Econometrics*, Philip Allan/Ballinger Publishing Company.

Pötscher, B.M. and Prucha, I.R. (1989): 'A Uniform Law of Large Numbers for Dependent and Heterogeneous Data Processes', *Econometrica*, **57**, 675–83.

Rao, R.R. (1962): 'Relations Between Weak and Uniform Convergence of Measures with Applications', *Annals of Mathematical Statistics*, **33**, 659–80.

Rockafellar, R.T. (1968): 'Integrals Which Are Convex Functionals', *Pacific Journal of Mathematics*, **28**, 525–39.

Rockafellar, R.T. (1971): 'Integrals Which Are Convex Functionals II', *Pacific Journal of Mathematics*, **31**, 439–69.

Trognon, A. (1987): 'Les Méthodes du Pseudo-Maximum de Vraisemblance', *Annales d'Economie et de Statistique*, **8**, 117–34.

Wald, A. (1949): 'Note on the Consistency of the Maximum Likelihood Estimate', *Annals of Mathematical Statistics*, **20**, 595–601.

White, H. (1982): 'Maximum Likelihood Estimation of Misspecified Models', *Econometrica*, **50**, 1–25.

White, H. and Domowitz, I. (1984): 'Nonlinear Regression with Dependent Observations', *Econometrica*, **52**, 143–61.

Wolfowitz, J. (1949): 'On Wald's Proof of the Consistency of the Maximum Likelihood Estimate', *Annals of Mathematical Statistics*, **20**, 601–2.

Wu, C.-F. (1981): 'Asymptotic Theory of Nonlinear Least Squares Estimation', *Annals of Statistics*, **9**, 501–13.

Index